*New Approaches
to Economic and Social
Analyses of Discrimination*

New Approaches
to Economic and Social
Analyses of Discrimination

Edited by
Richard R. Cornwall
and Phanindra V. Wunnava

PRAEGER

New York
Westport, Connecticut
London

Library of Congress Cataloging-in-Publication Data

New approaches to economic and social analyses of discrimination /
  edited by Richard R. Cornwall and Phanindra V. Wunnava.
    p.   cm.
  Includes bibliographical references and index.
  ISBN 0-275-93581-7 (alk. paper)
  1. Discrimination in employment.   I. Cornwall, Richard R.
II. Wunnava, Phanindra V.
  HD4903.N48 1991
  331.13'3—dc20   91-15504

British Library Cataloguing in Publication Data is available.

Library of Congress Catalog Card Number: 91-15504
ISBN: 0-275-93581-7

First published in 1991

Praeger Publishers, One Madison Avenue, New York, NY 10010
An imprint of Greenwood Publishing Group, Inc.

Printed in the United States of America

The paper used in this book complies with the
Permanent Paper Standard issued by the National
Information Standards Organization (Z39.48-1984).

10 9 8 7 6 5 4 3 2 1

Contents

Illustrations

FIGURES

TABLES

Preface and Dedication

Sadie Tanner Mosell Alexander: 2 January 1898 - 1 November 1989

T his volume is dedicated to the memory of Sadie Tanner Mosell Alexander, who died 1 November 1989 at the age of 91 while we were pulling this volume together. Dr. Alexander's successes and struggles epitomize the processes producing, as well as those resisting, inequality in our markets, first making Dr. Alexander's human capital unmarketable and then yielding to her persistent, thoughtful use of legal and collective instruments. We therefore dedicate our work to her.

Sadie Alexander was born 2 January 1898 to a prominent family in Philadelphia and attended secondary school in Washington, D.C. She studied at the University of Pennsylvania, receiving a bachelor of science degree with highest honors in 1918, a masters in economics in 1919, and a Ph.D. in economics in 1921.[1] She was the first African American woman to receive a Ph.D. in economics (and, by just one day, only the second Black woman to receive a Ph.D. in this country in any field). Unable to get any work despite receiving help from all her professors at Penn, she went to Durham, North Carolina, to work as an assistant actuary for two years for a Black-owned insurance firm. Being unfamiliar with and uncomfortable in the South, Dr. Alexander returned to Philadelphia. She married Raymond Pace Alexander, whom she had met when they were both undergraduates at Penn. Raymond Alexander had just completed Harvard Law School and passed the bar. Sadie Alexander decided to attend the Law School at the University of Pennsylvania, thinking "that at least I could work for him [her husband] when I graduate" [Jablow 1980]. Sadie Alexander was the first Black woman to graduate from the University of Pennsylvania Law School. In this she followed her father, Aaron Mosell, who had been the first African American to graduate from this law school. She then became the first Black woman to be admitted to the Pennsylvania bar and was the second woman of any race to hold the position of assistant city solicitor in Philadelphia. Dr. Alexander was the first African American woman to serve on a presidential commission when Harry Truman appointed her to his Committee on Civil Rights in 1946-48. She also served on John F. Kennedy's Lawyers' Committee for Civil Rights Under Law in 1963 and in 1981 served as chair of Jimmy Carter's White House Conference on Aging.

Sadie Alexander achieved much for women especially for African American women. She served as national secretary of the Urban League for twenty-five years and as head or member of Philadelphia's Commission on Human Rights for seventeen years. She and her husband worked throughout the 1930s initiating legal fights to open restaurants, hotels, and movie theaters to African Americans. "In the 1940's, Dr. Alexander [pressed] for the hiring of Blacks on the Penn faculty and the integration of the armed services. As a member of Truman's civil rights commission, she played a major role in that committee's findings . . . [which were] a foundation of the later civil rights movement" [St. George 1989].

This is a record of impressive achievements in the face of stubborn resistance. Can a person who is not a male European American realistically aspire to such achievements, or are these only the stuff of superheroines? This volume seeks to explore both the causes and the consequences of barriers to equality by race and gender in our society. Although a distinction between cause and consequence of social inequality cannot be rigorously sustained, it serves well to give an initial orientation to the different emphases of the chapters here. The first three parts start with the fact of inequality and detail how this affects the ways markets operate. The fourth part reverses this view by looking at how markets sometimes appear to sustain or even amplify social inequality and also looking at roles for public policy in mitigating these possible effects of markets.

To address these questions about social diversity, we offer methodological and ideological diversity, bringing together work by sociologists and economists, Marxists and neoclassicals, econometricians and verbal artists. We achieve not harmonious agreement but vital discussion of the impediments to equality. Our views range from new Classical Marxist ideas on rivalry among entrepreneurs and among ethnic groups to neoclassical supply-side, human-capital factors (education, intermittency, and culture as capital) as well as to demand-side factors including the costs of eliciting effort from workers, so-called "efficiency" wage theories, organizational inertia, and the costs of changing social relations in workplaces. Data are examined for evidence of segmentation of workplaces by gender as well as other criteria and for segmentation of business start-ups by geography and race. Each of the four parts of this volume has a brief introduction to place its chapters in the context both of this volume and of recent debates about inequality. We invite readers to skim these four introductions to survey what ideas are offered here.

This volume is the tangible fruit, after thoughtful revision in several cases, of the Eleventh Annual Middlebury Conference on Economic Issues held 6-8 April, 1989. This conference brought twenty-three scholars from around the nation together with an equal number of people from Middlebury College to discuss seventeen papers. This series of conferences is made possible each year through the generous support of Robert A. Jones, who has helped us host constructive debates on a wide range of topics in political economy. We especially want to acknowledge the essential institutional expertise provided by Sheila Cassin in overseeing all the nitty-gritty arrangements without which these dreams and schemes of "experts" would never see the light of barcode or human eye. We have been helped enormously by the numerous people here at Middlebury College who have been generous in many ways and especially Steven K. Metzler, who prepared the final copy of every word and digit in this volume with amazingly good humor and skill. We gratefully acknowledge the timely and careful indexing done by Helen Reiff as well as the significant financial support we received to prepare this book for publication from the Christian A. Johnson Distinguished Professorship in Economics. We also thank James and Tom Blake at the Computer Center at the State University of New York at Binghamton for help translating several disks from one format to another. We thank Jonathan F. Mowry, Sohail A. Shaikh, and Erica Nourjian, who gave us invaluable assistance when the details of organizing the tables, notes and bibliography required focused, careful labor. Finally, we very much want to make clear the support, patience, and encouragement of those who have been closest to our excitements and frustrations as we worked on this conference and book, especially Vijaya Wunnava, Kate Cornwall, and Rob Zeuner.

PART I

UNEMPLOYMENT: ALTERNATIVE EXPLANATIONS AND DISCRIMINATORY CONSEQUENCES

Any approach to theory, if it is to have an impact, must be based on facts that hit scholars over the head because of their clear inconsistency with prevailing theory. The first chapter of this volume does just that. Why has the unemployment rate for African Americans so constantly, across time, education, age, and sex, been roughly twice the level of unemployment for European Americans since 1954? To understand these striking results, it seems useful to look at explanations for unemployment and at how it is related to discrimination. The first part of this volume conducts such a survey and presents both new theoretical ideas and empirical results.

Steven Shulman gives a usefully succinct summary of standard theories of racial inequality in chapter 1. Using the context of the classic studies by Gilman [1965], Beller [1978], and Bonacich [1976] of the appearance between 1940 and 1954 of the racial gap in unemployment rates, it is found that Gilman's emphasis on wage rigidity is not enlightening in the face of recent evidence. Individual supply-side factors, that is, varying amounts of human capital, are found to be unable to explain much of the racial differential in unemployment rates. Similarly, on the demand side of the labor markets, the idea of subjective prejudice by employers or by customers of firms, statistical discrimination based on informational uncertainties, and divide-and-conquer models are also found to be inconsistent with the cyclical patterns of unemployment. Shulman presents a new model that he names the race relations model since it focuses on race as a social relation of production in its own right rather than as a result of some other more basic factor.

Chapter 2 by William Darity looks systematically at theories of unemployment and initiates a rather comprehensive look in this volume at the latest theoretical wrinkle in explaining (justifying?) unemployment: "efficiency" wage theory (EWT). The notion underlying EWT is that wages are raised above market-clearing levels to save on monitoring and supervisory costs in eliciting effort from workers. The idea that this disequilibrium process in markets for labor-power might be a critical factor producing unemployment and discrimination goes back at least to Stiglitz [1973]. Darity puts EWT in the context of the evolution of NeoKeynesian economic theory and offers a critical evaluation of its usefulness in understanding unemployment and wage differentials by race.

A concise, clear statement of EWT is given in chapter 3 by Michael Robinson and Phanindra Wunnava. They use the effort-regulation model of the firm stemming from Bulow and Summers [1986] where inequality results from different responsiveness by sex and by race to wage and supervisorial incentives to supply effort. For example, if men have lower turnover rates than women or higher supervision costs, they will receive relatively higher wage premia as firms minimize costs by substituting increases in wages for less supervision. Using 1983 Current Population Survey data, this chapter provides some evidence that two implications of the Bulow-Summers model are valid: (1) there is a different relationship between supervision costs and wages for males and females, and (2) the percentage of the work force that is female has a more negative effect on wages where monitoring costs are presumed to be higher; that is, in larger firms.

Robinson and Wunnava explore the consequences for inequality in pay by gender of the fact that women interrupt their careers more than do men. This line of inquiry goes back to the pioneering work by Gordon and Strober [1978] and is closely related to the comprehensive econometric investigation of this hypothesis by Solomon Polachek and Charng Kao in chapter 9 of this volume. Section II of chapter 2 takes the other side of this debate about the realism of the explanations for racial and sexual inequality offered by the Bulow-Summers model. It combines evidence by Denise Bielby and William Bielby on differences by gender in the responsiveness of effort to wages as well as evidence collected by Rhonda Williams on the implications of turnover rates by race to argue that the assumptions of the Bulow-Summers model are not valid.

The picture given in chapters 1 and 2 of the weaknesses of neoclassical approaches to the study of racial inequality and unemployment is followed in chapter 4 by Rhonda Williams' development of a Classical Marxist view. This continues the thinking of a long line of economists for whom inequity has been seen as the central asymmetry to be understood rather than viewed as an aberration to be explained with a few bandaids applied to the body-theoretic. This approach is of importance for two reasons. First, it is very different from the monopoly-monopsony, scheming-capitalists-divide-and-conquer-the-workers approach that many economists going back to Baran and Sweezy [1966] identify with Marxists and that has recently been given new and less monopolistically encumbered life by Reich [1981], among others. Rather, building on work on divisions by race (Spero and Harris [1931]) and sex (e.g., Hartmann [1982], Reskin [1988]), this view argues that "neo-Marxian models fail to address the extent to which 'white solidarity' can increase white workers' bargaining power vis-à-vis both capital and black workers." This complements and extends Shulman's race relations model of chapter 1 by making clear that existing econometric studies do not adequately allow for the endogeneity of race and gender in analyzing labor markets.

The second significant contribution of chapter 4 to the study of inequality in labor markets is to integrate analysis of the speeds and costs of operation of capital markets with the outcomes we observe in labor markets. This is an insight that will likely stimulate much future thinking and analysis of data. It complements and extends the suggestions Shulman made in chapter 1 about costs faced by firms as they adjust the racial composition of their workforce. This chapter also connects with the discussion in Part IV of this volume of the role of culture in many analyses of inequality, a discussion in which Williams ([1987a], [1988]) has played an important role. Thus chapter 4 plays a central role in sketching new directions for the analysis of inequality.

This volume contains several views of the usefulness of the notion that labor markets are segmented by race and gender. The explanation for dual labor markets has recently been revised by the Bulow and Summers' [1986] model which is used by Robinson and Wunnava in chapter 3. This assumption of a segmented market is important to the study by David Fairris and Lori Kletzer in chapter 7 of whether sexual inequality in earnings is increased or decreased by differentials in wages that compensate for variations in working conditions. Fairris and Kletzer find that this effect on sexual inequality differs according to whether one looks at the subordinate primary segment or at the secondary segment of labor markets. This complements the search for relevant microdifferences in organizations that lead to sexually segmented labor markets in chapter 5 by William Bielby and in chapter 6 by James Baron. The analytical approach of Baron is tied by Shulman in chapter 1 to the transformation between the 1930s and the 1950s from racially split labor markets to racially segmented labor markets. Shulman's account of racial segmentation is also closely related to Williams' account of racially divided labor markets in chapter 4.

1
Why Is the Black Unemployment Rate Always Twice as High as the White Unemployment Rate?

Steven Shulman

Racial inequality is not static. Over the course of this century, blacks have narrowed the wage gap by their willingness to fight prejudice and discrimination, to acquire education and skills, and to relocate when necessary. The consequent changes in white attitudes and federal law, as well as the periodic pressures created by industrial shifts and employer competition, have aided in the occupational advances that undergird the relative growth in the incomes of individual black workers. Although this encouraging trend slowed markedly over the 1980's, James Smith and Finis Welch [1986:vii] are surely correct to view it as "belying the widely held view that the relative economic position of blacks in America has been stagnant." The contours of racial inequality have changed along with those of American society as a whole.

An important exception – and unfortunately not the only exception – to this benign interpretation of racial history is the stubborn failure of the black unemployment rate to show any tendency to converge with the white unemployment rate. Yet this should not come as a surprise. The trajectory of American society has not taken the simple form of increasing enlightenment, and the changes in racial inequality have not simply been those of steady, if overly slow, advance. Overt bigotry is no longer an acceptable mode of public discourse; nonetheless, the election campaign of our current president reduced itself to the racist stereotype it fashioned in the image of Willie Horton. Residential and social segregation remains virtually as pervasive today as a quarter-century ago despite the growth in the black middle class. Old attitudes are resurrected with new names such as David Duke and skinheads. Thus it should come as no surprise that racial trends in labor market outcomes are not accurately summed up by the title of Smith and Welch's monograph, *Closing the Gap: Forty Years of Economic Progress for Blacks*. The gap has been closing only along some dimensions, only for some people, and only depending on how it is measured. A more optimistic conclusion than that cannot honestly (or at least accurately) be stated.

The accepted wisdom is that the stagnation in overall black living standards as compared to those of whites, whether measured by family incomes, poverty rates, employment-to-population rates, crime rates, infant mortality rates, or incarceration rates, is largely due to the dismayingly rapid formation of female-headed households, which has offset the gains made by individual black workers. It is frequently suggested that these changes in black family structure are a paradoxical by-product of public policies intended to help blacks in particular and the poor in general (e.g., Murray 1984), a suggestion that assumes that discrimination, the lack of opportunity, and the loss of hope are no longer sufficiently powerful to account for the allegedly self-destructive choices of young blacks. I will leave it to Elaine McCrate (see chapter 11) to dissect the presumption that the family choices of blacks are rational in terms of the supposed incentives provided by welfare, but irrational in terms of the opportunities that would otherwise await them, opportunities that many assert exceed those available to whites. Instead, I will discuss the contradictory racial trends in labor-market outcomes solely in terms of individuals in the labor force, a restriction that inevitably understates the black/white gap in standards of living, but that avoids the confounding factors of family structure and work disincentives allegedly created by welfare recipiency.

My topic is the black/white unemployment rate differential. I will not quibble with the official definition of unemployment.[1] Even by this measure, the black unemployment rate has consistently been about twice the white unemployment rate since 1954. My attention is thus confined to the employment prospects of individual blacks and whites in the labor force, a category that all agree captures the role played by labor-market discrimination per se. Is the persistence of a racial gap in unemployment rates due to supply-side or demand-side features of the labor market? How can it be reconciled with the trend in the wage gap among employed workers? What does it suggest about the explanatory power of the various models of discrimination?

My approach to these questions is presented in four main parts. In section I, I describe trends in the unemployment rate differential and on this basis pose the theoretical problems that motivate this chapter. In Section II, I show that the unemployment rate differential cannot be explained by the relative distribution of characteristics that blacks and whites bring to the labor market. This implies (in conventional economic terms) that the demand-side of the labor market, that is, employment discrimination, is to blame.[2] In the subsequent section, I argue that most of the commonly accepted models of discrimination fail to explain either the persistence or the cyclical changes of the unemployment rate differential. One model, however, is consistent with these trends and thereby displays the logical possibility (if not the empirical certainty) that the unemployment differential is a by-product of rational business decision making. This model is applied in section IV to explain the originating and sustaining forces behind the unemployment rate differential. I conclude that discrimination is endogenous to the normal economic processes of modern capitalism.

I. TRENDS OF THE UNEMPLOYMENT RATE DIFFERENTIAL

It is a truism that the black unemployment rate is twice that of the white unemployment rate. The proportionate constancy that the black/white unemployment rate ratio expresses, whether over time periods or between cohorts, explains its common usage as a measure of the unemployment gap. However, the ratio may conceal as much as it reveals. For example, assume that the black unemployment rate goes from 10 percent to 16 percent while the white unemployment rate rises from 4 percent to 8 percent. The ratio would fall from 2.5 to 2.0. Yet blacks have clearly suffered more than whites in this hypothetical downswing since their unemployment rate increased by six points while the white unemployment rate increased by only four points. Because the black unemployment rate is normally much higher than the white unemployment rate, changes that are absolutely greater for blacks can be proportionately greater for whites, making changes in the ratio difficult to interpret as an index of relative welfare. On the other hand, the unemployment rate difference varies widely between cohorts and over time and hence fails to express the proportionate constancy that is the most striking feature of the unemployment gap. For this reason, it is important to look at both the ratio and the difference in order to get a complete picture of movements in the unemployment rate differential.

Figure 1.1 uses seasonally adjusted quarterly data to chart the black/white unemployment rate ratio and difference against the total unemployment rate for the years 1954-81. The ratio hovers fairly steadily around 2, though it seems to decline somewhat from 1967 through 1971 and to rise somewhat from 1975 through 1981. Notice that the difference mirrors the total unemployment rate so closely that, with the exceptions of the sharp surges in total unemployment in 1971 and 1975, it would be tempting to conclude that the point spread between the black and white unemployment rates generally equals the number of percentage points of total unemployment. The relation is remarkably close.

Figure 1.1
Total, Ratio, and Difference of Black and White Unemployment Rates, 1954-1981

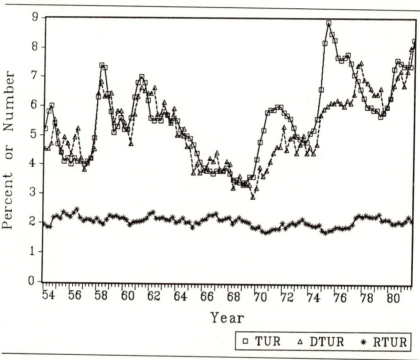

It is possible that the approximate equality between the unemployment rate difference and the total unemployment rate is sustained by the special employment problems of so-called secondary workers. As total unemployment rises, black teens may experience more than proportionate increases in unemployment due to their vulnerability to local labor-market conditions [Holzer 1988:46], thereby raising the overall measure of black unemployment. At the same time, white women facing less economic pressure to work may give up on searching for a job and drop out of the labor force, thereby reducing the overall measure of white unemployment. Trends such

Figure 1.2
Total, Ratio, and Difference of Black and White Unemployment
Rates for Women, Teenagers Excluded, 1978-1987

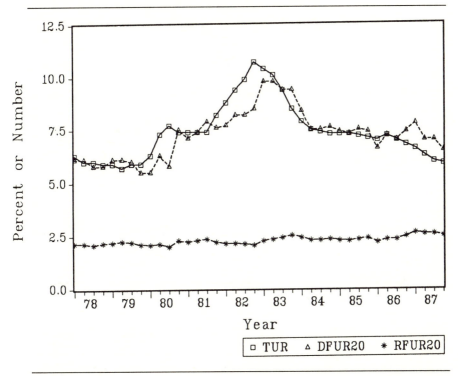

as these could account for the rising spread between the black and white
unemployment rates as total unemployment increases.

Figures 1.2 and 1.3 show that this explanation is false. These figures use
a newly revised series of seasonally adjusted quarterly data to chart the
unemployment rate ratio and difference against total unemployment for
the years 1978 through 1987. Unlike figure 1.1, these data are broken down
by sex and are restricted to workers 20 years old and over. Note that the
match between the unemployment rate difference and the total unemployment rate is, if anything, closer than that shown in figure 1.1. The sharp
upsurge in total unemployment in 1982 did not outstrip the unemployment rate difference as it did in 1971 and 1975 despite the fact that it ended
at a higher level. The female and male differences both track total
unemployment equally well. It appears as though the mapping of total
unemployment onto the unemployment rate difference must be explained
in terms of the experiences of persons fully committed to the labor market.

Figure 1.3
**Total, Ratio, and Difference of Black and White Unemployment
Rates for Men, Teenagers Excluded, 1978-1987**

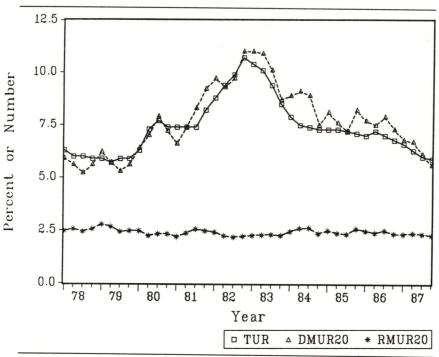

The approximate equality between the total unemployment rate (TUR)
and the unemployment rate difference (BUR – WUR) accounts for the
truism that the black unemployment rate (BUR) is constantly twice that
of the white unemployment rate (WUR). Arithmetically, it is easy to show
that

$$(BUR - WUR) = ([BUR/WUR] - 1)(WUR).$$

If we approximate that (BUR – WUR) = TUR, then it quickly follows that

$$(TUR/WUR) + 1 = BUR/WUR,$$

where the right-side term is the unemployment rate ratio. Since whites
comprise about 85 percent of the labor force, TUR and WUR are bound
to be fairly close. Consequently, their ratio will approximate unity, and
BUR/WUR will thereby fluctuate around two.

The key to explaining the constancy of the black/white unemployment rate ratio is thus the identification of (BUR – WUR) with TUR. Why should total unemployment consistently raise black unemployment above white unemployment by an amount approximately equal to itself? Or, phrased another way, since TUR and WUR change by roughly the same amount, why should black unemployment change more? Why is black unemployment more cyclically variable than white unemployment? It seems as though the question of the constancy of the racial unemployment gap

Table 1.1
Unemployment by Turning-Point Month

Date	TUR	ΔBUR	ΔWUR	Δ(BUR – WUR)
Nov 73(p)	4.8%	—	—	5.0
Mar 75(t)	8.6	5.8	3.5	7.3
Jan 80(p)	6.3	–2.2	–2.4	7.5
Jly 80(t)	7.8	2.3	1.5	8.3
Jly 81(p)	7.2	–0.3	–0.6	8.6
Nov 82(t)	10.7	5.3	3.3	10.6
Oct 88(p*)	5.2	–9.2	–5.0	6.4

Notes: Symbols used:
    UR =   unemployment rate
    Δ   =   change from preceding date
    T   =   total
    B   =   black only
    W =   white
    p   =   peak
    t   =   trough
    * The National Bureau of Economic Research has not declared Oct 88 to be a turning-point month. However, as of this writing, this is the most recent date with the lowest TUR of the 1980s expansion.

Sources: *Labor Force Statistics Derived from The CPS*, vol 2 (Seasonally Adjusted Data), Bureau of Labor Statistics, Bulletin 2096, September 1982, table D-26; *Revised Seasonally Adjusted Labor Force Statistics 1978-87*, idem, Bulletin 2306, March 1988, table A-24; *1989 Economic Report of the President*, table B-39.

is at heart a question of the extra sensitivity of black unemployment to overall labor market conditions.

Greater detail on the cyclical changes in black and white unemployment is presented in table 1.1. These figures show peak-to-trough and trough-to-peak changes in white and black unemployment (seasonally adjusted rates), where the latter has the advantage of being defined as "black only" rather than "black and other" (the "black-only" unemployment rate is usually a percentage point higher than the "black and other" unemployment rate). Since 1973, the United States has undergone three recessions and three expansions. It is notable that the black unemployment rate not only increased more than the white unemployment rate in every recession, but also fell less than the white unemployment rate in two of the three expansions. As a result, the black/white unemployment rate difference increased over the entire business cycle from the early 1970s through the early 1980s. In terms of employment, blacks suffered a steady erosion in their relative welfare during this period.

This observation qualifies the previous statement that black unemployment appears to be more cyclically variable than white unemployment. This is true in bad times – meaning that blacks bear the first and most severe brunt of unemployment – but not necessarily in good times. The failure of black unemployment to fall as much as white unemployment over the upswings is attributable to the declining strength of the expansions during this period: each successive peak was characterized by a higher unemployment rate until the mid-1980s. It took the long expansion of the mid-1980s for black unemployment to resume its historical tendency to fall to a greater degree on the upswing (as it did, for example, in the artificially exaggerated upswing of the 1960s [Gilroy 1974: 42]). As the labor market secularly slackens, the expansions shorten and weaken so that blacks never have a chance to make it to the head of the hiring queue. The traditional pattern of last hired-first fired is consistent with this trend: if employers give hiring preference to whites, then the ability of blacks to gain relative benefits from an expansion will depend upon its strength and duration.[3] Section II justifies the focus on employers (as opposed to the characteristics of black workers themselves), and section III explains why the last hired-first fired pattern has a basis in the profit-maximizing behavior of firms. Here it is sufficient to note that the educational and legal gains that blacks made over the 1970s were apparently unable to offset the last hired-first fired pattern. Only sustained labor-market tightness is capable of reducing the black/white unemployment gap.

The interaction of the last hired-first fired pattern with longer-term trends in aggregate unemployment can thus account for the cyclical and secular patterns of black unemployment, or, in other words, for the correspondence of the black/white unemployment rate difference with the total unemployment rate. As long as blacks are the first to lose their jobs in a recession, the unemployment gap will persist over long periods of time unless recessions are somehow eliminated, and it will rise in downturns, thereby displaying the marked countercyclical pattern described earlier. As long as blacks are the last to find jobs in an expansion, their relative increase in employment will depend upon the length and strength of the recovery. Consequently, the countercyclical pattern shifted so that it favored blacks in the 1960s and hurt them in the 1970s and early 1980s.

The immediate puzzle posed by these trends in the unemployment gap can be appreciated by comparison to the trend in the wage gap. Smith and Welch [1986, 1989] argue that the trend toward wage convergence from 1940 to 1980 reflects the trend toward educational convergence of black and white workers. Competition forces employers to efficiently utilize the available human resources, so that despite prejudice, blacks and whites will experience increasingly similar labor-market outcomes as they provide increasingly similar labor-market inputs. This argument can also be applied to the trend in the unemployment gap. Since specific training and general training are held to be complementary [Mincer 1971], a rise in black education should increase black acquisition of on-the-job training and thereby raise the cost of turnover to both the worker and the firm. Human-capital theory thus predicts that the trend in the unemployment gap should follow that of the wage gap.[4] Yet this is not what we observe.

The decline of the racial wage gap is primarily due to a drop in occupational segregation; indeed, the increasing overlap of the black and white occupational distributions [Farley 1984:46-50] is perhaps the best evidence that the human capital of blacks and whites has become more similar. If the trends in human-capital acquisition and wage growth are inconsistent with the trend in the unemployment gap, then it would follow that the occupational and industrial distributions of black workers can account for little of the gap. It is possible to test this proposition by calculating what the black unemployment rate would be if blacks within occupational and industrial categories experienced the same unemployment rate as the average within each category as a whole.[5] In 1987, for example, if blacks within each of six occupational categories had experienced the same unemployment rate as the average for each category, then their total unemployment rate would have been 6.2 percent. This compares to their actual unemployment rate of 13.0 percent, and an aggregate unemployment rate of 6.2 percent. This means that next to none of their excess unemployment can be explained in terms of their distribution *between* occupational categories; the problem is their higher rates of unemployment *within* occupational categories.[6] The same is true with respect to their distribution between industries: in 1987, if blacks had experienced the same unemployment rate as the average within each of nine industrial categories, their unemployment rate would have been 5.8 percent. In other words, their distribution between industries would actually lead one to predict that their unemployment rate would be lower than the average. This is the same conclusion to which the U.S. Commission on Civil Rights [1982:38] came on the basis of a different sample and measurement technique. Yet human-capital theory is in essence one of the distribution of blacks and whites between occupational and industrial categories. Just as the theory predicts that blacks and whites should receive the same wage returns from human-capital investments, it also predicts that they should receive the same employment returns.

The conclusion that human-capital theory cannot explain the black/white unemployment gap is justified more thoroughly in the following section, but it clearly applies with all the more force when the changes in popular opinion and federal law since 1964 are compounded with the trend toward educational convergence. The apparent reduction in the so-called discriminatory preferences of whites, both individually and collectively, in conjunction with the educational trends, should make blacks and whites increasingly similar in their vulnerability to overall labor-market conditions. Smith and Welch [1986:109] believe that "nothing on the unemployment side of the labor market counteracts the sustained economic progress of blacks on the wage side of the labor market." This is surely one of the most specious statements to be made by serious economists in recent years.[7] The persistence of the unemployment gap not only offsets the improvements in living standards made possible by wage gains, but it also confounds the standard explanation for the wage gains. How are we to reconcile these trends? The following sections consider supply-side and demand-side explanations for this question.

II. THE SUPPLY SIDE

Supply-side explanations concern the relative distribution of productivity influencing characteristics that black and white workers bring to the labor market. The role of such factors can be evaluated with both time-series and cross-sectional data. In terms of the former, the contradictory trends in the wage and unemployment gaps are difficult to reconcile because, as noted earlier, human-capital theory predicts that the two should move in the same direction. Although the human capital gap has narrowed [Farley 1984:16-33], the unemployment differential has, if anything, widened. In terms of the latter, if the black labor force had the same distribution of productivity-related characteristics as the white labor force but experienced its own rates of return, the unemployment differential would largely remain. Supply-side explanations cannot account for wage and unemployment differentials within comparable groups. Evidence to this effect is presented below.

Unemployment can be influenced by the composition of the labor force along the lines of sex, marital status, age, experience, education, and residence. I will consider each in turn. Because these are cross-sectional comparisons, the unemployment gap is measured by the ratio within subgroups at some given moment in time. The issue of the correspondence of the unemployment rate difference with total unemployment over time is taken up in the next section. However, to provide some sense of the continuity of these cross-sectional comparisons through time, 1988 figures will be contrasted with more detailed calculations based on earlier data from my dissertation [Shulman 1984a:ch. 3].

Figures 1.2 and 1.3 show that the unemployment rate differential is virtually identical between the sexes. This is because the historical gap between the male and female unemployment rates has been similar between the races. In fact, since 1984 the male/female difference has virtually fallen to zero for both blacks and whites. Both the black and white labor forces have become increasingly feminized over time, the former due to the decline in the black male labor-force participation rate and the latter due to the rise in the white female labor-force participation rate. Due to these trends, the relative sexual composition of the black and white labor forces has next to no impact on the unemployment rate differential. In May 1983 (arbitrarily chosen), for example, if blacks had had the same sexual distribution of their labor force as whites, the unemployment rate ratio would have been 2.36 instead of 2.34.[8]

Tables 1.2A and 1.2B show black and white unemployment rates and ratios by sex and marital status for 1988. Married persons with spouse present have considerably lower unemployment rates than other individuals. However, the contrast is as great among whites as among blacks, so that the black/white ratio among married persons with spouse present is actually higher than that for widowed, divorced, or separated persons. It

Table 1.2
Unemployment Rates by Family Type and Race, 1988

A. Among Men

Marital Status	Black	White	Black/White
Single	19.4%	8.5%	2.28
Married, spouse present	5.8%	3.0%	1.93
Widowed, divorced, separated	11.5%	6.1%	1.89

B. Among Women

Marital Status	Black	White	Black/White
Single	18.3%	6.6%	2.77
Married, spouse present	6.7%	3.6%	1.86
Widowed, divorced, separated	9.9%	5.5%	1.80

C. Percentage of Families with Unemployment

Family Type	Black	White	Black/White
Total	15.2%	6.8%	2.23
Married couple	13.0	6.2	2.10
Female headed	17.5	9.7	1.80
Male headed	16.5	9.8	1.69

Source: *1989 Handbook of Labor Statistics*, various tables.

is evident that even if blacks had the same labor-force distribution between sexes and family types as whites, they would still be about twice as likely to be unemployed. Indeed, table 1.2C shows that the relative likelihood of a black family experiencing unemployment is actually greater for married couples than for other family types. This is simply because there are two adults in a married couple who can be afflicted by unemployment, as opposed to one adult in other family types.

Age is another factor that can influence the probability of unemployment. Teenagers have especially high unemployment rates, so the more the black labor force is skewed toward teens, the more the unemployment rate differential will rise. However, the opposite can just as well be the case. In 1981, for example, white teens comprised 8.38 percent of the white labor force, while black teens comprised 7.53 percent of the black labor force. Though it is not always the case that teens comprise a larger percentage of the white labor force, the small fraction of teenagers in both labor forces means that racial differences in this factor cannot account for much of the unemployment gap. However, it is important to note that the unemployment rate ratio falls with age even among adults. Table 1.3A shows that in 1988, for example, the black unemployment rate and the black/white unemployment rate ratio fell steadily as age rose above 24 (although the blacks in the oldest category were still 60 percent more likely to be unemployed than similarly aged whites). The fall in the ratio with age

Table 1.3
Unemployment Rates by Age, Reason, and Schooling, 1988

A. Age

	Black	White	Black/White
Total	11.7%	4.7%	2.49
16-19	32.4	13.1	2.47
20-24	19.6	7.1	2.76
25-34	11.9	4.5	2.64
35-44	7.5	3.5	2.14
45-54	5.9	3.1	1.90
55-64	4.8	3.0	1.60

B. Reason

	Black	White	Black/White
Job losers	5.1%	2.3%	2.22
Job leavers	1.4	0.7	2.00
Reentrants	3.4	1.2	2.83
New entrants	1.9	0.5	3.80

C. Years of Schooling, > 24 years old

	Black	White	Black/White
Total	10.0%	4.0%	2.50
< 4 years high school	14.6	8.3	1.76
4 years high school only	11.2	4.6	2.43
1-3 years college	7.4	3.2	2.31
> 3 years college	3.3	1.5	2.20

Source: *1989 Handbook of Labor Statistics*, tables 28, 37 and 67.

contradicts the "vintage effect" [Smith and Welch 1989:528], which presumes that younger blacks enjoy greater opportunities than older blacks, and suggests that the improvement in wage offers may be a trade-off against a decline in employment offers. The decline in unemployment with age may mean that the younger age composition of the black labor force (due in large part to earlier mortality) may account for some fraction of the unemployment rate differential. Nonetheless, if the black labor force in 1981 had the same three-tier age distribution as the white labor force (teens, 20-34, and over 34), the overall unemployment rate ratio would have fallen from 2.12 only to 2.10. The relative age distributions of the black and white labor forces therefore have virtually no impact on the unemployment differential.

Age influences unemployment in part because it is a proxy for experience. Workers with less experience may have more difficulty finding work and may be more prone to be laid off when demand slackens. One measure of relative experience is the fraction of new entrants into the labor force. If proportionately more of the black labor force is composed of new entrants, then the unemployment gap will widen due to the need for new entrants to acquire skills and contacts. However, unemployment rates recalculated with new entrants subtracted out fall by about the same amount for blacks and whites, so that the ratio is virtually unaffected. The average adjusted unemployment rate ratio over the years 1969-79, for example, was 2.08, while the unadjusted ratio averaged 2.11.

Black workers may also be more likely to experience unemployment if they have spent time away from the labor force, thereby reducing their informational contacts, their employment record, and their acquisition of on-the-job training. Table 1.3B examines this possibility by breaking down unemployment rates by the reason for unemployment. Black reentrants (and, even more so, new entrants) do experience greater unemployment relative to their white counterparts than black workers with immediate experience, but even black job leavers are twice as likely to be unemployed as white job leavers. In any case, most black unemployment is concentrated among job losers, where the ratio well exceeds two. These figures force us to question why blacks are so much more likely to lose their jobs than whites, and why, if they leave the labor force or newly enter it, they have so much more trouble than similar whites in finding jobs. The distribution of blacks between experience categories would thus seem to have less to do with the unemployment gap than their relative probabilities of employment within experience categories.

Perhaps the most common belief is that black unemployment is relatively high because black education is relatively low. As noted earlier, the difficulty here is in reconciling the steady fall in the educational gap with the stubborn persistence of the unemployment gap. In March 1979, for example, if blacks had had the same educational distribution as whites, the unemployment rate ratio would have been 2.14 instead of 2.33. By March 1983, the white civilian labor force had completed a median of 12.8 years of schooling, while the black civilian labor force had completed a median of 12.5 years of schooling [also see Farley 1984:16-22]. The difference is hardly great enough to account for the unemployment differential. Table 1.3C shows black and white unemployment rates and ratios by schooling category in 1988. The ratio is actually greater for high-school graduates than for dropouts. It drops thereafter, but black college graduates were still well over twice as likely as white college graduates to be unemployed. Nor is this solely a product of older black college graduates suffering from the "legacy of discrimination." For persons who had completed at least one year of college in March 1983, for example, the ratio among 25-34-year-olds was 2.62; among 35-44-year-olds, 1.92; and among 45-54-year-olds, 1.44 [USDoL 1984:Tables B-2, B-13]. Even within educational categories, it appears (as noted earlier) that the unemployment gap displays a "reverse vintage effect" that may be due to the greater aspirations of younger blacks (or the greater desperation of older blacks). This observation lends little comfort to those who would have us believe, on the basis of an ill-founded generalization from academia and government to the private sector as a whole, that well-educated blacks face superior employment opportunities in comparison to well-educated whites.

The residential distributions of blacks and whites are similarly unable to explain their relative unemployment experience. In 1980, for example, if blacks had had the same four-region distribution as whites, the unemployment rate ratio would have been 2.37 rather than 2.25 for men and 2.27 rather than 2.29 for women. Table 1.4A shows that this comparison continued to hold in 1988 for a nine-region breakdown. Although the unemployment rate ratio varied substantially between regions, the lowest it fell was 1.83, and in some regions black unemployment was well over triple that of white unemployment. The same conclusion holds if we look at cities rather than regions. Table 1.4B shows that the unemployment gap was nearly as great in the suburbs as in the central cities and in rural as in urban areas. The contrast in the unemployment gap between poverty and nonpoverty areas (table 1.4C) was similarly small. The geographic distribution of the black labor force would thus seem to have little to do with the aggregate unemployment gap.

The data presented in this section suggest that excessively high black unemployment cannot be explained in terms of the characteristics of the black population itself. Furthermore, other analysts have come to the same conclusion with respect to racial gaps in labor-force participation.[9] Even if it were true (as is commonly supposed) that excessively high black

Table 1.4
Unemployment Rates by Residence, 1988

A. Region

	Black	White	Black/White
New England	5.5%	3.0%	1.83
Middle Atlantic	8.4	3.9	2.15
South Atlantic	9.0	3.7	2.43
East South Central	14.3	5.6	2.55
West South Central	15.7	6.6	2.38
East North Central	16.7	5.1	3.27
West North Central	13.5	4.1	3.29
Mountain	11.3	5.9	1.91
Pacific	10.9	5.1	2.14

B. Metropolitan

	Black	White	Black/White
Metropolitan			
Urban	11.8%	4.6%	2.56
Central cities	12.6	5.3	2.38
Suburbs	9.4	4.1	2.29
Nonmetropolitan			
Rural	10.9	4.9	2.22
Farm	7.6	1.9	4.00
Nonfarm	12.8	5.9	2.17

C. Poverty Areas

	Black	White	Black/White
Poverty areas	15.3%	7.9%	1.94
Nonpoverty areas	9.2	4.4	2.09

Source: *1989 Handbook of Labor Statistics*, tables 10 and 11.

unemployment and labor-force dropout rates are due to a greater fraction of young, poorly educated persons isolated in the central cities, it would still have to be explained why comparable whites are underemployed less; however, as this section has detailed, the black/white gap exists over virtually all population subgroups. Although a strong case can be made that black occupational mobility corresponds to changes in educational attainment, supply-side factors simply do not appear to provide very powerful explanations for the level or the trends in black employment itself.

This discussion should not be taken to suggest that supply-side factors play absolutely no role in the determination of the unemployment differential. It could conceivably be the case that the interaction between these factors is more powerful than each considered separately. Nonetheless, this author is not aware of any literature in which multiple regression models show human-capital factors accounting for a substantial fraction of the unemployment differential. Jackson and Montgomery [1986:139], for example, conclude that "the results from the different estimates using the NBER, NLS and CPS data sets suggest that differences in layoff or job-loss experiences between blacks and whites cannot be explained simply by differences in schooling or the geographic and age distributions of the respective populations. ... Of the conventional human capital variables, only tenure was consistently found to reduce job loss, layoffs, and discharges among blacks or to reduce the black-white differential in these rates." In any case, human-capital factors cannot be considered to be exogenous determinants of unemployment since discrimination may reduce the incentive to acquire human capital in the first place. Magura and Shapiro [1987], for example, show that the high unemployment experienced by black youth causes black high-school students to dropout, and not vice versa. Multiple regression models may thus overstate the impact of supply-side factors on the unemployment gap. The question is more acute when considered in a time-series sense. Everyone agrees that black/white human-capital differences have fallen over time. Why then has the unemployment differential remained unaffected?

III. THE DEMAND SIDE

Section I showed that any explanation of the black/white unemployment gap must account for three trends: (1) its long-term persistence, (2) its countercyclical fluctuations, and (3) the shifts in the countercyclical pattern resulting from the dependence of black employment gains on the strength and length of the upswing. It was also argued that these trends can be attributed to the interaction of overall labor-market conditions with the last hired-first fired pattern. This section will explain why the last hired-first fired pattern is a consequence of "rational" business decision making. The racial gap in unemployment can thereby be blamed upon systemic employment discrimination and as such can be considered to be an endogenous element of the modern capitalist economy.

Section II showed that distribution of various characteristics between blacks and whites cannot account for the size of the unemployment gap, let alone its secular or cyclical trends. If this is the case, it follows that the unemployment gap must be due to the discriminatory decisions of employers or, at the least, to the response of employers to the discriminatory pressures of white consumers or workers. Unfortunately, it is difficult to directly measure or test for the existence or extent of such discrimination. Far more data are available on worker characteristics than on the details of employer decision making. This institutional bias in the collection and release of data influences our understanding of racial differences in the dynamics of employment and unemployment. In particular, it results in a pronounced empirical slant toward human-capital models despite the fact that their results almost always leave a large portion of the racial gap unexplained [Swinton 1983:19]. Daniel Lichter [1988:771], for example, shows that between 1970 and 1982, "the significance of race [on underemployment] increased over time, regardless of age group, level of education, or temporal macroeconomic shifts." Nonetheless, the skew in the availability of data allows for the endless refinement of human-capital models, while the extent and mechanics of race discrimination go relatively unexplored.

Several suggestive models of discrimination are available, but in the absence of directly relevant data, the tests that have been made of the importance of labor-market discrimination are either indirect [e.g., Shulman 1987; Reich 1981] or based on small, geographically restricted samples [e.g., Culp and Dunson 1986].[10] This has encouraged orthodox economists to insist that the ordinary workings of the competitive marketplace are automatically prone to eliminate discrimination [e.g., O'Neill 1987]. Although there are several possible routes by which discrimination can be shown to boost profitability (and thus be reproduced by market mechanisms), the lack of direct data has kept these models in a speculative limbo. This is unfortunate since, in the absence of any evidence that excessive black unemployment is due to the characteristics of the black population itself, we must of necessity turn to demand-side explanations for the trends in the unemployment gap.

The lack of demand-side data forces the analysis in this section to pursue a different path than that of the previous section. Instead of resorting to "the facts," the question must be addressed theoretically. In contrast to the supply side, are there trends on the demand side that correspond to those of the unemployment gap? In particular, can the last hired-first fired pattern be explained in terms of the profit-maximizing behavior of firms? Such an explanation is suggestive rather than conclusive insofar as it only establishes the possibility of discrimination. Nonetheless, if demand-side dynamics can be shown to be theoretically consistent with the trends of the unemployment gap, the conclusion that discrimination is the cause of the unemployment gap would be strengthened. The empirical support for this conclusion could then be considered in part to be negative (insofar as supply-side factors cannot be connected to the unemployment gap) and in part to be positive (insofar as some studies do show that employment discrimination sustains the unemployment gap). Positive support is also provided in section IV in the form of an historical sketch of the origins and development of the unemployment gap. The need for more empirical research on employment discrimination is obvious.[11]

A demand-side explanation means that the link between aggregate unemployment and the spread between black and white unemployment must be shown to arise from the profit maximizing decisions of firms. Models of discrimination are the natural place to which to turn to establish such a link since they are designed to connect business behavior to discriminatory outcomes. If it can be shown that such models predict a rise in employment discrimination during a downturn and, conversely, a fall in an upturn, then it follows that they are consistent with the secular and cyclical trends of the unemployment rate difference. The persistent recurrence of high unemployment would prevent the racial unemployment gap from disappearing; the increase (decrease) in employment discrimination in a downturn (upturn) would make the unemployment rate difference fluctuate countercyclically; and the countercyclical pattern could shift with changes in the strength and length of the upturns by influencing the degree to which employment discrimination falls as the macroeconomy grows. Thus the models of discrimination must connect employment discrimination to overall labor-market conditions to be useful for our purposes.

Unfortunately, the most commonly discussed models of discrimination fail to do exactly that. This is due to their effort to analyze "discrimination in general" rather than distinguishing between the types of discrimination (e.g., employment, occupational, and wage) so as to dissect the labor market dynamics of each in particular. Discrimination is then held to be due to some fixed rationale that is implicitly invariant with respect to labor-market conditions.

Becker's *The Economics of Discrimination* [1957] is probably the most widely cited work in the field. He argues that discrimination stems from subjective prejudice or white "disutility" from associating with blacks. Yet if prejudice is taken as a given and not allowed to be endogenously dependent upon the anxiety of whites for job security in the context of recurringly slack labor markets, it is difficult to see how or why it would fluctuate cyclically. Indeed, Becker concludes that prejudice will result in segregation but not wage or employment differentiation (given a sufficient number of nonprejudiced employers), and the modern work based on his model presumes that discrimination is unlikely to persist in a competitive environment. This model is therefore inapplicable to the problem of employment discrimination in general and to its relation to aggregate labor-market conditions in particular.[12] Sowell [1981b:ch. 3], for example, argues that employment discrimination cannot be sustained because it increases the search costs of hiring, thereby assuming that labor markets are always tight enough to limit the supply of qualified white labor.

The other most commonly cited model of discrimination is based upon informational uncertainties: blacks are presumed to be riskier to hire if their characteristics (e.g., educational quality) are less well known than those of whites, or if the mean of their average group abilities is believed to be less than that of whites. Ascriptively based "statistical discrimination" then becomes a low-cost screening device in which black job applicants are treated on the basis of the perceived average characteristics of their group because information about each individual is imperfect and costly to obtain. They are therefore less likely to be hired or, if they are hired, to be allocated into jobs that require large investments in on-the-job training [e.g., Thurow 1975:170-177]. These models are superior to subjective prejudice models because they connect discrimination to profit maximization rather than "irrational" prejudice. However, there is no reason to expect informational uncertainty to fluctuate cyclically. Statistical discrimination models are therefore unable to connect discrimination to aggregate labor-market conditions. Furthermore, informational uncertainty falls rapidly after an applicant is hired, so that firms with long-term black employees should be less prone to practice statistical discrimination. Competition should then generalize this result. Consequently, models of informational uncertainty cannot explain the persistence of discriminatory decision making that results in inequality in excess of that created by actual human-capital differences. Indeed, imperfect information can be considered to be a type of barrier to competition that "alert entrepreneurs" should have an incentive to overcome [Darity 1989:339-340].

The subjective prejudice and statistical discrimination models stem from the neoclassical tradition, but institutional and radical economists have also contributed to this literature. Their models do predict the secular persistence of discrimination and in this sense are preferable to the neoclassical models. The institutional model is based upon the organizational rigidities that arise from the resistance of internal labor markets to change. Internal labor markets are insulated from competition in the external market. They maximize long-term profitability insofar as they stabilize production by governing the pricing and allocation of labor by administrative rules rather than the exigencies of supply and demand, and by establishing promotional ladders and other incentive systems that are based upon custom and allow for compromise between labor and management [Doeringer and Piore 1971]. According job privileges to white workers may be a custom that stabilizes relations between management and majority workers. For example, white workers may take it to be their customary prerogative that they compete among themselves but not with women and minorities, and that new hires get primarily drawn from a pool of their friends and relatives. Changing that custom (and its concrete consequences in terms of the mechanisms that establish job access and allocation) can be costly, risky, and time consuming. As Baron notes on page 127 of his stimulating contribution to this volume, firms display an "inertia associated with structures and procedures. Jobs and organizations are designed in ways that conform to economic pressures and sociocultural understandings present at the time of founding, which are likely to persist unless subject to intense pressures for change." Hence the pressure to stabilize production by maintaining a shared set of implicit agreements between management and white workers can result in an institutionalized resistance to occupational integration that can depress the demand for black labor.

This perspective is highly suggestive because it reconciles the persistence of discrimination with (external) market competition. However, in and of itself, it is not adequate to our purposes. First, it predicts that changes in the institutional environment, for example, due to legal intervention, should realign internal labor markets and reduce the sway of racial custom. This is in fact what we observe. The problem is in reconciling this with the persistence of the unemployment gap. Second, there is no reason to expect institutionalized rigidities to fluctuate cyclically. The internal labor market is defined in terms of its insulation from the instability of the external labor market. Finally, internal labor markets explain discrimination only in terms of the behavior of large firms; it remains to establish their effect at the aggregate level.

Radical models of discrimination are based on the presumption that capitalists and workers have intrinsically contradictory interests. The most commonly cited (at least by economists) of such models explains racial discrimination as a manifestation of the more fundamental dynamics of class conflict.[13] Employers can raise their profits if racial divisions inhibit labor solidarity and hence reduce the bargaining power of workers. This model predicts that discrimination will persist even in competitive conditions [Reich 1981]. Yet it is poorly suited for the analysis of the unemployment gap. Bargaining between labor and management largely concerns wages and working conditions, but only rarely directly addresses the issue of employment. No firm prediction can be made about the impact of bargaining power on employment since wages have a contradictory effect: they expand employment by adding to aggregate demand, but they contract employment by adding to the costs of production. Furthermore, to the extent that cyclical implications can be drawn out of this divide-and-conquer interpretation of discrimination, they would appear to suggest that discrimination would fall in a downturn. As unemployment rises, labor is weakened and wages fall so that the need for a divide-and-conquer strategy as a device with which to discipline labor would be diminished. Since bargaining between capital and labor is rarely directly applicable to the issue of employment, and since the pressure for employers to use divide-and-conquer strategies would seem to be greater in an expansion than a recession, this model does not appear to be well suited for the analysis of the unemployment gap.[14]

Although none of these models provide a satisfactory analysis of employment discrimination or its interaction with labor-market conditions, it is possible to do so by combining elements of each into a more cohesive discussion of race as a social relation of production. This approach views discrimination as contradictory, insofar as it may both raise and lower the costs of production, and as complex, insofar as it is composed of differing but related practices. Discrimination is therefore seen to be both continuous and changeable as a result of variations in its socioeconomic context. I call this approach the "race relations model" because it interprets race as a social relation of production in its own right rather than as a manifestation of some other underlying reality (such as class struggle, organizational rigidities, or informational uncertainties). The remainder of this section outlines this model and discusses its inferences with respect to labor-market conditions.

It has long been recognized that discrimination can increase the costs of production. However, it has been less well recognized that *ceasing* discrimination can also raise costs. Since costs can arise from both continuing discrimination and ceasing discrimination, the balance between them can be influenced by aggregate labor-market conditions. The race relations model thus predicts both the secular persistence and the countercyclical fluctuations of the unemployment differential.

The costs of continuing discrimination can consist of some combination of the following: (1) wage premiums paid to attract qualified white applicants, (2) longer search times needed to find qualified white applicants, and/or (3) lower production due to the hiring of less qualified white applicants. In other words, it is costly to forgo the hiring of qualified black applicants. It is a familiar argument that competition dictates that the firm that most efficiently employs its resources – including its human resources – will be able to capture market share from the discriminatory firm that, by definition, is striving to satisfy objectives other than maximum profits. Thus the models of discrimination which predict its persistence either are based upon barriers to competition (informational uncertainties or institutionalized rigidities) or assume that discrimination is an efficient method of utilizing human resources because it reduces worker collusion (divide-and-conquer).

This argument assumes that product markets are sufficiently competitive so that any loss in efficiency gets translated into a loss in market share. Even granting this dubious assumption, however, it does not follow that competition and discrimination are necessarily antithetical. It is also costly to cease discrimination; competition thus plays a contradictory role in the reproduction of discrimination, a role that varies with overall conditions in the labor market.

Ceasing discrimination can be costly due to the social character of production, that is, the organization of work in terms of worker/worker and worker/capitalist relations, and their impact upon output and incomes. On the one hand, workers must cooperate with each other to produce goods, but on the other hand, workers must be divided from each other to reduce labor solidarity and facilitate managerial control. Racial identification plays an important role in maintaining this balance. It enables management to establish (even if unconsciously) a hegemonic relation with its white workers, creating an overlap of interests and beliefs that offsets their

class conflicts at the expense of black workers. Consequently, its breakdown can increase costs to the firm by threatening the control of management and the security of white workers, resulting in lost output and/or
increases in the wage claims on income.

Reducing discrimination can lower productivity by disrupting traditional patterns of authority and association. The continuity of production
requires a stable relationship between the firm and its social environment.
Ceasing discrimination can thwart the implicit and explicit expectations
that bond the firm to its suppliers, customers, and governmental regulators,
which is why capitalism has been more prone to adapt to apartheid than
to erode it [Fredrickson 1988]. The continuity of production also requires
a stable relationship between management and labor within the firm. Thus
Doeringer and Piore [1971:136] argue that disrupting the established
channels of recruitment, screening, allocation, training, wage setting, and
promotion can "raise the inefficiency of the labor force adjustment process,
at least in the short run, thereby imposing costs on both the employer and
society. Only where the effect of discrimination has been to create a grossly
inefficient internal labor market will there be any offsetting benefits."
Ceasing discrimination necessarily changes previously successful employment practices. As long as there is a recurrent excess supply of labor, there
is little incentive for the firm to increase its risks by undermining the tried-
and-true procedures that have traditionally generated, selected, and de-
ployed an applicant pool. The firm thus minimizes risk and stabilizes
production by adopting the norms already present in its external and
internal environments.

Instability can also result as the rules regulating class conflict are undermined, as vested interests are unseated, and as competition increases for a
limited set of rewards. For example, reducing discrimination can increase
training costs and/or lower output if white workers resist the integration of
the work force, the diminution of their prerogatives, and the alteration of
an accepted wage and occupational structure. Hill [1989] argues that
unions have frequently functioned as the organizational vehicles for these
objectives; indeed, if this were not the case, it would be hard to understand
the historical opposition of most unions to racial integration. Ceasing
discrimination can lower output by disrupting the customary basis of labor
relations because, as Thurow [1975:107] argues, "group preferences about
a 'just' wage structure can have a major impact on production. Because it
can have an impact on productivity, it must be taken into account by the
employer." Furthermore, reducing discrimination may also impair team
efficiency. Cooperation is crucial for mistakes to be corrected and

opportunities to be recognized. This is particularly the case in the upper ranks where the nonstandardized and uncertain nature of decision making forces managers to rely heavily on trust, communication, and teamwork. Social homogeneity thus raises the team efficiency of managers. Breaking these bonds by bringing in women and minorities can be irrational for the cost-minimizing firm [Kanter 1977].

Disruption in the traditional patterns of authority and association, change in the rules of internal labor markets, alteration of the customary basis of labor relations, and reduction in team efficiency therefore are all reasons why ceasing discrimination can lower productivity. A reduction in discrimination can also mean greater wage costs due to the potential rise in labor solidarity [Reich 1981]. Discriminatory practices can therefore be costly and risky to change due to the impact upon employers, white employees, and organizational structure.[15] Thus, given that the social relations of race provide a context within which the firm must operate, the simple imperative of cost minimization can account for the perpetuation of discrimination. But since continuing discrimination can also raise costs as human resources are misallocated or as the government pursues policies that raise the risks and penalties for discrimination, the question arises as to the determination of the balance between these opposing pressures.

One answer notes that "discrimination" is a complex practice and in different ways influences wages, occupational attainment, and the probability of employment.[16] The pressures to minimize the costs of both continuing discrimination and ceasing discrimination may be resolved by reducing its costliest component (e.g., wage discrimination, which can be easily monitored) and concurrently intensifying the others (e.g., employment discrimination, which is difficult to prove). In other words, the types of discrimination may be trade-offs against one another. Firms may alter the margins they explore as conditions change, thereby changing the composition of (without making a net reduction in) their discriminatory practices.[17] Alternatively, the appearance of reducing discrimination may be created by de jure methods while the reality of discrimination continues de facto. Changing the appearance of discrimination may be sufficient to mitigate the pressures to cease discrimination without incurring the costs of actually changing discrimination itself.[18]

A final answer directly addresses our focus on labor-market conditions. It concerns the extent of the inefficiencies allegedly created by discrimination: if there exists an excess supply of labor, then the hiring of qualified white workers need not be forgone, search time need not be appreciably expanded, and wages need not be raised. Unemployment, in other words, reduces the costs associated with discrimination. It furthermore tends to increase the costs associated with ceasing discrimination. When labor markets are slack and work is scarce, workers place a premium on job security. White workers may choose racial solidarity over class solidarity if they face incentives to prefer job security over wage gains [Shulman 1989]. Thus the conflicts associated with reducing discrimination – conflicts over authority, prerogatives, incentives, custom and teamwork – all tend to increase when unemployment rises. The ability of white workers to protect "their" jobs and to maintain some influence over the hiring process becomes increasingly important as their occupational alternatives diminish. At the same time, management can maximize control and productivity and reduce labor solidarity and wages by giving priority to the interests of its white workers during a period when the costs of doing so are falling.

As unemployment rises, the costs of continuing discrimination thus fall and the costs of ceasing discrimination thus rise, so that incentives shift toward increasing discrimination. The opposite is the case in the upswing when human resources are scarce and opportunity costs are high for lost output. This approach thereby captures both the secular persistence and the countercyclical fluctuations of employment discrimination. The fact that blacks gained more than whites in the upswings of the 1960s and less than whites in the upswings of the 1980s can be attributed to the relative strengths of the expansions, and hence the relative reductions in employment discrimination, in those two decades. Policy efforts after the 1960s may have reduced wage discrimination among employed workers since it is relatively easy to measure and monitor by antidiscrimination agencies; but employment discrimination is more difficult to control since it coincides with the general drop in the demand for labor in recessionary conditions. Indeed, a drop in wage discrimination can encourage employment discrimination as the traditional demand for "cheap" black labor is choked off.

It is thus possible to explain the correspondence of the unemployment differential with total unemployment in terms of the rational behavior of firms. Changes in labor-market conditions shift the cost incentives of discrimination so that employment discrimination rises in downturns and falls in upturns. Demand-side dynamics can therefore be shown to be theoretically consistent with the movements of the unemployment differential.

IV. A SCHEMATIC APPLICATION

This section presents a schematic history of the black/white unemployment gap in an effort to show the applicability of the discussion of the race relations model of discrimination. The salient conclusions of this model are that: 1) the intensity of discrimination will vary with labor-market conditions in particular and with political or other factors in general that change the relative costs of continuing and ceasing discrimination, 2) the structure or composition of labor market discrimination may change as wage discrimination, occupational discrimination, and employment discrimination trade off against one another or alter their relative degree of importance, and 3) the pressures to cease discrimination may result in more changes in the appearance of discrimination than in its actual practice. I will use this perspective to outline the forces behind the emergence of the unemployment gap and the forces that have sustained it in the face of economic and political pressures against discrimination.

The emergence of a racial gap in unemployment represents a historically significant transition in the nature of black oppression that deserves more attention from researchers than it has thus far received. Edna Bonacich [1976:39] described it as a "reversal": black unemployment did not exceed white unemployment before 1940 and did not achieve the two-to-one ratio we now take for granted until 1954. She explained this phenomenon in terms of the New Deal's dissolution of the "split" labor market (differentially priced labor of equivalent quality). As the labor movement succeeded in legalizing unions and institutionalizing collective bargaining, the ability of employers to reduce costs by substituting black for white workers was reduced. Management and unions cooperated to preserve a racial division of labor [Hill 1989], the former to transform their previously repressive control over white labor (partially based on the threat of substitution of cheaper black workers) to a more sophisticated system of hegemonic control,[19] the latter to institutionalize job security. This reduced the demand for black labor so that total unemployment became unevenly divided along racial lines. Factors such as the mechanization of southern agriculture helped account for the emergence of the black/white unemployment gap, but changes in labor-market structure created by the pressures of white workers as well as management were necessary to sustain it through time. As Jill Rubery [1978:34] noted, labor-market segmentation (differentially employed labor of equivalent quality) results as much from the defensive actions of workers as from the offensive actions of management: "Workers act defensively to protect themselves from the competition of the external labour market, to obtain job security and higher wages, to the exclusion and possible detriment of those remaining in the unorganized sector." Employment discrimination thereby became rooted in the segmentation of the postwar labor market.

The transition from a split labor market to a segmented labor market represented the success of the efforts by white workers to insulate themselves from competition by cheaper black labor. Because blacks could not be paid less for the same work, they could not be used to threaten white workers; indeed, their isolation into a specific subset of jobs and their use as a buffer against recessions meant that discrimination now increased the job security of white workers. Given the reorganization of the industrial relations system created by the New Deal, capital shifted to occupational segregation and employment discrimination and away from wage discrimination as the most efficient margins on which to maximize the gains from discrimination.

The emergence of segmented labor markets was thus based upon systematic employment discrimination against blacks as part of the postwar compromise (or "labor accord") between organized white labor and management. Although industrial unionism was perceived to be more equalitarian than craft unionism, Herbert Hill [1989:191-192] concludes that "the great promise of the CIO, the promise of an interracial labor movement, was never realized....The CIO policy was at best an expression of abstract equality in contrast with the pattern of exclusion and segregation that persisted within the AFL. By 1955, when the CIO and AFL merged ... the CIO policy on race had become an empty formality." Despite being nominally committed to the goal of racial equality, the union movement promoted a labor accord that, according to Edwards and Podgursky [1986:21], "primarily organized white male workers." The gains for management were labor peace, stability, and productivity; the gains for white male labor were job security and rising real wages. The losses were everybody else's.

Although anticommunism has frequently been blamed for the triumph of business unionism over social unionism, the substitution of race consciousness for class consciousness is probably more important and in large part may account for the success of the anticommunist crusades. Hill [1989] comments numerous times on the role of race in the assimilation of white ethnics, their organization into labor unions, and its mitigating effect on class conflict. The accord of the postwar period represented the integration of unions into the system of managerial control, institutionalizing its hegemonic character (since management and labor now had common interests in increasing productivity) and at the same time establishing it as a racial system of social identification and job preference. This outcome, of course, was not simply a product of union connivance, but was due to a strategic alliance with management in the context of the long-standing beliefs and practices of white supremacy. Management took advantage of (and thereby perpetuated) racial ideologies and conflicts in its efforts to stabilize the labor process and establish hegemony over its white workers. This new system of industrial relations thereby altered the way in which business firms functioned, for it embedded these social codes in organizational structures. This accounts for the perpetuation of employment discrimination in the context of political and economic pressures to eliminate it.

Labor markets in the 1950s and especially the 1960s were relatively tight. These decades also saw the emergence of a powerful movement against racial discrimination that eventually resulted in a variety of pieces of legislation designed to outlaw discrimination and remedy its past effects. One result was the trend toward convergence in black and white educational attainment. Overt bigotry went out of fashion, and instead "equal opportunity" (however defined) became the watchword of the day. As a result of these developments, black occupational mobility increased more rapidly than white, so that occupational segregation declined. Yet the unemployment gap persisted. The reasons for this apparent paradox lay in the institutionalization of the system of white job preference created by the labor accord.

Baron, in chapter 6, surveys a variety of studies to support his argument that "social forces and discriminatory cultural beliefs prevalent when a job or organization is founded condition the way that positions are defined, priced, and staffed, becoming institutionalized within the formal structure and informal traditions of the enterprise." His concern is more with occupational segregation than with employment discrimination per se (though he uses the latter term), but his argument is clearly applicable to the question of the unemployment gap. The racial basis of the labor accord established job hierarchies that were socially as well as technically defined. Consequently, specific recruitment, screening, and allocative procedures were institutionalized to preserve this hierarchy that systematically excluded or marginalized black workers. Once in place, these job definitions and employment procedures became costly and risky to change, not least because powerful interest groups had an interest in seeing them maintained. The resistance of vested interests will create transactions costs (e.g., information blockages, resource withholding, and so on) that inhibit the alteration of racially based job hierarchies and that tend to substitute cosmetic changes for real changes. Minorities and women, for example, may find their jobs reclassified as "managerial" while the actual centers of decision making remain in the same hands as before. They still are not allowed to compete for white male positions in more than a token fashion. Occupational stratification is thus simultaneously a system of social differentiation in which white males are insulated from job competition and thus from aggregate unemployment.

In addition to his citations of other studies, Baron supports his argument with evidence culled from his analyses of the occupational structure and staffing of the California civil service system and of a sample of 415 firms. Evidence of the organizational endogeneity of racial job preference is also presented in the 1987 study by Jomills Braddock II and James McPartland. They surveyed a nationally representative sample of 4,078 employers to collect data on the mechanisms and criteria for hiring and promotion decisions. Four types of racial employment barriers were then specified and investigated: "segregated networks" at the candidate stage, "information bias" and "statistical discrimination" at the entry stage, and "closed internal markets" at the promotion stage. Their conclusion is worth quoting at some length:

Our research indicates that exclusionary barriers (1) continue to restrict equal employment even in the absence of intentional discrimination, (2) are imbedded in the structure of labor markets and major institutions of society, and (3) are reinforced by the usual unregulated incentive systems for employers.

We find many minorities continue to face the exclusionary barriers of segregated social networks, information bias, and statistical discrimination in finding entry positions, and these barriers contribute to the problems of closed internal labor markets frequently faced by minorities within the firm. . . . These barriers continue to exclude minorities unfairly even when there is no intention by employers to treat minorities any differently from other potential employees.

We find these barriers are kept in place in part because they are tied to the racial segregation of schools and neighborhoods that persists in modern society and to the white perceptions of racial group differences that derive from unequal educational and employment opportunities of the past and present . . . .

Not only are the continuing barriers sustained by major institutions of American society, but there are few strong incentives for employers to overcome these barriers. Indeed, the desire for cost-efficiency contributes strongly to keeping these barriers in effect. [Braddock and McPartland 1987:27-28]

The evidence and arguments presented by Baron and by Braddock and McPartland support the contentions of this chapter that discrimination becomes institutionalized due to the adaptive responses of organizations to their social environment, that ceasing discrimination is costly because it disrupts vested interests, ignites conflicts, and requires risky change in traditional personnel practices, and that the normal workings of the competitive market are unable to eradicate discrimination given the recurrence of high unemployment.

These forces created and sustained employment discrimination despite the relatively tight labor markets of the 1950s and 1960s. In other words, racial segmentation in the labor market offset the impact of low unemployment during this period. But as noted earlier, other political, legal, social, and educational developments would also have tended to raise the costs of discrimination and thereby reduce the racial gap in unemployment. The combination of these forces did reduce occupational segregation (though, as Baron notes, the occupational mobility of women and minorities is frequently limited and cosmetic and fails to redistribute power within the firm). Nonetheless, if labor markets had continued to be tight, it is conceivable that employment discrimination would have fallen as the costs of continuing it began to exceed the costs of ceasing it. But this did not occur. Unemployment secularly increased starting in the early 1970s, skewing the cost structure of discrimination back toward employment preferences for whites. By the inauguration of the Reagan administration, hostility toward measures to achieve racial equality was openly expressed by government officials and the subsequent decline in civil-rights enforcement further encouraged racial bias in employment practices. It took the long expansion of the 1980s for black unemployment to once again fall more than white unemployment. A renewal of high unemployment will bring in its wake a renewal of employment discrimination and the cycle will begin again.

Thus the contemporary period has seen employment discrimination continue as before, but for the opposite set of reasons. After World War II, labor market segmentation offset the pressure of tight labor markets to sustain employment discrimination. Since the mid-1970s, this set of forces has reversed, so that rising unemployment has offset the decline in racial job segmentation to sustain employment privileges for whites (aided and abetted, of course, by a permissive federal attitude toward discrimination). This schematic account of the unemployment gap thus illustrates that the forces at play are complex and contradictory, that they conjoin social relations, business practices, and economic and political conditions, and that their results could never be predicted in an a priori fashion. Nonetheless, it is theoretically feasible to predict that discrimination will not wither away on its own. As long as capitalism creates institutions which incorporate and reproduce their social environment and labor markets that consistently suffer from prolonged unemployment, it re-creates discrimination. This cycle suggests that discrimination does not decline so much as it periodically retreats, only to reemerge as economic and political conditions change. In the absence of a sustained policy effort – or a total realignment of society's basic institutions – racism will continue to debilitate our collective existence.

V. CONCLUSIONS

Given the changes in law and popular attitudes over the past quarter-century as well as the trend toward convergence in the educational and occupational attainments of blacks and whites, one would expect racial inequality in labor-market outcomes to have steadily fallen. This is true for wages but not for unemployment. It is difficult to attribute the latter to the characteristics that blacks bring to the labor market, especially in light of the human-capital rationale for the former. Unemployment differentials persist within cohorts defined along a number of dimensions as well as over time periods covering diverse conditions. This persistence is in reality due to the special responsiveness of black unemployment to aggregate labor market conditions. Since the supply side of the labor market cannot account for the sensitivity of black unemployment, the conclusion by default is that the demand side, that is, employer decision making, is to blame. This conclusion is strengthened by the ability of the race relations model to reconcile the secular and cyclical trends in the unemployment differential with aggregate labor-market conditions. The rational decisions of employers in response to changes in the costs of production result in fluctuations in employment discrimination that translate into the trends we observe in the black/white unemployment differential. This perspective can incorporate the changes the economy and polity have undergone in the postwar period to account for the maintenance of the unemployment gap in the face of varying cyclical and structural conditions.

Discrimination is capable of adapting to changes in its political and economic environment as long as there are incentives for it to be practiced. These incentives exist for both white workers and capitalists, the former in terms of job security and the latter in terms of the maximization of control and the minimization of costs. There is no necessary reason for discrimination to decline over time, especially given the propensity of a capitalist economy to create slack labor markets. The view that discrimination is a form of irrational business decision making fails to consider the social cohesion created by racial identification both among white workers and between white workers and capitalists, and the impact of that cohesion on output and incomes. Capitalism responds to discrimination in the same flexible, rational, and adaptive manner that it responds to all else in its environment. It uses discrimination like any other resource. It incorporates it, transforms it, and ultimately reproduces it.

2
Efficiency Wage Theory: Critical Reflections on the NeoKeynesian Theory of Unemployment and Discrimination

William A. Darity, Jr.

NeoKeynesian economics – distinct from the economics of Keynes [1936] – is the economics of price inflexibility, impediments, informational asymmetries, and the like. It is, in a nutshell, the economics of imperfection. While Keynes [1936] set as his theoretical task the demonstration that a capitalist economy would inevitably produce episodes of persistent less than full employment in the absence of lags, leaks, or frictions, the NeoKeynesians cannot conceive of such a story. Their orthodox impulses make it impossible for them to envision a circumstance where less than full employment would be generated under ideal vacuum conditions in a private-enterprise economy. NeoKeynesian economics is really neoclassical economics dressed up in the regalia of imperfections.[1] Simultaneously, NeoKeynesians doubt that there is a credible argument for the persistence of racial or ethnic discrimination in a competitive marketplace. Because they acknowledge the real-world occurrence of discrimination, just as they acknowledge the real-world occurrence of unemployment, they are led to advance a theory of discrimination that is rooted in the same types of imperfections that are the source of their theory of unemployment. The NeoKeynesian theory of discrimination also is the economics of price inflexibility, impediments, informational asymmetries, and the like.

As Steven Shulman suggests in the preceding chapter, there is intuition behind looking for links between theories of unemployment and of discrimination. However, the existence of such a link also means that where there are limitations to the NeoKeynesian account of the causes of unemployment, there also are limitations to the NeoKeynesian account of discrimination. It is the purpose of this chapter to explore these limitations and to demonstrate that the entire NeoKeynesian theoretical venture merely leads back to positions from which its practitioners have sought to escape. Ultimately, NeoKeynesian theory grinds toward the conclusion that unemployment (involuntary) and discrimination cannot persist or do not exist at all.

It is noteworthy that NeoKeynesian economics is heavily influenced by Joseph Stiglitz's style of microeconomics. Therefore, it is reassuringly neoclassical in its foundations. Economic agents are rational beings engaged in optimal decision making. Utility maximization and profit maximization animate the actions of participants in the economy. Barriers to the frictionless operation of the economy exist, however. They are not the consequence of state action, nor are they atavistic institutional holdovers from a prior, precapitalistic era. Instead, the barriers themselves are viewed as the outcome of optimizing behavior by economic agents in the face of some immutable imperfection, *the genesis of which is never really explained*. Given this immutable imperfection – a constraint of sorts on all participants' actions – economic agents adapt, constructing special arrangements that would appear suboptimal to the untutored eye. But in the face of the immutable imperfection, these special arrangements appear to be quite sensible, that is, optimal.

The core of Stiglitzian economics, then, is the postulate that there is at least one natural imperfection that conditions the world in which economic agents operate. The persistence of this imperfection is taken as a given; no substantive attempt is made to explain its presence or irreducibility. For example, when the imperfection is asymmetric information, the condition of uneven knowledge continues indefinitely in what otherwise appears to be a competitive economy. Taking this natural imperfection as a given, agents design ingenious arrangements that are based upon microeconomic optimization. One result is the monitoring/efficiency-wage literature to be discussed below. Another is the credit-rationing literature, the most interesting extension of which is the theory of adverse selection where borrowers know their own default propensity but the lenders do not. What is peculiar about this approach is that none of these agents who construct such intricate responses to an environment with informational asymmetries ever seeks to pursue economic activities that would eliminate the imperfection in the first place, although, implicitly, there are profits to be earned from such activities. Economic agents never mount a direct attack on the basic imperfection in Stiglitz's world.

In Keynes' [1936] own work, it was the general veil of uncertainty facing everyone that created an important role for credit and finance, not unevenness in the dispersion of knowledge per se among people. What varied in Keynes' world was the range of rules of thumb – or "conventions" – that economic agents adopted in response to the universal climate of uncertainty. Of particular significance from the standpoint of Keynes' analysis of investment activity and the theoretical possibility of an unemployment equilibrium was the uncertainty that enveloped the determination of the prospective yield on capital assets. For Keynes, ignorance about prospective yield was inherent in the inability of human beings to foretell the future, especially the relatively distant future. This was a universal ignorance.

One may wish to refer to uncertainty as an "imperfection" as well. If so, there might be an odd sort of grounds for rapprochement between Keynes and Stiglitz, but only a rapprochement of a marginal sort. There is a qualitative difference between Stiglitz's imperfections, which we can conceive of private actors devising schemes to overcome directly, and Keynes' grand imperfection, which can only be corralled in principle by state control over investment, that is, Keynes' "socialization of investment." In the NeoKeynesian world, some actors know economically relevant information that others do not know – and somehow *cannot* extract – but in Keynes' world *no one* can know how the future will affect the value of a capital-asset.

I. SOME DIFFICULTIES WITH THE NEOKEYNESIAN THEORY OF UNEMPLOYMENT

Admirably, for the NeoKeynesians, the phenomenon of involuntary unemployment, that is, unemployment that is not attributable to search activity nor induced by the alternatives posed by nonlabor sources of income provided by the state such as unemployment compensation or welfare, is a concept they want to take seriously. They take involuntary unemployment to mean a circumstance where individuals seeking work at prevailing wages are unable to find work. For the NeoKeynesian economist, then, there is some category of persons who fall between those who have employment and those who are not labor-force participants. The involuntarily unemployed seek work at the wages currently being paid, but there are insufficient positions available for them to be hired by employers.

This leads rather naturally to a fairly old diagnosis of the source of the problem, a diagnosis that would have been acknowledged as a potential and credible explanation for depression-level unemployment by economists whom Keynes [1936] would have labelled the "Classicals." A putative aggregate labor market fails to clear because of wage rigidity, whether nominal or real. The downward stickiness of wages leads to a condition of persistent excess supply of labor in the aggregate; hence jobs are rationed among all the potential claimants for positions.

In Keynes' time this would have been a rather unsurprising explanation for unemployment. Keynes [1936: 6] would have subsumed the search-theoretic explanation for unemployment under the heading of "frictional" unemployment – "unemployment due to a temporary want of balance between the relative quantities of specialized resources as a result of miscalculation or intermittent demand; or to time-lags consequent on unforeseen changes; or to the fact that the change-over from one employment to another cannot be effected without a certain delay, so that there will always exist in a non-static society a proportion of resources unemployed 'between jobs.'" This was not involuntary unemployment for Keynes.

But neither was unemployment produced by wage rigidity "due to the refusal or inability of a unit of labour, as a result of legislation or social practices or of combination for collective bargaining or of slow response to change or of mere human obstinacy, to accept a reward corresponding to the value of the product attributable to its marginal productivity" (Keynes: 6). In short, labor that was unemployed because it was unwilling or unable to underbid the existing workforce was voluntarily unemployed for Keynes. Therefore, involuntary unemployment had to amount to something else.

NeoKeynesian economics does not seek to interpret the dimensions of that "something else." In fact, I argue here that its stopping point is with the category of unemployment that Keynes himself characterized as "voluntary." Yet the rhetoric of the NeoKeynesians equates wage rigidity, or more generally imperfect price inflexibility, with involuntary unemployment (see Hahn [1987], Solow [1980], and Stiglitz [1986]). In fact, Solow's [1980] December 1979 presidential address to the American Economic Association amounts to a catalogue of reasons why wages are inflexible downward, including explanations for unemployment that anticipate the substance of all the arguments made in the NeoKeynesian literature of the late 1980's. The latter arguments, of course, emphasize the essential optimality of wage rigidity, subject to some aforementioned immutable imperfection.

In Solow's address [1980: 8-9], the following six major arguments are offered for the existence of wage rigidity and, hence, for unemployment:

1. Piecemeal wage reductions will be resisted by labor to maintain an

established contour of relative wages across occupations and across firms. This is an argument for nominal wage rigidity extracted from a portion of Keynes' early discussion in *The General Theory* where Keynes [1936: 13-15] sought to offer an explanation as to why it could be rational for labor to fight against nominal wage reductions while not resisting a reduction in the real wage engineered by a general price inflation. Solow bypasses Keynes' more fundamental point [1936: 7-13] that even if labor did accept cuts in money wages in either piecemeal or across-the-board fashion, there would be no assurance that labor thereby could reduce the real wage, due to the nexus that exists between nominal wages and the level of prices via aggregate demand.

2. A connection between labor productivity and the level of wages is posited. Higher wages elicit greater effort from labor, presumably at a diminishing rate, creating a profit motive for employers to raise wages above the level that will clear the labor market. This is the efficiency wage hypothesis that takes its absolute wage form[2] in the work of Stiglitz [1986] and its relative wage form[3] in the work of Bulow and Summers [1986] and Summers [1988].

3. A customarily understood "fair wage" prevails, which it is equally customarily understood should not be undercut by persons out of work. There may be harsh social sanctions against underbidding in the face of such widely accepted norms. The "insider-outsider" model of Lindbeck and Snower [1988] gives the suitably rational veneer to this type of argument.

4. Wages possess inertia due to the implicit agreement in wage contracts that laborers will be insured against the adverse effects of periodic unemployment by receiving higher than market-clearing wages while they are employed. This requires a fairly widespread consensus among the tastes of workers giving greater weight to higher wages over employment security, and it requires accompanying strictures against underbidding by those who do not share this consensus.

5. Collective bargaining arrangements lead to the establishment of long-term contracts – perhaps motivated by the rationale afforded by the implicit contracts literature – that lead to wage rigidity and employment fluctuations.[4] This is simply a variant of the trade-union-power argument of pre-Keynes vintage. It has led to the more recent controversies over whether the aggregate labor market is best characterized as a contract market, with accompanying wage rigidity, or as an auction market, with an accompanying flexprice view of wage determination. The empirical evidence, to say the least, is murky on which view is closer to reality (see

Kniesner and Goldsmith [1987] and Heckman and MaCurdy [forthcoming]).

6. Both employers and employees fear that any wage change made today will be difficult to reverse in the future when economic conditions change. If, for example, employers agree to higher wages today, they may fear that they will be unable to extract reductions in the face of an economic downturn. If employees accept cuts today, they may fear that they will be unable to receive increases when the economy goes on an upswing. Both parties have an incentive to maintain the status quo wage rate. In this case, wage stickiness is both upward and downward. Presumably a satisfactory scheme of indexation would overcome this problem, although frequently labor and management never can agree upon the appropriate index to dictate automatic variations in wage payments.

The most recent work in the NeoKeynesian/wage-rigidity literature boils all these arguments down to two major types – the efficiency wage hypothesis and the implicit contracts hypothesis (see Stiglitz [1986: 154]). The NeoKeynesians do not admit the theoretical possibility that there can be meaning to the concept of involuntary unemployment or less than full employment under a regime of flexible wages or, more generally, flexible prices. In contrast, Bobbie Horn and I have argued (see Darity and Horn [1983, 1987-88]) that Keynes' concept of involuntary unemployment is of sufficient generality to encompass flexprice regimes. In its simplest terms, Keynes' involuntary unemployment amounts to a circumstance where it is possible to raise the level of employment in the economy by expanding aggregate demand, regardless of what happens to wages, whether nominal or real.[5]

The NeoKeynesian literature starts with the presumption, as did Keynes' Classical precursors, that if there is unemployment, then wages must be too high. Keynes' involuntary unemployment need not start with such a presumption and is therefore open to the more empirically relevant possibilities that real wages can move acyclically or procyclically. Furthermore, from the standpoint of Keynes' criterion for the existence of involuntary unemployment, it is not a condition that besets individuals but instead is a condition that characterizes labor as a whole. Keynes' concept of involuntary unemployment also encompasses the phenomenon of *underemployment*, in the sense that Keynes viewed workers as involuntarily unemployed if they were engaged in work that was below the level of productivity they could attain in employment that would be available to them at higher levels of aggregate demand.

Let us focus exclusively on the efficiency wage hypothesis, especially since the implicit contracts hypothesis unequivocally is a theory of voluntary unemployment in Keynes' sense. In some earlier formulations, the efficiency wage hypothesis was an argument that arose out of the perception that, in developing countries, higher wages permitted workers to purchase improved levels of nutrition and hence perform better on the job. In the context of "modern industrial economies," the efficiency wage hypothesis takes on the character of an effort-elicitation problem. Workers will shirk unless wages are sufficiently high to induce them to put forth a better effort. There is a wage-productivity nexus of which employers are aware and accordingly they set wages in a manner that maximizes profits, cognizant that their wage-setting decision will affect the performance of their workers.

Why not simply fire those most predisposed to shirk and replace them with the unemployed, who presumably will work harder for lower wages? Here a Stiglitzian immutable imperfection – an information asymmetry in this case – comes into play. Individual workers know whether or not they will shirk, but the employers do not and are faced with a signal-extraction problem – they cannot determine with good (reasonable? sufficient?) accuracy which workers are the shirkers and which ones are not. Precisely why low-cost monitoring schemes do not become available is not made clear. The rational alternative is to pitch the wage rate at such a level that it minimizes the average worker's propensity to shirk relative to prospects for additional revenue on the margin. This seems to be the essence of the argument made by Bulow and Summers [1986] and Summers [1988]. Rebitzer [1988] appends a Marxist-influenced analysis of the labor process, but nevertheless ends up advancing another variant of the effort-regulation model where employer wage setting is designed to extract greater effort from employees. Bowles [1985] makes the connection between the supervisory costs of monitoring work effort and the size of the wage premium explicit so that if monitoring could be changed to cost less per worker, then the wage premium and the threat level of unemployment would decrease. In any case, the information asymmetry is clearly not immutable. A modern Austrian probably would argue that enterprises would emerge specializing in providing inexpensive external monitoring services to firms.

Several features of this type of argument are problematic. First, the wage rigidity does not really arise from the existence of a wage-productivity nexus. Rather, wage rigidity comes from the assumption that firms have wage-setting or monopsony power in their factor market, another imperfection the NeoKeynesians slip under the door again without explanation.[6]

Second, the connection between the costs of monitoring workers and the self-supervision that is induced by a combination of higher wages and the threat of being stuck in a trap of underemployment for a time is often too simplistic.[7] For example, Bulow and Summers [1986: 382] attribute the difficulty in "detection of shirkers" to the characteristics of primary sector jobs, the sector where they argue that the effort-elicitation problem is prevalent due to "the responsible character of primary-sector jobs." Of course, the reason why the "responsible character" of such jobs creates insuperable monitoring difficulties is never given.

Third, an odd presumption of this literature is the notion that all workers must be paid the same wage. But to induce improved performance through pay, one could link compensation to "output." [8] I presume that Wall Street brokers and investment bankers would fit into Bulow and Summers' category of primary-sector workers with jobs possessing a "responsible character"; ethical character, of course, is not an issue here. Bonuses, premiums, profit-sharing arrangements, etc., all create incentives for such employees to perform at a high level. But compensation for performance is ex post rather than ex ante, in the sense that the worker demonstrates that he or she has had a "good" year before he or she receives the Christmas extra. Here wages are tailored to individual performance. The feasibility of such ex post variable-wage schemes clearly depends on the cost to the firm of accurately monitoring each employee's actual contribution to the firm's long-run profits. This again underscores the hole in this approach's explanation which is based on "monitoring costs."

Fourth, in a related vein there is an intermediate form of worker policing that lies between external monitoring and individual self-supervision. Employees frequently work in groups on tasks. Employers could reward the group for performing the task successfully, whether it is on an assembly line or in a professional agency. The group members receive additional compensation based upon group performance. This creates an incentive for workers to police the members of their own group. Raising the average wage for all workers need not be the route taken to solve the effort elicitation problem.

Stranger still, it is not apparent that employment must necessarily fall under a regime where wages are sticky for efficiency wage reasons. In the absolute wage version of the hypothesis, it is easy to demonstrate that it is possible for both wages and employment to rise relative to the conventional situation where there is no wage-productivity nexus. In Summers' [1988] relative wage version, the higher efficiency wage is associated with lower employment, but in general the efficiency wage hypothesis does not, in and of itself, dictate a decline in employment.[9] The efficiency wage hypothesis is not necessarily a theory of unemployment.

Some final reservations about the efficiency wage hypothesis are of a strictly empirical sort. Leonard [1987] has found little evidence to support the notion that interindustry variation in wages is due to efficiency wage considerations. Bielby and Bielby [1988] looked for the dependence of self-reported effort on a number of human-capital factors and on earnings. The dependence on earnings was "not large . . . a doubling of earnings increases effort by just .04 on the four-point scale." In fact, the effect was not even significant for women, though the coefficient was very similar in size for men and women.[10] This casts doubt on the basis of EWT, namely, that average wage premia elicit significant increases in effort.

The piece of evidence that Bulow and Summers [1986] used to make their case was the Ford Motor Company's raising of wages from between $2 to $3 per day up to $5 per day in 1914. A more detailed study of the same case by Raff and Summers [1987] indicated that efficiency wage considerations led to Ford's decision, although they acknowledged that other explanations are possible and that it is an open question how generalizable the Ford instance is to other circumstances. In particular, they found that the archival record did not support the notion that Ford increased an efficiency wage premium to save on the costs of monitoring since these costs were minimal and were decreasing because of the technological changes Ford had introduced a few months earlier. Instead, they conjectured that this historical example may have had more to do with encouraging worker morale and discouraging collective action by workers in implicit bargaining over wages and working conditions [1987: S81-S83]. Suffice it to say that it remains unclear why NeoKeynesians have come to believe that costs of monitoring effort are a key imperfection in labor markets, with average wage setting serving as the optimal prod used by firms to regulate effort.

II. SOME DIFFICULTIES WITH THE NEOKEYNESIAN THEORY OF DISCRIMINATION

The most explicit presentation of a NeoKeynesian theory of discrimination appears in a section of the Bulow and Summers paper [1986: 397-404]. Their examples focus on gender discrimination and discrimination against younger workers, but presumably their argument could be extended to ethnic or racial discrimination as well. The question is: Do they in fact present a theory of discrimination or do they resuscitate a variant of human-capital theory as their explanation for earnings and employment differentials?

Bulow and Summers accept as a stylized fact the existence of a dual labor market, split between a primary and a secondary sector. The evidence for the existence of a dual labor market is probably at least as good as the evidence against it (see Dickens and Lang [1988]); even Kniesner and Goldsmith [1987] in a different context suggest that a more accurate characterization of the U. S. economy would point toward several labor markets with very different features from one another. But this is peripheral since Bulow and Summers do not belabor the question of whether there is a dual labor market or not. At base they postulate its existence and then proceed. It is not a bad postulate. What is less satisfactory is what comes next.

The secondary sector is one where wages are lower and turnover is higher, but "workers are monitored perfectly and thus have no possibility of shirking" [Bulow and Summers 1986: 382]. The "menial" nature of secondary-sector work makes "monitoring . . . costless." In contrast, as mentioned earlier, primary-sector workers are far more difficult to monitor; hence those higher quality jobs carry higher-wages.

But why are some groups of workers relatively more concentrated in the secondary sector, a sector where firms can even reduce wages without anticipating greater shirking, despite the fact that Bulow and Summers [1986: 398] assume that there are no productivity differentials between the groups of workers? Bulow and Summers ostensibly assume that the two groups of workers, men and women or blacks and whites or adults and youths, are equally able to perform the tasks in either sector. But all is not precisely as it seems. The two groups of workers are not the same on all nonascriptive dimensions; their propensities to separate from jobs differ:

A major characteristic of groups thought to be disadvantaged in the labor market is that they have a very high separation rate. . . . [T]he rate of labor force withdrawal is about 1% per year for males aged 25-59 but about 19% per year for women in the same age bracket. . . . [There also is evidence of] large age and race differences in separation probabilities as well. [Bulow and Summers 1986: 399]

Although the groups have the same capabilities, and experience is not assumed to affect ability to perform, the groups have different propensities toward turnover. The group with the higher mean propensity toward turnover requires an even higher wage to avoid shirking in the primary sector. Therefore, members of this group are more expensive workers on average. Since Bulow and Summers [1986: 400] postulate that all workers in the primary sector must receive the same wage rate, the compensating variation occurs in a reduced probability of members of the high-turnover group moving into the primary sector. To the extent that not all women have a propensity to high separation rates and not all men have a propensity to low separation rates, the NeoKeynesian theory takes on the flavor of a statistical discrimination argument [Bulow and Summers 1986: 401].

However, this model of discrimination really is the human-capital theory in disguise. The propensity toward separation affects the propensity to shirk. Shirking certainly is part and parcel of individual productivity characteristics; it is a behavioral propensity that has economic content. From the standpoint of employers, the propensity to separate is a component of the human-capital package that the worker presents at the hiring office.[11] Groups of workers are differentially allocated across the two sectors precisely because they are different in terms of their mean productivity performance in the primary sector.

Bulow and Summers do not inquire into the sources of the differential propensity toward separation. After all, if turnover is higher in the secondary sector, then workers concentrated in the secondary sector will display higher separation rates. But some other factor besides their higher separation rates – perhaps discrimination pure and simple – may account for their initial overrepresentation in the secondary sector.

Bulow and Summers [1986: 397] construct this peculiar argument to establish that discrimination can persist in competitive markets. But in a strict sense, theirs is not a model of discrimination. It is no more than a model of human-capital differences. Thus they do not resolve the puzzle they posed for themselves: they do not demonstrate how discrimination can persist under competitive conditions. They do not explain why similarly situated people are paid differently; the postulated gap in separation rates means that the groups are not similarly situated. Of course, one also can ask, just as Jones [1987: 1230] has asked: Why does dualism persist in the face of competitive conditions?

The efficiency wage explanation of racial inequality offered by Bulow and Summers can also be examined on its own terms.[12] Black over representation in the secondary sector would, in this context, explain persistent racial wage gaps. However, as noted by Bulow and Summers, this crowding cannot persist if blacks and whites are identical with respect to attributes and market behavior. Bulow and Summers then invoke turnover and separation rates to explain black/white wage inequality. Suppose that black workers have higher separation rates than white workers, ceteris paribus. Because workers with higher quit rates have a shorter anticipated stay in the primary sector, employers must pay them more to discourage shirking. Because high-turnover workers will shirk more at a given wage, employers avoid them, and they are crowded into the secondary sector.[13]

Bulow and Summers surprisingly insist that turnover rates are unrelated to productivity but then proceed to incorporate race by positing racial differences in worker behavior because "[o]ur model cannot explain discrimination" if blacks and whites are identical [Bulow and Summers 1986: 398]. However, the extant evidence on separation rates seriously threatens the chosen line of reasoning. Viscusi [1980] and Blau and Kahn [1981], after adjusting for personal and work characteristics, found that blacks are less likely than whites (and women are no more likely than men) to quit a job; Weiss's [1984] well-structured study suggested that white males are more likely to quit than nonwhite males, and that southern whites are particularly likely to quit their jobs. More recently, Boston [1988: 129-131] found that blacks have a longer median job tenure than whites. If these findings are reliable, then, according to the efficiency-wage/dual-labor-market/turnover discrimination model, blacks' earnings should exceed whites' earnings!

William Bielby reports in chapter 5 on his work with Denise Bielby [1988] that recent research on differences by gender in "internal standards of personal entitlement suggests that, all else constant, women can be expected to allocate more effort than men to work activities." Thus we would expect that women would require lower wage premia to elicit the same effort as men with the same levels of other human capital characteristics. This would imply that one unit of female effort would cost less than one unit of male effort and so would lead the Bulow-Summers model to forecast that women would predominate in the "primary" jobs and men would be "crowded" into the "secondary sector." To the extent that Bielby and Bielby's work suggests that the relation between effort and labor power is "exogenous" in the sense that it is largely sex-specific and "culturally prescribed"[14] rather than the result of individualistic optimizing decisions, we thus satisfy the key assumption of the Bulow-Summers model that sexual differences in effort elicitation are exogenous, but they are empirically in the wrong direction. This model again gives results that contradict clear evidence of inequality in occupations and wages.

Efficiency wage models of discrimination thus typify the aforementioned model-building practice. Theorists relax the assumption of identical workers (reminiscent of the human-capital tradition) and derive an equilibrium consistent with the phenomenon they desire to explain. Unfortunately, the quits data substantively challenge the model's ability to explain racial inequality. As indicated earlier, it is clearly inadequate theorizing, even on its own terms, to try to explain racial and sexual differences in earnings, let alone unemployment, on the basis of "exogenous" differences in turnover rates and to pretend that everything else is held constant.

Closely related to NeoKeynesian explanations making use of the efficiency wage rationale for slipping in imperfect competition are the overtly monopolistic "rent sharing" explanations of wage differentials that are not related to measurable differences in human capital. Thus Krueger and Summers [1987] explain the interindustry wage structure as the consequence of rent sharing in the presence of efficiency wages. Rents exist because of firm monopoly power in an imperfectly competitive economy - the world of inelastic product demand curves, monopoly power, and high concentration ratios. Because most high-wage industries are highly concentrated, earn high profits, and have labor costs that are a small portion of total costs, managers' rent sharing with workers is relatively less costly than it would be in labor-intensive industries.[15]

The rent sharing model also explains the observed pattern that high-wage industries pay high wages for all workers and occupations, differences among them such as monitoring and training costs and turnover rates notwithstanding. But, of course, this explanation goes too far. In fact, it contradicts the efficiency wage story since we are still left with the problem of why employers share rents with workers whose jobs are easily monitored. To suggest that rent sharing reflects managers' desire to "help" workers runs into the objection that these managers will be disciplined by an "efficient" capital market where takeover artists respond to shareholders who don't give a hoot about workers' well-being. We are left, at most, with the question of whether capital markets recognize what Yellen [1984] calls the "sociological" rationale for paying above-market-clearing wage premia: the morale-boosting, fairness-adhering, union-weakening versions of EWT presented by Akerlof [1982] and Akerlof and Yellen [1988] and suggested by Raff and Summers [1987]. In any case, we find EWT to be no direct help in understanding racial inequality in the operation of markets and firms.

III. ARE THERE ALTERNATIVES TO THE NEOKEYNESIAN ANALYSIS OF DISCRIMINATION?

There is a certain peculiarity to NeoKeynesian economics. Its explanation for unemployment is old-fashioned wage rigidity based on monitoring costs that are largely unexplored. Its explanation for group economic inequality is average differences between groups in potential productivity or in access to rent sharing that are also unexplained and that totally ignore the possibility of monitoring. Is this a case where there is much smoke from an intellectually tiny fire?

Perhaps the insider-outsider model of Lindbeck and Snower [1988] affords a superior basis for a theory of discrimination. Lindbeck and Snower have sought to explain why workers without employment do not undercut the wages of those on the job. Their answer has been fear of harassment and noncooperation by the insiders when the outsiders move into the workplace, having driven wages downward. One might imagine that the insiders are white laborers and the outsiders are black laborers.

But the long history of black workers' involvement in strikebreaking efforts after being excluded from union membership by white workers (see Spero and Harris [1931]) suggests that blacks have been willing to undercut the wages of the insiders. Moreover, Lindbeck and Snower do not explain why employers do not establish entirely new operations staffed entirely by the lower-cost outsiders, thereby avoiding the problem of merging hostile insiders with wage-cutting outsiders. The complaint that can be raised about Lindbeck and Snower's model as a basis for a theory of discrimination is that it does not lead to a theory of unequal wages or exclusion of blacks from employment. It leads instead to a model that yields as its long-run outcome a world of segregated work forces receiving uniform wages - as long as there are no productivity differences across the groups.

Orthodox economics is orthodox economics, either in its frictionless idealized mode or in its imperfectionist mode. It tends to give us neither a theory of unemployment nor a theory of discrimination. Instead, it tends to give us a framework of analysis that suggests that neither of these phenomena can exist or, at least, persist. The NeoKeynesians seem to want to have it both ways: they want to be orthodox enough to gain professional credibility readily and yet recognize the existence/persistence of unemployment and discrimination. Simply put, they cannot do so. This argument suggests that those who would understand both unemployment and discrimination would do well to explore the approach outlined by

Rhonda Williams in chapter 4, which answers the questions posed at the start of this section by linking the operation of capital markets to the persistence of unemployment and to the operation of discrimination in labor markets.

3
Discrimination and Efficiency Wages: Estimates of the Role of Efficiency Wages in Male/Female Wage Differentials

Michael D. Robinson and
Phanindra V. Wunnava

Recent work on efficiency wage models has increased our understanding of discrimination, as well as the operation of labor markets (Bulow and Summers [1986]; Bowles [1985]; and Akerlof [1984]). Bulow and Summers [1986] developed an efficiency wage model of labor markets that has direct implications for discrimination. They argued that the wage premia necessary to keep males and females from shirking differ because of relative quit rates. Discrimination results from the efforts of employers to limit the wage premia paid to females. In their work, no empirical tests of the hypothesis were presented.[1] We believe that directly testable hypotheses about sex discrimination can be derived from their model. This chapter will consider these issues and present the results of two empirical tests. We show that the average decrease in the earnings of each individual worker as the percentage of women in the workforce increases is more marked in large than in small plants. The second investigation reveals that for males there is a larger trade-off between supervision costs and wages than can be observed for females. These results indicate that some evidence exists that sex discrimination is in part the result of efficiency wages.[2]

I. THE NO-SHIRKING CONDITION AND DISCRIMINATION

Bulow and Summers [1986] derived the wage premia necessary to insure that primary-sector workers will not shirk under the assumption that workers maximize lifetime utility, dislike working, and may be fired for shirking in the primary sector. This premium is given by

(1) $$w_p - w_s = [ir/D] + [iqN/D(N-E)] \,,$$

where w_p is the primary-sector wage, w_s is the market-clearing secondary-sector wage, i is the intensity of work effort, q is the quit rate, r is the discount rate, D is the probability that a shirker will be caught and dismissed, N is the size of the work force, and E is the size of the primary sector.[3] The wage premium, $w_p - w_s$, must be larger for workers that are less likely to be caught shirking. In addition, higher quit rates lead to higher premia. Here is the source of discrimination hypothesized by Bulow and Summers. Since women have lower labor-force attachment, they will require larger wage premia than men. Employers attempting to minimize wage costs will prefer to place men in primary-sector jobs and women in secondary-sector jobs, with the result of occupational segregation and wage differentials.

If the disutility of work is related to work effort, then we can obtain an expression from (1) that relates work effort to the wage differential, quit rate, and probability of being caught shirking:

(2) $$(w_p - w_s) / \{(r/D) + [qN/D(N-E)]\}.$$

Bulow and Summers assumed that supervision is fixed and therefore that a single wage premium is associated with a level of work effort. In different circumstances, the amount of supervision may vary, and, in fact, firms may be able to add supervision at some cost. This implies that a combination of wage premia and supervision will be associated with a given work effort.

A simple efficiency wage model can be developed by considering a competitive firm facing price P for output and wage w for labor. Output Q is a function of the number of workers L and the intensity i with which they work. Work intensity, given by (2), relates effort to wage premia and supervision. Work intensity is a function of two factors: the amount of supervision S (which determines D, the probability of being dismissed for shirking, and which is obtained at cost g) and the wage premium, $x = w_p - w_s$. These assumptions give the following simple system:

(3) $$\text{Profits} = PQ - (w + x)L - gS \,,$$

(4) $$Q = f(L, i) \,,$$

(5) $$i = g(x, S) \,.$$

The firm's problem is to maximize profits by selecting L, x, and S, the amount of labor, the wage premium, and the amount of supervision. The first-order conditions are as follows:

(6) $\qquad Pf_L(L, i) = w + x,$

(7) $\qquad Pf_i(L, i)g_x(x, S) = L,$

(8) $\qquad Pf_i(L, i)g_S(x, S) = g.$

Condition (6) sets the marginal cost of labor equal to the marginal productivity of labor (given work intensity), (7) sets the marginal cost of increasing work intensity equal to marginal benefits of increasing intensity, and (8) sets the marginal cost of supervision equal to the marginal benefit of supervision. From (7) and (8) the following condition can be derived:

(9) $\qquad g_x(x, S)/L = g_S(x, S)/g.$

This condition sets the marginal cost to marginal benefit ratio for supervision equal to that for work intensity.

Using (9), we can see one possible source of male/female wage differentials as viewed by Bulow and Summers. Goldin [1986] and Bulow and Summers [1986] argued that $g_x(x, S)$ is greater for males than for females.[4] That is, the marginal gains in work intensity from increasing wage premia will be larger for males than for females. This may arise because of females' lower level of commitment to the job. If females plan to leave the job more often than males, it may be harder to persuade them to provide more intensity with a wage premium.[5] This implies that males and females working at the same intensity will have different levels of supervision and wage premia. This is consistent with the finding by Ragan and Smith [1981] that the wage reductions associated with high quit rates are larger for males than for females. Males will have larger wage premia than females (at the same intensity). Second, employers may perceive females as being more docile and easy to manage than males. This implies that the cost of supervision will be higher for males than for females and again that the wage premia offered to males will be higher than those offered to females working at the same level of intensity.[6]

Whichever explanation is accepted, firms treat males and females differently. Females will receive more supervision and lower wage premia for the same work intensity. It would be quite difficult for firms to achieve this mix with males and females working side by side at the same jobs. Therefore we would expect that firms would devise two occupations: one with high supervision and low wage premia and a second with low supervision and high premia. By channeling males and females to the appropriate occupations (that is, occupational segregation), firms could achieve the desired mix of supervision and wage premium for all workers.[7]

It is worth noting at this point the difference between this approach toward discrimination and the standard human-capital approach. Here, while the male/female wage differential does depend in part on differences in characteristics between males and females, the wage differential is rooted in the way in which employers extract labor power from the workers and not in the differences themselves. Further, the differences between males and females assumed by this model are not productivity differences.

II. TESTABLE HYPOTHESES

This section develops and tests two hypotheses that are implied by the preceding analysis. First we consider the relationship between plant size and the gender of employees in wage determination. Then we consider the relationship between supervision and earnings for males and females.

IIA. Plant Size and Percent Female

It is well known that wages are inversely related to the percentage of the work force that is female in an industry. We argue that this result can be explained by the efficiency wage model of discrimination. Further, this effect should manifest itself more in large firms because of increased supervision costs. Assuming that the work effort of females is less responsive to wage premia than that of males, employers would be more likely to fill primary jobs, again characterized by high wage premia, with males. Since this is the case, we can use the percentage of the work force that is female as a measure of the relative probability that a worker in the industry is in fact a secondary worker.

Next consider the case of plant size. If monitoring costs are related to plant size, wages should be determined differently in different-size plants. Suppose that there are two plants, one with perfect monitoring and the second with expensive and inefficient monitoring. In the first plant, all

Table 3.1
Variables Used in Efficiency Wage Model of Discrimination

Variable	Description
Experience (prior to current job)	Worker's age less education and tenure plus five
Experience^2	Experience squared/100
Sex	= 1 if male, = 0 otherwise
White	= 1 if white, = 0 otherwise
Education	Years of education
Tenure	Years of tenure
Tenure^2	Tenure squared/100
Union	= 1 if in Union, = 0 otherwise
Part-time	= 1 if works less than 35 hours per week
Percent union	Percent union at the 2-digit industry level
Percent female	Percent female at the 2-digit industry level

Other Control Variables

Region	Dummies for the nine Census Bureau regions
Occupation	Eight occupation dummies
Industry	Nine one-digit SIC code industries

(Estimates for these dummies are not reported due to space considerations, but are available on request from the authors.)

Size Categories (for table 3.2 and for "supervisory" variable in table 3.3)

Large	More than 100 employees
Small	Less than 100 employees

Plant Size Dummies (for table 3.3)

Size 1	Less than 25 employees
Size 2	25-99 employees
Size 3	100-499 employees
Size 4	500-999 employees
Size 5	1,000 and over employees

Table 3.2
OLS Wage Regression Results: Effects of Plant Size and Percent Female on Earnings

Variable	All Workers		Males Only	
	Large	Small	Large	Small
Intercept	1.665**	1.438**	1.818**	1.54**
	(29.14)	(32.29)	(25.25)	(25.72)
Percent Female	-0.373**	-0.115**	-0.450**	-0.215**
	(-10.11)	(-3.39)	(-8.15)	(-3.84)
Education	0.050**	0.043**	0.052**	0.047**
	(22.58)	(22.34)	(18.13)	(18.16)
Experience	0.009**	0.014**	0.011**	0.020**
	(8.31)	(16.04)	(7.01)	(14.61)
Experience^2	-0.017**	-0.028**	-0.016**	-0.038**
	(-5.44)	(-12.77)	(-3.46)	(-11.42)
Tenure	0.030**	0.029**	0.033**	0.029**
	(21.08)	(20.23)	(17.23)	(15.01)
Tenure^2	-0.057**	-0.058**	-0.060**	-0.059**
	(-12.57)	(-12.10)	(-10.68)	(-9.21)
Union	0.056**	0.199**	0.040**	0.219**
	(5.21)	(15.52)	(2.78)	(13.64)
Percent Union#	-0.041	-0.085	-0.106	-0.051
	(-0.80)	(-1.22)	(-1.63)	(-0.57)
Part-time	-0.127**	-0.127**	-0.201**	-0.179**
	(-7.93)	(-12.56)	(-6.53)	(-9.98)
Sex	0.182**	0.223**		
	(17.21)	(22.11)		
White	0.086**	0.041**	0.112	0.080**
	(5.96)	(2.90)	(5.22)**	(3.79)
Observations (N)	6,214	10,756	3,474	5,720
R-squared (adj)	0.53	0.47	0.47	0.43
F-value	188.75	246.34	84.75	117.54
Standard error	0.339	0.404	0.348	0.417

Notes: The dependent variable is the natural log of hourly earnings. Estimates were obtained by ordinary least squares. T-statistics are in parentheses.
** Significant at the 5% level.
Industry, occupation, and regional dummy coefficient estimates are available on request.
The unexpected sign on this variable may be due to a high correlation between Percent Female and Percent Union.

workers would be paid competitive wages, there would be no need for occupational segregation, and there would be little difference between male and female wages. In this case, the presence or absence of female workers tells us nothing about the level of wages. In the second plant, we would expect to observe large wage premia in primary-sector jobs and a sharp delineation between the primary and secondary sectors. Since the male workers would be more heavily concentrated in the primary jobs, we would expect the percentage of the workers that are female to be extremely important in wage determination. A plant with high monitoring costs that employed primarily males would pay much higher wages than a similar plant employing females. Since we believe that monitoring costs increase with plant size (Calvo and Wellisz [1978]), small plants should have low monitoring costs and large plants high monitoring costs. This implies that only in large plants will the gender mix of the workers contain information about the market-sector characteristics of the jobs.

The May 1983 Current Population Survey supplement contains data on plant size and allows us to test our hypothesis. Wage equations were estimated for small and large establishments using data for private-sector nonagricultural employees and including a measure for percent female at the two-digit level of the Standard Industrial Classification code. The equations were estimated for all workers and for males only.

Table 3.1 lists the variables used in the analysis and table 3.2 reports the regression results. The human-capital variables and labor-force-status variables have their expected signs. As predicted, the negative effect of percent female is much greater in magnitude for large plants than for small plants.[8] This suggests that the effect of the percentage of females is more pronounced where monitoring costs are larger.

IIB. Supervision Costs and Wage Differentials

Equation 9 indicates that there should be a positive correlation between supervision costs and wage premia for the profit-maximizing firm (Leonard [1987]). If the efficiency wage model of discrimination is correct, this relationship should be quite different for males and females. All things equal, an increase in supervision costs should lead to a larger increase in male than in female wages, since it is hypothesized that males are more responsive to wage premia. This occurs because an increase in supervisory costs leads to a change in the mix of supervision and wage premia used in obtaining effort from male and female workers. For example, in the extreme case where females are totally unresponsive to wage premia, increasing supervision costs would lead to higher male wages, no change in female wages, and a reduction in female employment.

In order to test this hypothesis, a measure of supervision costs had to be constructed; this measure could then be included in wage equations that were estimated using the data set described earlier (with the exception that part-time workers and nonwhites were included). Since data on the marginal cost of supervision would be impossible to obtain, estimates of average supervision costs were used. Average supervision costs in an industry are defined to be the dollars per hour per employee spent on supervision. Supervisors are defined as workers with three-digit occupations clearly identified as supervisory. The three-digit occupation codes make it relatively easy to identify supervisory workers in the industry. Because we believe that supervisory costs are much different in large and small plants, this measure was constructed separately for plants with more and those with less than 100 employees by two-digit industry SIC code. In order to construct the average cost measure, we first computed total supervisory costs per hour in the industry/plant size cell. This was simply the sum of the hourly wages of the supervisory workers. Total supervision costs per hour were then divided by the number of nonsupervisory workers in the industry to obtain average supervision costs per worker per hour. Clearly this measure represents a first approximation and the results should be taken in this light. It is also problematic to use an industry-level measure for supervisory costs that might better be constructed on the individual firm level.

The results from Table 3.3 indicate that there appears to be a correlation between wage premia and supervision costs. However, this relationship only holds for males. The relationship for females is not significant. In order to determine the importance of supervisory costs in total male/female wage differentials, we used a standard total differential decomposition, where the total differential can be expressed as:

$$TD = (b_m - b_f)X_f + b_m(X_m - X_f).$$

The first term on the right-hand side represents the unexplained differential and the second term the explained differential. Applying this technique reveals that 15 percent of the total male/female wage differential "is unexplained" by the different coefficients on supervision costs for males and females.[9] This tends to confirm the predictions made by the efficiency wage model of discrimination.[10]

Table 3.3
OLS Wage Regression Results: Effects of Supervision Cost on Earnings

Variable	Males Estimate	Females Estimate
Intercept	0.938	1.076**
	(23.68)	(20.86)
Average Supervision Cost†	0.082**	0.003
	(5.51)	(0.255)
Percent Female	–0.272**	–0.205**
	(–6.52)	(–5.81)
Education	0.045**	0.035**
	(21.83)	(15.44)
Experience	0.018**	0.007**
	(16.03)	(7.48)
Experience^2	–0.032**	-0.015**
	(–11.91)	(-6.02)
Tenure	0.029**	0.026**
	(19.58)	(16.58)
Tenure^2	–0.057**	–0.055**
	(–12.22)	(–9.70)
Union	0.143**	0.102**
	(12.26)	(7.41)
Percent Union#	–0.201**	–0.176**
	(3.42)	(2.22)
Part-Time	–0.174**	–0.074**
	(–11.37)	(–7.33)
White	0.0905**	0.014
	(5.69)	(1.05)
Observations (N)	8,241	7,420
R-squared (adj)	0.50	0.455
F-value	191.38	145.44
Standard error	0.40	0.36

Notes: The dependent variable is the natural log of earnings. Estimates were obtained by ordinary least squares.

T-statistics are in parentheses.

** Significant at the 5% level.

Industry, occupation, plant size, and regional dummy coefficient estimates are available on request.

† Average supervision cost is defined to be the dollars per hour spent on supervisory employees per nonsupervisory worker where supervisors are those workers in occupation codes 3-18, 303-306, 243, 413-414, 448, 456, 503, 613, 553-558, 633, 803, 843, 863. The measure was constructed by plant size (over and under 100 employees) for 40 two-digit industries. A descriptive table of the measure is available from the authors.

The unexpected sign on this variable may be due to a high correlation between Percent Female and Percent Union.

III. CONCLUSION

This chapter contains the results from an empirical study designed to test the predictions of an efficiency wage model of discrimination. Bulow and Summers in their 1986 paper argued that discrimination against women stems from the need for employers to pay wage premia to workers to inhibit shirking. Since women have lower labor-force attachment than men, the wage premia that would have to be offered for a given level of supervision exceed those that would have to be offered to men. Because of this, occupational segregation occurs.

Given the relationship between plant size and supervision, two hypotheses were made based on this discrimination theory. Since large plants have higher supervision costs, managers there will more likely pay large wage premia and need to discriminate. Small plants with low supervision costs will more likely pay competitive wages to males and females. Our results indicate that in fact wage effects associated with the percentage of females are larger in large plants.

A second approach taken was to attempt to distinguish the unexplained wage differentials between males and females that were associated with variables that measure supervisory costs. Our results indicated that male wages were positively correlated with supervision costs, while there was no significant relationship between female wages and supervisory costs.

4
Competition, Discrimination, and Differential Wage Rates: On the Continued Relevance of Marxian Theory to the Analysis of Earnings and Employment Inequality

Rhonda M. Williams

Contemporary economic theory has all but completed the burial of the idea that market discrimination explains racial wage differentials or differences in general pecuniary accomplishments across ethnic groups under competitive conditions. We need only await the eulogy.

(Darity and Williams 1985: 256)

Unfortunately, we are led to conclude that the competitive model cannot without substantial modification provide a plausible explanation of inter-industry wage variations.

(Krueger and Summers 1987: 18)

Economists use the word *competition* to describe an anonymous acceptance of market forces and *not* aggressive "rivalry" among individuals.

(Binger and Hoffman 1988: 98)

For those who use the neoclassical notion of "perfect competition" as the starting point from which to explain wage distributions in capitalist economies, the existence of persistent wage differentials between comparable black and nonblack workers lingers as a festering sore of inconsistency on the body theoretic. A more detailed diagnosis reveals that the injury is more than skin deep: substantive, long-lasting interindustry wage differentials (again between observably comparable workers) are also the norm in racially homogeneous cultures.[1] Indeed, as Krueger and Summers [1987] have recently documented, advanced capitalism's interindustry wage structure is remarkably consistent across time, cultures, occupations, and broad categories of workers. Simply put, there are high-wage and low-wage industries; the former deploy capital-intensive production techniques and

...gh profit rates, while the latter are labor-intensive, low-profit sectors. With obvious regret, the authors proclaimed that economists must abandon the preferred "competitive" model and embrace "imperfect" competition.

How did Krueger and Summers explain wage differentials that do not correlate with skill differentials - the general phenomenon of which black/ white wage gaps are a particular case? After much deliberation, Krueger and Summers pronounced that the interindustry wage structure is a consequence of "rent sharing" in an imperfectly competitive economy.[2] The rent sharing model offers an immediate explanation of racial wage and employment differentials between equally productive workers: black workers are disproportionately rationed into the ranks of the "non-rent-sharing" industries and the out-of-work. The only remaining question is how this comes about.

This chapter is not, however, an exercise in the further development of rent sharing and other models of imperfect competition as explanations of racial earnings and employment inequality. Indeed, chapter 2 suggested that these models are at odds with extant empirical evidence on racial turnover differentials and, in any case, repeat the conventional maxim that people with different quantities of human capital receive different wages. Rather, these models are but a reference point from which to further my exploration and development of explicitly *Classical Marxian* models of competition and discrimination.

The resurgent classical Marxian tradition (see Shaikh [1980], [1981a], [1981b], [1982a], [1982b]; Weeks [1981]; Semmler [1984]; Botwinick [1988]) conceptualizes competition between capitals as a dynamic and rivalrous process that generates tendencies toward *both* profit rate differentiation *and* equalization. Triumphant capitals have the means and motive to concentrate and centralize. Long-standing profit and wage differentials are an expected consequence of cost-cutting rivalry in a world of fixed capital, constant technological innovation, and persistent unemployment. This chapter develops a simple proposition: *The Marxian tradition's theory of competition among capitals explains the general phenomenon of sustained wage differentials between qualitatively similar workers.*

This chapter also extends previous works (Williams [1984], [1987b]; Darity and Williams [1985]; Darity [1989]) that analyze *racial job competition* within the working class. Racial (or, more generally, ethnic) job competition is a characteristic of racialized working-class formations in capitalist societies and conditions the racial distribution of wages and employment. Whereas previous works identify the ends and means of racially mediated competition within the working class, this chapter (1) advances the theoretical analysis of the competitively produced wage hierarchy and (2) identifies empirical and historical research agendas that can further our understanding of ethnically defined communities as participants in the reproduction of labor-market discrimination.[3]

I have organized the remainder of this chapter as follows. Section I uses the neoclassical conceptualization of competition as an occasion to ponder orthodox theorizing. Rent sharing and efficiency wage models of racial inequality provide recent examples of the theoretical tendencies of a tradition whose methodological signature is the propensity to reason from ideal types.

Section II begins the core of this chapter and serves as an introduction to the Classical Marxian tradition. It abstracts from differences among capitals and workers to consider the wage-labor relation for capital as a whole.[4] Section II briefly develops the by now standard Marxian analysis of dynamic capital accumulation as a process that, at the most general level, (1) segments the working class into the employed and the unemployed and (2) establishes the economic conditions for intra-working-class competition to avoid relegation to the reserve army of the unemployed.

Section III incorporates an explicitly Marxian conceptualization of competition, understood herein as the process of accumulation by self-expanding and rivalrous units of capital. After presenting the principal tenets of competitive theory, this section moves directly to Marxian competition's implications for wage differentials within and between industries. Botwinick's [1988] analysis of the relationship between profit and wage differentials orients this section.

Section IV concludes the core of this chapter by arguing that differentiated capital constitutes the material base for job competition between employed workers. In white supremacist or ethnically divided capitalist economies, workers (both men and women) frequently live and compete as members of race-ethnic groups. This penultimate section examines two literatures that speak to the emergence of white supremacy and class relations in capitalist societies. The first describes, interprets, and explains the evolution of the ideology and practices of racial domination; the second theorizes working-class formations in western Europe and the United States. These literatures provide a context within which to locate and expand the study of racial job competition between and within industries and between the employed and unemployed. Section V summarizes the chapter's main themes.

I. THINKING ABOUT COMPETITION: NEOCLASSICAL THEORY, EFFICIENCY WAGES, AND RACIAL EARNINGS INEQUALITY

This section (1) provides a methodological context within which to locate the neoclassical notion of "perfect" and "imperfect" competition and (2) briefly explores the *structure* of rent sharing and efficiency wage models as they are currently used to explain racial wage differentials (see chapter 2 for a more substantial critique of these models). The latter process allows us to concretely examine neoclassical theorizing in the face of empirical evidence that contradicts predicted competitive outcomes. This discussion will provide a background against which to compare section II's Marxian methodological approach.

As is well known, "perfect competition" is a state of affairs that defines a firm's behavior and market environment. The profit-maximizing (perfectly) competitive firm is first and foremost one among a large number of buyers and sellers; it is thus a "price-taker," not a "price-maker." In addition, (1) all agents possess complete information about production and consumption activities, (2) resources are perfectly mobile, implying free and rapid entry into and exit from the industry, (3) both production possibility and preference sets are convex, and (4) there are neither externalities nor collective behavior. In such a state of affairs, all disturbances yield but temporary deviations from the next long-term equilibrium. When they occur, exogenous cost-reducing technological innovations are quickly appropriated by all, and innovators reap but a momentary and tiny advantage; entry and exit eliminate extranormal profits that arise from changes in market demand or supply. Because each and every capitalist faces unlimited demand for his commodities, price wars are unnecessary and foolish. By construction, neoclassical theory sweeps away the war for market shares that dominates corporate boardrooms, business texts, and trade magazines: "In one stroke, the central characteristics of warfare among firms - the intention to fight, and the ability to damage - are eliminated by assumption." [5] Indeed, evidence of either direct rivalry or a decrease in the number of firms operating in an industry is deemed sufficient to label a market "imperfectly" competitive.

When confronted with such a perfect competition, the unwashed tend to question the legitimacy of the neoclassical undertaking. The faithful, in turn, have a patented response to the protest that "the assumptions of perfect competition are wildly inaccurate descriptions of capitalist market life." True believers will most likely recite the Friedmanesque instrumentalist chant: "The goal of positive science is the making of predictions; hence, the truth value of assumptions is largely irrelevant." [6] However, such disclaimers serve more to reveal the instrumentalist's philosophical isolation than his perspicacity. Most post-World War II philosophers of science have rejected the notion that science's only goal is prediction; modern positivists (the logical empiricists) insist that explanation is a very important objective of scientific practice and are surprisingly consistent in displaying a concern for the truth-value of assumptions (Williams [1987a]).[7] The neoclassical instrumentalist is clearly a "black sheep" in the positivist family. Among the neoclassicals, those concerned with the truth-value of their assumptions frequently toil in the fields of imperfect competition (e.g., noncooperative game theory).

To the extent that s/he is an instrumentalist, the contemporary ortho-dox theorist appears to be modern positivism's "illegitimate" child. I do not, however, wish to disavow instrumentalism on exclusively a priori grounds. It is logically possible that this method could, by chance, yield substantive insights into the regularities, contradictions, and proximate causal processes characteristic of capitalist development. However, I think that the particularities of neoclassical methodology make such an outcome highly unlikely. Specifically, I wish to extend Darity's argument from chapter 2 and propose that *all* orthodox theorists (and not just Neo-Keynesians) are clever practitioners of a rather paradoxical procedure, one consequence being the continued generation of models that are of limited value to the student of market-mediated racial inequality. In so doing, I will briefly explore an alternative, explicitly Marxian methodological tradition.

As a concept, perfect competition denies a commonly agreed-upon feature of business life, interfirm rivalry (actually, it denies several com-monly agreed-upon features, but the point can be made with just one). Consider Marxist critiques (Shaikh [1980], [1981b], [1982a]; Botwinick [1988]) of the neoclassical method. Shaikh and Botwinick argue that perfect competition is a conceptual ideal -type. It is commonly known that perfect competition's assumptions are at odds with the self-understanding that informs the activity of the accumulating class. The methodological implications of this construction are significant: rather than theorizing by abstraction from a conceptualization of the social totality, neoclassical theorists construct an ideal type and then proceed to study its properties.

In sharp contrast, Marx (and Marxists rooted in the epistemological tradition of "overdetermination," see Resnick and Wolff [1987: ch. 2]) begin quite differently. First, every social phenomenon, including the process of theorizing, is understood to be a condition of the existence of every other phenomenon - that is, "overdetermined." There is no aspect of social life that is presumed to be the "last-instance" determinant of all others. An overdeterminist epistemological standpoint implies that Marxian theory's emphasis on class relations is the delineation of a conceptual entry point, not the identification of an ontological essence. Theory's goal is therefore not the production of the essential "truths" of social life. Rather, theory's purpose becomes the specification of the the mutual overdetermination of class and nonclass processes that constitute the social totality.[8]

Theory thus begins with an overdetermined conceptualization of the social totality – what Marx termed the "real concrete." The real concrete is itself the product of a thought process. Theorizing's substance is the derivation of simpler determinations of the whole via successive rounds of abstraction. These simpler abstractions then become the components for the reconstruction of the whole, this time as a richer totality of relations and contradictions. Marx defined thinking's product as the "thought concrete." Knowledge is thus the transformative process that links concrete reals to thought concretes. Because thinking is both part of and overdetermined by the concrete-real, theorizing changes our understanding of the real concrete.

In this chapter, the relevant totality is the process of capital accumulation. Application of the method just described might imply that we first "abstract" from white supremacy (or, more generally, ethnic conflict) and begin by developing theoretical categories that facilitate the successive explanation of competition, employment, and wages in racially homogeneous economies. The next step is the successive incorporation of the relations and processes characteristic of specifically white supremacist (or, more generally, ethnically divided) social formations in order to describe and explain the racial distribution of work and wages.

For neoclassical theorists, perfect competition, as opposed to capital accumulation, is the entry point for the analysis of the racial distribution of employment and earnings. As a thought concrete, perfect competition prescribes that equals be rewarded equally, race notwithstanding. When confronted with empirical results that appear to contradict this normative "law," practitioners proceed to gather data to substantiate differences between workers that can redeem the original model. Steven Shulman's observation (chapter 1, section III) that "[f]ar more data are available on worker characteristics than on the details of employer decision making" is testimony to the relationship between the assumed validity of the perfect competition model and the categories used to collect data. The analysis of the relationship between worker characteristics and labor-market outcomes is, of course, the substance of the human-capital research agenda.

Models of imperfect competition are the other widely cultivated response to the gap between the competitive model's predictions and empirical evidence. The general practice is, of course, either to "relax" one or more of the initial, descriptively inaccurate assumptions or, as William Darity so decisively observed in chapter two, a more recent tendency is the invocation of "immutable imperfections," informational asymmetries being a contemporary favorite.[9] This, then, is the aforementioned peculiarity of the orthodox method: *The practitioner arguably engages in abstraction; however, her starting point is not a recognizable real concrete. Rather, she abstracts from her ideal type, perfect competition.*

An example germane to the topic at hand – racial employment and earnings inequality – will concretize this claim and conclude this section. Consider efficiency wage (EW) models as they have been applied to black/white wage inequality, recalling that this inequality is a particular case of the more general phenomenon of wage differentials between equally skilled workers. Although there are several EW models now in circulation (see Katz [1986]), they share a concern with the prevalence of non-market-clearing wages. Why do unemployed workers not bid down wages? The EW hypothesis is that workers' efforts depend on their wages – that is, the wage-labor contract is not self-enforcing, and successful capitalists must "elicit" work.[10] Moreover, workers know their propensity to shirk, but employers do not. Employers resist wage reductions because doing so may lower productivity more than it reduces wages, thus raising unit costs. Recalling perfect competition, EW theorists have "dropped" the assumption that employers have "perfect knowledge" of worker productivity.

Efficiency wage models of discrimination thus typify the aforementioned model-building practice. Theorists relax the assumption of identical workers (reminiscent of the human-capital tradition): because groups of workers differ in their separation rates, discrimination and wage inequality between "otherwise" comparable workers persist. However, as explained in chapter 2, this analysis is plagued by both conceptual problems and available data on worker terminations that challenge the EW model's ability to explain racial earnings inequality. Closely linked to the failure of EW models to describe adequately the costs of monitoring workers is the failure of the rent sharing model of imperfect competition to explain why capital markets fail to discipline managers who allegedly share the rents with those workers whose efforts are easily monitored (Krueger and Summers [1987]).

Both neoclassical methods – theorizing by constructing "deviations" from an ideal type – and explanations of the wage distribution seem wanting. I turn now to the Marxian tradition, wherein systematic inequality is conceptualized as a constitutive component of the social totality rather than viewed as an aberrant imperfection.

II. CAPITAL ACCUMULATION, COMPETITION, AND THE RESERVE ARMY OF THE UNEMPLOYED

In keeping with the methodology presented in the previous section, the core of this chapter begins by abstracting from differences among the employed to examine the differentiation of the working class into the employed and the reserve army of the unemployed. Even at this rather general level of analysis, we shall see that class relations differentiate the workforce, generate wage differentials not easily eliminated by labor mobility, and establish the basis for generalized competition within the working class.

For readers unfamiliar with the Marxian economics, Sections II and III provide a glimpse of this tradition. This overview draws heavily from the works of Shaikh [1978, 1980, 1981a, 1981b, 1982a, 1982b], Semmler [1984], Weeks [1981], Botwinick [1988], and, of course, Marx [1849, 1857, 1867, 1894]. These sections cannot serve as a substitute for systematic study of Marx or Marxists but they may provide a stimulus and motivation for such an undertaking.

IIA. Accumulation and Unemployment

Whereas neoclassical theorists only recently have begun to consider the unique properties of the wage-labor contract, such concerns are a long-standing component of the Marxian tradition. Indeed, a cornerstone of Classical Marxism is the thesis that capitalists must impose surplus labor time on workers in order to reproduce themselves qua capitalists. That which is distinctive about class relations under capitalism is that capitalists use the apparently voluntary institution of commodity production and exchange for the imposition of surplus labor. Labor power – workers' capacity to work – becomes a commodity under capital's class relations, and it is labor power that workers sell to capitalists. Labor power is conceptualized as a unique commodity in bourgeois economies because it is *the* commodity capable of generating surplus value – that is, value beyond what it costs to produce that same labor power. Labor power's value – the socially necessary labor time required for its reproduction – is the value of the workers' means of subsistence and includes the means to achieve a socially determined level of existence. Surplus value – the value that workers produce over and above their wage – is the source of profit and the goal (along with social control) of capitalist production.[11]

At this most general level of discourse, capital's ability to guarantee the successful imposition of surplus labor time in bourgeois society must be addressed. Two necessary class conditions must be satisfied.[12] First, workers must be separated from the means of production and "set free" from noncapitalist social relations of production. In Europe, this violent and disruptive process took many generations (see Marx [1867: part VIII]). Via enclosures, taxation, genocide, and "legally" established coercion (e.g., the Witch Persecutions of seventeenth-century Europe as described in Mies [1986: ch. 2]), capitalists and their collaborators separated peasants from the land and their possessions in order to compel work through the commodity form. In colonies, the process was equally bloody, albeit not identical. A second condition for accumulation is that capital must maintain control of the means of production. Capital's existence as a social relation of production thus requires the "primitive accumulation" of a working class and the reproduction of that class for capital. Sustained expansion both concentrates wealth in fewer and fewer hands and draws ever more populations into the ranks of the waged and unwaged.

Neoclassical theory's competitive labor market models accord primacy to the exchange relation between buyers and sellers of "labor." In sharp contrast, Marxists analyze labor markets in an explicitly dynamic context understood as being characterized by a class struggle over the imposition of surplus labor. Theories of unemployment highlight the depth of the differences between the two paradigms. In neoclassical theory, unemployment is the consequence of continuing market imperfections (some of which result in efficiency wages), search and signalling behavior, and exogenous factors (e.g., shifts in the composition of demand).[13] For Marx, unemployment was an expected outcome of continuing changes in the rate of capital accumulation, capital labor ratios, and labor-force participation (Marx: [1867: ch. 25]; Botwinick [1988: ch. 3]).

Consider capital accumulation when the capital/labor ratio - or, more precisely, the proportion into which capital advanced is divided into means of production (the value of constant capital) and wages (the value of labor power) - stays constant.[14] Under these circumstances, expanded accumulation increases the demand for labor power and thus produces upward pressure on the general wage level. This in turn causes the pace of accumulation and the demand for labor power to slacken, so that workers' wages begin to recede: "The rise of wages therefore is confined within the limits that not only leave intact the foundation of the capitalistic system, but also secure its reproduction on a progressive scale." [15] Herein we encounter the first limit on wages: the general wage level will not reach a level that completely throttles accumulation.

This discussion is limited because it abstracts from the class struggles that precipitate a key tendency within capital – that is, the increasing capital intensity (organic composition of capital, OCC) of commodity production. Marx ([1867]: ch. 10) vividly documented the evolution of English working-class power that compelled Parliament to legally limit the working day. Working-class activity thus limited capital's ability to increase the appropriation of surplus value by simply increasing the length of the working day. Marx defined the lengthening of the working day as a capitalist strategy to increase surplus value in its absolute form. Thereafter, capitalists' relative surplus value strategy sweeps onto the historical stage. When capitalists impose work and substitute means of production for labor power, productivity increases (less socially necessary labor time is required per commodity), and commodity values (and prices) decline, including the value of labor power. Labor power's value falls because the value of the means of subsistence falls; the ratio of surplus value to wages thus increases, and the basis for accumulation is thus reproduced on an expanded scale.

Two crucial results follow from this analysis. First, in contrast to the neoclassical theory of "exogenous" technical change, Marxian theory roots technical change in class struggle. Second, increases in the rate of accumulation need not entail proportionate increases in the demand for labor power:

On the one hand, therefore, the additional capital formed in the course of accumulation attracts fewer and fewer labourers in proportion to its magnitude. On the other hand, the old capital periodically reproduced with a change of composition, repels more and more of the labourers formerly employed by it. [16]

We therefore have two contradictory processes at work vis-à-vis the rate of accumulation and demand for labor power: general increases in the pace increase the demand, yet the increase in capital's organic composition reduces the demand for labor power. Marx's study of capitalist development led him to conclude that the latter effect would tend to dominate the former, thereby assuring that capital reproduces an expanding reserve army of the unemployed. That reserve army, in turn, is available for rapid deployment during periods of intensified accumulation and constrains workers' efforts to raise wages.

In the current period, the global reserve army grows. In the United States, government unemployment figures can obscure the growth of the surplus population unless traditional data are examined in conjunction with data on labor-force participation (and with an eye to employment in the state sector).[17] Employment to population ratios, alternatively referred to as employment rates, remain at historically low levels for both black and white men even after the increases from 1982 to 1988 (see U.S. Bureau of the Census [1988]; Dewart [1989]: 28). For blacks, however, the historical decline is most pronounced among young men who are not joining the labor force; among whites, older men are leaving the ranks of the employed (Christensen [1988]). The black/white unemployment gap continues to climb.[18]

The hidden unemployment of involuntary part-time (IPT) workers — women and men — is also unmeasured by the traditional unemployment rate. Boston's "marginalization rate" (MR = [IPT + unemployed + discouraged workers] / [employed + unemployed + discouraged]) displays both a huge racial gap and, apparently, secular increases, as the table below indicates. Recalling that 1982 was a low point in the employment cycle and 1970 was nearer a cyclical peak, we see that the two-to-one racial gap in narrowly defined unemployment rates (see chapter 1 by Steven Shulman) continues to approximate the racial marginalization ratio. Because 1970 and 1982 are very different points of their respective business cycles, these two points do not establish a secular increase. However, given that the nonteen male employment rates of the 1980s have not risen to their 1970s levels, it appears probable that we are experiencing a secular increase in marginalization rates.

Marginalization Rates

	Blacks	Whites
1970	15.3	7.7
1982	27.0	14.6

Note: See Boston [1988: 49].

IIB. Competition, Wage Differentiation, and the Reserve Army

I have so far argued that capital accumulation on an expanded scale reproduces a reserve army of the unemployed (Marx termed this tendency "the general law of capitalist accumulation"). As Marx noted, the reserve army is itself diverse, consisting of those unemployed because of secular or sector-specific downturns, those dispelled in periods of rapid technical change, those most recently "set free" from noncapitalist social relations of production (this setting free can occur in a variety of ways, of course), and those who are rarely, if ever, in capital's service.[19]

The reserve army has long been a key focus of the Marxian theoretical tradition and the politics informed thereby. Marxists are now expanding the analysis of the reserve army and competition within the working class.[20] Specifically, we argue that capitalists do not autonomously determine the composition of intra-working-class divisions. Gendered workers, in their cultural and racial diversity, actively participate in the processes that differentiate the unwaged from the waged and the high-waged from the low-waged. Botwinick [1988] provides a recent and cogent summary of the implications of this idea that is worthy of lengthy quotation:

First, given that this process of differentiation is an integral part of the general law of capitalist accumulation, it must also be considered when we attempt to assess the current relevancy of Marx's famous argument concerning capital's long run tendency to homogenize the working class. Second, the presence of these groups of workers who are in various degrees of desperation will often create an intense degree of competition and antagonism between employed and unemployed workers which is not merely generated by capital's attempts to divide and conquer the working class. Thus, as painful as this conclusion may be, we must begin to assess the extent to which employed workers, themselves, have often played an important role in the sustained differentiation of the working class as they attempt to protect themselves from this intense competition within the aggregate labor market.[21]

We must also recognize that actively employed workers who are attempting to protect (and improve) their standard of living must conduct their struggle against capital on two fronts. On the one hand, workers must continually struggle to resist capital's relentless attempts to deskill labor at the point of production. On the other hand, they must also find a way to protect themselves from capital's ready reserves of unemployed workers within the aggregate labor market.[22]

Botwinick's comments are of obvious significance to our examination of the general and specific tendencies of intra-working-class competition. Two additional observations are warranted. First, the strength of the argument does not rest on the existence of a racially divided working class;

indeed, this section deliberately abstracts from racialized working-class formations. Second, there is no a priori or historical reason to believe that entrenched, employed workers always have sufficient resources to thwart new competitors emerging from the reserve army. Recall, for example, the United States at the turn of the century. Between 1890 and 1910, emergent white male unions struck repeatedly and violently (and sometimes successfully) to displace black men from jobs they had long held. Brutally competitive job competition is no newcomer to U.S. capitalist development.[23]

The ends and means of working class job competition remain to be specified. Accumulation produces both the multidimensional general reserve army and "job-specific" labor reserves (many of whom already work, but at a lower wage); it produces the material base for substantive intraclass conflict among the employed as well. Subordinate workers are a potential labor reserve; indeed, from capital's perspective, they may be more easily mobilized than the unemployed. Insofar as workers define their objectives as the preservation of "job power" (that is, control over and/or input into the processes that define, create, and credential jobs and thereby delimit the eligible set of competitors and trainees) and the real wage, they are threatened by workers lower in the wage hierarchy. All workers confront the competition born of class relations in capitalist society. When workers compete as labor power, they participate in the composition of class relations, but not necessarily in a manner that equally empowers all.[24]

Workers' efforts to protect their incomes, prevent deskilling, and avoid the reserve army date back to early guilds and craft unions. In the United States, the American Federation of Labor reinforced the position of the free, skilled, white male laborer as the dominant wage earner. Within white working class formations, men's efforts to establish themselves as the primary or sole waged workers proved instrumental to the construction of husband patriarchy.[25] Within the working class as whole, this struggle does not proceed as random atomistic wage cutting. On the contrary, the combatants most often wage their war along lines demarcated by race and ethnicity.

But I am getting ahead of myself. My point is simply this: workers seeking to shelter themselves from bourgeois society's most fragile and despised existence – life among the low-waged and unemployed – have ample reason to create and wield weapons to shelter themselves from other members of the working class. Even at a level of analysis that deliberately abstracts from racial divisions and divisions within capital, we have derived a simple proposition: *Workers competing within capital as a whole are in conflict with both one another and capital over the creation and mobilization of job-specific labor reserves and the reserve army.*

The presence of the reserve army also has a limiting effect on the wage-equalizing tendencies of labor mobility. Recall that neoclassical competition presumes that labor mobility across sectors equalizes sectoral wage differentials in a full-employment economy. Marxian analysis, as we have seen, argues that unemployment is a permanent feature of capitalist economies. Hence when workers move from low-wage to high-wage sectors, the presence of the reserve army substantially moderates any tendencies for wages to rise among the low-waged. Also, as many have noted, labor mobility is costly for capital too. Training costs and more generally the costs associated with disrupting the social relations of the workplace mean that the wage gap between workers must be sufficiently large to make substitution of reserve workers for high-wage workers cost effective.[26] The reserve army therefore both limits and provides a foundation for wage differentials.

III. CAPITAL, COMPETITION, AND DIFFERENTIATION: A CONTEXT FOR THE ANALYSIS OF INTERINDUSTRY WAGE DIFFERENTIALS

I have examined the expansionary tendencies of capital as a whole, arguing that it is a process that differentiates the working class at the level of the social relations of production. Dynamic capital accumulation produces a surplus population whose presence chastens the demands of the employed; indeed, it creates material conditions for competition among workers that are not easily reduced to capitalists' intentionally collusive effort to "divide and conquer" the working class.

This section further specifies the process of capital accumulation by addressing the existence of multiple capitals. Part IIIA explores the Classical Marxian tradition's conceptualization of competition, that differs substantially from the "monopoly-capital" theory of capitalism's stages. This reading of capitalist competition explains the production of differentiated units of capital and thereby tendencies toward both the equalization and differentiation of profit rates. Part IIIB examines the processes of dynamic differentiation through which capitalist competition creates the possibilities for wage hierarchies.

IIIA. Capitalist Competition: Differentiation and Homogenization

Whatever their nontrivial differences with the neoclassical tradition, most modern radical economists locate themselves in a theoretical discourse defined by notions of "perfect" and "imperfect" competition. More precisely, many radicals (Marxists, neo-Marxists, post-Marxists, etc.) claim that Marx's conceptualization of competition was rooted in an analysis of the behavior of the price-taking firm. Moreover, the conventional wisdom holds that the past century brought the decline of the price-taker and ushered in the era of price-making "monopoly capital;" hence theoreticians should acknowledge the demise of competition by abandoning a competitive framework in the modelling of wages and prices in bourgeois economies.[27]

Yet an oppositional voice emerges from the theoretical wings. James Clifton, Anwar Shaikh, Willi Semmler, and John Weeks are prominent voices arguing for readings of both Marx and of capitalist competition that radically differ from the monopoly-capital tradition.[28] This emergent "Classical" Marxian tradition is the basis for this section's examination of rivalrous competition among capitalists.

Although they do not deny that capitalist relations have changed structurally and institutionally in the past century, Classical Marxists nonetheless posit a conceptualization of competition that dramatically differs from those popular among both orthodox economists and monopoly capital theorists. First, we understand that competition is a *rivalrous* activity and read capitalists' routinely observed struggle for market shares as a competitive battle. In this context, market prices vary according to the specific conditions of competition, but have, as "centers of gravity," market values that vary according to changes in the direct and indirect labor requirements of production. The "real-concrete" from which we begin is a production landscape where large amounts of fixed capital, price wars, advertising, and uncertainty are conditions of, but not barriers to, competition. Second, capitalist rivalry also creates tendencies toward the concentration and centralization of capital as winners absorb losers within and across industries. Finally, competition generates differentiation in production conditions, which is manifest as differentiated intraindustry profit rates as well as tendencies toward the equalization of rates of profit across industries.[29]

Marx began his analysis of capital by examining the properties of capital as a whole, and characterized it as a self-expanding, surplus- and commodity-producing set of class relations. "Competition" emerges because capital has many owners and managers. Single producers of a given commodity are not, however, beyond the clutches of competition, since they must still compete for a share of the total market. Accumulation is a process of rivalrous management and thus the consequence of self-expansion by different units of capital, each of which strives relentlessly to realize surplus value.

Within an industry, the struggle to expand value generates the battle over market shares. Although capitalists employ many weapons in the competitive struggle, the cheapening of their commodities is a crucial element of the battle plan:

Each individual capital strives to capture the largest possible share of the market and to supplant its competitors and exclude them from the market. (Marx [1863]: 484)

The one capitalist can drive the other from the field and carry off his capital only by selling more cheaply. In order to sell more cheaply without ruining himself, he must produce more cheaply, that is, increase the productive force of labour as much as possible. (Marx [1849]: 40)

The battle of competition is fought by cheapening of commodities. The cheapness of commodities depends, ceteris paribus, on the productiveness of labour, and this again on the scale of production. (Marx [1867]: 626)

The previous section described how class conflict over the length of the working day accelerated capital's need for mechanized techniques of production, that in turn require large outlays of constant (fixed) capital. But large absolute fixed costs require an expanded scale of output to generate low unit costs, that is, the covering of fixed costs requires an expanded market for that output. Insofar as cost-cutting technological change increases the capital intensity of production, the mass of constant capital is also increased. The innovating capitalist not only can sell his commodities more cheaply, he *must* sell more of them. Price reductions are a means to expanding markets.[30]

Price-cutting also can damage rivals. Today's cost-cutting innovator discovers that his rivals cannot and do not immediately adopt the new methods, due to fixed capital's nontrivial turnover periods (recalling Shulman's terminology of chapter 1, adjustment costs are significant). While the innovator's rivals cannot, in other words, immediately "junk" their old equipment, the innovator must cut prices to make room for an expanded output. But in so doing, he also wreaks havoc upon rivals still operating with older technologies and thus higher unit costs. The technological aggressor jeopardizes the laggard's market share, and the latter cannot respond in kind without substantially reducing his profit margins and rates. Furthermore, the price war threatens the high-cost producer's profit expectations substantially more than those of the low-cost aggressor. Botwinick ([1988]: 179) summarizes intraindustry competition as follows:

Given the presence of prolonged turnover periods for fixed capital, the dynamics of competition and technical change will normally result in the continual redifferentiation of profit rates within each industry. Capitals with the most advanced techniques will tend to have greater fixed capital outlays, higher capital/output and capital/labor ratios, lower unit costs, and higher profit margins. As prices are driven down they are likely to enjoy higher profit rates as well.

Marx analyzed competition *between* industries in volume 3 of *Capital*. He explored the consequences of competition between industries that operate with different organic compositions of capital (or capital/labor ratios)[31] and different rates of profit. Marx's argument (and extensions thereof) is straightforward: capital flows from sectors with low profit rates (the capital-intensive sectors) and toward sectors with high profit rates (the labor-intensive sectors). Market prices rise in the former and decline in the latter, generating a tendency for profit rate equalization. Competition thus redistributes value between sectors.

Here again, costs of adjusting fixed capital loom large: the real time required to enter and exit industries is a condition of competition. Capital moves more quickly into and out of labor-intensive industries, thus generating rapidly fluctuating profit cycles. The opposite holds for more capital-intensive sectors: their profit margins and prices will change more slowly. Large amounts of fixed capital imply higher adjustment costs and so capital enters and exits more slowly. Adjustment to fluctuations in demand appears as changes in capacity-utilization rates. Therefore, the tendency for profit rates to equalize across industries only occurs over an extended period of time.[32]

Shaikh ([1981b], [1982b]) has argued that Marx's analysis of the tendential profit rate equalization concludes at a high level of abstraction. The differentiation of interindustry conditions of production leaves open the question of which firm governs the conditions of interindustry capital mobility (and therefore the average or general rate of profit). Shaikh provides further specificity by developing the concept of "regulating capitals." Within an industry, the regulating capital is the enterprise with the best available and reproducible conditions of production. It is this capitalist that entering capitals seek to emulate and that tends to earn the average rate of profit vis-à-vis other industries. Shaikh [1982a] also has shown that the regulating capital's profit rate will not generally equal the *industry* average profit rate. On the contrary, the regulator's rate will exceed the industry average and serve as the goal of new industry entrants. It is the interindustry variations in the regulating profit rate that stimulate capital mobility.

From a Marxian perspective, the general rate of profit that we actually observe therefore is not an "equilibrium" price; on the contrary, it is the result of turbulent processes of movement of capital across industries and within industries. Within industries, innovations in the technical conditions (and social relations) of production differentiate profits; between industries, capital mobility creates a tendency for the equalization of profit rates between regulating capitals. At a given point in time, a variety of profit rates will exist. *Profit rate differentials within industries are the expected consequence of competitive capital accumulation and these differentials may persist for quite some time.*

IIIB. Workers and Differentiation: The Dynamic Constitution of the Wage Hierarchy

For wage theorists, the Classical Marxian tradition provides a rich framework within which to situate a general analysis of wage differentials between comparable workers and a specific model of black/white wage inequality.[33] Botwinick [1988] has provided the former – a detailed theoretical discussion of competitive wage differentials. This section concludes with a critical (and partial) summary of his model;[34] it completes the last logical step necessary for section IV's elaboration of a theory of racial job competition and black/white wage differentials.

First and foremost, Botwinick argues that a thorough Marxian analysis of competitive wage determination presupposes a detailed analysis of the differentiation of capital. Marx's notes indicate that he planned to write a separate volume on wage labor after completing volume 3 of *Capital*. His discussion in volume 1 is thus necessarily incomplete, although somewhat illuminating. For example, chapters 15 and 20 briefly link uneven technological change to the reproduction of low-wage industries and the masses of the working poor: workers released from innovating industries become the wage-dampening reserve labor force available to labor-intensive sectors. Excess labor reserves in turn reduce capital's incentive to introduce labor-saving machinery, that further contributes to uneven technical change. A similar phenomenon occurs *within* the most innovative industries: those employed in firms slow to adopt the newest cost-reducing methods will confront employers struggling to remain competitive via the reduction of wages.

Yet by no stretch of the imagination is this a determinate analysis of wages and profits. Botwinick's theory of wage differentials thus provides a fruitful beginning for such an analysis and warrants close consideration. One of his central objectives is the derivation of *limits* to wage increases in the context of differentiating conditions of capitalist production and profitability. Specifically, capitalist competition and the reserve army strictly limit wage variations; within these limits, workers' efforts to raise their wages will decidedly shape the distribution of wages between equally skilled individuals. When wages exceed these limits, profits go to zero.[35]

Botwinick begins with the following scenario: suppose that workers organize and raise wages in all the regulating capitals in hypothetical "industry A." For ease of exposition, he also assumes that interindustry competition has led to prices that equalize profit rates for all regulating capitals. Under these conditions, a wage increase immediately raises unit costs and therefore lowers profit margins and profit rates in A.[36] It is at this juncture that the competitive process comes into play:

The initial discrepancy in profit rates caused by the wage increases will eventually cause the rate of growth of supply within industry A to decelerate as capital flows more rapidly into other industries where regulating capitals are enjoying higher profit rates. Assuming a period of healthy accumulation, supply will tend to grow more slowly than demand, and the equalization of profit rates across regulating capitals within each industry will bring about a rise in relative prices for the regulating capitals suffering the original wage increase.[37]

Even this rather general level of analysis generates two nontrivial results. First, as long as the local wage increase remains within the limits of competition (developed below), there is no reason to expect immediate reductions in the actual level of employment (clearly a different result from that derived from the neoclassical short-run wage model); on the contrary, the expected outcome is a decline in the *rate of growth* of employment and output. Second, the price increase is conceptualized as a consequence of capitalist competition – that is, capital mobility – not monopoly pricing power.

The next task is a precise derivation of three *sets of limits* that constrain workers' efforts to raise their wages. "Limit one" derives from the conditions of immediate profitability and interindustry competition: it is "determined by the profit margins of the regulating capitals experiencing the wage increase." [38] "Limit two," derived from the state of intraindustry competition, is a function of the unit costs of the second most efficient producers (the subdominant capitals) in industry A. The final "Limit three" is determined by workers' ability to impose costs upon capitalists trying to obstruct the wage increases.[39] In what follows, I develop the reasoning behind each limit.

Limit one connects the "real time" required for industry A's slowed growth to generate a new production price with the necessary conditions for the regulating capital's economic survival: "In order for these capitals to survive this transitional period, . . . these wage increases cannot be permitted to cause rising unit costs to entirely wipe out the profit margins of the regulating capitals." [40] Hence Limit one: the wage increase cannot exceed the profit margin per unit of labor.[41]

A less obvious result, but a significant corollary of this analysis, is that (1) the regulating capitals' profit margins must be directly proportional to their capital/output ratios and (2) that profit margins per unit of labor for each industry vary proportionately to capital/labor ratios. Alternatively stated, *equal profit rates require unequal profit margins, and large profit margins provide more room for wage increases*. Thus, Limit one is consistent with the observation that capital-intensive industries are more attractive to workers seeking wage increases.[42]

Limit two is derived from the examination of intraindustry competition and answers the following question: At what point do wage increases jeopardize the regulating capital's position qua regulating capital? Limit two is a function of the difference between the unit costs of the regulating and subdominant capitals and requires that the unit costs of the former not exceed those of the latter.[43] If workers in the regulating capital push wages beyond this limit, rising prices will not be sufficient for the regulator to maintain its advantage over its rivals in the rate of profit it earns. If the regulating capitals lose their regulating status, they will try to reclaim lost position by reducing wages, thus making the initial wage increase difficult to sustain in the face of continued competition.

Botwinick also shows that if we compare two industries, one capital-intensive and one labor-intensive, Limit two will be larger in the former than in the latter, insofar as the percentage difference in unit costs is the same in each industry: [44]

At the very least, the above results certainly suggest that given roughly similar differentials in unit costs within various industries, many highly capital-intensive industries may have a larger potential range for wage differentials to develop within the confines of vigorous intra-industry competition. On the other hand, highly labor-intensive industries will tend to have a much more narrow potential for intra-industry wage variation.[45]

This describes the generally recognized phenomenon that labor-intensive industries are much more vulnerable to low-wage competition than their capital-intensive counterparts.

Botwinick's third limit answers a question that the previous discussion might prompt: If wage increases do indeed pose a nontrivial threat to profits, why would managers concede to any wage increases at all, even those that fell within the previously discussed limits? His answer is a straightforward application of the Marxian understanding of the the workplace as a site of class conflict. Simply stated, management's will is not hegemonic; organized workers can obstruct production and thereby impose costs on capitalists who resist wage increases. Workers' ability to do so is conditioned by the technical conditions of production (and, I would add, by state policies and the availability of labor reserves). Thus capitalists must compare the costs of wage increases to the cost of resisting those increases.

Consider, for example, the scale of a firm's operations and the level of its fixed capital investment.[46] During periods of labor-management strife, management can more easily maintain production if the workforce is small. However, if the operation employs a large number of workers, an effective strike can stop business as usual. Similarly, if workers stop production in a plant with a high level of fixed capital investment, the firm will sustain serious overhead costs during the strike period. Insofar as management explores relocation as a means of thwarting workers' efforts to raise wages, a large mass of undepreciated fixed capital will most likely slow management's movement; a small and/or old capital stock facilitates capital mobility (as do tax policies). Further, as many have noted, workers who are machine-tenders are costly to replace since the cost of replacing such workers includes training costs for new workers.

Botwinick's discussion of adjustment costs includes themes familiar to those rooted in discussions of the conditions that favor or hinder worker organization and high wages (e.g., Cartter [1975]; Freeman and Medoff [1982]). That which is new about his analysis is the context in which he locates the discussion. In the Marxian tradition, workers' struggles and strategies must be situated in the context of capitalist competition and accumulation. From the perspective of workers seeking stable employment and higher wages, capital is decidedly heterogeneous. Regulating capitals with high levels of fixed capital investment and high capital/labor ratios can more easily absorb wage increases than their competitors with low overhead and labor-intensive techniques of production. However, it is not monopoly power that explains the regulating capital's ability to absorb the wages; rather, it is "because competition requires these capitals to earn relatively high profit margins." [47]

IV. COMPETITION, DISCRIMINATION, AND DIFFERENTIATION: RACIAL CONFLICT WITHIN THE WORKING CLASS

We are now theoretically positioned to address black/white employment and wage inequality, a motivating concern of this chapter. Classical Marxian theory argues that competition *both* divides the working class into the employed and unemployed *and* dynamically reproduces a competitive wage hierarchy. Significantly, it also rationalizes the conventional wisdom regarding the structure of interindustry wages, that is, actually existing capitalist economies have demonstrated a surprisingly stable interindustry wage structure. As was noted at the chapter's beginning, there are high-wage and low-wage industries; the former are relatively larger, more profitable, and more likely to deploy capital-intensive production technologies than the latter (Krueger and Summers [1987]; Dickens and Katz [1987]).

IVA. Racial Formations and Competition Within the Working Class

When extended to the owners of labor power, Marxian competition is an intraclass rivalry dictated by the employment and wage hierarchy generated by capitalist competition. Workers in search of employment stability and wage growth have ample incentive to secure favorable niches in the industry-occupation matrix, both by excluding and displacing others. Entrenched workers also have reason to be wary of those lower in the wage hierarchy. In this context, worker strategies to shelter themselves from job competition are consistent with a desire to remain employed, protect themselves from employment shocks, and impose costs on employers seeking to use low-wage workers to reduce their wages. By controlling job definitions, information, training, and evaluation, the employed can build shelters to protect themselves from capital's efforts to reduce wages (and therefore costs) via the introduction of cheaper labor power. Like capitalists, workers try to "concentrate" their winnings. Job competition is thus the norm for capitalist economies, and the losers appear more frequently in capital's relative surplus population.

Yet labor-market combatants are not asocial individual wage cutters. On the contrary, self-identified (and gendered) racial and ethnic communities have emerged as the principal competitors. As an analysis of competition, Marxist theory thus provides a foundation for a general theory of ethnic inequality in capitalist social formations, wherein discrimination draws life from the self-interested activity of ethnic communities within the working class. It therefore offers a context within which to explore the general phenomenon of ethnic conflict in capitalist societies as diverse as South Africa, Great Britain, New Zealand, France, and Israel. Marxian competition also articulates an alternative theory of racial inequality within which to locate the particular case of black/white inequality in the U.S. working class.

In the United States – and, more generally, in most white supremacist bourgeois economies – "race" is deeply constitutive of workers' identity as struggling social subjects. "Race" is a mediating relation in the construction of class formations; it has repeatedly served as a locus of intraclass conflict (see Harris [1927]; Spero and Harris [1931]; Janiewski [1986]; Williams [1987b]; Darity [1989]; Hill [1976], [1984], [1985], [1989]). The prevailing "radical" wisdom (e.g., Reich [1981]) construes racial divisions as a threat to working-class solidarity: capitalists are the primary beneficiaries of a racially divided (and thus more easily conquered) working class. Marxist competition between labor powers implies that this analysis is fundamentally incomplete. The neo-Marxian models fail to address the extent to which "white solidarity" can increase white workers' bargaining power vis-à-vis both capital and black workers in the intraclass competition for employment and access to potentially high-wage sectors.[48] In other words, white workers can benefit from employment discrimination against blacks, that explains why they have and do participate therein.

Working-class communities are, of course, gendered. Among whites, male-dominated gender-based labor-market competition has been a crucial element of the construction of male dominance within the working class (see Hartmann [1982]; Walby [1986]; Bergmann [1986], [1989]; Milkman [1980], [1987]; Reskin [1988]). Theorists differ as to their analyses of working-class men's motivation for wielding gender solidarity to exclude women from their job turf. Some feminists (e.g., Reskin, Walby, and Hartmann) emphasize the connection between men's ability to exclude women from preferred sectors of the labor market and the concomitant creation of male privilege. This chapter challenges feminist theorists to racially disaggregate the male employment and wage hierarchy in their theories of male labor-market behavior. Glenn's [1985] documentation of a race-ethnic labor hierarchy among women suggests the need for gender-specific analyses of racial job competition.

This chapter presents an analysis of the economic foundations of competition among workers. It does not presume to offer a substantial contribution to the historical emergence of either racism or husband patriarchy within the working class. On the contrary, it presumes that "actually existing" Western bourgeois societies have developed as white supremacist patriarchies and explores the material foundation for gender-mediated racial conflict therein. There are, however, vibrant literatures that provide orienting perspectives that complement the framework presented here.

The first includes research that takes as problematic the racial and gender mediations of capitalist social formations. For example, Hartmann [1981], Walby [1986], and Pateman [1988] provide compelling feminist analyses of the emergence of white bourgeois and/or "civil" society as a modern patriarchy. Cox [1970], Said [1979], Fredrickson [1981], and West [1982] document the relationship between white supremacy and the past four centuries of capitalist development. Their research identifies the historical specificity of white supremacy as a set of social practices rooted in the European colonizing tradition, post-Enlightenment science, and the political and economic domination of "nonwhite" peoples. Mies [1986] examines the global emergence of racially mediated gender hierarchies in the context of "patriarchal accumulation."

A second tradition (see the essays in Katznelson and Zolberg [1986]) recognizes proletarianization as an important process in modernity, state formation, and the emergence of civil society. Katznelson [1986] describes a nonessentialist approach to theorizing class in capitalist societies. This method proposes that "class in capitalist societies be thought of as a concept with four connected layers of theory and history: those of structure, ways of life, disposition, and collective action." Katznelson's call for the need to understand working class communities as complex social formation is welcome. Shefter's [1986] essay on U.S. working class formations in the late nineteenth century emphasizes ethnicity as a locus of community identity. Yet neither Shefter nor Katznelson (in this context) pose as problematic the European immigrants' historical appropriation of "whiteness" as a positively valued cultural resource. How did "whiteness" subsume and transform ethnicity? How did the interplay of whiteness and ethnicity shape this and subsequent generations' political demands, forms of cultural expression, and organizations? The answering of these questions is crucial for a more complete understanding of U.S. working-class formations.

IVB. Marxian Competition in Context: Connections with Prior Research

An explicitly Marxist theory of discrimination intersects with and has implications for much recent research. For example, consider those who emphasize the cost-inefficiency of discrimination. If capitalist competition is a ruthless rivalry for market shares fought through the cheapening of commodities, how can managers afford to accommodate white (male) supremacy in the wage hierarchy? Our answer derives from the joint consideration of the composition of capital, the conditions of competition, and the intrafirm social relations of production.

Consider an employer for whom payments to high-wage, white male machinists constitute a large portion of labor costs. In this case, the cost savings from training and employing black female operatives might be substantial. However, if wage costs are a small portion of total unit costs, that is, production is capital-intensive, the net savings are considerably reduced. If this employer manages a regulating capital earning the general rate of profit, the pressures to reduce labor costs are further moderated by his competitive stature. But competitive conditions and the net cost savings derived from the technical conditions of production do not exhaust the manager's decision calculus. He must also include the costs of transforming a white male working environment into one that includes black women. *When sufficiently numerous and either tacitly or explicitly organized, dominant workers can make capital "pay" for ending discrimination.*

As Shulman ([1984b] and in chapter 1) has so carefully detailed, there are several paths through which ending white (male) privilege within the working class can be costly for capital. In the example at hand, the disruption of white male supremacy can distort white men's expectations about their authority and power vis-à-vis black women. Second, specific efforts at black inclusion may disrupt established procedures (formal and informal) for recruitment, screening, allocation, and training. The costs of reproducing the workforce thus increase. If white men overtly resist training black women (or, by analogy, if white men resist the inclusion of *any* women in their domain), training costs again increase. Similarly, white resistance to integration may generally impair team workplace cooperation. Because chronic unemployment among white men means that there exists a reserve from which to draw, cost-conscious managers could easily view black employment as a risky and expensive undertaking.

During periods of rapid accumulation, white workers' resistance to black employment should lessen because capital is creating new jobs; for capitalists, the threat of rising wages increases the incentive to employ and reallocate black labor (although blacks need not necessarily make employment gains relative to whites). During periods of general economic contraction, we would expect employment discrimination to increase: ending discrimination would increase white workers' vulnerability to unemployment, and continuing discrimination is less costly to capital. Shulman's [1984b] empirical work suggests that employment discrimination against blacks increased in the high-unemployment early 1980s.

Although my example focuses on occupation-based job competition, the costs of ending discrimination are mediated by the particulars of inter- and intraindustry competition. This poses a challenge to conventional discussions of job competition. Most theoreticians and strategists alike frequently construe job competition as rivalry for access to specific occupations, but accord limited significance to job competition (or, more frequently, occupational segregation) based on race or gender as a means of sorting workers among differentiated industries. My point here is not to discount occupational segregation as a pervasive means of securing white wage privilege vis-à-vis blacks (or white men's superordinate position to white women); rather, my analysis suggests that most previous theoretical work fails to accord sufficient attention to the competitively differentiated industrial structure as a domain of job competition.

Existing empirical work calls attention to the industrial distribution of workers by race and gender. Dean's [1988] examination of the wages and gender composition of occupation-industry groups revealed that men are concentrated in capital- and resource-intensive occupation-industry cells. Dean's data did not, however, allow her to sort the genders by race. Dickens and Katz's [1987] industry wage analysis reveals that ceteris paribus, female-dominated industries are low-wage industries. However, they shed no light on racial inequality by industry since their coefficient for "% black" varied from specification to specification. Reich's analysis of industries, wages, and profits ([1981]: 302) showed a sizable and significant negative relation between an industry's median white earnings and the percentage of nonwhites in its labor force. Higgs's [1989] survey of the pre-World War II South revealed that blacks were concentrated in low-wage occupations across all sectors, but also disproportionately employed in low-wage industries.

Few existing studies sort workers into race-gender groups. The use of "race" and "gender" dummies is, of course, problematic, because not all the women are white, and many of the blacks are women.[49] Williams [1990] demonstrated the existence of an intraindustry race-mediated gender wage hierarchy. The aggregate 1979 industry data showed that men of both races were more concentrated in high-wage employment than women; within each gender group, whites were more concentrated in high-wage positions than blacks.

Because of their single-equation specifications, existing studies do not explicitly test the job-competition hypothesis. That is, they do not entertain the hypothesis that *race-mediated job competition sorts blacks (men and women) into low-wage industries*. The testing of such a hypothesis requires the *simultaneous* estimation of a race (preferably, race-gender) employment composition equation in conjunction with a theoretically informed wage equation. In the former equation, "% black (female)" must be endogenous and determined by the industry wage, an endogenous variable, and other measures of the industry's relative desirability to workers. Such a specification incorporates the proposition that the racial composition of industry employment is itself an outcome variable.

Marxian competitive theory potentially demystifies the wage hierarchy and the reserve army. It provides a lens through which to comprehend both general wage inequality and the particulars of racial earnings and employment inequality. In the United States, black workers have yet to escape overrepresentation in the reserve army and among the low-waged; the analysis of intraclass racial rivalry developed herein constitutes an explanation of this phenomenon. This is a vital portal through which one must first proceed for any study of discrimination that seeks to understand the extent to which race is called into service to distribute work and wages within capitalist social formations.[50]

V. CONCLUSION

Capitalist accumulation is a rivalrous, competitive warfare that generates tendencies toward differentiation as well as homogenization; it is a process that reproduces both the relative surplus population and a distribution of earnings that cannot be explained simply in terms of the capacities of individual workers. Within and between industries, capital displays a hierarchy of profit margins and rates. For workers, capital's heterogeneity implies an uneven distribution of wage opportunities and a reason to devise strategies to secure and maintain access to preferred industries and occupations. Workers' fortunes, though uncertain, are inextricably linked to the relative competitive stature of their employers.

Bourgeois society exacts a high price for losing the competitive struggle for steady employment at a living wage. Losers are first and foremost prey to employment and wage variation; they are also vulnerable to the stigmatization and social engineering that a bureaucratized and materialist culture heaps upon the unwaged and low-waged. Marxian theory suggests that the past decade of white male resistance to "affirmative action" is not without economic foundation. Affirmative action is an effort to redistribute the destitution caused by capital's rivalry. In the United States, policies designed to *racially* redistribute employment and wages will be resisted by many white workers who have benefited from a state-supported (and gender-mediated) race privilege that allowed them to consolidate employment winnings. An overnight *racial* re-apportionment of employment and wage income would leave millions of whites (men and women) either unemployed or working at lower wages. Hence dominant workers will (and do) resist efforts to change the rules; [51] they marshal their intellectual, political, cultural, and economic resources to fend off the insistent outsider.

For blacks and nonblacks seeking to form interracial working-class alliances, this analysis poses a profound challenge. No longer can we simply say that white workers seeking to reproduce their privilege within the working class (that is, secure and maintain employment and their absolute real incomes, as opposed to their income relative to capital) are mindlessly working against themselves. Our analysis suggests that a Marxian conceptualization of competition restores a logical place for solidarity among ethnic communities seeking collectively to climb, rather than smash, the wage hierarchy.

PART II

LABOR-MARKET SEGMENTATION: EVIDENCE AND IMPLICATIONS OF GENDER BARRIERS

T he three chapters in this part explore the forces, largely from the demand side of labor markets, to split these markets into segments by gender with little mobility across the boundaries of these segments. Chapter 5 by William Bielby summarizes the empirical evidence challenging neoclassical explanations of the allocation of effort and job segregation by sex. This evidence indicates that men's and women's allocations of effort and the pattern of sex segregation between and within workplaces are not consistent with familiar explanations based on supply and demand in labor markets. It thus argues that there is a clear usefulness for alternative ways of understanding how men and women approach work and are sorted into jobs. Organizational inertia, bounded rationality, employee and employer interests, cognitive stereotypes, and sex-specific norms of entitlement are found empirically to shape job choices and personnel practices. In looking at neoclassical supply-side, demand-side, radical, and Marxist explanations for inequality by gender, Bielby finds that inadequate attention is given to ideologies of gender roles.

The very useful overview in chapter 5 of organizational rationales for sexual segmentation is continued by the extensive survey of organizational research in the following chapter by James Baron. Research on inequality in the workplace has long sought to distinguish the influence of characteristics that workers bring to their jobs (supply-side effects) from the features of firms or organizations offering the jobs (demand-side effects). Baron offers a detailed and very insightful view of distinctions among organizations that current research reveals to be important with special emphasis on inequality by gender. He argues for a more microscopic view than microeconomists usually employ: the specification of what constitutes a particular job, of the earnings associated with that job, and of the system for matching particular people with particular jobs all appear to be closely linked to ascriptive characteristics through psychological, normative, political, and historical factors. The conclusion is strong: organizational form matters if economists are to avoid bias in econometric analysis due to the omission of organizational variables.

This comprehensive survey of the institutional factors that segment the labor market, especially internal labor markets, by gender are followed by an exploration in chapter 7 by David Fairris and Lori Kletzer of how sexual segregation affects working conditions and earnings of men and of women. They find that in the subordinate primary segment of these markets, the pattern of wages across good and bad working conditions leads to doubt that the main explanation is supply-side choices by women. The tendency of differentials in earnings to compensate for differentials in working conditions is found to be stronger in the more competitive secondary segment. What is surprizing is that estimates of the gap in wages between men and women that do not control for working conditions may *underestimate* the extent of wage discrimination by gender in this sector: controlling for working conditions appears to increase the gap in wages between men and women. This is because women tend to have worse working conditions than men for those conditions with positive compensating payments. These results are surprising because they reverse the findings of the seminal work by Filer [1985] in this field. This suggests strongly that ignoring possible barriers in labor markets may bias estimates of the determinants of earnings. The particular classification of jobs used by Fairris and Kletzer goes back to Osterman [1975], although alternative categories are explored, including that due to Gordon [1986]. This chapter adds to the evidence of segmentation ranging from Dickens and Lang [1985] to Doeringer and Piore [1971] and Gordon, Edwards, and Reich [1982].

The work in this part has significant implications for the evaluation of efficiency wage theory (EWT) explored in the first part of this volume. In chapter 5, William Bielby expands on his research with Denise Bielby on differences by gender in the elicitation of effort. It is the effort-elicitation function that is central to the development in chapter 3 by Michael Robinson and Phanindra Wunnava of EWT. The critique in chapter 2 by William Darity of efficiency wage approaches relied, in part, on this work by Bielby and Bielby. The costs faced by employers in eliciting effort from employees are one type of transaction cost. Section V of chapter 6 offers conjectures on other types of transaction costs that affect the evolution of organizations.

Kletzer and Fairris argue that limits to the freedom of choice over working conditions bias estimates of compensating differentials as well as estimates of inequality in earnings. This reinforces the limits to conventional measures of discrimination which are explored in chapter 8 by Harriet Duleep and Nadja Zalokar. They illustrate how supply-side responses to differences in earnings that are based on ascription can bias conventional estimates of the costs of such discrimination. Chapter 9 by Solomon Polachek and Charng Kao develop further supply-side explanations for inequality in earnings. Their thorough development of the implications of differences by gender in plans to interrupt one's career provides a very insightful methodological and ideological complement to Bielby's comparison of gender differences in chapter 5.

5
The Structure and Process of Sex Segregation

William T. Bielby

$\mathbf{M}$y work, like that of several others contributing to this volume, seeks to understand the persistence of occupational segregation by sex and the sex gap in earnings. Neoclassical economists, of course, have an elegant, coherent theory of the sources of both occupational segregation by sex and earnings differentials: they come from the rational, utility-maximizing behavior of men and women within households and labor markets.

Sociologists view the situation differently. Indeed, depending on whom you ask, a sociologist might offer any of a number of explanations for sex differences in labor-market outcomes. Social psychologists would stress sex-role socialization. Feminist scholars would emphasize the "patriarchal" interests of male employers and workers. Marxists would tell a story about capitalists creating divisions in the work force in order to control labor and boost profits. Organizational theorists might talk about the unintended consequences of bureaucratic rules and procedures. Not surprisingly, sociologists from different camps often talk past one another.

However, sociologists are increasingly taking the work of neoclassical economists seriously. The language of "human capital," "statistical discrimination," and the like is increasingly part of the sociological discourse on gender and work. However, sociologists do not accept the neoclassical account uncritically. In this chapter, I first summarize how my research with James Baron and Denise Bielby challenges neoclassical explanations and then raise some issues concerning the promise and limitations of recent interdisciplinary approaches to the study of job segregation by sex and other forms of discrimination.

I. NEOCLASSICAL VIEWS

In a sense, it all starts with the household division of labor. Women prefer, get stuck with, or have a comparative advantage caring for children and the home. Because of that, they invest less in market human capital. For example, intermittent labor-force participation leads to less work experience and thus to lower productivity and flatter age-earnings profiles. Women rationally *choose* occupations that are easy to leave and reenter, where skills do not atrophy, and so on. These choices lead to occupational segregation and wage differentials (see chapter 9 by Solomon Polachek and Charng Kao; Polachek [1979]).

Becker [1985] has offered a clever twist on this explanation. People do not simply allocate time between household and market activities. They also allocate *effort*. Since women allocate more effort to household activities, they have less effort to allocate to work outside the home. So, even when men and women have the same *amount* of work experience, training, etc., women are less productive. An additional hour of women's work is less effort-intensive than one of men's work. As a result, women are worth less to employers and accumulate less market human capital with each additional hour of work. This leads to an explanation for both occupational segregation by sex and earnings differentials within occupations. Women choose less effort-intensive jobs, and they are less productive than men working on the same jobs.

There is, of course, another view of occupational segregation that admits to a certain kind of "discrimination," but only a *rational* kind of "statistical discrimination." In a world filled with uncertainty, employers cannot always know the relevant traits of job applicants. Suppose that there are important traits that are difficult to measure, but we know that, on average, women exhibit more (or less) of them than men. One example often cited is the likelihood of job turnover.[1] Suppose also that there are two kinds of jobs - those for which it is costly to replace a worker who quits and those for which it is not. Not knowing actual quit propensities, rational, profit-maximizing employers will reserve the former jobs for men and fill the latter with women, even if there is considerable overlap in the underlying distributions of quit propensities of men and women (Phelps [1972]; Aigner and Cain [1977]).

My research in collaboration with Denise Bielby (Bielby and Bielby [1988]) and James Baron (Bielby and Baron [1986]) suggests that despite the elegance of the neoclassical accounts, the world just does not work that way. Men and women employees do not act in a way that is consistent with neoclassical accounts, nor do employers.

II. EMPIRICAL CHALLENGES TO NEOCLASSICAL VIEWS: THE ALLOCATION OF EFFORT

Denise Bielby and I, using the 1973 and 1977 Quality of Employment Surveys, attempted to operationalize a human-capital model of the allocation of work effort (Bielby and Bielby [1988]). The hypothesized relationships derived from Becker's approach are summarized in Table 5.1 and the details of our analyses can be found in our 1988 article. Here I simply

Table 5.1
Hypothesized Effects: Determinants of Work Effort

Variable	Hypothesized Effect
FEMALE (0-1)	–
AGE (yrs)	inverted U
FAMILY STATUS	
Working spouse (0-1)	–
Nonworking spouse (0-1)	++ males; + females
Children 5 or younger (0-1)	– –females only
Children 6 or older (0-1)	– females only
HOUSEHOLD RESPONSIBILITIES	
Primary responsibility for child (0-1)	–
Child care hrs. (hrs)	–
Household chores hrs. (hrs)	–
MARKET HUMAN CAPITAL AND LABOR SUPPLY	
Part-time (0-1)	–
Part-year (0-1)	–
Schooling (yrs)	+
Labor force continuity (proportion)	+
Other family income (log $)	–
JOB ATTRIBUTES	
Earnings (log $)	+
Autonomy (1-4)	+
Self-employed	+
Occupation (10 major groups)	no hypothesis

Source: Bielby and Bielby [1988].

summarize the findings relevant to the issue of job segregation and earnings disparities.

Contrary to the clear implication from Becker's model, women do not exert less effort than men in the workplace in order to conserve effort for household activities. Compared to men with similar household responsibilities, market human capital, earnings, promotion opportunities, and job responsibilities, women allocate substantially more effort to work activities; the net sex difference is nearly one-half a standard deviation on the scale we use. To the extent that women do allocate effort away from the workplace in order to meet family demands, these trade-offs bring their work effort back to the level of the typical male with no such family responsibilities.

How could this be? We believe that the neoclassical model of the allocation of work effort is seriously flawed in several ways. First, it may be inappropriate to assume that the "stock" of effort to be allocated by an individual is fixed, analogous to a fixed stock of physical capital. For women to work just as hard as men, if not harder, despite their greater household responsibilities, women must be able to draw on a reserve of energy that is either not available to the typical male, or more realistically, that men choose not to draw upon. Stephen Marks, a sociologist who has written on this topic, [1977: 927] cites physiological evidence in support of his claim that "individuals have abundant and perpetually renewing [energy] resources." He suggests that individuals generate the energy needed to participate in activities to which they are committed and that they often feel more "energetic" after engaging in them. Our findings imply that as women add work roles to their family roles, they generate the energy necessary to fulfill their commitments to the two sets of activities.

A second factor ignored by human capital models is what social psychologists call "entitlement norms." The allocation to effort at work is influenced by internalized norms of a "fair day's work," which may differ by sex. Determinations of fairness are based on perceptions of contributions relative to rewards. Experiments show that men and women differ in how they invoke equity considerations in allocating effort and rewards. On average, women pay themselves less than men performing the same task, and women tend to undervalue their efforts relative to men (Lenney [1977]; Callahan-Levy and Messe [1979]; Major, McFarlin, and Gagnon [1984]). It appears that, on average, women have lower internal standards of "personal entitlement," and, in the absence of salient external comparison standards, they make fairness judgments based on application of same-sex norms about appropriate rewards (Berger et al. [1972], Crosby [1982]).

In a laboratory experiment designed specifically to examine sex differences in effort and standards of personal entitlement, Major, McFarlin, and Gagnon [1984] asked men and women to do as much work as they thought was fair for a fixed amount of money. They collected objective measures of the accuracy and efficiency of performance on the task as well as information on each subject's perceptions of his or her level of performance. They discovered that, on average, "women worked longer, did more work, completed more correct work, and were more efficient than men" (1409). At the same time, men and women did *not* differ in their self-evaluations of their performance, despite women's superior objective performance. Nor did men and women differ in their reports of satisfaction from the task. In short, laboratory research on sex differences in internal standards of personal entitlement suggests that, all else constant, women can be expected to allocate more effort than men to work activities.

Third, structural features of workplaces might reinforce sex differences in entitlement norms. For example, research on sex segregation in the workplace suggests why same-sex norms about rewards for performance persist. Most men and women work in sex-segregated jobs (Bielby and Baron [1984], [1986]; Reskin and Hartmann [1986]). Consequently, many women lack information on both the numerator and the denominator of the "equity ratio" of reward to effort for men's work. According to social psychologists, it is precisely when external bases of social comparison are unavailable that individuals rely on internal, same-sex norms (Berger, Zelditch, Anderson, and Cohen [1972]; Berger, Rosenholtz, and Zelditch [1980]; Austin [1977]). Major, McFarlin, and Gagnon found that when external comparison information was available, neither sex relied on same-sex norms to make judgments of fair pay for a given task. Thus equity research suggests why employers might have a stake in a sex-segregated workforce: as long as women lack information about the reward structure for men, they will be willing to work for less pay. (Moreover, husbands of working women benefit by avoiding responsibility for household activities, despite the fact that their wives expend as much or more energy as they do at work.)

Fourth, another aspect of our analysis calls into question the extent to which decisions about work and family are made in a deliberately self-conscious, rational manner. Bielby and Bielby [1988] found that men's work effort is greatly influenced by family demands, while the effects of "human-capital" investments such as schooling and labor-market experience are relatively weak. In contrast, compared to men, women's work effort is less strongly influenced by family demands, but is more strongly affected by investments in market human capital. For example, a man with child-care responsibilities reduces his work effort, but a woman in the same situation does not. At the same time, a man with meager investments in "market human capital" – education and labor-market experience – does not decrease his work effort, but a woman with comparable investments does decrease her work effort. This suggests that individuals take sex-specific culturally prescribed roles for granted. Women do not adjust their effort allocations in response to household responsibilities, and men do not adjust their effort allocations in response to workplace investments.

It appears that individuals *do* rationally reflect upon their efforts when they cannot fall back upon culturally prescribed roles. Men confronted with household responsibilities reduce their work efforts, as do women with meager investments in market human capital. For men, some level of work effort may be culturally prescribed and "taken for granted" regardless of investments in education and training. For women, a certain level of work effort may be culturally prescribed and "taken for granted" regardless of the level of household responsibilities. Moreover, the level of effort allocated to work by a woman with heavy household responsibilities is at least as large as that allocated by men with no such responsibilities at home.

In sum, Becker's human-capital model of the allocation of work effort provides a plausible explanation for both sex segregation and wage differentials by sex. However, our research and other social psychological studies call into question some basic premises of this model. The assumption of a fixed stock of effort may be unrealistic, the social psychological processes may be more complex than what is typically assumed about "economic man," and segregation of men's and women's jobs may reinforce sex differences in social psychological processes.

III. EMPIRICAL CHALLENGES TO NEOCLASSICAL VIEWS: NONECONOMIC BASES OF STATISTICAL DISCRIMINATION

James Baron and I set out to analyze how men and women in the same general line of work are sorted into different firms and into different jobs within firms (Bielby and Baron [1984], [1986], [1987]; Baron and Bielby [1985]). Figure 5.1 shows the issue schematically. Consider an occupation like "electronics assembler" that is 40 percent female. Suppose that three firms in an industry employ electronics assemblers and that each of these firms uses assemblers in three of its job titles. In the hypothetical example, firm 1 relies disproportionately on male workers, firm 2 relies dispropor- tionately on female workers, and firm 3 relies on a balanced mix of male and female workers. In firm 1, each of the jobs is staffed disproportionately by men, and in firm 2, the opposite is true. In firm 3, however, the first job is staffed exclusively by men, and the second and third jobs exclusively by women. We can imagine other patterns besides the one depicted in figure 5.1 for an occupation that is 40 percent female. For example, in a world without statistical discrimination, we might find the sex composition of specific jobs normally distributed around 40 percent female. In any case, according to neoclassical models of the labor market, knowledge of differ- ences between firms and jobs in work requirements and differences between the sexes in job traits should explain how men and women in mixed occupations get distributed across firms and jobs.

Figure 5.1
Hypothetical Distribution of Workers in a Mixed Occupation Across Firms and Jobs

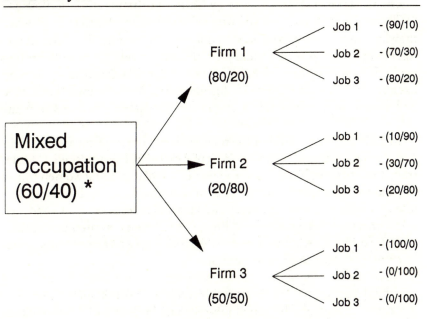

* Ratio of Male Workers to Female Workers

Baron and I assembled data like this for several hundred California firms studied by the U.S. Employment Service in the late 1960s and 1970s. That is, we looked at how firms hiring from a sex-mixed labor pool staffed their jobs as a function of firm and job characteristics. Neoclassical models suggested the following hypotheses: scale, bureaucratization, and job-specific training are related to turnover costs, so if women are more likely to quit, they should be underrepresented in firms and jobs where these costs are high. If employers statistically discriminate based on turnover costs, women should be excluded altogether from jobs where these costs are high. The remaining job traits we looked at are job-relevant skills. Women have been shown to perform better, on average, on traits such as verbal skills, motor coordination, finger dexterity, interpersonal skills, and stamina under repetitive, monotonous working conditions. Men have been shown to perform better, on average, on numerical skills, spatial skills, and upper body strength. Thus the distribution of men and women across jobs should reflect differences in jobs in the extent to which they require these sex-linked traits.

Our most startling finding was that California firms in the late 1960s and 1970s rarely employed men and women in the same job titles. Even when drawing from a sex-mixed labor pool for a work role like "electronics assembler," firms reserved some job titles exclusively for men and others exclusively for women. That is, firms either employed male workers exclusively or female workers exclusively, or, if they employed both, men and women were completely segregated by job title, as in firm 3 in figure 5.1.

In addition, we found that the relationships between firm and job traits and the sex composition of work were exactly as hypothesized. "Male" traits were positively related to the likelihood of excluding women from a job and the effects of "female" traits were in the opposite direction. Our research indicates that employers exclude women from some jobs and men from others (in the same general line of work) based on their perceptions of group differences between men and women in job-related traits. That is, employers statistically discriminate.

However, our findings did not support the neoclassical version of statistical discrimination. Statistical discrimination is efficient only when it is costly to measure the actual job-relevant traits of individual workers. The factors that made the greatest difference in whether men or women were employed were not the subtle and difficult-to-measure factors like turnover costs. They were physical demands and finger dexterity. Men are assigned the jobs perceived to involve heavy work and women – *in the same occupation* – are assigned the "light" work. Women are assigned jobs defined as "detail" work, and men are not.

According to neoclassical economists, employers are sacrificing profits in order to sustain the type of sex segregation we observed. Our measure of physical demands was whether a job required lifting more than twenty five pounds. In most of the firms we studied, no woman would be assigned to these jobs, regardless of that woman's own physical strength. Yet it is simple and inexpensive to devise a test to learn whether a female (or male) job applicant is capable of lifting twenty five pounds. Similarly, it should be easy to devise a simple test that would allow an employer to observe whether a male (or female) job applicant could successfully complete a task requiring finger dexterity. Given that they were drawing from sex-mixed labor pools, why did employers persist in sustaining almost complete job segregation by sex? We had access to narrative material about the employment practices in these California firms, and analyses of these qualitative materials suggested several important factors.

Policies. In many of the firms studied by the Employment Service, it was a matter of company policy not to employ women in certain jobs and to favor employing women in others. Jobs closed to women were typically perceived to be physically demanding and those favoring women usually involved "detail" work. Curiously, while we often came across policies specifying that women were preferred for certain jobs, we rarely encountered official *prohibitions* against men being employed in these jobs. Yet in practice, men rarely were employed in predominantly female jobs unless they were supervisors and in that case, they would almost always have distinct job titles.[2]

There are at least two reasons for the lack of any explicit prohibition against using men in specific jobs, despite the nearly perfect segregation in practice. First, if female labor is less expensive, employers have no incentive to employ men in the same job categories as women, even if the company has no policy against doing so. Second, prohibitions against women working in certain jobs often originated in protective legislation (even if these regulations no longer applied), and thus complying with government regulations was often the original rationale for having a policy on women's work. No similar regulations mandated policies on men's work.

Organizational inertia. Once a sex-based division of labor is established, it becomes "taken for granted," sustained over the years unless some deliberate effort is taken to undo it.[3] This was especially evident in the exclusion of women from jobs perceived to be physically demanding. California laws prohibited the employment of women in jobs requiring heavy lifting until these laws were struck down in 1971. Yet our data showed that the exclusion of women from so-called physically demanding jobs was just as widespread through the late 1970s – when the practice was illegal – as it was during the period before 1971. We also saw this inertia in data from firms analyzed by the Employment Service at two points in time, typically six or seven years apart. The sex-based division of labor rarely changed over that six- or seven-year period, even when total employment fluctuated substantially, *unless* there was some deliberate effort taken to undo sex segregation.

Cultural stereotypes. Cognitive psychologists have demonstrated that we all use stereotypes, or cognitive schema, as a cognitive shorthand we invoke to achieve economy in perception (Ashmore and Del Boca [1981]). Of course, the particular stereotypes we hold about sex roles are widely shared and continually reinforced in our culture. Despite what is assumed by neoclassical models of discrimination, the profit motive is not necessarily strong enough to overcome the cognitive processes that lead to the use of stereotypes. Thus it may be that employers make hiring decisions based on widely shared *misperceptions* of differences in the average traits of men and women. To complicate matters further, statistical discrimination can lead to "self-fulfilling prophecies," or what social psychologists call "expectancy confirmation sequences" (Darley and Fazio [1980]). That is, employers expect certain behaviors from women and assign them to routine tasks and dead-end jobs. Women respond by exhibiting the very behaviors employers expect, reinforcing the stereotype. Moreover, social psychological research suggests that employers are more likely to attend to and retain information that confirms stereotypes, ignoring behavior by women that does not fit their expectations.[4]

Given the kind of data available to Baron and me, we had no direct evidence of cultural stereotypes held by specific employers or managers about men's work and women's work. However, such stereotypes were invoked quite often in policies regarding the employment of women in "heavy" work and in "detail" work. Indeed, it was not uncommon to encounter a policy prohibiting employment of women in certain jobs because of heavy lifting requirements and to then find in detailed job analyses by the Employment Service that these jobs required no heavy physical labor. In other words, the work is often labelled as "heavy work" because it is done by men.

Interests. Finally, the extreme sex segregation we discovered within mixed occupations could not have been sustained without someone's interests being served. It is not difficult to see how employers might have an interest in sex segregation. For example, our research on the allocation of effort suggests that segregation sustains sex-specific norms of entitlement. Male employees who view integration as a threat to their wages may resist the assignment of women to the job titles they hold. However, not at all clear from existing research are the circumstances under which male workers have the capacity to act on these interests, given employers' economic incentive to substitute cheap female labor for expensive male labor. Although my research with Baron on statistical discrimination did not get at the interests issue directly, other work we have done suggests a slight tendency for greater segregation in settings where male workers have substantial market power (Bielby and Baron [1984]).

IV. CONCLUSION: RECONCILING ALTERNATIVE PERSPECTIVES ON THE STRUCTURE AND PROCESS OF SEX SEGREGATION

We can identify six more or less distinct kinds of explanations for a single phenomenon: sex segregation in the workplace. These explanations are (1) neoclassical, based on models of statistical discrimination and investments in human capital; (2) social psychological, emphasizing socialization and internalized norms; (3) institutional, emphasizing the intended and unintended consequences and inertia of organizational arrangements; (4) cultural, emphasizing taken-for-granted notions of men's work and women's work, often shared by both men and women; (5) political, stressing the different interests of male employers and employees with respect to maintaining the status quo; and (6) patriarchal, emphasizing the common interests of male workers and employers in maintaining a sex-based division of labor.

The research my colleagues and I have pursued has sought to test neoclassical explanations of gender differences in the workplace, not to offer fully developed alternatives. In posing tentative accounting for our findings, we have drawn on both institutional approaches to the structure of work and social psychological theories of entitlement norms. Of course, these areas are no longer beyond the purview of neoclassical economics. For example, Williamson ([1975], [1985]) explains variation in organizational structures with the concept of economizing on transaction costs, and "efficiency wage" theorists invoke entitlement norms to explain interindustry wage differentials (Krueger and Summers [1987]; Akerlof and

Yellen [1988]).

It is customary to applaud cross-disciplinary efforts, and the blurring of the boundaries between sociology and neoclassical economics may eventually lead to a comprehensive explanation of job segregation by sex that is consistent with the empirical evidence on the subject. By incorporating "sociological factors" (e.g., institutional barriers, entitlement norms), neoclassical models may be able to more faithfully represent the factors that slow the rate at which market forces erode discrimination in pay and job assignment. Moving in that direction requires continued commitment to the neoclassical assumption that were it not for various "drags" on the system, market forces would inevitably discount ascriptive factors like race and gender in valuing otherwise comparable labor inputs.

Adapting the neoclassical model in this way has appeal due to the power of the model's formal analytical properties. However, the pervasiveness and persistence of job segregation by sex seems too far at odds with the imagery of even the most extreme adaptations of the model (for a similar view, see the concluding paragraph of William Darity's contribution to this volume, chapter 2). For example, it is difficult to imagine what kinds of "transaction costs" could explain the nearly universal job segregation of men and women *within the same occupation* that Baron and I found across a wide variety of organizational settings. That such segregation would persist is especially problematic from a neoclassical perspective, since the rationale was typically based on stereotypical perceptions of men's and women's job aptitudes, often with little basis in the actual duties men and women performed on the job. Indeed, on more than one occasion a labor economist has suggested to me that the kind of uniform sex segregation within occupations that Baron and I detected simply cannot exist in the real world!

Radical and Marxist economists who study discrimination have always been more open than their more orthodox colleagues to incorporating concepts and findings of sociologists. Furthermore, the kind of persistent job segregation by sex detected in my research with Baron is fully consistent with their models. Represented in this volume by the contributions of Rhonda Williams (chapter 4) and Steven Shulman (chapter 1), radical and Marxist models are built upon an imagery of conflict and struggle over control of the workplace among contending groups defined by race, class, and gender. In attempting to account for the persistence of the racial gap in unemployment, Shulman moves this line of theorizing forward by addressing the economic and social costs of dismantling discrimination. According to this perspective, job segregation and other forms of discrimination are likely to persist in the absence of any exogenous shock or direct intervention that changes the social relations among contending groups.

However, while radical and Marxist approaches appear more consistent with the findings of our research, I am not yet prepared to accept their models. My reservation is based on the absence of gender as a cultural or ideological phenomenon in their explanations of segregation and other forms of discrimination. Instead, their models are driven by the logic of systemic properties like concentration and monopolization and the self-interested, rational action of social groups (e.g., employers, white male workers) intent on preserving their privileged positions in the division of labor (Darity and Williams [1985]). Based on my research and my reading of the work of other sociologists, I have come to believe that gender is more than a dimension along which the labor force is segmented and that gender ideologies are a strong, semiautonomous force shaping segregation and other manifestations of socioeconomic inequality. I have yet to see this notion of gender and ideology incorporated into formal models of discrimination, but I can illustrate the empirical reality of the issue with two examples.

The first concerns the circumstances under which women were demobilized from factory jobs in the automobile industry after World War II. In the most definitive study to date on the topic, Milkman [1987] documented that the women who held these jobs performed at least as capably as the men they replaced. She also showed that many of the women mobilized by the automobile industry during the war wanted to keep their jobs. Moreover, at the war's end, the automobile manufacturers could no longer rely on "cost-plus" government contracts and therefore should have been more sensitive to labor costs after the war than during the war. Furthermore, Milkman showed that the unions that represented the interests of white male workers had virtually no power to influence management policy regarding hiring preferences and job assignments. In short, management appeared to have both the incentive and the ability to rely disproportionately on women during the tremendous expansion in employment during the years following the war.

Such behavior by employers would be consistent with both neoclassical and neo-Marxist approaches to the labor market. Instead, Milkman showed that management acted on a strong preference for young, male veterans and went to great lengths to purge women from all but the traditionally female job classifications. Perhaps management feared that female substitution in the automobile factories would destabilize labor relations and were taking into account one of the costs of dismantling discrimination emphasized in Shulman's chapter in this volume. However, there is little evidence that the very decisive actions taken by management to demobilize women were based on an informed view of the costs of possible resistance by male workers. Instead, for reasons that are difficult to explain from any perspective emphasizing economic self-interest (or class interest), employers concluded that women ought not to hold these jobs once men returned from war.

My second example comes from research I have done in collaboration with Denise Bielby (Bielby and Bielby [1991]) empirically testing Jacob Mincer's [1978] neoclassical model of family migration decisions among dual-earner couples. According to the model, couples maximize family well-being. When a husband or wife is confronted with a job advancement requiring geographic relocation, the couple migrates when that person's gain is greater than the cost of disrupting his or her spouse's career. Otherwise, there is no net gain to the family, and family well-being is maximized by forgoing the job opportunity at the new location.

Figure 5.2
Reluctance to Relocate Due to Family Considerations, by Sex,
Spouse's Earnings, and Gender-Role Beliefs

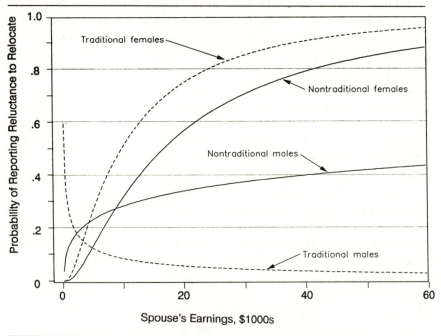

Spouse's Earnings, $1000s

Presumably, the risk to joint family earnings due to a relocation increases with the level of earnings of the spouse whose career will be disrupted. If so, then the neoclassical model predicts that reluctance to relocate for a new job should increase directly with the level of the spouse's earnings. Accordingly, it was not surprising when data from the 1977 Quality of Employment Survey showed spouse's earnings to be the strongest predictor of a reluctance to relocate for a much better job in a new location. What was surprising (from the neoclassical perspective) was that the net effect of spouse's earnings was highly contingent upon both gender and gender-role beliefs. As figure 5.2 illustrates, traditional males – those who believed in the primacy of the husband's role as provider and who disapproved of working mothers – were not influenced at all by their wives' earnings. In contrast, traditional females were extremely sensitive to their husbands' earnings. In effect, such women expressed reluctance to relocate for job advancement unless their husbands earned very little. Holding nontraditional gender-role beliefs had opposite effects on men and women. Compared to traditional women, nontraditional women were more inclined to pursue job advancement at a new location, while the opposite was true for nontraditional men compared to traditional men. In other words, our results showed that among those holding traditional beliefs, men were likely to put their private career interests ahead of the interest of overall family economic well-being (contrary to the assumption of the neoclassical model), while women behaved altruistically toward the family, maximizing family well-being instead of personal well-being (consistent with Mincer's assumption). However, the relationship was sharply mediated by gender-role beliefs, and the sex differences in orientation toward self and family were substantially attenuated among those holding nontraditional beliefs.

Thus our research suggests that traditional gender-role ideologies sustain women's disadvantages in both workplace and family dynamics. Traditional notions of women's role provide a rationale for job segregation and statistical discrimination in the workplace, and those same beliefs make it more difficult for women than men to pursue job opportunities (which in turn can reinforce stereotypes and provide a rationale for statistical discrimination). In short, gender-role ideologies appear to directly shape the extent to which husbands and wives define and act upon their interests.

In sum, in an important sense, the economic theories of segregation and discrimination – neoclassical supply-side, demand-side, radical, and neo-Marxist – are neutral with respect to gender (and race). In these theories, whichever group happens to have fewer resources or less predictable traits or arrived last when either capital or "good jobs" were being allocated happens to end up disadvantaged. The ideological content of cultural idioms of gender and race have no causal impact in any of these theories.[5] Curiously, this is true even when these theories are borrowed by sociologists, who, in recent years, have been captivated by theories that purport to explain social behavior as the outcome of "rational action" (Hechter [1983]; Coleman [1990]). Yet the examples I have cited suggest that culture and ideology might have considerable explanatory power in more fully accounting for both persistence and change in job segregation and other forms of discrimination. At least at a descriptive level, sociocultural factors are impossible to ignore in any close empirical investigation of these phenomena. However, it is quite clear that we have a long way to go before such factors are fully incorporated into our theoretical and analytical models of discrimination.

6
Organizational Evidence of Ascription in Labor Markets

James N. Baron

Theories of discrimination and labor markets have, at least until recently, treated organizations or firms for the most part as black boxes.[1] Organizations are assumed to structure work, design rewards, and allocate personnel so as to satisfy some broad technical or societal imperative, which is taken as exogenous and determinative. Organizations are simply the arenas in which these larger imperatives are played out. This black box treatment of organizations has been as conspicuous in sociologists' functional theory of stratification (Davis and Moore [1945]; Lenski [1966]; Treiman [1977]) as in economists' human-capital models of labor-market attainment. The former theory argues that firms must pay an occupation what it is worth, where worth is determined by societal importance; according to the latter (human-capital) theory, firms must pay workers what they are worth, where worth is determined by the value of the skills and training needed in a given line of work and the relative supply and demand of individuals available to perform that work. Both theories thus implicitly assume that organizations design wage rates so as to allocate and motivate labor efficiently. Enterprises allocate individuals to their highest and best use because if they did not do so, some other organization would bid away the individual's services by offering a higher wage, which could be paid because the individual would be more productively employed. Returns to individual ability and experience are similarly rationalized in these accounts.

Accordingly, in sociologists' status-attainment formulation, the economy (and society in general) is seen as undergoing progressive differentiation and functional specialization - what Parsons [1951:480-535] referred to as "institutionalized rationalization." As a result of this continual upgrading, organizations rely increasingly on education and ability (and decreasingly on social origins and ascriptive traits) in assigning individuals to positions within the division of labor (Blau and Duncan [1967: ch. 12]). This view argues that the positive returns to schooling and experience observed in stratification research obtain because they promote organizational efficiency, as well as the smooth functioning of the entire social structure, by optimizing the match between workers, tasks, and rewards. Yet the term "organizations" is conspicuously absent from the index of Blau and Duncan's seminal study within this tradition, *The American Occupational Structure*, despite the fact that Peter Blau is one of our most distinguished organizational theorists. Apparently, institutionalized rationalization and universalism were assumed to be so pervasive and inexorable that differences in employment regimes across organizations were not essential objects of study.

This inattention to organizational arrangements is equally puzzling when one considers public policy concerns. For example, debates about the likelihood of reducing long-standing inequalities by increasing educational attainment among women and nonwhites hinge on assumptions about when, how, and why firms use educational criteria in staffing decisions. Yet few studies of inequality have examined that topic directly (e.g., Collins [1975]; Cohen and Pfeffer [1986]). Moreover, most social policies aimed at changing the distribution of labor-market opportunities and outcomes are targeted toward organizations, rather than individuals, if only because it is much more difficult administratively and politically to design, implement, enforce, and evaluate policy interventions aimed at individuals or households than at workplaces. Given that fact, inattention to organizational arrangements and policies shaping the distribution of rewards is all the more unfortunate.

To be sure, recent economic models concerning transaction costs, firm-specific human-capital investment, efficiency wages, gift exchange, implicit contracts, and the like have provided much greater richness to economists' investigations of organizations and labor markets. However, as Granovetter ([1985], [1988]) has observed, when economists tackle issues of internal organization, they typically propose formal models that represent institutions, contracts, and governance arrangements as optimal solutions to ubiquitous problems of moral hazard, adverse selection, and aversion toward effort and risk. Granovetter noted some of the conceptual and empirical shortcomings of such adaptive stories, as have I elsewhere (Baron [1988]). Because work organizations are arenas of ongoing social and political interaction, and not simply combinations of factor inputs and atomized individuals, organizational arrangements are influenced by cultural, political, and social psychological forces, and not simply by technical considerations and the logic of "principal-agent" relationships.

Understanding something about the sociology and social psychology of work organizations is therefore likely to inform our understanding of employment outcomes, including the extent of ascription in labor markets. Organizations influence the observed distribution of career outcomes in at least three key ways: by deciding what a given job entails (and drawing boundaries among jobs); by determining what a given job is worth; and by matching specific types of workers to particular positions.

Accordingly, I begin by surveying some results from recent research on these three issues, which illustrate how models of efficient labor markets and rational employers seem to miss some important empirical facts.[2] The evidence suggests that social forces and discriminatory cultural beliefs prevalent when a job or organization is founded condition the way that positions are defined, priced, and staffed, becoming institutionalized within the formal structure and informal traditions of the enterprise. After surveying various strands of this evidence, I try to weave them together. I suggest how recent work in psychology and sociology can illuminate the propensity toward ascription in a specific organizational setting, the likelihood of collective action by organizational participants aimed at supporting or eroding that ascription, and the success of organizational antidiscrimination efforts. The portrait that emerges has implications not only for economists' efforts to understand how labor markets operate, but also for their recent theories of how organizations function. In the concluding sections of the chapter, I discuss these implications, as well as some profitable directions for future research.

I. WHAT IS A JOB? ORGANIZATIONAL ARRANGEMENTS AS SOCIALLY ENDOGENOUS

Economists tend to view organizational arrangements, such as the specification of duties and the structure of reporting relationships, as deriving from a technologically mandated production function. Organizations structure activities in order to maximize productive efficiency and then staff positions accordingly. However, there is substantial evidence to suggest that the way in which roles and organizations are structured and evaluated is not independent of who is performing a specific activity. In other words, one organizational basis of ascription glossed over in economic accounts is the tendency for positions occupied by women and minorities to be structured and evaluated differently.

For instance, members of high-status social groups (e.g., males, especially whites) are substantially more likely to be allocated to unique job titles in organizations. Table 6.1 shows the numbers of full-time employees (by sex and race) in the California civil service who were the sole occupant of their job title as of March 31, 1985. Column 1 of table 6.1 indicates that women and nonwhites are clearly underrepresented in one-person titles. (The distribution of full-time employment by sex and race for the entire civil service is shown in parentheses in column 1.) Columns 2 through 4 demonstrate that these results are not due solely to the concentration of women and nonwhites in the lower reaches of the state's occupational structure: even within the high-status categories of "supervisory professionals" and "supervisory administrative staff" personnel, as well as in the highest-paying civil-service jobs, one finds the same pattern of underrepresentation of women and nonwhites in one-person classes.

Similar patterns were evident in a diverse sample of private-sector organizations that I have analyzed with William Bielby. In 415 organizations that we studied, there were 2,699 one-person jobs. Men occupied 91.9 percent of these jobs, while they represented 79.9 percent of the 206,335 employees in the sample. As in table 6.1, this overrepresentation persisted even after taking into account the different occupational distributions of men and women.[3]

Of course, this kind of evidence does not demonstrate causality: it could be that positions having certain characteristics that favor specialization attract white males and repel women and minorities, rather than the attributes of the incumbents shaping the way positions are defined. However, several types of evidence support the interpretation that ascriptive characteristics play a causal role. First, a wealth of recent theory and research addresses cognitive and social psychological biases governing social categorization (Brewer and Kramer [1985]). That work indicates an "in-group" bias in social categorization whereby more elaborate and differentiated schemas are adopted to describe in-group members and their activities. Brewer and Kramer summarized experimental results showing that even perceptions of facial distinctions, as well as of personality and behavioral characteristics, are more fine-grained among members of one's own in-group. In contrast, out-group members tend to be homogenized and their differences underestimated. Kanter [1977: ch. 8] has described this process and its effects in examining how the statistical rarity of women in organizations reinforces stereotypical generalizations about all women.

Table 6.1

Full-Time Incumbents of One-Person Job Titles in the California Civil Service: Distribution by Sex and Race, March 1985

		Category		
	All Full-time Workers	Supervisory Professionals	Supervisory Admin.Staff	Jobs with Starting Pay of $4000+/Month
Number of one-person titles (total full-time workers in category)	780 (123,212)	152 (9,664)	65 (4,087)	109 (1,438)
Breakdown by Sex and Race:				
White males	66.5% (38.6%)	74.3% (63.7%)	67.7% (50.2%)	82.6% (70.7%)
White females	13.1% (27.1%)	8.6% (12.9%)	15.4% (22.4%)	8.3% (6.0%)
Nonwhite males	15.3% (17.3%)	13.8% (18.0%)	12.3% (17.5%)	9.2% (15.9%)
Nonwhite females	5.1% (17.1%)	3.3% (5.5%)	4.6% (9.9%)	0.0% (7.4%)

Note: Figures in parentheses show percentage distribution by sex and race for all full-time employees within the category, i.e., for all state civil servants in column 1, all supervisory professionals in column 2, all supervisory administrative staff personnel in column 3, and all occupants of jobs with monthly starting pay of $4,000 or more in column 4.

An important corollary result from the social psychological literature is that the process of categorization is self-perpetuating. A set of categories, once in place, reinforces perceptions of distinctiveness across those categories, even if the categorization is entirely capricious. Numerous controlled experiments show that arbitrary categorizations of subjects into groups that are presumed to have different abilities or qualities can induce the distinctions in attitudes and behaviors that were expected and that were ostensibly the justification for the categorization (for reviews, see Rosenthal and Rubin [1978]; Fiske and Taylor [1984]; Messick and Mackie [1989]).

Social psychological studies also highlight how categorization and differentiation can be used strategically by high-status individuals or groups to segregate themselves from those of lower status, preserving their advantaged position and distinctive status within the larger society. This suggests that whatever "natural" cognitive tendencies or biases exist regarding differentiation can be heightened when an interest exists for distinguishing lower-status or out-group members. It also suggests that the struggle for power and legitimacy is often a struggle over social and organizational categories, with less powerful individuals and groups striving to have themselves recategorized to garner status and privilege (Reskin [1988]).

The tendency documented above for men and whites to monopolize one-person organizational job titles illustrates these processes. White men typically have preeminent influence in most organizations, and they enjoy a privileged position within the larger social order. Accordingly, it seems plausible that white men have a more elaborate and differentiated schema of the work that they do than they do of "women's work" and "minority work," which has become institutionalized within the formal structure of organizations.

Strang and Baron [1990] provide similar evidence of the ascriptive dimension of job structures. Analyzing job titles within the California civil service, they find the most extensive proliferation of detailed job categories within those lines of work that are most integrated by gender and race, controlling for a number of other variables that are likely to influence the extent of job-title proliferation. (They also document that this proliferation is not gender- or race-neutral, but rather contributes to job segregation of women from men and whites from nonwhites within occupations.) Although their cross-sectional results do not demonstrate causality, they are certainly consistent with experimental and historical work showing that the entry of women or nonwhites into lines of work previously dominated by white males fosters new detailed categories and statuses that reestablish segregation.

Occupational classification schemes also provide interesting examples of this kind of in-group bias in job categorization. Consider, for instance, the classification of various social sciences that appears in the third edition of the *Dictionary of Occupational Titles* (U.S. Department of Labor [1965]). The *DOT* is of special interest because it is a template on which many organizational job-classification systems are built. The job-classification system used in the *DOT* was developed principally by Sidney Fine and other vocational psychologists working for the U.S. Employment Service. Accordingly, it is interesting to observe that the third edition of the *DOT* contains fifteen distinct "master" job titles pertaining to psychology, as well as twenty related or synonymous titles.[4] In contrast, there are nine distinct titles (and no synonyms) listed in sociology, ten master titles (and three related synonymous classifications) in economics, four master titles (two synonyms) in anthropology, and only two master titles (no synonyms) describing political science.

These differences do not correspond closely to differences in the size of the disciplines involved (as indicated, for instance, by census occupational data), and it is thus difficult to believe that they reflect variation in the true specialization of skills and functions across fields (see Cain and Treiman [1981: 260]; Scoville [1969: ch. 2]). Rather, those who played the greatest role in creating the *DOT* apparently were more sensitive to distinctions within their own profession than in allied behavioral sciences, differentiating tasks within their own discipline more finely and homogenizing the activities of professionals in other fields. The efforts of those who created the third edition of the *DOT* to capture what people typically do in a job, and not merely the official duties or dominant technology of jobs (Fine [1968: 4-5]), no doubt exacerbated such tendencies.

Another form of evidence that ascriptive characteristics help mold how jobs are defined is archival. "Smoking guns" are rare in contemporary efforts to unearth discrimination, but there were fewer taboos about such things in previous decades. Accordingly, in many of the data sets I have studied, one finds explicit statements by those charged with designing employment systems averring that race and sex were taken into account in designing jobs and pay systems. For instance, in a recent class-action sex-discrimination lawsuit against the state of California, the judge was particularly struck by an internal memorandum drafted in 1934 by a state government official explaining job-classification procedures. The document stated that in establishing the initial salary schedules for civil-service jobs, in addition to market and skill factors, "certain supplemental factors were also taken into consideration, namely, the ... age, sex, and standard of living of the employees normally recruited for a given [job]" (Becker [1934: 62]). Presumably the specifications of jobs and divisions among them were equally influenced by ascriptive stereotypes.

Bielby and I similarly encountered numerous instances of managers or employers being explicit about such matters before there were potent legal sanctions against such practices (Bielby and Baron [1986]). For instance, in one pipe-manufacturing establishment studied by the Employment Service at three time points (described in Baron and Bielby [1986]), increases over time in the size of the male production workforce produced proliferation of job titles (within a line of work that had not changed over time and that had formerly been done within a single undifferentiated job classification), so that the establishment could preserve male privilege by providing additional promotion opportunities to these men during good times.

Another illustration is that within the 415 establishments Bielby and I studied, more than 75 percent of the " personnel managers" were male, while five-sixths of the "personnel clerks" were female. It was not uncommon for small- to medium-sized organizations to have either one or the other, that is, a single person doing personnel work, classified as a manager if male and as a clerk if female. To illustrate this tendency, I identified all firms in the Bielby and Baron sample having someone (but no more than one full-time person) performing a specialized personnel role (based on the detailed DOT occupational codes assigned to their job). I reasoned that these are all firms in which there is enough personnel-related activity to occupy up to one full-time-equivalent specialist, and therefore it is likely that the job activities of these personnel specialists are fairly similar across these firms. (It seems unlikely that a "personnel manager" in any of these enterprises would be doing much real managing, for instance, given no subordinates specializing in personnel matters to manage.) There were 49 establishments falling into this category for which the relevant data were available. Of these, 19 used a professional or managerial job title to refer to their personnel specialist: "personnel manager" (nine men, six women), "director of industrial relations" (two men), or "employment interviewer" (two women). The remaining 30 organizations used one of two clerical titles: "payroll clerk" (two men, twenty seven women) or "timekeeper" (one woman). Thus 28 of these 30 clerical positions were staffed by women, whereas 11 of the 19 "managerial" slots were staffed by men ($p <$ .001). Bielby and Bielby [1989] reported similar patterns in the structure of job titles within the Hollywood television industry.

Nor were the U.S. Employment Service analysts who collected these data immune from ascriptive stereotypes in classifying work roles. One analyst studying a musical instruments manufacturing company in 1961, for instance, encountered one woman and four men in an entry slot called "crook operator." He prepared separate job analysis reports for the woman versus the men on the following grounds:

The female Crook Operator was written as a separate job because she did not do any of the work of the four male Crook Operators, and she was on a lower skill level. The five workers, male and female, were classified [by the firm] as Crook Operators because they comprised the Crook Department. . . . Nor was the female Crook Operator being or going to be trained to do the work of the male Crook Operators, further indicating the need for a separate definition. (Job Analysis Schedule 2901950 [1960]).

Yet the same establishment was revisited ten years later by another analyst, and the three men and one woman then employed as "crook operators" were found to do identical work (Job Analysis Schedule 2914602 [1970]). Employment Service procedures seem to have changed more during the ensuing decade than the woman's job tasks, suggesting that the first analyst's conclusions largely reflected stereotypes about the relative craft abilities of male and female workers.

In short, there are powerful cultural and psychological forces shaping the design of organizational arrangements that are often given short shrift in efficiency-oriented models of labor markets and firms. While unequal labor-market outcomes are obviously due in part to differences in the kinds of positions occupied by members of different social groups, presumed differences among social groups are also an important *cause* of distinctions among work roles within an organizational division of labor. The historian Margo Conk [1978] has noted how, for instance, the U.S. Census Bureau imposed distinctions among detailed occupations based on perceived sociocultural distinctions (e.g., of sex and race) among the kinds of people who typically did different kinds of jobs. Ironically, variations in occupational distributions have subsequently been invoked to "explain" differences in socioeconomic standing by sex and race, when these differences helped to define the occupational classification in the first place!

Why does the social basis of organizational and occupational categorization matter? One reason it matters is that various studies, which I review below, show that jobs done by in-group and high-status members are also likely to be judged as worth more than other jobs.[5] This in-group bias favoring job categorization is therefore quite significant for pay discrimination. Specialization of job titles also confers other important advantages to incumbents, providing monopoly power, special recognition and expertise, and opportunities for idiosyncratic bargaining.[6] This is allegedly why industrial unions traditionally advocated detailed job titles. Moreover, the tendency to proliferate vertical distinctions and inflate the worth of jobs done by in-group members provides the foundations for longer career ladders and narrower spans of control than in lines of work in which workers have been homogenized and fewer distinctions recognized (Baron and Bielby [1985]; Strang and Baron [1990]). In short, conceptualizing and operationalizing discrimination solely in terms of unequal returns to individual human-capital or occupational characteristics ignores the subtle (yet powerful) ways that ascriptive distinctions are incorporated into organizational structures governing jobs, pay, and promotions.

II. WHAT IS A JOB WORTH? THE ORGANIZATIONAL CONTEXT OF BIAS

Evidence from diverse sources suggests that positions dominated by women and nonwhites are evaluated as worth less than positions that are otherwise comparable (in terms of skills and requirements) but dominated by men and whites. Various laboratory experiments demonstrate that men and women generally ascribe less worth to work performed by women (Major, McFarlin, and Gagnon [1984]; McArthur [1985]; Deaux [1985]), and case studies of job-evaluation systems have often uncovered biases (for reviews, see McArthur [1985]; England and Dunn [1988]). Studies of occupational prestige suggest that men and women ascribe less prestige to female-dominated jobs than to stereotypically "male" jobs (Bose and Rossi [1983]). Other research reports positive relationships (cross-sectional and longitudinal) between the percent white male in an occupation on the one hand and average monetary rewards on the other, even controlling for average occupational skills, vocational requirements, and labor-market factors (Treiman and Hartmann [1981]; England, Chassie, and McCormack [1982]; Strober [1984]; England, Farkas, Kilbourne, and Dou [1988]; Strober and Arnold [1987]; Parcel [1989]; as well as chapter 3 by Michael Robinson and Phanindra Wunnava and chapter 7 by David Fairris and Lori Kletzer in this volume). Similar results linking the demographic composition of jobs to their relative pay have been reported for diverse organizations (Rosenbaum [1985]; Pfeffer and Davis-Blake [1987]; Baron and Newman [1989], [1990]). These findings are the clarion call for comparable worth advocates.

While psychologists tend to attribute such findings to deeply ingrained cognitive biases, organizational research suggests that they are very much dependent on context. Tetlock [1985], for instance, argues that many of the cognitive biases and heuristics documented by psychologists largely vanish in contexts where individuals are accountable for the outcomes of their decisions. On the other hand, other biases reflect not bounded rationality or effort aversion but rather the desire to view oneself in a particular light, and they may be exacerbated when individuals are accountable for or otherwise heavily invested in the outcomes of an action (R. Kramer, personal communication). In short, those who claim that there is a ubiquitous "devaluation" of work done by lower-status workers may be as naive as those who claim that the market always prices jobs fairly.

Some of my recent work has examined how organizational arrangements, the prevalence of various interest groups, and characteristics of jobs affect the tendency toward biased judgments of job worth (Baron and Newman [1989], [1990]). We analyzed how the prescribed pay rates attached to jobs in the California civil service vary (net of job requirements) with the demographic composition of incumbents. We focused on the officially prescribed entry pay rates attached to jobs within the civil-service salary system, rather than analyzing the average wages received by job incumbents. This dependent variable obviously ignores variations in the actual pay received by incumbents in a given job. However, it has the virtue of being unaffected by sex or race differences in human capital, productivity, and the like among workers in a job. In other words, ours is a measure of prescribed or normative wages. If one observes, for instance, that female-dominated jobs are ranked lower in the normative wage hierarchy than otherwise comparable male-dominated jobs, this cannot be attributed to unmeasured human-capital or productivity differences among incumbents. To assess the net effects of sex and race composition on the perceived worth of jobs, we controlled for job content by using various detailed occupational distinctions (used by the state itself to represent differences in job requirements and responsibilities), as well as estimates of educational and experience requirements listed in civil-service job descriptions (see Baron and Newman [1989]).

Like other researchers, we found substantial net penalties associated with the presence of women and nonwhites in jobs, both cross-sectionally and in longitudinal analyses examining how changes in demographic composition between 1979 and 1985 affected a job's standing within the pay hierarchy of California state government. However, the magnitude of these penalties depended on various contextual factors. Among jobs dominated by women or nonwhites, the devaluation of pay was substantially greater when there were fewer objective criteria for gauging performance. This result is consistent with social psychological work documenting that decision makers rely on social criteria of proof more in settings lacking objective evaluative standards (Cialdini [1988]).

We also found that positions occurring in the fewest state agencies and having the fewest incumbents displayed the least ascription in pay setting, even though one might have expected from psychological theory that the rarity of these positions would make them more prone to stereotyping and devaluation. There are several possible explanations for this finding. One is consistent with stories emphasizing specific human capital: these idiosyncratic jobs may be the ones in which specific human capital is particularly important and in which employers therefore have a greater incentive to set pay rates without bias so as to attract the right person for the job. Another story, suggested to us by people knowledgeable about the workings of the civil-service system, puts more emphasis on organizational politics. Within a bureaucratic personnel system, changing job definitions and pay rates often requires an advocate willing to lobby for these changes. Women or nonwhites who perceive themselves as underpaid may be more likely advocates – and more successful in their advocacy – when they are the sole incumbent of a job or are in a job that exists only within one agency, where it is easier to mobilize one's colleagues. In contrast, collective action may be more difficult in larger, multiagency job classifications. Of course, if organizations benefit economically by undervaluing jobs done by women and racial minorities, then the savings are also greatest in the largest, most generic jobs, especially because these large classifications often anchor the pay for other positions (Dunlop [1957]). Given internal equity pressures, which are especially prevalent in state bureaucracies (where salary information is public), recalibrating the relative worth of these generic jobs would no doubt be much more problematic (see Bridges and Nelson [1989]).

In short, even if psychological propensities to devalue work done by women and nonwhites are greater in idiosyncratic positions, there appear to be countervailing economic, political, or organizational forces that result in the greatest bias within the most heavily populated job classes. These data represent state government employment, which may not constitute a competitive labor market, but the results suggest that it is actually generic job categories that are "closest" to external market pressures where ascriptive criteria figure most in assigning pay rates.

Our analyses uncovered certain organizational conditions that mitigate biased evaluations of job worth. Strong collective bargaining units committed to pay equity by sex, for instance, have lessened the devaluation of "women's work" within the California civil service (Baron and Newman [1990]). So, apparently, has employment growth. Theories of occupational crowding imply that the entry of women (or nonwhites) into a line of work depresses the wage rate by creating excess supply. If a work role becomes typed as worth less when women enter it, one might expect that women's entry would be less conspicuous and threatening to male occupants under conditions of growing demand for the job or occupation than under circumstances of decline. We found this to be the case in longitudinal analyses of prescribed pay rates of jobs between 1979 and 1985 within the California civil service (Baron and Newman [1989]).

In sum, the organizational and occupational context and the presence of various interest groups influences the extent of ascription in gauging what positions are worth. We have found the same to be true in studying the extent of gender-based job assignment (or sex segregation) within organizations. I turn next to that research.

III. WHO GETS WHAT JOB? ORGANIZATIONAL AND ENVIRONMENTAL FACTORS AFFECTING THE SUCCESS OF JOB INTEGRATION EFFORTS

IIIA. Historical Founding Conditions and Structural Inertia

Organizational theorists have argued that environmental conditions present at the time an enterprise is founded tend to be indelibly imprinted on its structure (Stinchcombe [1965]). Organizations adopt structures and procedures that are not only appropriate economically at the time of founding, but that also correspond to broader social understandings about how a specific type of enterprise ought to look and ought to be run. Once rationalized systems of personnel administration became accepted as an essential component of modern bureaucratic enterprise, for instance, they spread quickly to new firms and industries lacking many of the characteristics (such as high turnover, large size, and a unionized work force with firm-specific skills) that had supposedly necessitated such innovations in the first place (Meyer and Rowan [1977]; Tolbert and Zucker [1983]; Baron, Dobbin, and Jennings [1986]).[7]

Once in place, organizational structures and procedures demonstrate considerable inertia (Meyer and Brown [1977]; Hannan and Freeman [1984]). The influence of historical founding conditions and inertial pressures on labor-market outcomes has been documented in several empirical studies my colleagues and I have conducted. For instance, we recently studied patterns of job integration by sex in California state agencies between 1979 and 1985 (Baron, Mittman, and Newman [1991]). Employing linear partial adjustment models, we examined how organizational characteristics affected both the target level of integration that each state agency was capable of achieving and the rate at which state governmental organizations approached their targets. Gender segregation was measured using the index of dissimilarity across jobs (Duncan and Duncan [1955]) and an information-theoretic measure of segregation developed by Theil and Finizza [1971]. While these two indices involve somewhat different assumptions about how segregation should be measured, both assess how skewed the observed distribution of men and women is across job titles relative to the distribution of men and women within the organization as a whole.

We specified that the target level of integration in each agency depended on its division of labor (how finely job titles were differentiated) and on the degree of gender balance (or imbalance) in agency employment. Whether one regards a highly detailed division of labor as a tool by which employers willfully segregate or as a benign constraint imposed by the organization's size and technology, agencies will clearly have a harder time displaying an integrated workforce when employees are more finely classified across job titles. Similarly, whether an organizational workforce dominated by one sex reflects discrimination or external labor-supply constraints, agencies with a balanced workforce are capable of faster job integration than those in which one sex is an extreme minority.

We postulated that the speed with which each state agency approached its target level of integration depended on a number of organizational characteristics, including the agency's size and age; gender and race composition; occupational composition; growth rate; promotion and turnover rates; unionization; budgetary dependencies (proportion of funding coming from the federal government or state legislature, as opposed to user fees and other independent sources); the tenure and gender of its chief executive; the degree of scrutiny to which each agency was subject from the legislature; [8] the extent of oversight by the State Personnel Board (a watchdog agency that monitors and enforces compliance with antidiscrimination policies); the objectivity of each agency's outputs; [9] and controls for period effects. Thus, in interpreting the results summarized below, it is important to bear in mind that each effect reported is net of all other factors controlled in our analyses, and that when I speak of an agency's rate of progress or reform, I am referring to the speed with which it adjusted toward its specific integration target.[10]

Consistent with theories of organizational inertia, our longitudinal analyses revealed that younger state agencies, established during an era of intense concern with workplace equity, exhibited somewhat faster progress toward gender integration than older organizations did.[11] Similar evidence of the effects of founding conditions existed at the job level; there was less devaluation by race and sex among civil-service jobs founded after the late 1970s, when the state government began paying closer attention to comparable worth, than among otherwise comparable jobs founded previously (Baron and Newman [1989], [1990]; also see Kim [1989]). These results call into question an assumption underlying many economic models of organizations and labor markets, namely, that the structure of jobs and organizations observed reflects the exigencies of productive efficiency. Rather, the organizational literature underscores the inertia associated with structures and procedures. Jobs and organizations are designed in ways that conform to economic pressures and sociocultural understandings present at the time of founding, which are likely to persist unless subject to intense pressures for change.

Organizational theorists have claimed that structural inertia is greater not only in old organizations, but also in large organizations compared to small ones. Large organizations invariably must decentralize their activities, and the delegation of authority and power usually impedes coordinated, centralized efforts by organizations to adapt to environmental pressures and changes. Consistent with that prediction, our analyses of state agencies and other studies in diverse samples of establishments document that larger organizations are more segregated and are slower to integrate over time (see Bielby and Baron [1984]; Lyson [1985]). This result does not simply reflect the tendency for large enterprises to have a more detailed division of labor (which would promote the appearance of greater segregation by reducing the number of incumbents per job title), which these studies control for in different ways.

IIIB. Interests

Various groups within organizations are likely to perceive an interest in either sustaining or undoing ascriptive job assignments and reward allocations. Because discriminatory organizational arrangements are often inert and may provide substantial economic and social benefits to the majority, the rate at which they abate in a given organizational setting is likely to depend on the constellation of interests favoring or opposing equal treatment.

Obviously, the aggrieved minorities themselves represent potentially important interest groups opposing such practices. Sociologists have argued that minority groups are more powerful and prone to collective action when their relative numbers increase in an organizational setting (Kanter [1977]). In a sample of predominantly small organizations in California's private sector, which had been studied by the U.S. Employment Service between 1959 and 1979, job segregation varied inversely with the percentage of female employees in an establishment, even after controlling for occupational composition and other organizational characteristics likely to affect segregation levels (Bielby and Baron [1984]). Similarly, in longitudinal analyses of California state government agencies between 1979 and 1985, organizations employing a sizable (and increasing) proportion of women displayed faster gender integration than otherwise comparable agencies, again even controlling for relevant organizational and occupational constraints (Baron, Mittman, and Newman [1991]).

Of course, these effects might have nothing to do with the political actions of the minority groups involved, but rather simply reflect labor-supply constraints. For instance, agencies having a large (or increasing) percentage of women may integrate faster because they are less constrained by sex-specific labor supply than other organizations. However, while labor supply obviously shapes gender-based job allocations within organizations, it is far from the entire story. I base this inference on four facts. First, we have found persistent segregation across jobs and organizations even in settings where gender-based differences in labor supply seem minimal, such as detailed occupations that employ both men and women (Bielby and Baron [1986]). In occupations involving a mixture of traditionally "male" and "female" characteristics (e.g., physical lifting and repetitive dexterous work, respectively), both women and men were employed, but hardly ever in the same job classes or organizational settings. In other words, both sexes were available for this kind of work, but their assignment to specific work settings appeared to depend principally on whether a specific employer typed the role as more "appropriate" for men or women. This brings me to the second piece of evidence undercutting labor-supply explanations: Employment Service analysts explicitly recorded employers' ascriptive stereotypes with amazing frequency; a number of illustrations are cited in Bielby and Baron [1986].

Third, in analyzing segregation trends in the California civil service, labor-supply constraints affecting an agency's capacity to integrate were proxied in several ways. For instance, we allowed the agency target to depend on the overall percentage of women in the organization, and our specification of the speed of adjustment controlled for the occupational composition of each agency. Fourth, we conducted numerous supplementary analyses to examine whether the effect of having a large contingent of women on rates of gender desegregation merely reflected labor-supply differences across organizations. For instance, we examined alternative measures of job segregation for each agency that standardized for the degree of segregation within the entire occupational structure of the California civil service.[12] These measures thus take as given the degree of labor-market segregation within the civil service as a whole, examining only how segregated each agency is in its jobs relative to the degree of segregation in the statewide occupational labor markets from which it draws. In these supplementary analyses, the effects pertaining to the percent female in each agency were weakened, but not eliminated. The evidence, then, suggests that the relative size of disadvantaged constituencies in an organization has a direct net effect on the speed with which discriminatory job assignments abate, which is not due solely to labor-supply considerations.

Unions are another constituency whose effects on segregation have received considerable attention. Analyzing a sample of predominantly small, private-sector California enterprises from the 1960s and 1970s, Bielby and I found that unionized establishments tended to exhibit higher levels of sex segregation (Bielby and Baron [1984]). Recent analyses of the California state government agencies in the 1980s produced similar results: integration was slower in agencies having a larger proportion of workers in job classifications covered by collective bargaining units (Baron, Mittman, and Newman [1991]). In supplemental analyses, however, much of the negative effect of unions on rates of integration vanished once we controlled for the amount of segregation in the occupational labor markets of the civil service as a whole. In other words, the barriers to integration associated with the presence of unions apparently reflect the sex-segregated nature of occupations from which unions draw their members, rather than direct political opposition by unions.

IIIC. Organizational Leadership

Some perspectives on organizational evolution emphasize the role that leaders play in adapting organizations to the environment. In economic models, two rational employers facing the same production function are typically presumed to organize in roughly the same way and pursue similar objectives. In contrast, the organizational literature has suggested and documented that leaders can matter in shaping organizational evolution.

Our analyses of state government agencies revealed that organizations headed by female leaders were slightly faster to integrate by sex than otherwise comparable agencies run by men. We also found a positive effect of turnover among agency leaders on speed of job integration by sex. In the public sector, however, executive succession is closely linked with changes in political administration. Indeed, the effects of the gender and turnover of leaders on agencies' adjustment toward their integration targets appear to be due principally to the change of political administration that occurred in 1982-83, when the Republican George Deukmejian replaced the liberal Democrat Jerry Brown.[13]   Integration was occurring fairly consistently at the time most Brown appointees were replaced (1983 to early 1984) and then declined precipitously during the first year (1984-85) that Deukmejian's appointees (disproportionately men) had complete control over budgets and hiring. This was also the period of lowest executive succession, following the spate of postelection political appointments (see Baron, Mittman, and Newman [1991]). Thus the widespread turnover of leaders that occurred after the 1982 election definitely wrought change in agency practice, consistent with other organizational research showing that leadership succession is a key way in which bureaucracies overcome inertia and realign themselves with a changing environment (e.g., Meyer [1975]). However, given the lag between the Deukmejian appointments and agency responses, it appears that executive succession associated with the Republican gubernatorial victory in 1982-83 actually *depressed* progress toward gender-integration targets. In other words, changes at the top did indeed facilitate organizational change in this case, but not in the direction of reducing ascription.

It might be argued that we found effects of leader characteristics and turnover on segregation patterns only because we were looking at a sample of public-sector organizations. Economists have frequently observed that state governments operate in a protected environment (e.g., Killingsworth [1985]), sheltered from competitive pressures that might reduce or eliminate the latitude for leaders to shape organizational practice in their own vision. This may be true. However, there appears to be considerable anecdotal evidence that top-level organizational commitment has also influenced antidiscrimination efforts in the private sector (e.g., Shaeffer and Lynton [1979]; O'Farrell and Harlan [1984]; Bielby and Baron [1984]). Moreover, such an argument implies that leaders in the public sector who are committed to antidiscriminatory policies can indulge their tastes because they are shielded from market pressures, whereas private-sector managers do not have this luxury. Interestingly, this seems to contradict Becker's (1971) oft-quoted claim that it is precisely the competitive pressure built into the market that will erode discrimination in the workplace. Can one have it both ways?

Agency theorists might answer yes (D. Baron, personal communication). Female leaders may have "tastes against discrimination," which they indulge as a form of managerial perquisite, just as it has been argued that male executives may display "tastes for discrimination." However, recall that our statistical models controlled for a number of characteristics of agencies that would seem to affect the ability of managers to indulge their "tastes," such as organizational size, age, budgetary dependencies, degree of external scrutiny, and the like. Therefore, the tendency for women leading agencies to promulgate faster change than their male counterparts does not seem attributable to some obvious difference in the kinds of organizations they lead or the environmental pressures they face. The point here is that most analyses of labor-market discrimination ignore *who* heads a given enterprise. Our results for state government agencies, in contrast, suggest that it matters a fair bit: female leaders and pre-Deukmejian leaders seem to have been more responsive to pressures for employment equity.

IIID. Environmental Pressures and Constituents

Finally, organizational theory and research also provide some clues about how an organization's success at reducing ascriptive job assignments might be affected by its environment. Although organizations are subject to inertia, they are not immune to external pressure. Like other researchers (e.g., Salancik [1979]; Freeman [1981]; Beller [1984]; Leonard [1984]; Burstein [1985]), we found that state agencies subject to the strongest external pressures for reform exhibited faster integration. For instance, agencies that had been targeted and sanctioned by the state government's own watchdog organization, the State Personnel Board, integrated more rapidly (Baron, Mittman, and Newman [1991]). Similarly, agencies whose mandate makes them most subject to oversight by the state legislature integrated faster than agencies having more autonomy. However, we found little evidence that the extent of budgetary dependence on the state legislature per se influenced agencies' progress toward job integration. This finding is consistent with recent work in political science, which argues that legislative committees overseeing government agencies face many of the classic principal-agent problems (asymmetric information, monitoring difficulties, and conflicting goals), and therefore "the budget is simply not a very dependable control mechanism" (Moe [1987: 487]).

IIIE. Summary

Clearly, there are other important determinants of job integration whose effects I have not discussed. For instance, Cohn [1985]) has shown that if job segregation has the effect (never mind the aim) of paying women less than men, then employers presumably have more economic incentive to segregate when their technology is labor-intensive and when there is a clear division between "good" and "bad" jobs in the establishment (also see Bridges [1980], [1982]; Lyson [1985]). I have focused on some particular characteristics of organizations – their structures, leaders, internal constituencies, and external environments, some of which are less clearly related to economic considerations – that influenced the rate of progress toward gender integration in several diverse samples of organizations. By illuminating the propensity toward bias in a specific work setting, the sway of interests and environmental pressures favoring or opposing discrimination, and the success of efforts to eradicate discrimination, theories of organizational behavior and change have much to offer those interested in labor markets, ascription, and changing patterns of socioeconomic opportunity.

IV. LOOSE COUPLING AND ORGANIZATIONAL RESPONSES TO ANTIDISCRIMINATORY PRESSURES

Organizational scholarship also reminds us of the distinction between formal organizational structures and policies on the one hand and actual practices on the other. The less than perfect correlation between the two is probably not accidental, but rather an important way that organizations retain the flexibility necessary to adapt to uncertain and rapidly changing environments (Weick [1976]). Just as organizations are not realistically portrayed by the production functions of economic theory, neither are they meaningfully represented by the organization charts and policy manuals of administrative science.

This point is important because it helps explain, I believe, why we often find more evidence of egalitarian *reforms* by organizations than we do of egalitarian *outcomes*. For example, examining field notes prepared by U.S. Employment Service analysts, Bielby and I found fewer employers explicitly mentioning policies restricting women's employment based on physical demands of work after 1971 – when the California Supreme Court declared such policies unconstitutional – than beforehand. However, we found that women were actually somewhat more likely to be excluded from jobs involving heavy lifting after 1971 than they had been previously (Bielby and Baron [1986: 784-785]).

Once again, labor-supply stories can explain this, but I do not find them compelling in this particular instance. For example, our conclusions about the increased relevance of physical lifting requirements in differentiating "women's" from "men's" jobs were based on regression analyses predicting the presence of women in specific job titles within gender-mixed occupations in our sample. A labor-supply story would have to explain why women "chose" to enter the very same detailed occupations as men in a given organizational setting, but not the specific job titles having a physical lifting requirement well within the capacities of any female who has ever had a child. We found numerous instances of this phenomenon:

[In one ordnance establishment,] 555 women were employed as "Assemblers," while 243 men were employed as "Production Workers," both entry jobs involving the same duties and sharing the same detailed DOT code. Job analyses indicated few differences between the two slots, except that men occasionally lifted more than 25 pounds, the limit that women could then legally lift without a special permit. Of course, a separate job title is not required to capture that distinction, and in most other respects, the jobs were identical. In fact, in certain respects, the women's job appeared more demanding, according to the job analyst. (Baron and Bielby [1985: 242]).

Our analyses of California government agencies uncovered similar evidence of the limits of antidiscriminatory reforms. I noted above that gender integration was faster in state agencies cited for past discrimination by the State Personnel Board. The board identified certain targeted job classifications in which specific employment objectives were to be reached, but their sanctions were also intended to reduce segregation throughout the entire job structures of the agencies involved. Yet segregation declines in the cited agencies were entirely attributable to integration in the targeted job classes; in fact, in two of the three organizations involved, the remaining job classifications actually became slightly more segregated over the period studied (Baron, Mittman, and Newman [1991]).

This result brings to mind Smith and Welch's (1984) findings: comparing occupational distributions obtained from employers (via the Equal Employment Opportunity Commission [EEOC]) and from employees (via the Census Bureau), they concluded that much of the apparent " job integration" in response to the targeting of industries by the EEOC and Office of Federal Contract Compliance Programs (OFCCP) simply reflected cosmetic reclassifications of disadvantaged workers into "managerial" and related categories. These findings suggest the ability of organizations to segregate their desegregation efforts, as it were, compartmentalizing their activities to respond to specific internal constituencies and external pressures without undertaking wholesale reforms (also see Leonard [1989]). While this might reflect a conscious effort to subvert the intended aims of targeting, an intriguing alternative is that it simply illustrates the tendency for social systems to respond to pressures for costly or disruptive changes in a selective and limited way. That tendency, of course, generally has tremendous adaptive value, as ecologists have demonstrated, since overresponsiveness to environmental forces could quickly cripple any complex system. This is not to endorse the outcome in this case, but only to offer a possible explanation for it.

Organizational theory and research suggest that formal structures and policies are especially likely to be divorced from actual practice in certain circumstances: when the organization lacks a clear and certain core technology; when it is large and bureaucratic, yet faces a turbulent environment putting a premium on flexibility; when entrenched interests have been able to institutionalize their control over organizational activities; and when formal rules and structures are important sources of external legitimation (see Scott [1987: 261-264]). These are the settings in which we might therefore predict the largest gaps between official organizational postures and actual outcomes, including those involving employment equity.

In sum, attention to what goes on inside organizations underscores the difference between organizational "accounts" and actual practices and suggests when antidiscriminatory policies and reforms may mask the perpetuation of ascriptive outcomes. There is a methodological implication here as well. Social scientists and policymakers often assess labor-market trends (including discrimination) based on official statistics reported by organizations to government agencies, statistics that represent a particular kind of organizational account or social construction (Starr [1987]). The organizational context of labor-market outcomes is thus critical not only because organizations shape the reality of discrimination, but also because they can manipulate the very statistics and perceptions that frame public policies and discussions concerning discrimination. The examples described above should serve to illustrate how the social scientist's datum or trend is often the manager's strategically created fiction.

V. IMPLICATIONS FOR THEORIES OF ORGANIZATIONS AND ORGANIZATIONAL CHANGE

Sociologists and social psychologists have no first principles concerning organizations or discrimination analogous to economists' theory of the firm or of competitive labor-market dynamics. They do, however, have a number of useful ideas and research findings about how cognitive, social, and organizational factors influence the way jobs are defined, evaluated, and staffed, including the role that ascriptive distinctions play in these processes. I have summarized various strands of research relevant to these concerns. Although these different studies were not guided by an over-arching conception of organizations, their findings seem to mesh rather nicely. Accordingly, this section tries to weave these strands together, suggesting what can be learned from these findings about how organizations evolve.

First, I have noted how economic and cultural forces prevalent when an organization is founded become indelibly imprinted on its structure and practices. I have suggested how this may have operated with regard to the structuring of jobs and wage rates in the California civil service, and work with Bielby reveals similar patterns among organizations in the private sector (Bielby and Baron [1984], [1986]). Once in place, personnel structures, like many features of organizations, exhibit inertia, especially in the absence of external pressure, circumstances conducive to internal collective action, or changes in organizational leadership that can mobilize forces for change.

In the case of job titles and wage rates, their initial ascriptive nature was likely to be self-reinforcing for several reasons. First, research on social comparison processes indicates that people tend to make fairness comparisons vis-a-vis those in the same role and who share the same ascriptive characteristics (Runciman [1966]; Major and Forcey [1985]; and section

II of the preceding chapter by William Bielby). The job segregation of women from men and of blacks from whites reduces the contact that the disadvantaged have with the privileged and strengthens the tendency for women and minorities to restrict their fairness comparisons to others within their own social group and organizational role. Moreover, initial stereotypes about the difficulty or importance of a particular job and about the worthiness of its incumbents are also likely to be reinforcing, given well-documented psychological tendencies for role expectations to be internalized and for outcomes that confirm stereotypes to be recalled and attended to more than disconfirming ones (Hamilton [1981]).

The inertial character of organizational arrangements challenges perspectives in economics and administrative science that view enterprises as continually adapting to changes in their resource and political environments. To be sure, transactions-cost approaches provide some clues as to why organizational arrangements might exhibit inertia. The same logic of bounded rationality that explains why employer stereotypes are more likely to be confirmed than dispelled is embraced by Williamson [1975] in explaining the rise of stable hierarchies that supplant flexible market transactions. In addition to such cognitive considerations, Williamson also highlights the resource-related costs associated with implementing organizational changes and the relationship-related costs when individuals work closely with one another, making staffing changes particularly costly and disruptive.

However, I have emphasized throughout this essay that organizations are not simply aggregations of physical resources and technical interdependencies, but also arenas in which social relations, political contests, and cultural forces shape the enterprise. Accordingly, I believe that there are several other kinds of transaction costs associated with organizational changes, including those required to eradicate ascriptive personnel practices, to which economic theories might give greater attention. First, once a coalition or subunit obtains power in an organization, it is not likely to cede power easily and may strive to institutionalize its privileged position, preventing structural adaptations that would better align the organization with its changing environment. Subunits do this routinely in all-too-familiar ways, such as controlling the information gathered by and distributed within the organization; structuring organizational career ladders to reinforce the privileged position of a specific occupation, function, or division; and resisting changes in strategy or policy that would reduce the centrality of the subunit's contribution (Pfeffer [1981]).

While this can obviously be costly for an organization, so can efforts to realign the organization's structure with its changing environment. In a decentralized enterprise, subunits typically possess some measure of expert power or informal influence and there is not likely to be an overriding consensus on goals. Under these conditions, changes to the status quo subject the organization to what Milgrom and Roberts [1988] have termed "influence costs": efforts by specific constituencies to mold changes to their own benefit. To some extent, there are economies of scale in bickering; opening up one set of issues for renegotiation reduces the perceived costs of visiting other issues as well. Few of us spontaneously debate our soulmates about where the coffee mugs should be stored or whether to store them upside down or right-side up, but the process of moving to a new residence often precipitates extended debates about such minutiae. (The tendency for relocations to produce such squabbles may account for the oft-noted correlation between leaving a residence and leaving a relationship.) Such influence costs are especially great in settings characterized by goal dissensus and perceptions of inequity among the parties, such as the personnel systems of the state governmental agencies I studied, which are public and highly visible. Subjecting the job-classification and salary systems of the civil service to a major overhaul no doubt involves significant influence costs.

There is a related cost associated with organizational adaptation often overlooked in economic models of formal organization. As various organizational theorists have noted, much of the control that organizations are able to exert over members stems from the taken-for-granted nature or legitimacy of rules and standard operating procedures (e.g., Perrow [1979: 150-152]; Edwards [1979: ch. 9]). According to this view, the triumph of rational bureaucracy and the detailed division of labor are due largely to the subtle and invisible ways they control actors' premises, not simply the technical efficiencies they generate. Planned change efforts can potentially threaten that premise control by demonstrating to members that their organization is essentially a collection of wills, some of whom have triumphed, and that structures and procedures are consciously chosen, rather than natural outgrowths of tradition or the spirit of rationality. While this insight may be personally liberating, it is not clear that it promotes organizational goal attainment: tradition and standard operating procedures provide a firmer foundation for many deeds (including dastardly ones) than does a superior's "Because I said so!"

Institutional economists have observed, for example, that wage differentials in organizations tend to assume the status of customary law, retaining force long after the circumstances warranting these differentials have changed (e.g., Kerr [1954]; Doeringer and Piore [1971]; Elbaum [1984]). The definitions of jobs and distinctions among them are often equally tenuous and mysterious. It is sometimes argued that what threatens managers and executives most about comparable worth, for instance, is not the recalibration of women's work, but rather the task of explicitly legitimating *their own* privileged job definitions and pay standing vis-à-vis the rest of the organization. In short, one factor sustaining inertia in organizations and employment relations is the taken-for-granted nature of past practice and the "legitimation costs" involved with exercising managerial discretion to make changes.

Organizational theories provide some insights regarding when these costs are likely to be greatest. In older organizations and those with a high-tenure workforce, one is especially likely to observe vested interests favoring the status quo and greater legitimacy associated with existing traditions and patterns of working relations. In organizations that are decentralized, highly differentiated, and/or socially heterogeneous, goal conflict and a loss of centralized control typically increase "influence" and "legitimacy" costs when attempts are being made to move the enterprise in a unified direction.[14]

The empirical analyses I summarized suggest that inertial tendencies are not insurmountable, however. I identified some factors that appear to have strengthened the impact of past traditions and stereotypes on job assignment and reward allocations and other factors that had the opposite effect. For instance, consistent with field work and social psychological experiments, we found that ascriptive reward allocations, institutionalized long ago within California's civil-service structure, were most intransigent in work roles having vague or ambiguous performance standards. In situations of evaluative uncertainty, organizational actors are especially likely to fall back on past heuristics, including cultural stereotypes, in making judgments.[15]

Stated differently, undoing discrimination requires effective collective action on the part of affected groups. The absence of clearly defined performance standards in a job is one factor that makes effective collective action trickier for incumbents advocating organizational reform.[16] I summarized other evidence suggesting greater progress toward workplace equity in settings where economic, political, and social forces favor collective action by the disadvantaged or discourage resistance by their opponents, including: jobs and organizations that are growing, where the "pie" is expanding enough to reduce the perceived threat by those favoring the status quo; settings where activist unions have a strong presence and in which women and minorities represent a relatively large share of the work force; and in job classifications having few incumbents and occurring in few organizational settings, where it is easier for incumbents to mobilize and less costly for organizations to remedy pay inequalities.

Some of our other empirical results imply that vested interests favoring discrimination operate with greater force in shaping opportunities and rewards for current organizational members than for future generations. In the California civil service, for example, we found that the growth rate had a much stronger positive effect on job integration by sex than did the rate of internal promotion (Baron, Mittman, and Newman [1991]). I believe this partly reflects the fact that it is easier for organizations to alter long-standing policies and practices with regard to future members than in dealing with existing employees, among whom implicit contracts and organizational traditions have developed. Accordingly, groups who have benefited from ascriptive job assignments and reward allocations may tolerate changes that affect how people are treated in the future more than changes affecting those currently employed. This makes it easier politically for an organization to integrate by growing (and changing the rules and practices governing hiring of new employees) than by altering the allocation of jobs and rewards among current members. The same line of argument may also explain the apparent lagged effect of Deukmejian's political appointments who, unconstrained by past practice, implicit contracts, and long-standing commitments to redress prior discrimination, slowed the pace of agency progress toward integration targets.

Consistent with other research, our analyses of private- and public-sector organizations reveal that external pressures helped reduce ascriptive job and reward assignments. Yet organizations appear less responsive to such pressures than some theoretical perspectives imply. Our results indicate that enterprises respond selectively to external pressures, especially when they possess some source of institutional autonomy, such as a mandate that minimizes the degree of scrutiny from legislators. The framework outlined in this section suggests where and why we might see continued labor-market ascription, even if discriminatory "tastes" vanished. Indeed, if these tastes have abated more rapidly than have the circumstances favoring inertia, this may help explain the loose coupling we seem to observe between organizational reforms aimed at eliminating ascription and tangible organizational outcomes.

VI. SUMMARY AND IMPLICATIONS FOR FUTURE RESEARCH

In the organizational world I have described, the extent of ascription is affected not simply by employer tastes, labor supply, the legal environment, and economic transaction costs, but also by psychological, political, and normative factors shaping organizational change and sustaining the status quo in a given setting. Drawing on my own research, I have described how some of these factors affect three facets of discrimination: how ascriptive characteristics figure in the way jobs are defined, evaluated, and staffed in organizations.

The clear implication of literature I have reviewed is that organizational form matters, which economists have increasingly recognized not only in studying labor markets, but capital markets as well (e.g., Jensen and Meckling [1976]; Fama [1980]; Holmstrom and Tirole [1989]; Baker Jensen, and Murphy [1988]). Organizational scholarship by sociologists has something to say to economists interested in the evolution of organizational forms. Most recent formal theorizing by economists about organizations is of the multiple-equilibria genre, in which two contemporary organizations doing the same task may exhibit quite distinct forms because each adopted a different (but equally efficient) initial solution, that preordained a specific developmental path. I have suggested how and why various social and political considerations are likely to influence which organizational forms are viable; of these, which one a particular enterprise adopts; and how (whether) it changes over time.[17]

In particular, differences in founding conditions and environmental contingencies have a large impact on the rate at which ascription abates in labor markets, making organizations differentially responsive to economic, political, and other pressures, including those concerning equity in the workplace. In their black-box treatment of the firm, neoclassical economists have often tended to see the environment as relatively unproblematic, because small firms in competitive situations are viewed as facing nearly identical market forces over which they have little or no control. However, organizational research has shown that this is not the case; firms adopting identical organizational forms can exhibit extremely different relations with their environments, and a single market environment typically supports diverse organizational forms (Baron and Bielby [1984]). Organizational theorists have devoted considerable attention to conceptualizing and measuring the factors that make an enterprise vulnerable to external pressure, that insulate it from outside scrutiny, and that facilitate the adoption of various innovations (including state-of-the-art personnel techniques), thereby influencing how and when an organization adapts to changing environmental demands. They have also devoted substantial attention to the role that organizational leaders can play in shaping the evolution of the enterprise. Applying these tools to the study of employment practices promises to enrich both organizational analysis and labor-market analysis.

For instance, to the extent that organizations founded during the same historical period are expected to respond similarly to pressures for change – including pressures to change the employment relationship – it becomes critical to distinguish birth cohorts of organizations and industries in empirical research. Labor-market researchers routinely group individuals into birth cohorts in an effort to capture historical patterns affecting career outcomes. Similar groupings of jobs, organizations, and industries would be equally informative (see, for instance, Stinchcombe [1979]; Bridges [1982]).

This organizational literature clearly has other implications for future research on labor markets and discrimination. Some of these are self-evident. For instance, if there are systematic differences across organizations in the way jobs are structured, compensated, and staffed, then this heterogeneity may bias estimates of the effects of both demand (e.g., market structure) and supply (e.g., worker education) characteristics in econometric analyses of employment-related outcomes (see, for instance, the following chapter by David Fairris and Lori Kletzer).

However, an organizational approach also has more fundamental (and vexing) implications for how we conceptualize and measure labor-market processes, including the extent of discrimination. For instance, recent labor-market research has documented two intriguing empirical facts: stable firm and industry differences in occupation-specific wages (e.g., Dickens and Katz [1987]; Groshen [1989]); and a tendency for the distribution of wages within organizations to be compressed relative to the distribution of inputs and outputs (Frank [1984]; Lazear [1989]). Many recent economic explanations for both of these stylized facts have invoked sociological and social psychological notions about equity and social comparison. Pay compression is rationalized by arguing that firms would lose more from the discord, turnover, and haggling that large pay differentials encourage than they would gain. Similarly, many economists invoke equity considerations to explain the tendency for certain firms and industries to pay above-market wages (in all occupations): key employees are paid wage premia to engender feelings of loyalty, and the remaining employees are paid above-market wages in order to preserve internal equity, for the reasons just mentioned.

Economists' recent recognition of equity considerations is a welcome development, as inequity represents one type of organizational transaction cost that I emphasized above. However, I suspect that the other sorts of transaction costs to which I alluded – the influence and legitimation costs of attempting to undo long-standing organizational practices, including those governing pay – may also help explain pay compression within firms and the stability of wage differentials across firms and industries. In short, greater attention to organizational structures, processes, and histories will be necessary in order for economists to clarify and test the predictions of different efficiency wage stories (see chapter 3 in this volume by Michael Robinson and Phanindra Wunnava).

I have argued that powerful cognitive, social psychological, political, and cultural forces shape how jobs get defined, evaluated, and staffed with profound implications for labor-market outcomes. Accordingly, researchers should not take an organization's division of labor and salary schedules for granted, but rather look closely at their determinants and consequences. Studies examining differences across organizations in the way specific work roles came to be defined – and the implications of those differences for workers' outcomes – would be invaluable. Of course, the requisite data are often scarce, particularly for private-sector firms, because of confidentiality restrictions and the fact that few firms possess systematic and consistent personnel records over substantial periods of time. This means that the data that do exist may represent atypical organizations (e.g., firms either proud enough of their personnel practices or sufficiently threatened by a lawsuit to divulge the data to a researcher). Consequently, social scientists must collaborate to devise ways of overcoming these biases and limitations. One (expensive) approach is for researchers to assemble new data sets containing longitudinal information on representative samples of organizations, their jobs, and employees. Another strategy would involve piggybacking on existing sample frames, such as those used by governmental agencies that routinely monitor organizations. Alternatively, an increasing number of researchers have acquired data on career histories for individuals in specific public- or private-sector organizations, either through research or consulting activities. It may make sense to commission "meta-analyses" of their results in order to determine how and why personnel systems and employee outcomes vary across diverse organizational forms.

I highlighted how various interest groups within organizations affect the extent of ascription. This implies that we are likely to do much better in predicting individuals' labor-market outcomes if we know something about the various constituencies seeking to retain or overturn ascriptive employment practices within their work setting. Treating employment relations and outcomes as if they were the result of individualized deals between an employer and an employee overlooks how an individual's opportunities and attainments are affected by social and political ties in the workplace (Granovetter [1985]). Our results suggest that a valuable form of human capital possessed by some disadvantaged workers is the political clout that comes with their group being a sizable presence within an organization. This topic is well worth additional study in understanding who gets what and why.

Economists of various stripes have begun paying greater attention to the role of organizational arrangements in shaping employment relations and labor-market outcomes. By encouraging their efforts, perhaps this chapter abets the raiding of sociologists' turf by the economists (who would no doubt call this intellectual rent seeking). However, integrating economic and sociological insights into organizations is likely to improve our understanding of discrimination, our policies to eliminate it, and the quality of scholarship in both disciplines.

7
Working Conditions, Segmented Labor Markets, and Gender Discrimination

David Fairris and
Lori G. Kletzer

The literature on gender discrimination suggests that conventional human-capital measures explain, at best, less than half of the average male/female wage gap (Mincer and Polachek [1974]; Corcoran and Duncan [1979]). When detailed occupational categories are accounted for, however, the unexplained portion of the wage gap falls significantly (Treiman and Hartmann [1981]), suggesting that, all else constant, women are segregated into occupations at the low end of the earnings hierarchy. Other forms of segregation and other kinds of discriminatory pay practices may exist as well, explaining the remaining portion of the wage gap. Blau [1977] found, for example, that even within very narrow occupational categories, male/female wage differences exist across firms and industries, with jobs in high-wage firms being filled disproportionately by men.

Job segregation may result not from discriminatory labor-market practices but from the optimal decisions of women facing the same labor market constraints as men. According to this view, preferences are the driving force behind observed labor-market outcomes. One hypothesis along these lines is that occupational segregation and the related evidence on wage differences may reflect the different occupational choices of men and women owing largely to their differing expectations of the extent of labor-force participation over the life cycle.[1]

Alternatively, the empirical results on the male/female wage gap when occupational categories are accounted for may stem from the fact that working conditions differ across occupations (and across firms within occupations), and that women choose jobs with less onerous work characteristics, the monetary compensation for which is also less. According to this theory, the wage gap between equally qualified men and women in the labor market may be due, in part, to equalizing differences for the differing conditions of their work. The addition of occupation controls to a standard human-capital wage equation containing a gender variable may merely be capturing some of the differences in working conditions across jobs held by men versus women.

In a recent study utilizing occupational-level data, Filer [1989] found that controlling for a wide variety of working conditions caused the variable "percent female in the occupation" to become largely insignificant in explaining the variation in occupational earnings. This runs counter to earlier results by Treiman, Hartman, and Roos [1984], who found the "percent female" variable to be negative and statistically significant in explaining median occupational earnings of workers, even after controlling for differences in working conditions across occupations.

An attempt to untangle the specific interaction between the male/female wage gap and working conditions is contained in Filer [1985]. Using data on individuals from the 1977 Quality of Employment Survey, Filer found that adding measures of working conditions to conventional estimated wage equations for males and females increased the explained portion of the average wage gap by over a third (p. 433). The implications of this result are not at all clear, however. The theory of compensating wage differentials assumes a competitive labor market in which costless mobility allows workers to equalize differences in overall labor compensation at the margin. In order to equalize differences in nonmonetary aspects of employment across jobs, compensating payments must be positive for undesirable working conditions. The working conditions in Filer's study point to the existence of negative and statistically significant compensating payments for a number of undesirable working-environment characteristics.

Empirical work involving the theory of compensating wage differentials ignores much of what we have learned about labor-market rigidities and worker immobility from institutional analyses of internal labor markets and labor-market segmentation. Negative estimated compensating payments for onerous working conditions may result from the fact that the labor market is segmented, with good wages and working conditions in some segments, bad wages and working conditions in others, and significant barriers to mobility between segments. Studies that have incorporated working conditions into the analysis of the male/female wage gap have failed to do so in a manner consistent with the existence of noncompeting groups in the labor market, and as a result, their findings may be misleading.

Our goal in this chapter is to explore the interaction between working conditions, occupational segregation, and the male/female wage gap allowing for labor-market segmentation. In section I we review the theory of compensating wage differentials and introduce labor-market segmentation into the analysis of compensating payments. Section II presents the empirical model and the results of our analysis. In section III we discuss the findings and their implications for the literature on gender discrimination.

I. COMPENSATING PAYMENTS AND SEGMENTED LABOR MARKETS

The theory of equalizing differences in the labor market originates with the work of Adam Smith. In volume 1, chapter 10 of *The Wealth of Nations*, Smith offered five explanations for the existence of wage differences across workers, one of which was the relative agreeableness or disagreeableness of the work. Smith reasoned that, other things equal, competitive labor markets would produce outcomes in which "the whole of the advantages and disadvantages of the different employments ... must ... be perfectly equal or continually tending toward equality" [1937: 100]. Since the nonpecuniary rewards from work clearly vary across jobs, monetary compensation must also differ if "the whole" is to be equalized.

Rosen's [1974] model of hedonic prices and its application by Thaler and Rosen [1975] to the risk of injury on the job clarify the determinants of compensating payments in competitive markets. In these models, utility-maximizing worker/consumers are assumed to possess different preferences over bundles of wages and working conditions, and profit-maximizing firms are assumed to contain different internal costs of improving working conditions. Equilibrium compensating payments result from a worker/employer matching process involving labor mobility between firms, and their magnitude depends upon, among other things, the distribution of tastes and production technologies among the respective agents. Labor turnover forces recalcitrant firms with disagreeable working conditions to either provide monetary compensation or improve the quality of the work environment.

Generally, empirical tests of the theory take the form of estimated wage equations with a set of working-conditions characteristics added as explanatory variables. Working-conditions variables that have appeared in previous tests include the risk of death, working with machines, hard, fast, or repetitive work, and the like. With the exception of the risk-of-death

variable (whose estimated coefficients are generally positive and significant), the results of such tests have been wildly inconclusive. The
sometimes-negative, sometimes-positive nature of these estimated compensating payments has provoked a number of responses in the literature
(see Smith [1979] and Brown [1980] for useful reviews of the literature).

Segmented labor markets theory can be traced back to the work of J.
S. Mill on noncompeting groups. Mill argued that differential access to
schooling and variations in certain attributes from one's upbringing, such
as personal style, caused labor markets to be segmented, preventing some
people from moving easily into privileged occupations. As a result, he
stated, "the really exhausting and the really repulsive labors, instead of
being better paid than others, are almost invariably paid the worst of all,
because performed by those who have no choice" [1900: 372].

More modern theories of noncompeting groups in the labor market by
Doeringer and Piore [1971] and Gordon, Edwards, and Reich [1982]
describe a segmentation of the labor market into primary and secondary
sectors, with the primary sometimes divided into even finer segments, such
as the independent and subordinate primary, based on the autonomy of the
worker and the status of the job. In both presentations, the primary sector
is described as containing jobs with good pay, stable employment, room for
advancement, and decent working conditions. The secondary sector
contains just the opposite.

The division between primary and secondary sectors is based on the
presence of internal labor markets in the former and their absence in the
latter, the implication being that the secondary sector relies predominantly on competitive labor-market forces to allocate labor within the
firm.[2] Doeringer and Piore [1971] ascribe the growth of internal labor
markets to technological developments in production that brought forth
the need for significant on-the-job training by workers and thereby made
labor turnover increasingly costly to employers. For Gordon, Edwards, and
Reich [1982], the historical development of internal labor markets is due
not so much to employers' efficient organizational responses to new
production technologies as to the superiority of internal labor-market
arrangements for eliciting work effort from workers.

While the empirical task of dividing the labor market into primary and
secondary sectors carries with it some degree of arbitrariness, studies
utilizing data at the level of manufacturing industries (Oster [1979]),
occupations (Reich [1984]), and individuals (Osterman [1975]; Rumberger and Carnoy [1980]; Dickens and Lang [1985]) have all found
evidence supporting the segmentation hypothesis. The last set of studies,

for example, found significantly lower rates of return to schooling and labor-force experience in estimated wage equations for workers in the secondary sector. None considered a set of working conditions in their analyses of wage determination.

If the labor market is in fact segmented, with good wages and working conditions in the primary segment, bad wages and working conditions in the secondary segment, barriers to mobility from the latter to the former, and structurally different mechanisms for labor allocation and wage determination between sectors, then the failure to separate the segments for individual analysis may produce biased results. The existence of this particular pattern of wages and working conditions across sectors implies, moreover, that the improper pooling of labor-market segments may produce negative estimated compensating payments.

Figure 7.1 illustrates this issue. Assume that a particular element of the work environment is measured continuously along the horizontal axis in such a way that increases in the working-conditions measure implies a

Figure 7.1
Biased Estimation of Compensating Differentials

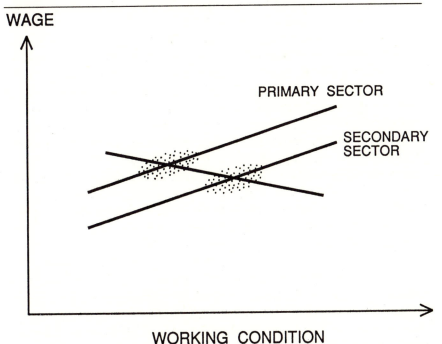

worsening of workplace quality. Wages are measured on the vertical axis. The slope of the estimated wage/working-conditions relation is the compensating payment.[3] Assuming that the pattern of wages and working conditions across segments is as discussed above, we can see that even though positive compensating payments may exist in both the primary labor market (the locus of points to the upper left) and the secondary labor market (the locus of points to the lower right), a failure to divide the segments for separate analysis may nonetheless yield estimated compensating payments that are negative.

It is not immediately obvious what we expect to find in the structure of wages across working conditions upon separating the labor-market segments for individual analysis. The secondary labor market is sometimes compared to the labor market of textbook competitive theory (e.g., Doeringer and Piore [1971: 167]), with high rates of turnover and little formal attachment of workers to firms. This might imply the existence of an active labor market in which firms compete for scarce labor and are thereby forced to pay compensating wage differentials. On the other hand, high rates of labor turnover may merely be a sign of a labor market in a state of flux, in which worker mobility is no indication of movement to something better, and competitive tendencies toward equalizing differences are largely nonexistent.

Compensation for disagreeable work is inherent in the structure of wages in the primary sector, since job-evaluation schemes common to internal labor markets regularly account for the conditions of work in the determination of wages attached to jobs. However, it is also true that most workers in the primary labor market are involved in long-term employment relationships that are shielded from the forces of market competition. Custom, tradition, and bargaining power influence the intertemporal structure of compensation for a given worker, as well as the structure of compensation across workers within an internal labor market.[4] While the present value of the benefits stemming from primary-sector employment must exceed the alternatives open in the general labor market, there may exist little tendency toward the equalization of differences across observationally equivalent workers in primary labor market settings.

While we have arrived at no a priori judgment concerning the structure of compensating payments in either of the two labor-market segments, the point of this discussion for the literature on the male/female wage gap is that any attempt to explore the link between working conditions and the extent of wage discrimination between men and women must do so in an empirical model allowing for structural differences between segments of the labor market. This is particularly important for discussions of gender discrimination because of the interaction between gender and preferences for working conditions (Filer [1983]); gender and the likelihood of secondary labor-market status (Gordon, Edwards, and Reich [1982]); and the quality of working conditions in different labor-market segments (Gordon, Edwards, and Reich [1982]).

II. EMPIRICAL TESTS AND RESULTS

To examine the effect of working conditions on measures of the male/female wage gap in separate segments of the labor market, we estimated different specifications of the standard semilog earnings function:

$$(1) \qquad \ln W_i = X_i b + e_i ,$$

where W_i is hourly earnings for individual i, X_i is a vector of individual and job characteristics, and e_i is a normally distributed error term. The sample was drawn from the 1977 *Quality of Employment* Survey. We chose this cross-sectional survey because it offers a wide assortment of working-conditions variables. Our sample included private, nonagricultural wage and salary workers, not self-employed, between the ages of 18 and 65, working at least ten hours per week, and earning more than $1.25 per hour. We used the categorization in Osterman [1975] to divide the sample into segments. Osterman divided the primary sector into upper (independent primary) and lower (subordinate primary) tiers based on the degree of autonomy in the job, where autonomy is the "freedom to set one's hours, freedom to set and keep personal standards, freedom to shape a product to one's sense of worth" (Osterman [1975: 512]). Jobs without these characteristics of autonomy were assigned to the lower (subordinate) primary sector. Following Doeringer and Piore [1971], Osterman's secondary sector contained jobs with low wages, employment instability, little or no opportunity for advancement, and no due process. We excluded the independent primary sector because it contained only 52 workers. After this exclusion, the sample size was 757.[5]

The categorical working-conditions variables were coded such that an increase in the value of a variable indicated a "worsening" of workplace quality. If the labor market offers compensating wage differentials for disagreeable work, all of the estimated coefficients on our work-environment variables should be positive. Summary statistics and variable

Table 7.1

Statistics for the Sample from the 1977 Quality of Employment Survey

	All	Subordinate Primary	Secondary
Experience	17.235	17.651	15.704
	(12.167)	(12.161)	(12.104)
Experience^2	444.927	459.219	392.307
	(550.424)	(558.138)	(519.176)
Tenure	4.940	5.069	4.466
	(1.882)	(1.858)	(1.894)
Tenure^2	27.940	29.149	23.511
	(18.564)	(18.558)	(17.947)
Log Hourly Earnings	1.635	1.710	1.364
	(.532)	(.527)	(.457)

Proportion of Sample:

	All	Subordinate Primary	Secondary
Married	.681	.708	.580
Living in Urban Area	.697	.694	.705
Living in the South	.499	.494	.517
Living in NE or NC	.501	.506	.483
Male	.613	.657	.449
Collective Bargaining	.343	.360	.284

Plant Size:

	All	Subordinate Primary	Secondary
1-9	.153	.154	.151
10-49	.285	.281	.297
50-99	.120	.126	.099
100-499	.210	.212	.203
500-999	.072	.060	.116
1,000-1,999	.052	.050	.058
2,000+	.108	.116	.076

Industry :

	All	Subordinate Primary	Secondary
Mining	.028	.031	.017
Construction	.072	.073	.068
Durable	.181	.205	.091
Nondurable	.123	.131	.091

Table 7.1 (continued)

	All	Subordinate Primary	Secondary
Industry			
Transportation & Public Utilities	.092	.094	.085
Wholesale & Retail Trade	.184	.179	.205
Finance, Insurance & Real Estate	.072	.066	.091
Business & Personal Services	.029	.022	.057
Professional Services	.211	.191	—
Occupational :			
Professional & Technical	.144	.184	—
Managerial	.117	.148	—
Sales	.028	.035	—
Clerical	.174	.133	.324
Service	.097	.008	.426
Private	.002	—	.011
Craft	.188	.239	—
Operatives	.198	.234	.063
Laborer	.039	.019	.176
Education :			
Grades 1-7	.029	.022	.057
Grade 8	.039	.035	.051
Grade 9-11	.127	.116	.170
Grade 12 or equiv.	.407	.395	.449
Some College	.187	.185	.193
Jr. College	.041	.046	.023
College Graduate	.086	.099	.040
Grad Training	.084	.102	.017
Working Conditions :			
My job is/requires (1 = strongly agree, 4 = strongly disagree):			
No New Learning	1.791 (.795)	1.756 (.775)	1.919 (.852)
Lacks Freedom	2.387 (.866)	2.354 (.860)	2.508 (.880)

Table 7.1 (continued)
Statistics for the Sample from the 1977 Quality of Employment Survey

	All	Subordinate Primary	Secondary
Working Conditions			
Lacks Creativity	2.339	2.275	2.572
	(.856)	(.858)	(.808)
Meaningless	1.963	1.929	2.086
	(.702)	(.691)	(.730)
My job is/requires (1 = strongly disagree, 4 = strongly agree):			
Work hard (hard)	2.875	2.862	2.924
	(.775)	(.784)	(.741)
Repetitive	2.647	2.571	2.929
	(.866)	(.874)	(.774)
My job is/requires (1 = very true, 4 = not at all true):			
No Advancement	2.698	2.674	2.788
	(1.048)	(1.044)	(1.061)
Bad Commute	1.837	1.824	1.890
	(.996)	(.983)	(1.042)
Bad Hours	1.842	1.870	1.738
	(.914)	(.909)	(.928)
Danger* (yes)	.727	.738	.685
	(.446)	(.440)	(.466)
Working outside in bad weather (yes)	.291	.299	.261
	(.454)	(.458)	(.440)
Observations (N)	757	592	165

Notes: Standard deviations are in parentheses.
* Danger = 1 if respondent answered yes to the presence of one of the following in the workplace: dangerous chemicals; danger from fire, burns, or shock; air pollution from dust, smoke, gas, or fumes; things stored dangerously; dangerous tools or machinery; risk of catching disease; risk of traffic accident while working; risk of personal attack by people or animals; dangerous work methods.

definitions are presented in table 7.1.

To establish a "baseline" measure of the gender wage gap, we estimated equation (1) without controls for occupation or working conditions. These results are in table 7.2, column 1. Across occupations, men earned 26.3 percent more than women. Controls for broad occupational group are added in column 2. Within these groups, the gender wage gap was narrowed, as the estimated male coefficient fell to 21.8 percent, a decrease of 17.1 percent from the column 1 results. This reduction in the estimated male/female wage gap is consistent with the findings in the occupational segregation literature.[6] The reduction in the male coefficient implies that women are in lower-paying occupations than men, but does not address the question of why female occupations pay less than male occupations.

A comparison of columns 1 and 3 reveals that the wage gap also fell when working conditions were added to the estimated wage equation. This result is consistent with Filer [1985]. It suggests that women tend to be in jobs for which the overall working-conditions compensation is less than the compensation for the working-conditions of jobs held by men. Notice, however, that these results do not necessarily indicate that women have better working conditions than men. The reduced wage gap may occur because compensating payments are positive and women are in jobs with "better" working conditions, or because compensation is negative and women have "worse" working conditions.

In order to draw the conclusion that the sex composition of occupations is important in explaining wage differences, all other characteristics of workers and their jobs must be held constant, including working conditions. Adding occupation to the "baseline" estimate lowered the male coefficient by 17.1 percent (columns 1 and 2), while adding occupation to the "baseline" plus working conditions estimate lowers the male coefficient by 13.0 percent (columns 3 and 4).[7] Thus our results are generally consistent with Treiman, Hartmann, and Roos [1984] in suggesting that occupational segregation seems to be an important force explaining the observed gender difference in wages, independent of controls for working conditions. The cause of this segregation remains an open question.

Segmented labor markets theory points to the existence of structural differences in compensation, working conditions, and the gender composition of employment across certain segments of the larger labor market. As a preliminary check for structural differences, the sample used in table 7.2 was broken down into two segments: (1) subordinate primary and (2) secondary. Results for the subordinate primary and the secondary sectors

Table 7.2
Subordinate Primary and Secondary Sectors Together

	(1)	(2)	(3)	(4)
Male	.26343***	.21835***	.23648***	.20564***
	(.03471)	(.03689)	(.03725)	(.03843)
Education:				
High School	.10004**	.05334	.08228	.05231
	(.06046)	(.06008)	(.06016)	(.06020)
Some College	.24447***	.15272***	.22211***	.15877***
	(.0655)	(.06633)	(.06574)	(.06674)
College Grad	.41771***	.27296***	.38657***	.28212***
	(.07613)	(.07902)	(.07636)	(.07917)
Grad Training	.59920***	.42604***	.57523***	.44667***
	(.08174)	(.08793)	(.08276)	(.08852)
Experience	.00935***	.00734	.00878**	.00767**
	(.00460)	(.00451)	(.00457)	(.00451)
Experience²	−.0001	.00002	.00003	.00002
	(.00009)	(.00009)	(.00009)	(.00009)
Tenure	.13398***	.12667***	.13511***	.13023***
	(.04123)	(.04045)	(.04105)	(.04070)
Tenure²	−.00914***	−.00944***	−.00949***	
	(.00426)	(.00417)	(.00423)	

Working Conditions

Lacks Freedom		-.01251 (.01867)	-.00762 (.01853)
Hard		.01436 (.01939)	.01227 (.01921)
Repetitive		.04269*** (.01818)	-.03158** (.01804)
Dangera		-.03214 (.03464)	-.01014 (.03538)
Bad Hours		.01367 (.01647)	-.01934 (.01644)
No Advancement		.03862*** (.01444)	-.03230*** (.01437)
Weather		.05397* (.03675)	.03317 (.03690)
Bad Commute		.01557 (.01455)	.01595 (.01438)
Lacks Creativity		.03278* (.02088)	.03237* (.02078)
Meaningless		.01198 (.02395)	-.00789 (.02369)
No New Learning		.04171*** (.02123)	-.02891 (.02177)
Plant Size:			
50-99	.06106 (.04726)	.04814 (.04631)	.04077 (.04634)
100-499	.00903 (.04014)	.02264 (.03926)	.01739 (.03970)
500-999	-.00922 (.05924)	.02260 (.05821)	.02554 (.05824)

Table 7.2 (continued)
Subordinate Primary and Secondary Sectors Together

	(1)	(2)	(3)	(4)
Plant Size:				
1,000+	.16589***	.19711***	.15736***	.18237***
	(.04794)	(.04072)	(.04878)	(.04825)
Collective Bargaining	.15077***	.16392***	.17495***	.17611***
	(.03307)	(.03357)	(.03329)	(.03386)
Constant	.74021***	.96051***	.97628***	1.06439***
	(.1226)	(.1329)	(.1624)	(.1655)
Occupation[b]		j		j
Industry	x	x	x	x
Observations(N)	757	757	757	757
R-squared (adj)	.4767	.5043	.4913	.5094

Notes: Standard errors are in parentheses.
Other variables included in each equation: dummy variables for urban, South, marital status.
aSee definition of danger in table 7.1.
bOccupational dummy variables: managerial, sales, clerical, craft, operative, laborer, service, private (professional and technical excluded).
j Joint test for occupations is statistically significant at 5%.
x Industry dummies were included in the regression.
*Statistically significant at 15% (two-tailed test).
**Statistically significant at 10% (two-tailed test).
***Statistically significant at 5% (two-tailed test).

are presented in tables 7.3 and 7.4, respectively.[8]

In the subordinate primary sector (table 7.3), adding working conditions had a negative effect on the male/female wage gap: working conditions lowered the male coefficient by 12.9 percent (columns 1 and 3). If estimated compensating wage differentials were positive, this would suggest that women are in jobs with "better" working conditions. However, the estimated working conditions coefficients were mixed.[9] Many of the estimates were negative, not positive; for example, jobs with disagreeable hours (represented by the variable "Bad Hours") or that are repetitive ("Repetitive") or provide no opportunity for learning ("No New Learning") had negative and statistically significant compensating payments. These negative coefficients are problematic for the equalizing differences hypothesis. However, recall that a central characteristic of jobs in the subordinate primary sector is the presence of internal labor markets, administrative structures that shield jobs from competition and create an environment where compensating wage differentials might not be expected.

In the secondary sector (table 7.4), the addition of working conditions to the "baseline" estimate (a comparison of columns 1 and 3) increased the male-female wage gap by 16.4 percent. This result suggests that the extent of gender discrimination in the secondary sector is underestimated when controls for working conditions are absent. Also, in contrast to the subordinate primary-sector results, there is some weak evidence of positive compensating wage differentials in the secondary sector (jobs that are hard ("Hard") pay a wage premium, as do those with work tasks that require less creativity ("Lacks Creativity")).[10] Thus, contrary to Filer's [1985] more general results, women in the secondary sector are in jobs with worse working conditions, for which they receive positive compensating payments.

One of the remaining questions concerning the accuracy of our findings is the endogeneity of labor-market segments. If workers choose occupations (and therefore labor-market segments) based on expected earnings and other job characteristics, then the factors influencing workers' labor market locations (primary versus secondary) are likely to be correlated with their observed wages, creating the potential for endogeneity bias in our results. We investigated this issue using the switching regressions model found in Lee [1978]. We first estimated a maximum likelihood probit for labor-market sector and then estimated wage equations for the subordinate primary and secondary sectors, incorporating estimated Mills ratios from results of the first-stage probit. The results of

Table 7.3
Subordinate Primary Sector

	(1)	(2)	(3)	(4)
Male	.27183***	.26605***	.23683***	.24335***
	(.04131)	(.04568)	(.04481)	(.04759)
Education:				
High School	.04373	.01918	.02414	.00753
	(.07543)	(.07607)	(.07532)	(.07650)
Some College	.17626***	.11662	.15519**	.11532
	(.08099)	(.08323)	(.08146)	(.08391)
College Grad	.33942***	.24467***	.31087***	.24511***
	(.09147)	(.09524)	(.09170)	(.09555)
Grad Training	.50026***	.41363***	.49445***	.43508***
	(.09998)	(.1053)	(.1010)	(.1065)
Experience	.00762	.00627	.00740	.00647
	(.00546)	(.00544)	(.00541)	(.00545)
Experience²	.00003	.00006	.00003	.00005
	(.00011)	(.00011)	(.00011)	(.00011)
Tenure	.11466***	.11270***	.12721***	.12359***
	(.04914)	(.04899)	(.04903)	(.04927)
Tenure²	-.00723*	-.00778	-.00857	-.00874*
	(.00501)	(.00500)	(.00500)	(.00501)
Working Conditions				
Lacks Freedom			-.01150	-.00477
			(.02254)	(.02271)
Hard			.00112	-.00461
			(.02283)	(.02294)

160

Repetitive			.03284* (.02110)	-.03007* (.02118)
Danger[a]			-.03378 (.04192)	-.02565 (.04321)
Bad Hours			-.03293** (.01948)	-.03437* (.01973)
No Advancement			-.04754*** (.01703)	-.04036*** (.01718)
Weather			.05256 (.04328)	.04981 (.04370)
Bad Commute			.02438 (.01738)	.02104 (.01736)
Lacks Creativity			.02958 (.02516)	.03179 (.02538)
Meaningless			.00696 (.02871)	.00531 (.02861)
No New Learning			-.04174* (.02558)	-.02957 (.02592)
Plant Size:				
50-99	.06314 (.05437)	.05934 (.05423)	.05599 (.05421)	.05566 (.05444)
100-499	.02337 (.04701)	.02766 (.04665)	.02564 (.04748)	.02821 (.04752)
500-999	.04224 (.07543)	.03852 (.07480)	.04962 (.07513)	.04318 (.07494)
1,000+	.17352*** (.05571)	.18527*** (.05529)	.16035*** (.05671)	.16965*** (.05668)

Table 7.3 (continued)
Subordinate Primary Sector

	(1)	(2)	(3)	(4)
Collective Bargaining	.13054*** (.03805)	.15992*** (.03918)	.14978*** (.03869)	.16880*** (.03983)
Constant	.79501*** (.1470)	.96145 (.1577)	1.03347*** (.1912)	1.11569*** (.1982)
Occupation[b]		j		j
Industry	x	x	x	x
Observations (N)	592	592	592	592
R-squared (adj)	.4361	.4495	.4485	.4546

Notes: Standard errors are in parentheses.
Other variables included in each equation: dummy variables for urban, South, marital status.
[a]See definition of danger in table 7.1.
[b]Occupational dummy variables: managerial, sales, clerical, craft, operative, laborer, service (professional and technical excluded).
j Joint test for occupations is statistically significant at 5%.
x Industry dummies were included in the regression.
*Statistically significant at 15% (two-tailed test).
**Statistically significant at 10% (two-tailed test).
***Statistically significant at 5% (two-tailed test).

162

Table 7.4
Secondary Sector

	(1)	(2)	(3)	(4)
Male	.17521***	.13253***	.20399***	.18328***
	(.06480)	(.06064)	(.06910)	(.06448)
Education:				
High School	.10455	.01439	.11476	.02255
	(.09624)	(.08778)	(.09629)	(.08847)
Some College	.25449***	.12878	.19326*	.07412
	(.1079)	(.09900)	(.1106)	(.1018)
College Grad	.18112	.10498	.16981	.05750
	(.1626)	(.1510)	(.1607)	(.1521)
Grad Training	.49343***	.42875***	.65087***	.51772***
	(.2107)	(.1898)	(.2214)	(.2010)
Experience	.01876***	.01949***	.01174	.01426*
	(.00841)	(.00760)	(.00881)	(.00802)
Experience²	-.00031**	-.00033***	-.00011	-.00018
	(.00019)	(.00017)	(.00019)	(.00018)
Tenure	.17306***	.19545***	.21321***	.23739***
	(.07401)	(.06682)	(.07595)	(.06934)
Tenure²	-.01493***	-.01860***	-.01988***	-.02336*
	(.00194)	(.00718)	(.00813)	(.00743)
Working Conditions				
Lacks Freedom			-.02776	-.01335
			(.03289)	(.02986)
Hard			.12359***	.11444***
			(.03832)	(.03689)

Table 7.4 (continued)
Secondary Sector

	(1)	(2)	(3)	(4)
Repetitive			-.04525	-.02903
			(.03751)	(.03401)
Danger[a]			-.04519	.01340
			(.06086)	(.05719)
Bad Hours			.03895	.03951*
			(.03007)	(.02748)
No Advancement			-.03264	-.02893
			(.02808)	(.02545)
Weather			-.00198	-.03235
			(.07108)	(.03487)
Bad Commute			-.03374	-.03318
			(.02786)	(.02546)
Lacks Creativity			.06461*	.03832
			(.03588)	(.03328)
Meaningless			-.02650	.00623
			(.04189)	(.03869)
No New Learning			-.03608	-.03235
			(.03790)	(.03487)
Plant Size:				
50-99	.05044	.06256	.10236	.11015
	(.09563)	(.08610)	(.09609)	(.08713)
100-499	.00725	.01345	.03363	.04190
	(.07459)	(.06710)	(.07392)	(.06696)

	(1)	(2)	(3)	(4)
500-999	-.03926	-.02285	-.05019	-.05815
	(.09190)	(.08358)	(.09164)	(.08411)
1,000+	.15119*	.20283***	.19529***	.22533***
	(.09249)	(.08412)	(.09563)	(.08681)
Collective Bargaining	.26184***	.31668***	.27725***	.32036***
	(.06790)	(.06554)	(.06872)	(.06609)
Constant	.86753***	.93846***	.71863***	.75203***
	(.2178)	(.1963)	(.2903)	(.2846)
Occupation[b]		j		j
Industry	x	x	x	x
Observations (N)	165	165	165	165
R-squared (adj)	.5196	.6132	.5479	.6329

Notes: Standard errors are in parentheses.
Other variables included in each equation: dummy variables for urban, South, marital status.
[a]See definition of danger in table 7.1.
[b]Occupational dummy variables: clerical, service, private household (operatives and laborers excluded).
j Joint test for occupations is statistically significant at 5%.
x Industry dummies were included in the regression.
*Statistically significant at 15% (two-tailed test).
**Statistically significant at 10% (two-tailed test).
***Statistically significant at 5% (two-tailed test).

Table 7.5
Probability of Subordinate Primary Employment

	(1)	(2)
Male	.50523***	.47859***
	(.1158)	(.1342)
Education:		
High School	.39084**	.32450*
	(.2071)	(.2135)
Some College	.59458***	.48132***
	(.2301)	(.2398)
College Grad	1.1000***	.96582***
	(.3036)	(.3167)
Grad Training	1.42805***	1.22733***
	(.3409)	(.3549)
Experience	−.00342	−.00376
	(.00560)	(.00576)
Tenure	.09127***	.08253***
	(.03445)	(.03558)
Collective Bargaining	−.01906	.03465
	(.1213)	(.1265)
Working Conditions		
Lacks Freedom		.06840
		(.07060)
Hard		−.10283
		(.07413)
Repetitive		−.19876***
		(.07231)

166

Danger		.04800
		(.1304)
Bad Hours		.09762
		(.06335)
No Advancement		-.03513
		(.05507)
Weather		-.08123
		(.1359)
Bad Commute		-.09242***
		(.05507)
Lacks Creativity		-.05316
		(.07748)
Meaningless		-.12425
		(.09051)
No New Learning		-.02527
		(.07841)
Constant	-.40629***	.91483**
	(.2704)	(.4986)
Log L	-363.88	-353.18

Notes: Specification of each equation includes dummy variables for urban, South, marital status.
Standard errors are in parentheses.
* Statistically significant at 15%.
** Statistically significant at 10%.
*** Statistically significant at 5%

Table 7.6
Earnings Functions with Selectivity Correction

	Subordinate Primary		Secondary	
	(1)	(2)	(3)	(4)
Male	.18400*	.17389***	-.63242	-.29607
	(.1198)	(.08672)	(2.593)	(.5380)
Education:				
High School	-.03018	-.02198	-.50782	.15225
	(.1165)	(.08937)	(1.986)	(.3699)
Some College	.06804	.09050	-.67002	.27151
	(.1567)	(.1086)	(2.979)	(.5345)
College Grad	.16361	.19854	-1.57623	.32504
	(.2406)	(.1600)	(5.655)	(1.092)
Grad Training	.29387	.36901***	-1.8811	.87999
	(.2810)	(.1788)	(7.607)	(1.448)
Experience	.00805	.00799	.02252	.01121
	(.00524)	(.00523)	(.02877)	(.00854)
Experience ^{2}	.00003	.00003	-.00027	-.00011
	(.00011)	(.00010)	(.00057)	(.00017)
Tenure	.09369*	.11280***	.04263	.22216***
	(.05391)	(.04989)	(.4777)	(.1099)
Tenure ^{2}	-.00667	-.00818	-.01646	-.01938***
	(.00488)	(.00482)	(.02408)	(.00713)
Working Conditions				
Lacks Freedom	-.02202			-.01794
	(.02510)			(.07771)

	(1)	(2)	(3)	(4)
Hard	.09391 (.1160)	.01541 (.02794)		
Repetitive	-.07873 (.2253)	-.00940 (.03940)		
Danger	-.04067 (.07614)	-.04044 (.04142)		
Bad Hours	-.06586 (.1116)	-.04523*** (.02391)		
No Advancement	-.04195 (.04511)	-.04243*** (.01760)		
Weather	-.01871 (.1060)	-.05954 (.04312)		
Bad Commute	-.05860 (.1044)	.03588** (.02173)		
Lacks Creativity	.05242 (.06921)	.02839 (.02618)		
Meaningless	-.03677 (.1370)	.02263 (.03336)		
No New Learning	-.04800 (.04291)	-.03743* (.02503)		
Plant Size:				
50-99	.09235 (.08608)	.05422 (.05300)	.06415 (.05388)	.04509 (.2888)
100-499	.04175 (.06453)	.02595 (.04622)	.02504 (.04630)	.01402 (.2218)
500-999	-.04094 (.08369)	.05178 (.07309)	.04688 (.07386)	-.03586 (.2781)
1,000+	.19363*** (.08369)	.16291*** (.05503)	.17577*** (.05455)	.15107 (.2692)

Table 7.6 (continued)
Earnings Functions with Selectivity Correction

| | Subordinate Primary | | Secondary | |
	(1)	(2)	(3)	(4)
Collective Bargaining	.13089***	.14171***	.29271	.26571***
	(.03769)	(.03895)	(.2166)	(.07340)
Constant	1.18043***	1.15495***	-.13644	1.23026
	(.5068)	(.2334)	(3.197)	(2.171)
Lambda	-.41898	-.31724	2.1124	.25104
	(.5235)	(.3705)	(6.708)	(1.493)
R-squared	.4357	.4472	.5189	.5533

Notes: Specification of each equation includes dummy variables for urban, South, marital status.
Standard errors are in parentheses.
* Statistically significant at 15%.
** Statistically significant at 10%.
*** Statistically significant at 5%.

this estimation are reported in tables 7.5 and 7.6. The selectivity coefficients are, in all cases, statistically insignificant, and the findings from the ordinary least squares (OLS) estimation appear fairly robust to changes in estimation technique.

It is worth noting that the probit results reveal that men are more likely to be employed in the subordinate primary sector than are women, holding human capital characteristics constant. Years of education and job tenure are also positively related to subordinate primary employment. The estimated effect of gender is only slightly smaller when working conditions are added to the probit equation (column 2). Individuals who report that their jobs are repetitious are less likely to be employed in the subordinate primary sector, as are individuals who report that travel time is inconvenient.

While the switching regression results suggest that endogeneity of segments is not a serious problem for the OLS sectoral wage equations, an issue we have not addressed is the effect of using a priori judgments to define labor-market segments. Both the OLS and switching regression techniques use prior judgments in determining labor-market segments. The method of endogenous switching with unknown regimes introduced by Dickens and Lang [1985] addresses this problem. However, the Dickens-Lang technique is difficult computationally, particularly for data sets like ours with a relatively small sample size and a large number of explanatory variables. Without a larger data set, attempts to address this issue using the Dickens-Lang technique are unlikely to be fruitful.

III. DISCUSSION

Past attempts to explore the interaction between working conditions and the male/female wage gap have found that controlling for work characteristics reduces the estimated wage gap (Filer [1985]). However, the existence of structural differences across labor-market segments suggests that specifications assuming a competitive labor market may yield misleading results. When we allow for segmentation in the labor market, an interesting pattern emerges in the results on estimated compensating payments and the link between working conditions and gender discrimination.

In the secondary sector of the labor market, where the only statistically significant working conditions coefficients are also positive ("Hard" and "Lacks Creativity"), there exist at least weak tendencies toward equalizing differences in pay. This may be due to the fact that the secondary sector is more reliant on competitive labor markets for allocating labor resources.[11] Contrary to results for the entire labor market, the introduction of working conditions into estimated wage equations increases the estimated male/female wage gap in the secondary sector.[12] For the addition of working conditions to have this effect on the estimated gender wage gap, women must have "worse" working conditions when compensating payments are positive and/or "better" working conditions when compensating payments are negative. The statistically significant working-conditions coefficients may arguably shed the most light on which of the two effects is dominant. As seen from table 7.7, women report "worse" working conditions for both Hard and Lacks Creativity variables and each generates positive compensating payments.

The results for the subordinate primary segment of the labor market reveal no general tendency toward wage payments that equalize differences in working conditions. Given the prominence of internal labor markets in the subordinate primary sector, where employment relationships are long-term and where labor resources are allocated by a combination of custom, tradition, and merit, the absence of such a tendency is perhaps neither surprising nor particularly troubling. However, the results may also stem from a categorization procedure that fails to accurately capture the subordinate primary labor market, or from the fact that the subordinate primary sector itself contains a number of separate and distinct labor market subsegments that, when pooled, provide misleading results. Both possibilities strike us as plausible lines for further inquiry.[13]

The introduction of working conditions to estimated wage equations in the subordinate primary sector reduces the estimated wage gap. This suggests that women have better working conditions than their male counterparts when positive compensation for disagreeable working conditions exists and/or worse working conditions when such compensation is negative. If only the former pattern were present, an explanation involving unrestrained rational choice and the different preferences of men and women over working conditions might be the most plausible. But the appearance of this second pattern of wage differentials across working conditions would give cause for seriously qualifying that interpretation.

The results do not reveal a clear pattern of combinations of compensating payments and relative working-conditions quality; however, we also find little evidence for the existence of positive compensating wage differentials in the subordinate primary sector. Looking only at the statistically significant working-conditions coefficients, for example, work

Table 7.7
Sample Means for Working-Conditions Variables

	All		Subordinate Primary		Secondary	
	Male	Female	Male	Female	Male	Female
Lacks Freedom	2.271**	2.573	2.247**	2.563	2.423	2.578
	(.868)	(.839)	(.852)	(.839)	(.919)	(.845)
Hard	2.825**	2.955	2.819*	2.945	2.857	2.978
	(.799)	(.729)	(.793)	(.762)	(.838)	(.652)
Repetitive	2.525**	2.836	2.462**	2.783	2.894	2.957
	(.864)	(.835)	(.855)	(.873)	(.825)	(.732)
No Advancement	2.578**	2.891	2.530**	2.953	2.833	2.750
	(1.035)	(1.041)	(1.032)	(1.013)	(1.024)	(1.095)
No New Learning	1.764	1.832	1.725	1.814	1.974	1.873
	(.772)	(.829)	(.747)	(.825)	(.867)	(.841)
Bad Hours	1.920**	1.718	1.938**	1.738	1.820	1.670
	(.923)	(.887)	(.907)	(.901)	(1.003)	(.859)
Bad Commute	1.915**	1.714	1.888**	1.700	2.064**	1.747
	(1.014)	(.954)	(.997)	(.946)	(1.097)	(.978)
Lacks Creativity	2.260**	2.464	2.216**	2.392	2.500	2.631
	(.834)	(.877)	(.815)	(.927)	(.894)	(.730)
Meaningless	1.989	1.919	1.947	1.894	2.217**	1.978
	(.722)	(.668)	(.703)	(.669)	(.783)	(.668)
Danger	.830**	.574	.840**	.559	.772**	.608
	(.378)	(.496)	(.366)	(.497)	(.422)	(.491)
Weather	.418	.097	.411**	.099	.456**	.093
	(.493)	(.287)	(.492)	(.299)	(.501)	(.292)

Table 7.7 (continued)
Sample Means for Working-Conditions Variables

	All		Subordinate Primary		Secondary	
	Male	Female	Male	Female	Male	Female
Ln Wages	1.8149**	1.3411	1.858**	1.4138	1.5842**	1.1811
	(.4863)	(.4688)	(.4816)	(.4883)	(.4473)	(.3785)

Notes: Standard deviations are in parentheses.
 * Means are significantly different at 10%.
 ** Means are significantly different at 5%.

that is repetitious or provides few opportunities for promotion is associated with a significant wage reduction and women report being in jobs that are worse in both respects compared to men. Lower wages are also associated with inconvenience in working hours; however, men report more inconvenience than women with regard to this working condition.

The general devaluation of women's work is an important theme in the institutional literature on gender discrimination.[14] The fact that men and women face different job-evaluation schemes and different promotion ladders (Treiman [1979]; Remick [1984]; Hartmann [1987]) may lend insight into possible explanations for some of our results.[15] For example, if for working-conditions characteristics shared in common by both men and women the attached weights determining the wage are greater for men than for women, a pattern of observed negative compensation could occur. Men would have higher wages for any given work quality level, but the lower payment for undesirable work that employers face in the case of female jobs could produce an incentive for them to worsen the quality of working conditions for women relative to men.[16] The short promotion ladders found in women's occupations would only serve to exacerbate these observed differences in wages.[17]

Earlier work has shown that there exist differences in the returns to education and experience in the primary and secondary sectors of the labor market. The results of our analysis suggest that the segments contain structurally different compensating payments as well. Identifying the differing institutional arrangements that support gender discrimination in different segments of the labor market is a fruitful area for further research. Policies that address the problem will be successful to the extent that they are tailored to the institutional forces that perpetuate discriminatory practices. Our results give further credence to the view that these forces may not be the same in separate segments of the labor market.

It seems equally crucial that we begin to explore further the nature of labor-market segmentation. For example, does the process of segmentation owe its origin to the creation of efficient institutional arrangements for labor allocation (Doeringer and Piore [1971]), to the need for controlling workers in very different production settings (Gordon, Edwards, and Reich [1982]), or to the payment of efficiency wages (Bulow and Summers [1986])? More important, perhaps, is the question of the role that gender itself plays in the segmentation process. To date, gender categories have entered the analysis of segmented labor markets in rather ad hoc ways, largely after the segments themselves have been created.[18]

IV. CONCLUSION

This chapter has focused on the role of working conditions in explaining the male/female wage gap in the context of segmented labor markets. Tendencies toward equalizing differences in labor-market outcomes appear to be stronger in the secondary segment of the labor market than in the subordinate primary segment. Estimates of the wage gap that do not control for working-conditions differences may understate the extent of wage discrimination in the secondary sector since women tend to have worse working conditions than men for those conditions for which positive compensating payments exist. The tendencies toward equalizing differences are not very great in the subordinate primary segment of the labor market, where internal labor markets serve as the primary allocative mechanism. While controlling for working conditions reduces the male/female wage gap in this sector, the pattern of wages across working conditions makes it difficult to attribute this reduction to the unhindered choices of women.

PART III

SUPPLY-SIDE RESPONSES TO INEQUITY

When there is ascriptive inequity, when groups of people face unequal situations in markets because of their races or genders, how do they respond? This part of the volume explores how our analysis must be adapted to incorporate the responses made by people who face such inequity in markets. These chapters look at both racial/ethnic inequity and sexual inequity and both find that measures of discrimination that ignore the responses people make to the inequity they face, especially in markets for labor, severely bias these measures – though sometimes the bias is to make the inequity appear smaller than is justified (suggested by chapter 8) and sometimes the bias is in the opposite direction (suggested by chapter 9).

In chapter 8, Harriet Duleep and Nadja Zalokar draw on a recent series of studies, completed by themselves and by other colleagues at the U.S. Commission on Civil Rights, entitled Incomes of Americans, of the earnings of several groups relative to those of non-Hispanic whites. These studies describe great inequality within ascriptive groups as well as between groups. Duleep and Zalokar argue that conventional decompositions following Oaxaca [1973] of the total earnings differential between two groups into explained (due to measured differences in productivity) and unexplained, or discriminatory, portions may be misleading since they ignore possible responses people may have already made to inequity they anticipated when they acquired education or chose where to look for work, etc. Further, the conventional approach to measuring discrimination only uncovers the amount of discrimination faced on average by members of a particular group as a whole and thus such records can obliterate discrimination experienced by different subgroups within this group. The conven-

tional averages also ignore any distinction between 'market discrimination' and 'market segregation,' a distinction which Duleep and Zalokar
suggest is important for analysis of racial inequity.

In a complementary supply-side analysis, Solomon Polachek and Charng
Kao look at the responsiveness of women and men to expectations of
interruptions in careers and to their anticipated peak salaries. At the time
of entry into a career, e.g., at the completion of an M.B.A. degree, men and
women may have equal salaries, but may anticipate significant differences
in both peak salaries and in interruptions to raise children, etc. as found by
Gordon and Strober [1978] and updated by Strober [1982]. In a pioneering
study, Mincer and Polachek [1974] traced the economic implications of
such inequality in expectations and in chapter 9, Polachek and Kao
introduce expectations of lifetime rates of work participation into Ben-
Porath's (1967) life-cycle model of human-capital formation to show how
expectations about intermittent periods of wage and nonwage work can
affect investments in human capital and they devise a technique for
estimation that incorporates this component of human capital. They find
substantial similarity between the results using data from the 1960 and
1980 U.S. censuses and from the 1987 Taiwan Manpower Utilization
Survey. They show that between 70 and 90 percent of the observed male/
female wage gap can be explained, resulting in an unexplained portion of
10 to 30 percent, which is far lower than the 40 to 60 percent which is
estimated conventionally.

Thus differences in anticipated lifetime earning/work options can lead
to "talking career, [but] thinking job" as Machung [1989] found for female
seniors at Berkeley in 1985. That differences in potential earnings may lead
to differences in perceived productivity played an important role in the
arguments in chapter 2 by William Darity, chapter 3 by Michael Robinson
and Phanindra Wunnava, chapter 4 by Rhonda Williams, and Chapter 5
by William Bielby. Chapter 11 by Elaine McCrate also provides some
evidence of adaptation to discrimination; namely, that anticipated premarket and market discrimination may explain why teenage women
become mothers rather than concentrating on schooling and post-school-
ing investment. By attempting to quantify more of the unobserved
differences among people rather than just attributing unexplained differences in earnings to either "culture" or "discrimination," chapter 9 is
closely related both to chapter 11 by McCrate and to chapter 12 by
Stephen Woodbury. Finally, by focusing on supply-side responses rather
than demand-side factors in the search for causes and institutions which
maintain social inequity, the chapters in this part provide a clear comple-

ment to the ideological tone of Steven Shulman's discussion in chapter 1 of the racial gap in unemployment and the discussion in the previous part of this volume by William Bielby, James Baron, David Fairris and Lori Kletzer of gender barriers.

8
The Measurement of Labor-Market Discrimination When Minorities Respond to Discrimination

Harriet Orcutt Duleep and
Nadja Zalokar

Labor-market discrimination may not affect all individuals within a minority group equally. Some subgroups may experience greater discrimination than others, and some labor markets may be more discriminatory than others. When one is formulating policies to combat discrimination, it is important to know where to direct antidiscrimination efforts. Essential to this endeavor is determining where labor-market discrimination is worse: for which groups and subgroups and for which labor markets.

Using micro data from the 1940 through 1980 censuses, we have examined in a series of studies entitled *Incomes of Americans* the earnings of several minority groups relative to those of non-Hispanic whites.[1] Our comparisons of the earnings of minority groups with those of whites have provided information about variations in the relative earnings of minorities over time and by educational level, region of residence, age, and occupation. In undertaking the *Incomes of Americans* studies, our hope was that the comprehensive information we assembled would be useful to policymakers and civil-rights enforcement agencies in assessing where we are and where we need to go as we strive for equal opportunity for all Americans. Yet despite our finding great diversity in the measured incidence of discrimination across minority groups and across individuals within minority groups, we question in this chapter the extent to which estimates of minority/majority earnings differentials adjusted for differences in productive characteristics can serve as a useful guide to policy. Should policy efforts be focused on groups and labor markets where measured adjusted earnings differentials are greatest? We argue that labor-market discrimination may or may not be worst where adjusted earnings differentials are largest.

This chapter examines the implications of taking into account responses by individuals to discrimination. We argue that because individuals act, when possible, to minimize the effect of discrimination on their economic status, differences in adjusted earnings do not necessarily indicate where discrimination is worst. To understand fully the effect of discrimination on members of minority groups, it is necessary to develop theoretical and empirical models that take minority responses to discrimination into account.

I. BACKGROUND

The conventional economic analysis of labor-market discrimination derives from the theory of labor-market discrimination developed by Becker in his seminal work, *The Economics of Discrimination*. According to Becker's basic model of employer discrimination, the size of the wage differential between equally competent minority and majority members depends on two factors: (1) the shape of the distribution of employers by the extent to which they discriminate and (2) the size of the minority group.

A simplified version of Becker's employer discrimination model is illustrated in figure 8.1, which shows demand and supply of minority

Figure 8.1
Becker's Employer Discrimination Model

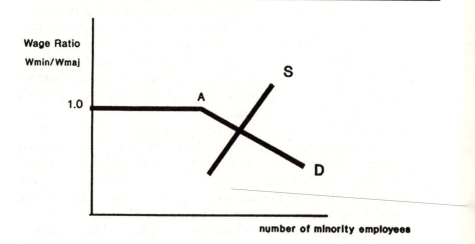

workers at different relative wages under the assumption that majority and minority workers are perfect substitutes. The demand schedule for minority workers, D, shows the total number of jobs that will be offered to members of the minority group at each minority/majority wage ratio. This demand schedule is formed by arranging the offers of employers according to the extent to which they discriminate. Employers who discriminate least are placed furthest to the left. Figure 8.1 assumes that no employers actually prefer members of minority groups, so that no jobs are forthcoming at a wage ratio greater than one; that a limited number of employers are indifferent between minority and majority workers, so that a fixed number of jobs are offered at a wage ratio equal to one; and that at successively lower wage ratios below one, more and more employers are willing to employ minority workers, and more and more jobs become available.

Given this demand schedule, the market equilibrium minority/majority wage ratio is determined by the position of the supply curve. If the supply curve intersects the demand curve to the left of point A, the equilibrium wage differential will be zero. If it intersects to the right of point A, minority workers will receive lower wages than majority workers. If the supply of minority workers increases, the equilibrium wage ratio falls. Becker referred to the resulting difference in compensation between equally productive members of the minority group and the majority group as "market discrimination."

Of course, discrimination may stem from prejudice on the part of employees or of consumers, prejudice that can, in turn, affect employers' decisions about hiring minority workers. Becker also discussed employee and consumer discrimination. One of his central results was that in the case of employee discrimination by majority workers who are perfect substitutes for members of the minority group, "market segregation" arises, with minority workers working in some firms, majority workers working in other firms, and integrated firms only existing to the extent that there exist nondiscriminatory majority employees. Yet because the wages of the minority group are equal to those of the majority group, there is no "market discrimination," as defined by Becker.

The theoretical framework developed by Becker was given empirical content by Duncan [1968], Oaxaca [1973], and Blinder [1973], who developed methods for measuring "market discrimination" but did not consider "market segregation." The standard approach to measuring market discrimination, usually called the "Oaxaca method," arose from their work. It is based on the following two regressions:

$$\ln y_i^{min} = \Sigma_j (X_{ij}^{min} \beta_j^{min}) + u_{ij}^{min}, \text{ and}$$

$$\ln y_i^{maj} = \Sigma_j (X_{ij}^{maj} \beta_j^{maj}) + u_{ij}^{maj},$$

where y_i denotes the earnings or wages of individual i and the X_j's include variables linked to a worker's productivity, such as education, experience, and region of residence. Then the overall average earnings differential between the majority and minority groups can be decomposed into the parts due to (1) productivity differences and (2) discrimination:

$$\overline{\ln y}^{maj} - \overline{\ln y}^{min} = \Sigma_j(\overline{X}_j^{maj}\hat{\beta}^{maj} - \overline{X}_j^{min}\hat{\beta}^{maj}) + \Sigma_j(\overline{X}_j^{min}\hat{\beta}^{maj} - \overline{X}_j^{min}\hat{\beta}^{min}).$$
$$(1) \qquad\qquad\qquad\qquad (2)$$

Specifically, the estimate of discrimination given in term (2),

$$D_{\overline{x}} = \Sigma_j \overline{X}_j^{min}(\hat{\beta}^{maj} - \hat{\beta}^{min}),$$

represents the difference between the logarithm of the wage earned by an average minority worker and the logarithm of the wage earned by a majority worker with the same productive characteristics as the average minority worker.[2]

Yet, from a policy perspective, it would be useful to know variations in market discrimination within a minority group as well as the average amount of market discrimination experienced by members of the minority group. Thus the Oaxaca approach for measuring market discrimination might be usefully supplemented by estimating an array of minority/majority earnings ratios, evaluated at different values of education, region, occupational groupings, and other variables that could help pinpoint where efforts to combat discrimination should be focused. In our work on the *Incomes of Americans* studies, we have made some efforts to evaluate earnings differences between minorities and non-Hispanic whites at various levels of key explanatory variables. Our work shows extensive variations in relative earnings across subgroups of minority groups.

Duleep's study of Asian Americans (Duleep [1988]) revealed that although the average American-born man in several Asian groups earns nearly as much or as much as a non-Hispanic white man with comparable skills and characteristics, highly educated Asian men earn less than their white counterparts. Further, Duleep found that the relative earnings of Asian men adjusted for productive characteristics also vary extensively according to region of residence. For instance, American-born Chinese men, three-quarters of whom live in the West, earn as much as non-Hispanic white men in California and more in Hawaii. Yet in the East, they earn 17 percent less than comparable non-Hispanic whites. American-born Filipinos, who on average earn substantially less than whites, earn as much as whites in the East and North Central regions of the United States.

In their study of black men, O'Neill et al. [1986] found that the relative earnings of black men also vary by level of education and region. Except for the youngest age group, the weekly wages of black men fall compared to those of white men as their education rises. In all age groups, black men earn substantially less relative to their white counterparts in the South than in the rest of the country.

Comparing black and white women, Zalokar [1990] found that when other characteristics are controlled for, the relative hourly wages of black women increase rather than decrease with education, as is the case for men. The hourly wages of black women with thirteen or more years of schooling actually exceed those of comparable white women. As is the case for black men, there are sizable regional differences in the relative wages of black women after controlling for other characteristics. Whereas the average black woman outside of the South earns 6 percent more than a comparable white woman, the average southern black woman earns 6 percent less.

II. MINORITY RESPONSES TO DISCRIMINATION

Our work points to a great diversity in the incidence of market discrimination across individuals within minority groups. Can we then conclude that where adjusted earnings differentials are greatest, discrimination is worst? Should policymakers channel their resources toward those groups and subgroups with the largest adjusted earnings differentials? More generally, what can we infer from variations in adjusted earnings differentials? Do they necessarily indicate where discrimination is worst, where attention should be focused, or where a situation has improved? Can such variations in adjusted earnings differentials be useful guides to public policy? [3]

Pondering these questions leads us to look again at the definition of discrimination offered by Becker. The emphasis on "market discrimination" by empirical followers of Becker may have caused researchers to lose sight of the true meaning of labor-market discrimination. Conventional empirical analysis appears to imply that if there is no market discrimination, then there is no discrimination problem; or, alternatively, if market discrimination is lower in one area than in another or in one set of vocations than in another, then there is less of a discrimination problem in the area or set of vocations exhibiting lower market discrimination.

These assertions do not necessarily follow. If members of a minority group are forced to take actions or to make decisions because of discrimination, then this represents a discrimination problem, even if they do not experience "market discrimination." For instance, a black family that cannot buy a home in a particular area is discriminated against even if the family is able to find an equally nice home at the same price in another community. This situation can be regarded as just as serious as if the family could not find an equally nice home or was forced to pay a higher price for its home. Yet measures of "market discrimination" would point to a discrimination problem only if the black family could not find an equally nice home or had to pay a higher price for its home. These concerns suggest that we should adopt a broader definition of what constitutes a discrimination problem. From a policy and legal perspective, discrimination is a problem if it induces an outcome or action that would not occur in the absence of discrimination.

The adjusted earnings differential approach of measuring discrimination (the Oaxaca method) focuses on uncovering market wage outcomes rather than the existence of discriminatory practices. It ignores actions that may be taken in response to labor-market discrimination and hence considers only one dimension of the discrimination problem.[4] Moreover, actions taken because of discrimination may themselves affect the level of market discrimination, making it difficult to know how to interpret measures of market discrimination.

One type of action that the adjusted wage differential approach ignores is the job-search behavior by members of a minority group that faces discrimination in a given labor market. Minority persons who are in a labor market that includes a significant number of discriminatory employers may have to search longer for a job that pays according to their qualifications than they would in the absence of such employers. They are not guaranteed that they will find a nondiscriminatory employer at the first place they apply for a job. This will be true even if there is a sufficient number of nondiscriminatory employers to ensure that the entire supply of minority workers can be hired at nondiscriminatory wages. Thus in figure 8.2,

Figure 8.2
Wage Ratio With and Without Discrimination

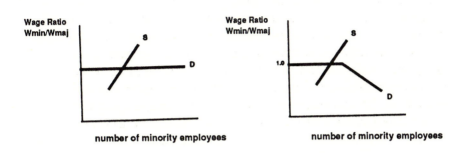

minority workers in the second labor market may have to search longer for a job than those in the first, even though there is no minority/majority wage differential in either market.[5]

Implicit in most of the empirical formulations of Becker's model is the assumption that the supply of a minority group in a labor market is inelastic with respect to the extent of discrimination in the labor market; that is, that minority members supply the same amount of labor regardless of the degree to which they are underpaid relative to comparable majority members.[6] It seems likely, however, that persons will reduce the quantity of labor they supply where their wages are depressed by discrimination. More generally, they will act to minimize the adverse effects of discrimination on their economic status.[7] Their actions may be as individuals, as families, or as groups. Individuals may alter their human-capital investment patterns, acquiring more or less education or training for different occupations in response to wage discrimination.[8] Moving from one region to another, as exemplified by the large twentieth-century migration of southern blacks to the North, may also be a response to discrimination. Self-employment may be another. Developing an economic niche that is controlled by members of the minority is another potential way of minimizing the effects of discrimination, as is seeking out alternative and less discriminatory consumer clientele.[9]

The type of response and the extent to which members of minority groups respond to discrimination in a given labor market depends on the costs to them of pursuing alternatives. By lowering the costs of alternatives, close-knit family structure, group cohesiveness, and mechanisms of social trust may be instrumental in facilitating certain responses. For instance, empirical work by George Borjas [1986] on the self-employment of immigrants provides evidence that the family plays an important role in determining who is self-employed. Particularly if there is discrimination in credit markets, the cost of pursuing self-employment may be lower for families than for individuals. For instance, families can pool savings to generate the capital necessary for self-employment ventures. As a result, groups characterized by a stable family structure may be more likely to pursue the self-employment alternative.

Group cohesiveness also lowers the cost of pursuing self-employment. Ivan Light [1972] has argued that a critical factor underlying the ability of a group to develop entrepreneurial activities is its use of informal methods of financial cooperation such as the rotating credit system "an association formed upon a core of participants who agree to make regular contributions to a fund which is given, in whole or in part, to each contributor in rotation" (Ardener [1964: 201]).[10]

Jiobu [1988] pointed out that in order for a minority to develop an economic niche or, in his words, to hegemonize an economic arena, the minority group must have some kind of leverage, such as "special knowledge or skills, a willingness to engage in businesses that the majority will not, or cannot, engage in" [225]. As an example, Jiobu pointed to the early Japanese immigrants who developed a niche in agricultural production by planting specialized crops that were labor-intensive, relying on family labor, applying scientific farming techniques, and using marginal lands that would respond to their farming methods. They further secured this niche by developing their own produce wholesaling. Jiobu argued that the social networks within the Japanese community facilitated this step: "Whether the wholesale produce business was unique in its requirements for informal trust is difficult to know. The point here, though, is that trust was required and that ethnicity reinforced it" [228].

As mentioned above, seeking a less discriminatory consumer clientele is another response to labor-market discrimination. Whether groups seek out less discriminatory customer markets depends upon the availability of such markets. For instance, Gary Becker [1971] suggested that nonwhite college graduates partially avoided white discrimination by catering to their own market.[11]

A relatively large fraction of non-white college graduates were, indeed, in occupations that cater to a segregated market: in 1940 about 50 percent of non-white graduates were doctors, dentists, clergymen, teachers, or lawyers, while only 35 percent of white graduates were engaged in these professions. The opportunities to cater to a segregated market were probably more available to southern graduates since the non-white market is both large (relative to supply) and more segregated there. Fewer opportunities to avoid discrimination are available to non-white high school graduates: the same fraction of whites and non-whites were in occupations not catering to segregated markets.[12]

Indeed, Zalokar [1990] found that in 1940, when discrimination against black women was very severe, after controlling for characteristics such as education, southern black women were less likely to be in professional occupations than southern white women. However, they were more likely to be teachers.[13]

The higher the cost to minority members in a particular labor market of pursuing alternative employment, the less elastic is their supply to this labor market. A continuum can be imagined: the higher the cost of

Figure 8.3
Effects of Discrimination Depend on Elasticity of Supply

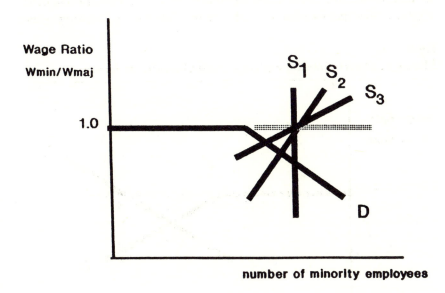

alternatives, the less likely minority members are to respond to discrimination. In the limit, the minority group's supply to the labor market can be completely inelastic. Thus, although all three groups in figure 8.3 supply the same amount of labor in the pictured labor market in the absence of discrimination, the costs of pursuing alternative employment are higher for members of group 2 than for members of group 3. For members of group 1, the costs of pursuing alternatives are prohibitively high and thus their equilibrium supply is the same as if there were no discrimination in this particular labor market. While measures of market discrimination will correctly show that labor-market discrimination is more costly in terms of forgone wages for group 1 than for group 2 and for group 2 than for group 3 (since their equilibrium wages relative to the majority are successively higher under discrimination), it is nonetheless true that from the viewpoint of the demand for their services, members of all three groups experience the same amount of discrimination in the labor market depicted here. Note that it is possible that groups 1 and 2 have more inelastic supply curves to this particular market because they face greater discrimination elsewhere. However, it is important for measures of discrimination to differentiate discrimination in this market from discrimination in other markets, since policy efforts can be better directed by knowing where

Figure 8.4
Effects of Discrimination on Wages and Quantity of Labor

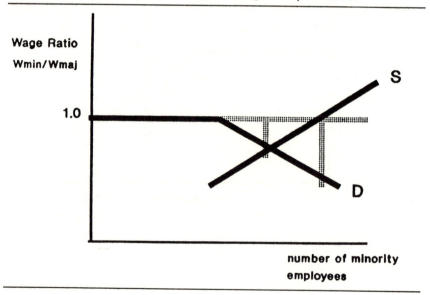

discrimination is worse.[14]

To the extent that members of a minority group respond to discrimination or to expected discrimination (i.e., to the extent that their labor supply is elastic), the quantity of labor supplied by members of a minority group to a given labor market will be smaller than it would have been in the absence of discrimination, and the observed earnings differential will be smaller than it would have been in the absence of this response (in the case of perfectly inelastic labor supply). If the minority group pictured in figure 8.4 had not responded to discrimination in the labor market and had supplied the same quantity of labor as in the absence of discrimination, the earnings differential between the minority and the majority groups would have been twice as large as the observed differential.[15]

Search costs, which are a function of the shape of the distribution of the intensity of prejudice across employers, will also induce a supply response if they are sufficiently high. As search costs go up, less labor will be supplied to a given labor market at each relative wage ratio. This corresponds to a leftward shift of the supply curve and may reduce the size of the earnings differential below what it would otherwise have been.[16]

Not only will a response to discrimination in a given labor market affect the quantity of labor supplied by minorities in the labor market, but it may also affect the characteristics of minority labor supplied to the discriminatory market, causing further difficulties with using market discrimination as a measure of the amount of discrimination in a labor market. To understand this, suppose that minority members differ according to nonproductive or ascriptive characteristics such as skin color, accent, or culture, and that those with nonproductive characteristics more similar to those of the majority group are less discriminated against than their counterparts who are more different. Then, rather than facing a unique demand curve (holding productive characteristics constant) in the discriminatory labor market, as is usually assumed, members of the minority group face different demand curves depending on how different they are from the majority group. The more similar individuals are to members of the majority group, the more elastic would be the demand curve they face. Assuming that all members of the minority group have the same alternatives elsewhere, discrimination will induce those who are the most different from the majority to seek these alternatives, whereas those who are most similar to the majority will remain.[17] Since these are precisely the minority members who face the least discrimination, measures of market discrimination based on adjusted earnings differentials for the discriminatory labor market will tend to underestimate the extent of discrimination

Figure 8.5
Different Demand Curves for Labor Depending on Ascriptive
Characteristics

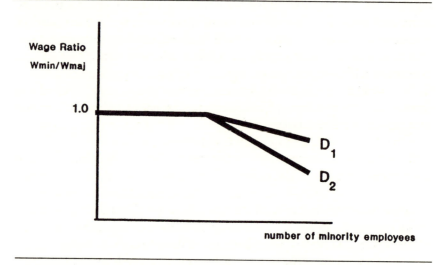

against "average" members of the minority in that labor market.

As an example, figure 8.5 shows hypothetical demand curves for lightly complected blacks (D1) and darkly complected blacks (D2). The costs of remaining in this labor market are greater for persons facing the second demand curve. Thus as long as all members of a minority group face the same costs of pursuing alternative employment, minority members facing the second demand curve will be more likely to leave this labor market.

The differential response by minority members in this situation creates a selection bias. Those who remain in a discriminatory labor market are not necessarily representative of those who would have been there in the absence of discrimination. Thus in the absence of a response, the earnings differential could be larger not only because of a larger number of minority persons in the labor market but also because minority members remaining in a discriminatory labor market may have different ascriptive characteristics than those who would have been in the market in the absence of discrimination.

Of course, it is also possible that the minority members remaining in a discriminatory labor market may have different productive characteristics than those who would have been there in the absence of discrimination. This situation, too, gives rise to a selection bias. Suppose that workers differ in their abilities. In the face of wage discrimination lowering their wages, only the most able minority members remain in the labor market, since only they can earn enough in the face of discrimination to make it worthwhile. The less able minority members leave for other labor markets, depressing wages for all workers in those labor markets. In this situation, researchers relying on market discrimination measures may underestimate the degree of discrimination in the discriminatory labor market and overestimate the degree of discrimination in other labor markets. [18]

As an example, suppose that there are two occupations, doctors and construction workers, and that discrimination against minority doctors is very severe, but there is no discrimination against minority construction workers. As a result of discrimination, only minority members with exceptional abilities (but unobserved by the econometrician) become doctors, and as a result, they earn comparably with average white doctors (but less than they would have earned in the absence of discrimination). Minority members who would have been less able doctors in the absence of discrimination become construction workers instead. If their ability as construction workers is the same as the average, then wages for all construction workers will be lower than they would be in the absence of discrimination, but there will be no minority/majority wage differential. On the other hand, if the would-be doctors are rather poor construction workers (if the skills and talents that make good doctors are negatively correlated with the skills and talents that make good construction workers), they will earn less than the average construction worker, and an apparent minority/majority wage differential will arise if these skills cannot be measured. By lowering the average ability of minority construction workers, the entry of the would-be doctors makes it appear, if one relies on adjusted earnings differentials as measures of market discrimination, that there is discrimination in the market for construction workers when in fact there is not. On the other hand, since only the most able minority doctors remain, adjusted earnings differentials measures of market discrimination indicate that there is no market discrimination against minority doctors when in fact there is a lot.[19]

This section has considered several ways in which minority responses to labor-market discrimination can cause measures of market discrimination to provide misleading evidence concerning the extent of discrimination in specific labor markets. First, market discrimination measures are affected by the elasticity of supply of minority labor to discriminatory labor markets. If minority labor supply to a discriminatory labor market is relatively elastic, market discrimination measures will show less discrimination in that market than if minority labor supply is relatively inelastic. One problem that results is that it is difficult to use market discrimination to compare the degree of discrimination across minority groups or across labor markets. For instance, minority groups with good alternatives outside of discriminatory labor markets will appear to face less discrimination in the discriminatory labor markets than minority groups with fewer alternatives when in fact they face the same degree of discrimination.

Second, in labor markets where employers, unions, or other institutions that determine access to jobs vary according to the extent to which they discriminate, minority members may face greater job search costs than majority members as they search for jobs with less discriminatory employers. These search costs may decrease the quantity of labor supplied by minority workers in a specific labor market and possibly raise their relative wage. Here again, market discrimination measures may provide misleading information as to the extent of discrimination in specific labor markets.

Third, if minority workers differ according to ascriptive traits that are discriminated against or according to unobserved productive characteristics, minority members' responses to discrimination may differ according to these traits or characteristics, causing selection bias problems to arise. In these situations, market discrimination measures will be biased measures of the impact of labor-market discrimination on the wages of workers who would be in the labor market in the absence of discrimination.

The empirical emphasis on market discrimination and adjusted wage differentials as measures of discrimination fails to account for the effects of these supply responses on relative wages and therefore may fail to reflect accurately the degree of discrimination in a labor market. Looking at adjusted earnings differentials without taking into account supply responses may lead to the erroneous conclusion that there is no discrimination in a particular labor market when in fact there is a lot, or that there is less in one labor market than in another when in fact the reverse is true.

III. MARKET DISCRIMINATION AS A MEASURE OF THE COSTS OF DISCRIMINATION TO MINORITIES

The main thrust of section II is that the traditional emphasis on "market discrimination" as a measure of discrimination results in underestimation of the extent of discrimination faced by minority members, because minority members respond to discrimination in such a way as to minimize its effects. A truer measure of the extent of discrimination might be the

Figure 8.6
Market and Potential Discrimination

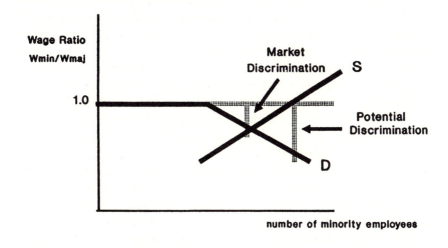

wage differential that would occur if minority members did not respond to discrimination, that is, the wage differential that would occur if their labor supply were completely inelastic at the quantity that would have obtained in the absence of discrimination. We will refer to this measure as "potential discrimination." It is the wage cost minority members would incur in the face of discrimination if they supplied the same amount of labor and held the same jobs as they would have in the absence of discrimination.

Figure 8.6 illustrates the distinction between market discrimination and potential discrimination. Note that if there were no minority supply responses to discrimination, market and potential discrimination would be one and the same. Empirical estimates of potential discrimination would, of course, require estimating the supply curves of minority members to discriminatory labor markets to determine the number of minority members who would be in the labor market in the absence of discrimination.

Not only does market discrimination underestimate the extent of discrimination in the labor market, but it also underestimates the costs of labor-market discrimination to minority members. In general, minority members would have to be given a wage increase greater than the amount of market discrimination to restore them to the utility level they would have reached in the absence of discrimination. Thus market discrimination is, very loosely, analogous to a compensating variation type of measure of the cost of discrimination in that it uses the prices in effect after discrimination has been implemented.[20] However, it is an underestimate because, as argued above, even if the wage increase were paid to those experiencing discrimination, it would not, in general, restore them to the hypothetical level of utility they would have experienced in the absence of discrimination.

Potential discrimination, on the other hand, is loosely analogous to an equivalent surplus concept in that it holds the quantity of labor at the hypothetical "original" level that would have obtained in the absence of discrimination.[21] Thus potential discrimination generally overestimates the costs of discrimination to minority members. Of course, this last statement is true only in the neoclassical case where minority members' utility depends solely on consumption and leisure. If minority members receive disutility from the existence of discrimination in and of itself, say from a reduced sense of self-esteem, potential discrimination may also be an underestimate of the costs borne by minority members. Since discrimination is illegal, regardless of the extent of pecuniary damages, the notion of potential discrimination, which holds quantities at the nondiscriminatory levels, is clearly the relevant concept for judicial measurements and for policy purposes directly pursuant to judicial decisions.

IV. CONCLUSION

Our concern at the U.S. Commission on Civil Rights to uncover not only the average extent of discrimination experienced by members of minority groups, but also variations in the incidence of discrimination within minority groups, has led us to consider minority responses to discrimination. When attempting to measure the extent of discrimination facing subgroups within minority groups as classified by education, region, occupation, and so on, we became aware that minorities might alter their characteristics in response to differential discrimination across these categories (i.e., that they might change categories), and that this response could affect our ability to discover in which categories discrimination is worst.

Thinking about minority responses to discrimination has led us to reconsider the use of adjusted earnings differentials as a guide to policy. We have argued that because of minority responses to discrimination, the adjusted earnings differentials approach may provide misleading information as to where efforts to combat discrimination should be focused.

Moreover, market discrimination may not be the appropriate measure of the costs of discrimination, in terms of utility loss, to minorities. Rather, it represents a lower bound on these costs. Our proposed alternative measure, potential discrimination, gives a measure of particular relevance to judicial proceedings. Our inquiry also clearly suggests that further research on a utility-theoretic approach to establishing measures of discrimination that are useful for public policy purposes is warranted.

Our analysis suggests that a fuller understanding of the nature of the minority supply responses to labor-market discrimination would be helpful for assessing the likely costs of discrimination to minority groups and for determining where antidiscrimination efforts should be directed. In particular, we have argued that knowing the quantity and the characteristics of labor that would be supplied by members of a minority group to given labor markets in the absence of discrimination could be crucial for pinpointing where discrimination is worst.

These arguments suggest that future research should study minority supply responses to discrimination. One possible avenue for future research may be to study the mobility strategies of minority groups, or the strategies by which they overcome discrimination and raise their economic status. Not only would such a study help us to discover where minority members would be employed in the absence of discrimination, but, in addition, it might illuminate reasons why some groups have succeeded in raising their economic status where others have failed.

Another possible avenue for future research is to address the selection bias problem that may result from minority responses to discrimination by using the two-stage procedure developed by Heckman [1979]. For instance, estimates of discrimination in the private sector should correct for the possibility that some minority members have reacted to labor-market discrimination by becoming self-employed. Similarly, estimates of discrimination at high levels of education should correct for the possibility that some minority members have chosen to limit their education.

Learning where discrimination is worst may require a shift in research emphasis from measuring earnings differentials to collecting information on the number and nature of discriminatory encounters experienced by minority members. In this regard, an experimental approach could be followed wherein minority and majority members with the same set of characteristics seek jobs in a given labor market.[22] Data could be collected on their job offers (i.e., search time, nature of job, wage offer, and so on) to see if the opportunities for minority members were substantially worse than those for members of the majority. Note that such an experimental approach would provide information that is "uncontaminated" by minority responses to discrimination.

Alternatively, a greater emphasis in our data-collection efforts could be placed on identifying barriers to the labor-market success of minority groups. For instance, an in-depth comparative study of the career paths of minority and majority business-school graduates might reveal much about the extent of discrimination faced by minority members.

Becker [1971: 58] wrote, "Market discrimination refers to the incomes received by different groups and ignores their distribution in employment; market segregation refers to their distribution in employment and ignores their incomes." With respect to this distinction, Becker cautioned that "many serious errors have been committed because of a failure to recognize that market segregation and market discrimination are separate concepts referring to separate phenomena." However, these two phenomena are related, and it is not clear that one can really determine the extent of the discrimination problem in a given labor market without also considering the market segregation problem. To guide where policy efforts should be focused, market discrimination and market segregation need to be viewed as joint outcomes.

9
Lifetime Work Expectations and Estimates of Gender Discrimination

Solomon W. Polachek and
Charng Kao

E conomic success is unevenly divided. Some groups' earnings far outpace earnings of others, so that earnings variations can be considered more the norm than the exception. Because of this, numerous research efforts have been devoted to understanding earnings distribution.

Despite valid economic arguments explaining earnings variations, it is problematic to explain why certain demographic groups such as women, blacks, and Hispanics tend to fall into the lower tail while other groups such as Jews, Catholics, and Asians are prone toward the upper end of the spectrum. Similarly, even within these groups there are variations. Earlier Cuban immigrants fare better than Mexicans, Puerto Ricans, or other Hispanics, though recent Cuban immigrants have been less successful.[1]

If unequal opportunities caused by unfair hiring practices cause these patterns, then the economy is failing to fully utilize highly productive employees, so that these inefficiencies can justify government intervention. On the other hand, if differing individual choices cause unequal economic outcomes despite equal opportunity, then government intervention could lead to distorted allocation of resources and inefficiencies within the economy. In this case, rather than helping disadvantaged groups, government intervention hampers economic efficiency so that in the long run all end up suffering. Thus the comprehension of demographic differences has become an important topic not only for researchers, but for policymakers as well.

One way to understand demographic earning differentials is to compute a discrimination coefficient representing the proportion of the wage gap unexplained once one controls for productivity differences. Obviously these resulting discrimination measures can be over or underestimated depending upon the implementation of the procedure.

One error that predominates is the omission of lifetime work expectations, including expectations concerning periods of intermittency so common among women, especially wives with children.[2] Life-cycle human-capital accumulation models dictate that expected intermittency affects human-capital investment and earnings long before one actually drops out. Not considering future work expectations leads to severe overestimates of discrimination, thereby causing erroneous policy implications.

In this chapter we outline a life-cycle model to show how these intermittency expectations affect human-capital investment, and how, in turn, differences in investments affect earnings long before one drops out of the labor force. Given the importance of these expectations, we devise an estimation procedure incorporating such work expectations. The approach is applied to the United States as well as Taiwan. In both cases, between 70 and 90 percent of the male/female wage gap can be explained, thereby implying discrimination coefficients around 10 to 30 percent, far lower than the 40 to 60 percent current estimates. To illustrate its robustness, the technique is applied to other demographic groups with equal success.

I. CURRENT APPROACHES TO ESTIMATE DISCRIMINATION: DECOMPOSITION OF RESIDUALS

Typically the discrimination coefficient is measured in one of two ways.[3] One can compare male earnings to what females would earn if they had male characteristics; or one can compare female earnings to what males would earn if they had female characteristics. In a nondiscriminatory world, no wage differentials would emerge from either of these comparisons, for in such a world, why would men and women of comparable characteristics receive differing wages?

The usual methodology entails regressing wages on individual characteristics. This yields earnings functions for males and females that can be denoted $g_m(x_m)$ and $g_f(x_f)$, so that

$$(1) \qquad \overline{Y}_m = g_m(\overline{x}_m)$$

and

(2) $\qquad \overline{Y}_f = g_f(\overline{x}_f)$

where the subscripts m and f refer to males and females, respectively, and the overbar denotes mean values. These equations imply that mean male and female wages can be computed by substituting male and female characteristics into respective male and female earnings functions.

Now define functions representing what males would earn with female characteristics and what females would earn with male characteristics:

(3) $\qquad \overline{Y}_{mf} = g_m(\overline{x}_f)$

and

(4) $\qquad \overline{Y}_{fm} = g_f(\overline{x}_m)$

equation (3) can be viewed as the "mean" female wage if a woman had a male earnings structure, and similarly equation (4) can represent the "mean" female wage if a man had a female earnings structure. The difference $\overline{Y}_{mf} - \overline{Y}_{fm}$ depicts the difference in earnings that can be explained by differences in male and female attributes. Hence $(\overline{Y}_{fm} - \overline{Y}_f)/(\overline{Y}_m - \overline{Y}_f)$ is the portion of the wage gap explained by differences in characteristics, while $d = [1 - (\overline{Y}_{fm} - \overline{Y}_f)/(\overline{Y}_m - \overline{Y}_f)]$ is the unexplained portion. By convention, d defines discrimination. However, a similar conceptualization applies when using equation (3). The difference $(\overline{Y}_m - \overline{Y}_{mf})$ represents the earnings differential attributable to sex differences in characteristics; $[(\overline{Y}_m - \overline{Y}_{mf})/(\overline{Y}_m - \overline{Y}_f)]$ is the proportion of the gap explained by attribute differences; and $d_2 = [1 - (\overline{Y}_m - \overline{Y}_{mf})/(\overline{Y}_m - \overline{Y}_f)]$ as discrimination. The only difference between the two approaches is that approach one uses the female earnings function (g_f) as a basis while approach two uses the male earnings function (g_m). Since in general $g'_m > g'_f$, approach two yields higher measures of discrimination and, on average, is more readily used for policy purposes (Oaxaca [1973]; Malkiel and Malkiel [1973]; Corcoran and Duncan [1979]; Corcoran, Duncan, and Ponza [1983]). Some advocate an average of both these alternatives by using a dummy gender variable in a wage regression [Polachek (1975a)].

In general there is no a priori reason to favor g_m over g_f or vice versa. It is perhaps for this reason that a weighted average of male and female earnings functions is often used. This most easily can be accomplished by pooling the male and female sample and restricting both male and female coefficients to be equal. Of course, the simplest application of this technique is to assess discrimination as the gender coefficient in an earnings equation run jointly for men and women,

$$(5) \qquad\qquad y = g(x,G) ,$$

where G is a dummy gender variable. Examples include McNulty [1967], Cohen [1971], Fuchs [1971], Kamalich and Polachek [1982] as well as chapter 7 by David Fairris and Lori Kletzer.

Explicit in these computations is that discrimination is measured solely by differences in the regression coefficients (including intercepts) between g_m and g_f (or solely by the coefficient of the gender dummy variable G if equation 5 is used), while the explained portion of earnings differentials emanates from gender differences in attributes. One problem, however, is that it is not necessarily true that differences in attributes are nondiscriminatory while structural differences (measured as differences in estimated coefficients) are discriminatory. In what follows, we illustrate why.

First, take the case of differences in attributes. These are considered nondiscriminatory because often individual labor-market characteristics such as schooling, including type of curriculum, choice of college major, etc. are determined well before work commences. Even aspects of work history such as on-the-job training, job turnover, mobility, occupation, and industry are not considered a product of discrimination However, is it really valid to hold one's current employer constant or society nonculpable? Is it not possible that society discriminates in opportunities of skill acquisition? Do all have access to comparable schooling (e.g., see chapter 11 by Elaine McCrate)? Are all workers laid off with equal probability in the business cycle (e.g., see chapter 1 by Steven Shulman)? Do all receive equal advice concerning school and other training opportunities? Even unmeasurable differences may be induced by discrimination. Motivational differences such as gender-related differences in upbringing can be caused by societal stereotypes. Thus both to the extent that society discriminates and to the extent that employees expect future discrimination while on the job, factor-endowment differences can result. To treat factor-endowment differences as nondiscriminatory is simply wrong. For example, observing that women have lower tenure may merely be an artifact of employers not permitting women to accumulate tenure.

Second, structural differences need not be discriminatory. For example, division of labor in the home implies differential husband/wife specialization in work and home activities. This implies that identical attributes can have different impacts on earnings. For the male, being married has, at least in the past, implied specialization in market activities. On the other hand, for women, this same variable implies a specialization in nonmarket activities. This means that a marital-status adjustment in a wage regression would yield misleading results. For men, being married raises wages because of the increased human-capital investment associated with a stronger lifetime work commitment. For women, being married lowers wages because of smaller investment incentives. In this case $g'_m > g'_f$, and for good reason.[4]

Most studies interpret such a structural difference to be discrimination. However, such structural differences can merely result from optimizing behavior by the family and can occur even in the absence of labor-market discrimination. For example, since on average, women are less educated and less experienced than their husbands even at the start of marriage,

Figure 9.1
Female Age-Earnings Profiles

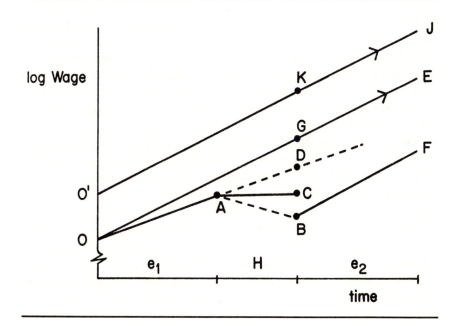

division of labor and specialization may be optimal to maximize lifetime family income.[5] Figure 9.1 illustrates these biases most succinctly. Line segment OABF represents the typical female age-earnings profile. Line segment O'KJ is the male profile. Distance BK is the male/female wage gap. The first approach to measuring discrimination, described above, seeks to define what women would earn if they had male characteristics. This amount is depicted by point D and implies that BD of the BK wage gap can be explained. The unexplained residual DK reflects discrimination.

We contend that this procedure overstates discrimination by improperly accounting for human capital.[6] Specifically, continuous work expectations (i.e., H = 0) increase human-capital investments. This increased investment can raise expected female earnings to G and K, thereby wiping out what is thought to be discrimination. Such increases in investment can occur as early as school by studying more market-oriented fields or can occur after graduation by seeking jobs with greater training opportunities. Current studies neglect the fact that labor-force expectations affect school and job choices and this leads these studies to overstate discrimination. This is the bias considered in this chapter.

II. EXPECTATIONS AND EARNINGS AUGMENTATION

That lifetime work expectations affect human-capital investments is obvious even from the very simplest life-cycle models.[7] Clearly, less work over one's lifetime decreases investment incentives throughout life. Even decreased work hours during limited periods can have dramatic effects, as intertemporal ramifications turn out to be extremely important. In what follows, we take a simple life-cycle model to illustrate the importance of these intertemporal effects on human-capital investment.

For simplicity, assume a model depicting decisions under a regime of perfect certainty.[8] Similarly, assume an individual decision maker whose objective is to maximize the present value of lifetime income.[9] A typical such objective can be illustrated as

$$(6) \qquad \text{Max } J = \int_{t=0}^{T} Y(t) \, e^{-rt} \, dt \, ,$$

where Y(t) represents period t's take-home earnings, consisting of the difference between one's potential earnings E(t) and one's investment in the future I(t). Thus

(7) $Y(t) = E(t) - I(t)$.

Potential earnings in period t are

(8) $E(t) = N(t) W(t)$,

where one's potential working hours are $N(t)$ and one's wage is $W(t)$.

Future investments can take on many forms. One common form is a productivity-enhancing investment at least partly paid for by the worker.[10] Another is the worker posting an assurance bond.[11] In either case, the current cost, $I(t)$, to augment future earnings can be expressed as

(9) $I(t) = S(t) W(t)$,

where $S(t)$ equals the number of potential working hours set aside in time period t to augment future earnings power. Take-home pay $Y(t)$ equals disposable income, so that

(10) $Y(t) = E(t) - I(t) = N(t) W(t) - S(t) W(t)$.

Substituting (10) into (6) yields

(11) $\text{Max } J = \int_{t=0}^{T} [N(t) - S(t)] W(t) e^{-rt} dt$.

For simplicity, assume that investment in time period t augments earnings in the very next time period. A simple function describing the rate at which investment $S(t)W(t)$ augments earnings is

(12) $dW(t)/dt = W'(t) = f[I(t)]$

such that $f' > 0$ while $f'' < 0$.[12] A simple illustration is

(13) $W'(t) = b_0 I(t)^b 1 = b_0 [S(t)W(t)]^b 1$.

Maximization of (11) under condition (13) implies maximization of the Hamiltonian

(14) $H = [N(t) - S(t)] W(t) e^{-rt} + \mu(t) \{b_0 [S(t)W(t)]^b 1\}$

with respect to $S(t)$.[13] First-order conditions yield

(15) $\qquad \partial H/\partial S(t) = -W(t)\, e^{-rt} + \mu(t)\, b_0 b_1 S(t)^{b_1-1} W(t)^{b_1} = 0,$

(16) $\qquad \mu'(t) = -[N(t)-S(t)]\, e^{-rt} - \mu(t)\, b_0 b_1 S(t)^{b_1} W(t)^{b_1-1},$ and

(17) $\qquad W'(t) = b_0 [S(t)W(t)]^{b_1}.$

Equation (15) implies that each period's investment is obtained by equating forgone earnings with the present value of increased future earnings. This yields an investment time path

(18) $\qquad I(t) = [b_0\, b_1\, W]^{1/(1-b_1)},$

where $W = \mu(t)e^{-rt}$, the current dollar equivalent of marginal benefits, and

(19) $\qquad \mu(t) = \int_{t=0}^{T-t} N(t)\, e^{-rt}\, dt.$

Over the life cycle, investment declines monotonically if per period labor-force participation is constant, but need not decline monotonically if labor-force participation is rising or expected to rise:

(20) $\qquad \partial I(t)/\partial t = -1/(1-b_1)\, [S(t)W(t)]^{b_1/(1-b_1)} \partial W'(t)/\partial N(t+j),$

where

(21) $\qquad W' = -N(t)\, e^{r(t-T)} + re^{rt}\!\int [N(\tau) - N(t)] e^{-rt}\, d\tau.$

Expectation of labor-force intermittency implies evaluating

(22) $\qquad -\partial[I(t)]/\partial N(t+j) = -1/(1-b_1)[S(t)W(t)]^{b_1/(1-b_1)}$
$$\partial W'(t)/\partial N(t+j),$$

which from the above is clearly negative. The sooner in one's life cycle one expects intermittency, the greater is the detrimental effect on investment.

III. A PROCEDURE FOR INCORPORATING EXPECTED LIFE CYCLE INTERMITTENCY

Almost all current analyses of sex wage differentials omit expectation from consideration.[14] Yet as we have seen, expectations may be an important potential wage determinant, since they affect an individual's investment incentives. To augment the wage-decomposition analysis, expectations must be added as a wage determinant. However, this is complicated. First, expectations are not observed. Second, expectations do not enter a wage function directly, but instead enter by influencing an employee's willingness to invest in human-capital and deferred-compensation schemes. One can capture this investment by predicting how much a rational planner would invest given his or her expected lifetime labor-force participation. The sum of these investments is directly proportional to earnings. The rate of proportionality is the rate of return to investment. This implies a wage function

$$(23) \qquad y_i = g^*(K_i, X_i, G_i),$$

where K is the appropriately measured human capital based on expected lifetime work expectations. It is comparable to $W(t)$ in the previous section. The variable X depicts exogenous individual characteristics affecting wages but not human capital or discrimination.[15] Adding gender, G_i, yields a measure of sex earnings differentials that adjusts for this appropriately measured human-capital stock. Interpreting the coefficient of G_i to represent discrimination would be consistent with the above definition of a discrimination coefficient. Linearizing (23) yields

$$(24) \qquad y_i = a_0 + a_1 K_i + a_2 X + \partial G_i + e_i.$$

The a_1 coefficient measures the rate of return to investment. As indicated, K in this equation depicts "expected lifetime work-adjusted" human capital.

Measurement of K is tricky because it is unobservable. Using panel data to identify a discrimination coefficient is no help because discrimination is not individual-specific. Thus it is not identifiable even with panel estimation schemes and K must be estimated. The procedure is best illustrated by graphically representing equations (15) and (19).

First-order condition (15) depicts the marginal costs and benefits of earnings-enhancing investment. These are illustrated in figure 9.2, in which MC represents the marginal costs of investment and μ_1, μ_2, ...with $\mu_T = 0$ coinciding with the horizontal axis. From (19) we see that $\mu(t)$ decreases as t increases. This depicts the marginal benefits at succeeding ages.[16] The intersection of MC and μ_t determines investments I(t) in each period. If labor-force participation is constant and invariant, I(t) declines monotonically since $\mu(t)$ decreases with t. On the other hand, as illustrated by equation (21) investment need not decline monotonically when labor-force participation varies over the life cycle. Clearly, then, knowledge of MC and $\mu(t)$ determines one's human capital investment I(t) in each period t. For any individual aged t*, human-capital stock (earnings potential) equals the sum of all past investments (minus depreciation):

$$(25) \qquad K(t^*) = \sum_{t=0}^{t^*} [I(t) - d\,K(t)] = \sum I_N(t),$$

where d equals depreciation and I_N is investment net of depreciation.

To measure K(t*), one must estimate I(t), which is determined by equating marginal costs (MC) and marginal gains (μ) of investment. End-

Figure 9.2
Marginal Costs and Benefits of Earnings Enhancing Investment

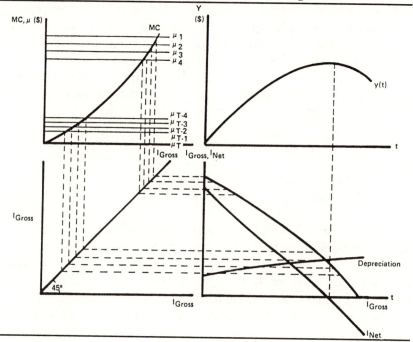

of-life restrictions within the maximization process are used to estimate depreciation (d).

If both the MC and μ functions are known, $I(t)$ can be estimated as the solution of the equation relating MC and μ, as in (15). On the other hand, a priori knowledge of $I(t)$ and $\mu(t)$ enables one to solve for MC. First MC is estimated for married males. This MC curve should apply to all population strata, if all are equally able. Our approach then is to assume the married-male MC curve for all and to compute $I(t)$ for single males and for single and married females based on their $\mu(t)$ curves. This is done for five educational levels separately.

IIIA. Estimating $I(t)$ for Married Males

The marginal cost (MC) function is obtained by equating each period's gross investment $[I(t)]$ with each period's marginal revenue $[\mu(t)]$. We first describe how to estimate $I(t)$, then $\mu(t)$, and finally the simultaneous solution of both functions. This is done for five educational levels (Ed = 1, ..., 5).

Married-male net investment $[K_N(t)]$ can be computed from traditionally computed age-earnings profiles. Accordingly, observed earnings can be specified as

(26) $$\ln y(t) = \ln y_0 + r \int_0^t K'(\tau)\, d\tau = \ln y_0 + b_1 t - b_2 t^2,$$

when $K'(t) = [b_1 - 2b_2 t]/r$, as is usually assumed in traditional earnings function estimation.[17]

Net investment at time t as a proportion of earnings power is

(27) $$K'(t) = (1/r)\partial[\ln E(t)]/\partial t$$

$$= (1/r)\,(b_1 - b_2 t)\{b_2/[1 - (b_1 + b_2 t)]\},$$

which, when expressed in dollars, is

(28) $$I_N(t) = [(1/r)(b_1 - b_2 t)]\, E(t)$$

$$= [(b_1 - b_2 t)]\exp[\ln y_0 + b_1 t - 1/2 b_2 t^2]\{b_2/[1 - (b_1 + b_2 t)]\}.[18]$$

To obtain gross investment [I(t)], depreciation must be computed and
added to net investment [$I_N(t)$]. To compute depreciation, recall that the
life cycle dictates that gross investment I(t) equal zero at the end of the life
cycle when t = T. This means that depreciation only occurs during year T,
so that depreciation can be computed as the ratio of net investment in work
year T divided by total accumulated human capital in year T. Thus

(29) $d = I_N(t)/K(T),$
where

(30) $K(T) = \sum\limits_{0}^{T} K'(t).$

The dollar value of I(t) can then be computed as

(31) $I(t) = I_N(t) + d\,K(t).$

IIIB. Estimating μ

Marginal gains are easily computed based on equation (19)

$$\mu(t) = \int\limits_{0}^{T-t} N(t)\, e^{-rt}\, dt$$

where N(τ) is an individual's expected labor-force participation at each
age τ. These labor-force participation rates are estimated from aggregate
data based on education, marital status, and age. Marginal investment
gains are computed separately for married and single males and for married
and single females.

IIIC. Estimating the MC Function

Equating I(t) with μ(t) yields MC. In line with those that hypothesize
heterogeneity across schooling groups, the MC curves are computed for
five educational levels [MC(S)] to allow for the differing human-capital
production functions associated with each schooling group.[19] We assume
that men, women, singles, and marrieds are of equal ability, so that the MC
curves vary across demographic group only by schooling level.

IIID. Estimating Human Capital for Each Demographic Group

Gross investment for single males and for single and married females relative to married males can be computed by equating MC and μ. This yields I(t) for these groups. Applying depreciation rates yields net investment $[I_N(t)]$, and summing yields expected capital-stock [K(t)] values under the assumption that females have the same earnings opportunities as males, but different lifetime work expectations. These K(t) values can then be used in the context of equation (24) to account for expected lifetime labor-force participation when estimating male/female wage differentials. Further sex differences in effort are included to the extent that expected lifetime labor-force expectations determine on-the-job effort.

IV. RESULTS

This estimation procedure is adopted for both 1960 and 1980 U.S. census data as well as data from the Taiwan Manpower Utilization Survey dated May 1987. Since the U.S. data is familiar, we concentrate on the Taiwan data. The Manpower Utilization Survey is a micro-data supplement to the monthly Labor Force Survey. It contains detailed information on 59,666 individuals, of which 17,326 are privately employed. A frequency distribution is given in table 9.1 and variable definitions are given in table 9.2.

To anchor the results to U.S. data, standard earnings functions are presented in table 9.3. It is interesting to note that the coefficients are very similar to those obtained for U.S. data. Rates of return to schooling are about 6 percent; the earnings functions appear quadratic; and male/female wage differentials are about 36 percent. Also like the United States, sex wage differentials differ by marital status (table 9.4). Single females earn 22 percent less than single men, yet married women earn over 50 percent less.[20]

As indicated, these sex wage differentials are often used to depict discrimination. However, we argue that these measures are biased. Although numerous biases are possible, we concentrate on that bias caused by omitting expected lifetime work behavior. To address the effects of omitted labor-market work expectations on wages, we calculate age-specific human-capital stock based on expected lifetime labor-force participation using the procedures described above. These are then used in equation (24).

Table 9.1
Sample Distributions of Ages, Marital Status, and Occupations by Gender for Taiwan

	Male		Female		Total	
	Obs	%	Obs	%	Obs	%
Total	10,041	100.00	7,285	100.00	17,326	100.00
By Ages						
15-19	745	7.42	797	10.94	1,542	8.90
20-24	1,324	13.19	2,117	29.06	3,441	19.86
25-29	2,335	23.25	1,363	18.71	3,698	21.34
30-34	1,783	17.76	1,001	13.74	2,784	16.07
35-39	1,250	12.45	751	10.31	2,001	11.55
40-44	729	7.26	448	6.15	1,177	6.79
45-49	727	7.24	395	5.42	1,122	6.48
50-54	468	4.66	222	3.05	690	3.98
55-59	442	4.40	138	1.89	580	3.35
60-64	238	2.37	53	0.73	291	1.67
By Marital Status						
Single Never been-Married	3,806	37.90	3,458	47.47	7,264	41.98
Married, Spouse Present	5,986	59.62	3,460	47.49	9,446	54.52
Other Ever Married	249	2.48	367	5.04	616	3.55

By Occupations						
Professional	482	4.82	356	4.9	834	4.8
Managerial	118	1.21	10	0.1	128	0.7
Clerical	996	9.94	1,584	21.7	2,580	14.9
Sales	868	8.61	439	6.0	1,307	7.5
Service	508	5.10	645	8.9	1,153	6.7
Manual	7,073	70.42	4,251	58.4	11,324	65.3

Source: See text.

Table 9.2
Variable Definitions

LnY: Log value of hourly wage rate in current NT $
Edu: Years of schooling completed
Market experience variables:
    Exp : Age – Edu – 6
    Exp2: Square term of Exp
DMR: = 1, if married; = 0, else
DSEX: = 1, if females; = 0, else
SEXMR: Interaction term of sex dummy and marital-status dummy
LNHR: Log value of weekly working hours
Occupational dummies:
    DOC1 = 1, if professional workers; = 0, else
    DOC2 = 1, if managerial workers; = 0, else
    DOC3 = 1, if clerical workers; = 0, else
    DOC4 = 1, if sales workers; = 0, else
    DOC5 = 1, if service workers; = 0, else
    The "manual workers" group is used as the reference group.
Industry dummies:
    DIN1 = 1, if mining, quarrying and agricultural sector; = 0, else
    DIN2 = 1, if manufacturing; = 0, else
    DIN3 = 1, if utilities; = 0, else
    DIN4 = 1, if transportation and communication; = 0, else
    DIN5 = 1, if construction; = 0, else
    DIN6 = 1, if commerce; = 0, else
    DIN7 = 1, if finance and insurance; = 0, else
    The personal and other services group is used as the reference group.

Dummy variables for Survey job location:

DAR1 = 1, if northern region; = 0, else

DAR2 = 1, if central region; = 0, else

DAR3 = 1, if southern region; = 0, else

The eastern region is used as the reference group.

DRE : = 1 if working in an urban area; = 0, else

Firm size Dummies:

DFR1 = 1, if large size (with employees greater than 500); = 0, else

DFR2 = 1, if medium size (with employees less than 500, but greater than 100); = 0, else

DFR3 = 1, if small size (with employees less than 100, but greater than 30); = 0, else

Firm size with employees less than 30 is used as the reference group.

Table 9.3
Wage Equations for the Populations of Married-Spouse-Present and Single-Never-Been-Married, in Taiwan

	(1)	(2)	(3)
Constant	5.1413	5.1858	5.2810
	(.0681)	(.0699)	(.0688)
Education	.0647	.0353	.0325
	(.0012)	(.0015)	(.0014)
Experience	.0446	.0389	.0374
	(.0010)	(.0009)	(.0011)
Experience^2	−.0007	−.0007	−.0007
	(.00002)	(.00002)	(.00002)
LNHR	−.5247	−.5099	−.5431
	(.0165)	(.0158)	(.0157)
DFR1		.2308	.2116
		(.0127)	(.0125)
DFR2		.1845	.1705
		(.0091)	(.0090)
DFR3		.1496	.1412
		(.0083)	(.0082)
DIN1		.0570	.0619
		(.0188)	(.0185)
DIN2		.0197	.0331
		(.0120)*	(.0118)
DIN3		.0921	.1100
		(.1201)*	(.1180)*

DIN4	.2509 (.0148)	.2391 (.0146)
DIN5	.0677 (.0142)	.0726 (.0139)
DIN6	.2249 (.0183)	.2162 (.0180)
DIN7	.1296 (.0191)	.1378 (.0188)
DOC1	.2876 (.0165)	.2813 (.0162)
DOC2	.5096 (.0357)	.4831 (.0351)
DOC3	.1810 (.0108)	.1593 (.0106)
DOC4	.1128 (.0148)	.1079 (.0146)
DOC5	.0566 (.0146)	.0597 (.0144)
DAR1	.0851 (.0228)	.0767 (.0224)
DAR2	.0372 (.0232)*	.0242 (.0228)*
DAR3	-.0373 (.0231)*	-.0520 (.0227)
DRE	.0463 (.0065)	.0468 (.0065)

Table 9.3 (Continued)
Wage Equations for the Populations of Married-Spouse-Present and Single-Never-Been-Married, in Taiwan

	(1)	(2)	(3)
DSEX	-.3651	-.3772	-.2228
	(.0066)	(.0066)	(.0093)
DMR		.1621	
		(.0095)	
SEXMR		-.2885	
		(.0123)	
Observations (N)	16,710	16,710	16,710
R-squared	.3754	.4502	.4692
F-value	1,986.75	563.23	561.17

Notes: Dependent variable is log value of hourly wage rate.
Standard errors are in parentheses.
All variables not marked * are statistically significant at 5 percent.

Table 9.4
Wage Equations Stratified by Marital Status for Taiwan

	Singles		Marrieds	
	(1)	(2)	(3)	(4)
Constant	6.3457	5.9729	5.1151	5.4119
	(.1086)	(.1130)	(.0879)	(.0893)
Education	.0572	.0432	.0581	.0204
	(.0017)	(.0020)	(.0016)	(.0020)
Experience	.0565	.0503	.0321	.0244
	(.0015)	(.0015)	(.0019)	(.0018)
Experience^2	-.0011	-.0010	-.0005	-.0005
	(.0001)	(.0001)	(.0001)	(.0001)
LNHR	-.8540	-.7890	-.4472	-.4389
	(.0265)	(.0262)	(.0207)	(.0196)
DFR1		.1259		.2484
		(.0177)		(.0170)
DFR2		.1067		.2008
		(.0122)		(.0126)
DFR3		.0931		.1531
		(.0110)		(.0117)
DIN1		.2368		.0885
		(.0299)		(.0253)
DIN2		.1432		-.1080
		(.0145)		(.0186)
DIN3		.2451		-.0352
		(.1664)*		(.1605)*

Table 9.4 (Continued)
Wage Equations Stratified by Marital Status for Taiwan

	Singles		Marrieds	
	(1)	(2)	(3)	(4)
DIN4		.2959		.1274
		(.0204)		(.0214)
DIN5		.1286		.0081
		(.0166)		(.0224)*
DIN6		.2967		.0951
		(.0263)		(.0252)
DIN7		.1920		.0496
		(.0234)		(.0286)
DOC1		.1972		.3402
		(.0200)		(.0250)
DOC2		.3688		.5533
		(.1009)		(.0394)
DOC3		.0663		.2284
		(.0139)		(.0155)
DOC4		.0493		.1529
		(.0180)		(.0223)
DOC5		.1322		−.0345
		(.0185)		(.0211)*
DAR1		.1173		.0486
		(.0333)		(.0296)*

220

	(1)	(2)	(3)	(4)
DAR2		.0769		-.0133
		(.0338)*		(.0301)*
DAR3		-.0169		-.0775
		(.0338)*		(.0299)
DRE		.0278		.0638
		(.0086)		(.0092)
DSEX	-.1658	-.1746	-.5235	-.5138
	(.0084)	(.0090)	(.0095)	(.0094)
Observations (N)	7,264	7,264	9,446	9,446
R-squared	.3642	.4218	.4273	.4820
F-value	829.28	219.45	1,008.11	359.24

Notes: Standard errors are in parentheses.
All variables not marked * are statistically significant at 5%.

221

Table 9.5
Wage Equations for Males and Females (Aggregate) for Taiwan

	(1)	(2)	(3)	(4)	(5)	(6)
Constant	14,945.7	5,786.2	-5,189.1	-3,238.6	7,962.8	3,977.5
	(61.8)	(261.0)	(360.8)	(391.2)	(323.5)	(299.5)
Education			991.3	607.2		
			(15.8)	(19.1)		
Experience			636.8	550.8		
			(12.8)	(12.2)		
Experience^2			-10.2	-9.3		
			(0.3)	(0.3)		
LNHR		15.2	19.3	21.1	16.5	17.8
		(1.1)	(1.2)	(1.1)	(1.2)	(1.1)
DIN1				115.1	586.8	617.6
				(247.0)*	(261.1)	(235.9)
DIN2				13.5	393.0	410.1
				(155.2)*	(166.5)	(150.5)
DIN3				1,632.2	2,467.0	2,806.8
				(1,577.7)*	(1,695.4)*	(1,531.9)
DIN4				2,709.2	3,807.6	3,221.9
				(239.5)	(255.9)	(231.4)
DIN5				1,807.1	2,388.3	2,308.8
				(194.7)	(207.4)	(187.4)
DIN6				316.1	413.9	582.0
				(186.2)*	(200.0)	(180.7)
DIN7				1,376.3	1,834.6	1,785.4
				(250.4)	(268.9)	(243.0)
DOC1				4,329.5	6,579.7	3,508.6
				(216.2)	(215.4)	(201.1)

DOC2				13,514.7	17,644.4	10,456.4
				(467.6)	(491.0)	(459.1)
DOC3				1,882.0	3,685.1	1,545.0
				(141.5)	(133.7)	(125.8)
DOC4				1,351.6	2,767.6	1,122.0
				(194.9)	(203.6)	(185.9)
DOC5				294.8	888.0	326.2
				(192.3)*	(205.1)	(185.6)*
DFR				1,729.6	2,065.6	1,413.3
				(100.3)	(106.8)	(97.1)
DAR				1,173.9	1,361.3	1,171.2
				(79.4)	(85.1)	(77.0)
DRE				536.0	497.8	362.0
				(83.8)	(89.8)	(81.2)
DSEX	-5,495.4	-1,648.7	-4,143.5	-4,240.8	-5,365.0	-2,210.3
	(95.7)	(92.4)	(86.3)	(87.3)	(89.8)	(96.3)
EHC			.0634			.0499
			(.0007)			(.0008)
Observations (N)	16,710	16,710	16,710	16,710	16,710	16,710
R-squared	.1663	.4145	.3676	.4418	.3551	.4735

Notes: Standard errors are in parentheses.
All variables not marked * are statistically significant at 5 percent.

223

Table 9.6
Wage Equations for Single Males and Females for Taiwan

	(1)	(2)	(3)	(4)	(5)	(6)
Constant	12,145.3 (68.6)	7,415.9 (333.8)	-116.1 (417.3)	-1,190.6 (452.6)	7,181.5 (395.6)	4,390.4 (373.5)
Education			662.9 (18.4)	515.3 (21.9)		
Experience			598.8 (16.2)	537.6 (15.9)		
Experience^2			-11.4 (0.4)	-10.4 (0.4)		
LNHR		3.8 (1.4)	7.5 (1.4)	10.9 (1.4)	8.1 (1.5)	9.1 (1.4)
DIN1				1,723.1 (319.9)	2,434.2 (346.9)	2,054.6 (320.3)
DIN2				1,109.2 (151.4)	1,464.6 (165.2)	1,237.4 (152.6)
DIN3				1,720.3 (1,783.3)	3,512.5 (1,949.9)	2,426.1 (1,800.0)*
DIN4				3,195.4 (282.2)	4,234.8 (307.2)	3,494.5 (284.3)
DIN5				2,370.8 (218.5)	3,120.7 (236.8)	2,732.9 (218.8)
DIN6				922.5 (178.0)	1,191.9 (194.5)	1,009.8 (179.6)
DIN7				1,720.8 (250.2)	2,188.5 (273.3)	1,906.2 (252.3)
DOC1				2,492.1 (213.5)	4,350.8 (216.4)	2,818.4 (204.4)

	(1)	(2)	(3)	(4)	(5)	(6)
DOC2				10,367.2	14,274.4	8,349.3
				(1,080.2)	(1,174.1)	(1,096.5)
DOC3				446.4	1,903.3	943.7
				(149.5)	(146.9)	(138.3)
DOC4				214.3	1,302.9	424.9
				(193.4)	(206.3)	(192.1)
DOC5				1,156.0	1,543.5	1,214.9
				(198.7)	(216.2)	(199.7)
DFR				753.7	993.2	740.3
				(110.5)	(119.9)	(110.9)
DAR				1,036.2	1,224.0	1,048.0
				(85.7)	(93.5)	(86.5)
DRE				218.8	334.6	283.0
				(89.4)	(97.7)	(90.2)
DSEX	-2,462.2	-1,352.1	-1,940.1	-1,938.6	-2,740.1	-1,605.0
	(99.3)	(92.0)	(90.0)	(96.1)	(102.0)	(99.4)
EHC		.0652				.0540
		(.0015)				(.0015)
R-squared	.0783	.2695	.2939	.3492	.2208	.3363

Notes: Standard errors are in parentheses.
All variables not marked * are statistically significant at 5 percent.

Table 9.7
Wage Equations for Married Males and Females for Taiwan

	(1)	(2)	(3)	(4)	(5)	(6)
Constant	16,754.6	5,006.8	-4,777.1	-557.3	9,070.6	5,102.1
	(88.9)	(381.5)	(600.4)	(641.5)*	(446.1)	(439.3)
Education			1,063.3	515.4		
			(23.6)	(28.4)		
Experience			583.1	444.0		
			(26.9)	(25.1)		
Experience^2			-9.2	-7.5		
			(0.5)	(0.5)		
LNHR		23.2	21.0	23.2	22.8	24.7
		(1.6)	(1.7)	(1.6)	(1.6)	(1.5)
DIN1				-757.5	-1,437.2	-1,133.7
				(361.0)	(367.0)	(347.6)
DIN2				-936.7	-1,163.5	-1,057.6
				(264.1)	(270.9)	(256.5)
DIN3				2,183.5	1,791.3	2,549.9
				(2,294.9)*	(2,356.0)*	(2,230.5)*
DIN4				1,903.2	1,862.6	1,794.1
				(360.2)	(369.7)	(350.0)
DIN5				1,001.4	569.2	892.5
				(306.4)	(313.6)	(297.0)
DIN6				236.5	160.2	100.8
				(320.9)*	(329.0)*	(311.5)*
DIN7				1,134.7	1,100.9	1,119.1
				(407.6)	(418.4)	(396.1)
DOC1				6,410.4	8,442.6	4,945.8
				(357.3)	(340.5)	(339.6)

	(1)	(2)	(3)	(4)	(5)	(6)
DOC2				13,876.0 (561.9)	16,708.2 (558.4)	11,571.4 (551.3)
DOC3				2,736.9 (220.9)	4,425.5 (198.7)	2,430.2 (197.7)
DOC4				2,356.8 (318.3)	3,535.3 (317.4)	1,999.6 (304.2)
DOC5				−760.1 (302.5)	−720.4 (308.1)	−1,002.0 (291.8)
DFR				2,005.9 (149.8)	2,263.5 (152.6)	1,848.7 (145.0)
DAR				1,410.6 (119.7)	1,622.2 (122.4)	1,367.8 (116.1)
DRE				825.1 (127.9)	999.1 (131.1)	746.2 (124.3)
DSEX	−7,539.2 (146.3)	−1,917.1 (159.4)	−5,775.9 (137.0)	−5,653.1 (135.0)	−6,378.4 (132.2)	−2,009.1 (161.9)
EHC		.0592 (.0011)				.0385 (.0012)
Observations (N)	9,446	9,446	9,446	9,446	9,446	9,446
R-squared	.1663	.4259	.3849	.4769	.4484	.5057

Notes: Standard errors are in parentheses.
All variables not marked * are statistically significant at 5 percent.

227

Table 9.8
Wage Equations for Married Females and Males for the United States

Variables	1960		1980	
	(1)	(2)	(3)	(4)
Constant	-3,620.50	662.9	19,656.70	-7,993.96
	(25.95)	(9.4)	(72.03)	(38.20)
Education	476.47		1,207.40	
	(60.84)		(94.78)	
Experience	175.19		472.60	
	(23.88)		(41.53)	
Experience^2	-2.80		-6.94	
	(21.42)		(28.99)	
Hours	0.89		166.42	157.88
	(27.66)		(47.85)	(45.33)
Weeks			212.78	227.86
			(68.68)	(73.73)
Exp Cap Stock		0.102		0.115
		(80.7)		(101.28)
Sex	-3,032.0	-324.70	-7,741.26	-1,717.21
	(54.87)	(5.07)	(96.31)	(16.84)
Observations (N)	28,065	28,065	69,271	69,271
R-squared	.29	.30	.43	.43

Notes: Also adjusted for years married.

The 1960 sample consists of white married-once-spouse-present males and females not employed by the government.

The 1980 sample consists of married males and females.

In addition, control variables are included for region, size, occupation, and industry.

228

Table 9.9
Wage Equations for Single Females and Males for the United States

Variables	1960 (1)	1960 (2)	1980 (1)	1980 (2)
Constant	-2,193.9 (17.99)	-919.13 (8.0)	-18,117.2 (30.88)	-7,389.79 (16.29)
Education	253.73 (25.75)		866.17 (29.34)	
Experience	139.23 (19.00)		478.62 (18.68)	
Experience²	-2.23 (13.28)		-8.04 (13.09)	
Hours		1.16 (33.99)	125.44 (15.28)	131.71 (15.54)
Weeks			247.87 (35.34)	251.69 (34.73)
Exp Cap Stock		0.044 (20.22)		0.086 (25.96)
Sex	-671.17 (11.90)	-486.41 (7.70)	-2,424.12 (14.64)	-1,377.94 (7.91)
Observations (N)	6,572	6,572	7,142	7,142
R-squared	.29	.36	.13	.30

Note: In addition, control variables are included for region, size, occupation, and industry.

229

Table 9.10
Wage Equations for Single and Married Males for Taiwan

	(1)	(2)	(3)	(4)	(5)	(6)
Constant	12,145.3 (107.7)	5,733.6 (389.4)	-6,217.6 (514.5)	-4,321.1 (555.0)	5,421.2 (465.4)	3,270.1 (436.6)
Education		1,039.9	640.0 (22.4)	(26.9)		
Experience			749.2 (22.5)	640.0 (21.5)		
Experience^2			-12.7 (0.4)	-10.9 (0.4)		
LNHR		13.7 (1.8)	12.4 (1.8)	16.5 (1.7)	16.5 (1.8)	17.7 (1.7)
DIN1				13.3 (330.6)*	-71.6 (345.6)*	367.4 (321.8)*
DIN2				55.7 (229.8)*	260.9 (242.5)*	544.9 (225.8)
DIN3				2,657.3 (1,947.8)*	3,470.7 (2,057.3)*	4,039.8 (1,914.3)
DIN4				2,551.9 (312.9)	3,191.0 (329.4)	3,189.7 (306.5)
DIN5				1,504.2 (261.6)	1,791.4 (274.8)	2,072.8 (255.8)
DIN6				685.0 (291.2)	992.3 (306.9)	1,109.5 (285.6)
DIN7				800.7 (398.6)	1,385.3 (420.6)	1,343.8 (391.4)
DOC1				4,757.2 (304.1)	7,294.9 (297.4)	4,020.1 (289.4)

	(1)	(2)	(3)	(4)	(5)	(6)
DOC2				13,263.7	17,136.4	11,212.4
				(544.8)	(556.8)	(540.3)
DOC3				1,950.0	4,187.0	1,722.9
				(223.0)	(213.7)	(208.8)
DOC4				1,074.3	2,573.3	1,088.1
				(266.8)	(273.6)	(257.5)
DOC5				−986.2	−861.2	−1,124.1
				(302.7)	(315.5)	(293.7)
DFR				1,439.1	1,950.0	1,394.6
				(154.4)	(161.3)	(150.8)
DAR				1,415.9	1,613.3	1,339.3
				(114.5)	(120.6)	(112.5)
DRE			1,983.6	740.4	886.2	647.6
			(162.9)	(119.4)	(126.0)	(117.4)
DMR	4,609.3	1,549.7		1,991.4	4,097.7	1,092.1
	(138.1)	(130.0)		(154.0)	(123.8)	(127.4)
EHC		.0573				.0422
		(.0010)				(.0011)
Observations (N)	9,792	9,792	9,792	9,792	9,792	9,792
R-squared	.1035	.3378	.3061	.3892	.3182	.4098

Notes: Standard errors are in parentheses.
All variables not marked * are statistically significant at 5 percent.

231

Table 9.11
Wage Equations for Single and Married Females for Taiwan

	(1)	(2)	(3)	(4)	(5)	(6)
Constant	9,683.1	1,456.2	-4,481.6	-3,449.8	2,088.9	-322.7
	(75.6)	(313.4)	(418.0)	(461.9)	(373.9)	(360.7)
Education			715.4	418.0		
			(20.0)	(24.1)		
Experience			337.6	284.5		
			(18.4)	(17.6)		
Experience²			-5.4	-4.9		
			(0.4)	(0.4)		
LNHR		20.6	21.6	21.7	20.1	21.4
		(1.3)	(1.3)	(1.3)	(1.3)	(1.3)
DIN1				583.2	70.8	318.8
				(356.3)*	(363.0)*	(341.5)
DIN2				143.8	110.4	313.2
				(192.3)*	(198.2)*	(186.6)*
DIN3				-687.7	-989.9	-1,164.0
				(2,684.2)*	(2,768.3)*	(2,603.2)*
DIN4				1,968.7	2,261.3	1,869.7
				(421.8)	(434.9)	(409.2)
DIN5				2,044.0	1,758.1	1,990.4
				(340.3)	(349.6)	(328.9)
DIN6				414.2	382.7	497.3
				(210.2)	(216.8)*	(204.0)
DIN7				2,064.8	2,071.8	2,260.1
				(270.4)	(278.9)	(262.4)
DOC1				3,694.4	5,241.9	3,607.4
				(275.1)	(266.8)	(256.7)

DOC2				6,846.9	7,980.2	6,416.6
				(1,269.4)	(1,307.0)	(1,230.4)
DOC3				1,537.9	2,821.7	1,756.9
				(162.8)	(145.9)	(141.7)
DOC4				976.0	1,861.9	1,163.7
				(259.8)	(262.0)	(247.5)
DOC5				1,275.0	1,410.6	1,434.4
				(222.6)	(229.2)	(215.6)
DFR				1,556.9	1,697.5	1,531.5
				(111.5)	(114.0)	(107.4)
DAR				1,089.7	1,275.6	1,047.2
				(94.5)	(97.0)	(91.5)
DRE				399.4	535.8	332.1
				(101.9)	(104.9)	(98.8)
DMR	−467.7	1,518.1	−415.1	−120.1	−804.7	1,717.2
	(107.1)	(105.0)	(143.1)	(137.4)*	(101.8)	(100.5)
EHC		.0872				.0640
		(.0021)				(.0021)
Observations (N)	6,918	6,918	6,918	6,918	6,918	6,918

Notes: Standard errors are in parentheses.
All variables not marked * are statistically significant at 5 percent.

233

Table 9.12
Wage Equations for Single and Married Males for the United States

Variables	1960			1980		
	(1)[a]	(2)[b]		(1)[a]	(2)[b]	
Mrst	3,001.82	534.65		2,030.41	389.19	
	(14.71)	(2.64)		(11.27)	(2.16)	
Exp Cap Stock		0.11			0.11	
		(28.20)			(81.90)	
Observations (N)	3,167	3,167		41,164	41,164	
R-squared	0.06	0.25		0.28	0.25	

Notes: [a] Also adjusted for Hours and Weeks.
[b] Also adjusted for Education, Experience, Experience^2, Hours, and Weeks.

Table 9.13
Wage Equations for Single and Married Females for the United States

Variables	1960				1980			
	(1)[a]		(2)[b]		(1)[a]		(2)[b]	
Mrst	−624.76		−148.26		−1,516.44		−578.29	
	(8.03)		(1.71)		(15.62)		(6.04)	
Exp Cap Stock			0.04				0.08	
			(11.35)				(54.00)	
Observations (N)	2,350		2,350		28,107		28,107	
R-squared	0.06		0.07		0.41		0.40	

Notes: [a] Also adjusted for Hours and Weeks.
[b] Also adjusted for Education, Experience, Experience^2, Hours, and Weeks.

Table 9.5 illustrates these results for Taiwan. The gender variable (DSEX) depicts male-female wage differentials. The gap is NT$ 5,495 for the entire population (column 1), NT$ 4,144 (column 3) adjusting for schooling and potential market experience (age minus education minus six), and NT$ 4,241 when also adjusting for industry, occupation, and region, as well as city and firm sizes (column 4). Roughly 25 percent of the male-female wage gap is explained, implying a 75 percent discrimination coefficient.

When account is taken of human-capital stock based on lifetime work expectations, the wage differential is reduced to between NT$ 1,649 and NT$ 2,210. This implies that about 70 percent [i.e., (5,495 – 1,649)/5,495] of the wage differential is explained, rather than 25 percent as in usual models. Similar results are obtained within marital-status groups (tables 9.6 and 9.7). For singles, 45 percent of the NT$ 2,462 gap is explained. For marrieds, this figure is 75 percent [(7,539 – 1,917)/7,539]. Note that although the traditionally computed wage differentials (column 3 of tables 9.6 and 9.7) are larger for marrieds than singles (NT$ 5,653 versus NT$ 1,938), the new adjusted differentials are relatively similar, being between NT$ 1,352 and NT$ 1,917 (column 2) and between NT$ 1,605 and NT$ 2,009 (column 6).

Tables 9.8 and 9.9 illustrate the results for the United States. Here we compare 1960 and 1980 U.S. census data (1/1,000 samples). We refrain from describing the data since they are readily available. Again, the relevant coefficients are the values obtained for the dummy gender variable (Sex). Two columns are presented for each year and stratum, one in which adjustments are made for traditional human-capital variables (age, education, and weeks and hours of work), and one that incorporates the expected capital-stock variable.

The coefficient –3,032 represents the 1960 dollar difference in earnings. The coefficient –324.7 represents the male/female earnings differential when appropriate account is taken of life-cycle differences in labor-force expectations. As can be seen, 89 percent [(3,032-324)/3,032] of the earnings differential can be explained when human-capital accumulation is fully incorporated. (This is actually an understatement because the 3,032 differential already adjusts for age, experience, and hours of work.) For 1980, the explained differential amounts to 78 percent [(7,741 – 1,717)/7,741]. When one adjusts further by occupation, industry, location, length of marriage, and number of children, these differences are reduced further, in some cases becoming insignificant. For singles (table 9.9), between 38 and 43 percent of the wage gap is explained.

To lend credence to these results, similar computations can be performed using groups for which sex discrimination is not an issue, such as analyzing wage differentials within a given gender class. An example would be marital-status wage differentials. Here married men earn far greater wages than single men, while single women earn more than marrieds. We analyze these marital wage differences for both Taiwan and the United States, with the results for Taiwan in tables 9.10 and 9.11 and those for the United States in tables 9.12 and 9.13.

In Taiwan, married males earn NT$ 4,609 more than singles. This gap is reduced to NT$ 1,984 when one controls for education and experience. However, when one controls for expected lifetime labor-force participation, the gap closes farther to NT$ 1,550. Lifetime labor-force participation's explanatory power is increased further when occupation and industry are added as controls. Here lifetime labor-force expectations explain 75 percent compared to 50 percent of the wage gap. Married Taiwanese females earn NT$ 467 less than their single counterparts. This gap is completely eliminated when one controls for lifetime work expectations.

Similar findings are obtained for the United States. In 1960, 82 percent of the $3,000 earnings premium married males received could be explained by married/single life-cycle differences in labor-force participation [(3,002 − 535)/3,002]. Likewise about 76 percent of the $625 premium single women obtained could be explained by lifetime labor-force participation. For 1980, these explained differentials amounted to 81 and 62 percent, respectively.

V. CONCLUSIONS

In order to put earnings variations in proper perspective, many researchers attempt to parcel wage differentials into "explainable" and "unexplainable" portions, with the unexplained portion denoting "discrimination." Discrimination measures, however, can be upward or downward biased. One error that predominates in current analyses is omitting lifetime work expectations, especially periods of intermittency so common among women with children. Such expected intermittency affects human-capital investment and earnings long before women actually drop out. Not considering future work expectations causes severe overestimates of discrimination.

In this chapter, we outlined a life-cycle model to show how these intermittency expectations affect human-capital investments. We then devised an estimation technique that incorporates life-cycle work expectations. The approach was applied to U.S. data as well as data from Taiwan. In both cases, as much as 80 percent of the male/female wage gap could be explained, thereby reducing the discrimination coefficient to about 20 percent.

To illustrate robustness, the technique was applied to an entirely different case, one not involving sex discrimination at all. Here the technique worked with equal success. Expected lifetime labor-force participation explained between 60 and 75 percent of the marital-status earnings gap for men and a slightly greater proportion of the marital-status gap for women.

Although this procedure was applied to explain earnings variations, it may be equally applicable to other aspects of discrimination. Clearly the speed with which one receives promotions in job ladders is related to lifetime labor-force expectations. Yet such expectations are as yet not appropriately incorporated. The same holds true of job mobility and other work decisions.

Unlike other techniques, the results presented here reveal low levels of discrimination. This means that differences in individual characteristics create wage differentials more so than differences in earnings structure. One should not take this to mean that there is no discrimination. Instead, the results indicate that discrimination is mostly societal: social custom, perhaps encouraged by government tax policies, motivates a division of labor in the home which causes women to have lower lifetime work expectations. This, in turn, decreases women's incentives to acquire earnings-enhancing skills.

PART IV

MARKETS: SOCIAL AMPLIFIERS OR DAMPERS? IS AN ACTIVE POLICY NECESSARY/EFFECTIVE?

The final part of this volume is a fitting conclusion to a book dedicated to someone who, in 1921, was the first African American woman to get a Ph.D. in economics and who then found that this human capital was unmarketable. Sadie Alexander went on to devote her life to addressing inequality by race and gender with legal weapons, laying groundwork for the civil rights movement of the 1950s and 1960s. Do markets, especially labor markets which determine valuations for Ph.D.'s in economics, serve to amplify or to dampen invidious social distinctions or must they be supplemented by affirmative public policy? The four chapters in this part measure inequality innovatively in social areas (entrepreneurship in inner-city black communities, teenage motherhood, black immigration, and education in the South) and each asks what the role is of markets in mitigating social inequality.

Chapter 10 by Timothy Bates focuses upon the interaction between inner-city ghettos of African Americans and the rest of the economy, an interaction that works to preserve these ghettos as depressed and underdeveloped enclaves within a prosperous economy and which suggests an analogy to dependency theory of international economic inequality, offering insights and institutional richness lacking in models of internal colonialism (e.g. Blauner [1972] and Tabb [1970]). This study utilizes data on characteristics of business viability from a new data source: samples of African-American- as well as European-American-owned firms that were operating in 1982 in 28 large metropolitan areas. These data are analysed to determine the traits of survivors as opposed to those whose business operations had ceased by late 1986. This is part of a larger ongoing research effort formulating and analyzing the Characteristics of Business Owners

(CBO) data base by the Bureau of the Census, in which Professor Bates has played a key role.

The empirical findings indicate that firms owned by well-educated African Americans are increasingly locating in nonminority sections of metropolitan areas. Facing weak internal markets, increasingly stripped of entrepreneurial talent, and redlined by commercial banks, the ghetto economy really has no prospect of generating the internal economic development that could produce jobs and incomes for its residents. Markets in the inner-city minority communities have collectively failed to overcome the constraints imposed upon business viability by the ghetto milieu.

This exploration of the role of economic forces preserving and amplifying social inequality is extended in chapter 11 by Elaine McCrate's exploration of the relation of inequality in economic incentives to differences in teenage childbearing. McCrate used 1986 National Longitudinal Survey of Youth (NLSY) data on young women to test whether young mothers could in fact reasonably expect low earnings, independently of the consequences of teenage childbearing. Contrary to the popular belief that certain teenage mothers are irrational (i.e., do not value education and work realistically), she argues that premarket discrimination in the form of lower quality schooling and anticipated market discrimination in employment offer a better explanation of racial and class disparities in teenage childbearing. Her results indicate that postponing childbirth in order to concentrate on schooling is ineffective for poorer, black women as a means of getting higher pay. Consequently, programs to reduce teenage motherhood may not lead to significant improvements in the mothers' later economic status. Thus in order to reduce poverty, her analysis calls for directly improving educational quality and job opportunities for poor women.

McCrate's chapter joins Woodbury's work in chapter 12 on earnings differentials of black immigrants in challenging cultural determinist theories of social inequality based on unobserved cultural/human-capital differences. During the 1980s, controversy grew around the interpretation of earnings differentials that could not be explained by observable factors such as labor-force experience and schooling. Whereas during the 1970s these unexplained earnings differentials were attributed largely to discrimination (Blinder [1973]; Oaxaca [1973]), in the early 1980s there was a harkening back to "culture-of-poverty" arguments (for example, Moynihan [1965]) that these differentials should be viewed as reflecting unobserved differences in human capital or cultural traits (Sowell [1981b], [1983];

Chiswick [1983a], [1983b]; Loury [1984]). Because this cultural/human-capital interpretation raises fundamental questions about the importance of racial discrimination and the role of markets in the United States, it has met strong counterarguments (Williams [1987a], Darity [1989]).

Woodbury follows an approach developed by Chiswick [1978] to estimate several earnings functions for foreign-born black men using data from the 1980 census of population. His findings raise questions about attributing unexplained earnings differentials solely to culture or unobserved human capital and point to the existence of significant labor-market discrimination against black immigrants. He finds that: (1) the earnings profiles over time of black immigrants differ dramatically from the earnings profiles of other groups of immigrants with earlier black immigrants earning less than more recent black immigrants – a puzzling result suggesting that discrimination is tangible by its decrease for more recent immigrants; (2) the return to education for black immigrants for whom English is their native language is as low as the return to education for other groups of immigrants for whom English is, at best, a second language; and (3) the unexplained earnings differentials for black immigrants, the gap which is the central focus in the debate between culture versus discrimination, greatly exceed the unexplained differentials for other groups of immigrants independent of language proficiency.

Closely related to debates about culture versus discrimination are arguments that "background differences" appear to be more important than "market discrimination to attainment of black-white economic parity" (paraphrased from a statement by Freeman [1981] and argued by O'Neill [1990]). Divisions among those making and refuting these arguments reveal deep and intense ideological splits among social scholars. Yet despite one's predisposition on the role of market versus nonmarket factors, one can still address the effectiveness of antidiscrimination interventions in markets. Chapter 13 by James Heckman looks at the effects of governmental policy on racial inequality: Did the legal changes in the mid-1960s cause a "discontinuous" narrowing of the racial gap in earnings? There are plausible arguments on both sides of this question, but Heckman looks at disaggregated data for the South and argues powerfully that though, of course, we cannot prove causality, there is a strong case for the effectiveness of Title VII of the Civil Rights Act of 1964 and related affirmative-action measures. This chapter continues this vital debate on the effectiveness of affirmative social policies, directly and intuitively summarizing and addressing the arguments by Freeman [1981], Smith and Welch [1984 and 1989], Jaynes and Williams [1989], Jaynes [1990],

Leonard [1990] and O'Neill [1990].

These final four discussions offer a fitting cap to the earlier chapters in this volume: what are the effects of markets on social distinctions? The earlier chapters described the feed back from social distinctions to markets: how do social distinctions affect markets? They began by observing the remarkable persistence of inequality by race and gender contrary to the very American belief in the efficacy of education. This persistence was described when looking at unemployment (chapter 1 by Steven Shulman and chapter 2 by William Darity), earnings (chapter 4 by Rhonda Williams), job-allocation (chapter 5 by William Bielby and 6 by James Baron) and working-conditions (chapter 7 by David Fairris and Lori Kletzer). The desire to disentangle market forces from social forces drove Solomon Polachek and Charng Kao's analysis of differences in earnings by gender in chapter 9 as well as Michael Robinson and Phanindra Wunnava's analysis in chapter 3. This same impulse lay behind Harriet Duleep and Nadja Zalokar's consideration of how to meaure market inequality in chapter 8. The diversity of these studies reflects the complexity of the social construction of markets: the ocean we all ride in is turbulent, but we beckon any student of society to swim extensively within this volume.

10
Circular Causation in Social Processes: The Case of the Ghetto and Black-Owned Businesses

Timothy Bates

Creation of viable small businesses commonly entails (1) involvement of talented and capable entrepreneurs who have (2) access to financial capital to invest in the business ventures, and (3) access to markets for the products of their enterprises. Absence of one or more of these three elements of business viability has traditionally handicapped many of the small firms that have operated in inner-city minority communities. Within these neighborhoods of large metropolitan areas, neither the black-owned businesses nor the nonminority enterprises are flourishing. These firms have collectively failed to overcome the constraints imposed upon business viability by the ghetto milieu. Facing limited access to financial capital, the ghetto firms that most commonly persist are small in terms of sales and employment relative to their counterparts located in other geographic areas. Human capital is typically not being retained: the black establishments that remain in business are more likely to be headed by high-school dropouts than college-educated entrepreneurs.

Section I of this study discusses interactions between the ghetto and the rest of the economy that work to hinder economic development. Given the realities of the ghetto milieu, the development role that black businesses could possibly assume is spelled out. The result – a theory of ghetto economic development – is designed to generate testable hypotheses about the role of black enterprise in the ghetto economy.

A unique set of data that describe black and nonminority businesses operating in 28 large metropolitan areas (described in section II) permit tests of these hypotheses. The results, presented in sections III and IV, suggest that highly educated business owners employing larger financial capital inputs are more likely to create viable firms than poorly educated cohorts whose inputs of financial capital are less bountiful. Black owners possess, on average, less of the inputs that are associated with business viability and their access to debt capital is restricted relative to the accessibility experienced by most of their nonminority counterparts. While it is true that limited access to capital as well as markets handicaps ghetto-oriented businesses irrespective of owner racial background, it is the black business community that suffers disproportionately from these constraints.

I. THE ECONOMIC DYNAMICS OF THE GHETTO

The urban ghetto is a depressed enclave within a prosperous economy: flows of income, resources, and people interact with conditions of poverty and underdevelopment in a system of circular causation that maintains the ghetto as a characteristic feature of the national economy. The pattern of the ghetto economy is one of self-reinforcing influences: (1) poverty reinforces the conditions that lead to poverty; (2) resources that might lead to economic development are drained out.

IA. Ghetto Defining Mechanisms

Ghetto-bound black populations include large numbers of individuals who are in a very real sense the "rejects" of American society. Mainstream America rejects individuals who do not meet the standards established for membership in the diverse subsystems that make up the larger social order. In our society, race is a criterion for acceptance or rejection. Racially defined ghettos make up one of the major subsystems into which society's rejects congregate.

People rejected from the socioeconomic system are not scattered at random. Rather, they tend to be collected at specific points. Particularly bizarre behavior, for example, takes some people to mental hospitals, while crimes draw others to prisons. Traits other than race that cause one to gravitate to the ghetto include poor education, low skills, inability to speak English, or poor adaptability to the behavior patterns of the dominant society.

The subsystems that hold society's rejects are separated from the central sectors of the social order by various types of barriers. Mental hospitals and prisons are walled and policed by armed guards. The ghetto, in contrast, is defined by barriers that are social and economic. The ghetto is not cut off completely from the rest of society and a substantial number of its residents eventually manage to move up and out into other sectors of society; others, meanwhile, move down and into the ghetto. Escape from the ghetto is often a process that stretches across generations. Parents arrive from foreign lands, lacking educational credentials, not fluent in English, and lacking marketable skills, and are relegated to the ghetto subsystem. Their children, in contrast, develop the educational background and the English fluency that enable them to penetrate the economy's high-wage sector; they move up and out, having surmounted the barriers that held their parents in the ghetto subsystem.

Ghetto barriers, unfortunately, prove to be insurmountable for the majority of its residents. Mobility outward is not based entirely on merit or even income; race is an important criterion for movement outward. The fact that the ghetto is a depository for people rejected from society influences the attitudes of the rest of society toward the ghetto. These attitudes are reflected in inadequate provision of public services, such as education, which tends to preserve ghettoization and to reduce the upward mobility of ghetto residents. The socioeconomic barriers that define the ghetto subsystem show up in the economic statistics in such forms as high rates of unemployment and relatively low income levels.

Mechanization of cotton picking provides an example of how ghetto mechanisms work. The black sharecropper in the Mississippi Delta region in 1950, poor, uneducated, and possessing only agricultural skills, was redundant there in 1955 due to mechanization. Cast out of one subsystem, he moved to a place that would accept the rejects created by agricultural mechanization. Partly by choice and partly because there was no other place to go, he ended up in the urban ghetto. Once caught in the ghetto subsystem, the ex-sharecropper was in the grip of barriers that tended to block his upward mobility and to perpetuate his poverty. Low incomes mean poor food, bad housing, and poor health. These conditions tend to reinforce low labor productivity, thus perpetuating low incomes. The drain of resources out of the urban poverty area – manpower, capital, and income – serves to reinforce poverty. The public services that might overcome part of the deficiencies in private incomes are substandard. Deficiencies in the educational systems, in particular, lead to low skill levels and low productivity. Life in the ghetto economy, therefore, is something of a vicious circle: (1) poverty often reinforces the conditions that lead to poverty, and (2) those ghetto residents who do move up and out take with them much of the entrepreneurial talent that development of the ghetto economy would require.[1]

IB. The Drain of Resources

Examination of the ghetto residents themselves indicates the chief factors that cause rejection from the dominant society:

1. Race: blacks, Puerto Ricans, Mexican Americans, and other minorities.
2. Recent arrival: from the rural South and Puerto Rico, as well as foreign countries.[2]
3. Cultural differences: persons whose background deviates from white middle-class culture.[3]
4. Low productivity: low earning power resulting from lack of skills, poor education, bad health, old age, and related factors.

Those who achieve high productivity as well as high earnings, plus assimilation into mainstream white culture, normally opt to leave the ghetto; most residents remain.

The chief resource of the ghetto economy is labor, and the largest income flow into the ghetto is derived from employment. In most ghettos, a substantial minority of the labor force is employed in middle-income jobs and a few actually attain high-wage employment. The higher-income individuals are the ones who are most likely to move up and out. Transfer payments supplement earned income, primarily through the welfare system, food stamps, social security, and medicaid.

Income flows out of the ghetto in much the same way as capital and labor. Ghetto residents buy goods produced elsewhere in stores that are typically owned by outsiders. Internal flows of income that might support greater economic activity and higher incomes within the ghetto are largely absent. Rather, ghetto income flows support economic activity elsewhere. A study by Oakland, Sparrow, and Stettler [1971] of the Hough area in Cleveland, based on household spending diaries, documented the outflow of income from ordinary household spending. It found that the marginal propensity to spend in Hough was 0.13: for each additional dollar of family expenditures, only thirteen cents was spent in Hough. Income flows such as these exacerbate inner-city underdevelopment. Money too often passes through urban ghettos "without lingering long enough to turn over several times and thereby generate incomes for other of the community's residents." [4]

If the dollars that ghetto residents bring into their communities are spent several times within the community, then additional economic activity is generated that will tend to benefit other ghetto residents. If local businesses were owned by neighborhood residents who would, in turn, spend their incomes in the community, even more money would stay within the ghetto economy and resultant multiplier effects would be correspondingly greater. This line of reasoning constitutes part of the logic behind promoting local ownership of ghetto businesses.

The goods purchased in any community are largely imported and ghettos, in this respect, are like any other urban area. In most communities, however, a significant portion of the retail and wholesale establishments are owned locally and the incomes of the owners are largely spent locally. A chain of spending and respending is set up that adds strength and variety to the local economy. Ownership of rental housing by community residents also promotes rechanneling of purchasing power back into the local economy, with attendant multiplier effects. Yet ghetto rental housing is owned overwhelmingly by outsiders and the monthly rent checks do not come back into the ghetto to support other enterprises or employees.

Probably the greatest flow of capital out of ghetto areas takes place in rental housing. Minimal maintenance of housing facilities enables land-lords to withdraw their capital from their real-estate investments.[5] Ulti-mately, the property will be worthless because of wear and tear, but while it is being used up, the owner can realize a nice cash flow while he takes out his capital. The fact that some property owners are withdrawing their capital by failing to maintain their structures causes surrounding owners to do likewise as a matter of self-protection. One deteriorated building draws down the value of surrounding property. These "neighborhood effects" cause housing disinvestment to be a self-reinforcing process that tends to accelerate once it begins. Rental housing owned by ghetto residents is subject to the same economic forces that lead to property deterioration generally in the ghettos. Local ownership, therefore, may not induce landlords to maintain properties in neighborhoods where buildings are deteriorating.

Capital also flows out of ghettos through deterioration of public facili-ties. Fiscally strapped older cities have a universal tendency to maintain facilities in middle- and upper-income areas and to put the priorities of the ghetto last. Schools, libraries, and medical facilities therefore deteriorate, parks run down, and streets and curbs go unrepaired.

Financial institutions have traditionally done a minimal job of servicing the loan demands of ghetto households and businesses. A substantial portion of the savings of the urban ghetto goes into banks and savings and loan associations (S & Ls) whose investment policies draw funds out of the area and into business loans, mortgages, and other investments elsewhere.[6] Little comes back to support the ghetto economy or promote its development.

Development of an area's financial sector typically stimulates economic growth by mobilizing savings that would otherwise be held as idle cash balances. Households and businesses depend upon the availability of such funds to finance economic functions beyond those supportable by their current internal capacity to raise funds. The mere existence of financial institutions, however, provides no assurance that ghetto areas will experience increased development by participating in the financial intermediation process. Local savers undoubtedly enjoy the benefits of safety and convenience that financial institutions provide, but local borrowers may not have access to the pool of savings that banks and S & Ls assemble.

Banks and S & Ls owned and controlled by ghetto residents can potentially reverse the savings drain by pooling and investing the savings of area residents to finance local economic development. This constitutes an important rationale for supporting creation and expansion of minority-owned inner-city financial institutions. Certain economic facts of ghetto life, however, constrain the behavior of financial institutions that are actively collecting deposits and lending to a ghetto clientele. These institutions are mobilizing the savings of a clientele whose incomes are, on average, lower and less stable than those of nonminorities. Their mean deposit account sizes, therefore, are well below the national averages for corresponding types of financial institutions. Smaller account size necessarily means more paperwork and extra teller labor time per deposit dollar, and this raises expenses relative to deposits.[7] Banks and S & Ls that are actively lending to ghetto borrowers face a loan demand function characterized by higher risk than that faced by nonghetto institutions. When financial institutions serve a ghetto clientele, their financial performance tends to reflect the economic disparities that characterize inner-city minorities versus the rest of society. Black-owned banks and S & Ls have, in fact, experienced relatively high operating expenses and loan losses, as well as lower and less stable annual profits compared to their nonminority counterparts. While this has not undermined the viability of most black-owned financial institutions, it has tended to limit their size and scope. Consequently, they have been unable to reduce substantially the drain of savings from ghetto areas.

Ghetto economic development therefore tends to be undermined by drains of savings, housing capital, and infrastructure. Income flows rarely strengthen and support other sectors of the ghetto economy because of their tendency to drain out quickly, supporting economic activity located elsewhere. The most serious drain that exacerbates ghetto poverty, however, is one that has grown in intensity in recent years. The ghetto's chief resource is labor, and its best products have increasingly been departing by way of the educational system and the high-wage economy. Drawn by opportunities outside of the urban poverty areas, many of the most intelligent, capable, and imaginative young people have moved into the economic mainstream, where rewards are greater and opportunities are wider. Programs that enable some to escape the ghetto serve to preserve and reinforce ghettoization for many more. The best and the brightest are drawn out of the ghetto to serve themselves and contribute to the further advancement of the dominant society.

Expanded opportunities for bright minority youth are consistent with restricted opportunities for most. In subtle ways, widened opportunities support the very economic processes that create and preserve the urban ghetto and poverty in America. They tend to draw intelligent and capable members of minority groups into the affluent mainstream, away from the underclass. Some become committed fully to the ideology of individual achievement. Meanwhile, those who remain caught in the ghetto are told that the fault is theirs, that if they had the initiative to seize opportunities, they too could have been affluent.

This ideology of individualism provides a rationale for not attacking the roots of the problem, the forces that work to block mobility out of the ghetto for most of its inhabitants. Blacks find themselves divided into groups of haves and have-nots, divisions that correspond to similar patterns in the overall society. Politically, this tends to undermine the united action of black groups; those who a generation ago would have been the leadership class of the ghetto are today increasingly divorced from its concerns.

IC. Black Business Impact on Ghetto Resource Drains

Business ownership is one alternative available to well-educated blacks that normally does not entail leaving the ghetto. Retention of local entrepreneurial talent is one of the prerequisites for reversing ghetto resource drains and generating a cumulative process of growth. As mentioned above, local ownership of businesses tends to strengthen internal income flows, thus increasing the regional multiplier.

To envision the impact of locally owned businesses upon the ghetto economy, it is useful to categorize them into two distinct groups:

1. Businesses serving predominantly a ghetto clientele: retail, most service industries, and small-scale construction.

2. Businesses serving larger markets, either metropolitan-area markets or, in a few instances, national markets: manufacturing, wholesale, transportation, and large-scale construction.

Both types of firms promote ghetto development, but the ghetto-oriented firms are inherently limited in their ability to alleviate ghetto economic problems. While those serving the local market may help to slow ghetto resource drains – creating, in the process, jobs and income – firms serving broader markets are the only ones capable of actually reversing the outward resource flow. Firms serving regional or national markets can potentially create vitally needed net inflows of resources into ghetto economies.

It is essential to understand why black-owned businesses that serve a ghetto clientele are unlikely to alter significantly the local economic landscape. Most fundamentally, the state of these ghetto enterprises reflects the economic circumstances of their clientele. The inner city is not a favorable environment for the economic development of most lines of business. Weak internal markets in ghetto areas reflect the obvious fact that poor people possess minimal purchasing power. The plentiful supply of cheap labor is an advantage to certain kinds of ghetto businesses, but markets and capital are other ingredients of enterprise success and both are in short supply. Lack of capital and weak internal markets are the major problems facing black-owned firms, but they do not complete the list of obstacles: high insurance rates, high incidence of economic crime, weak infrastructure, and poor public services, among others. The problems of markets and capital, in combination with these other ghetto attributes, are sufficient to minimize the economic development potential of a black business community that is oriented toward servicing a ghetto clientele.

The elements of a viable ghetto economic development strategy include (1) developing lines of business that can utilize the ghetto's supply of abundant labor and (2) relying heavily upon nonghetto sources for both capital and markets. The process of economic development in the urban ghetto requires fundamental changes in the flow of resources. To date, however, the vast majority of black-owned businesses have focused entirely upon serving a ghetto clientele. This sector of the business community is most useful for assisting economic development only when other forces have generated rising incomes for ghetto residents. Assume, for example, that ghetto businesses in fields such as construction and manufacturing succeed in attracting large-scale procurement contracts from corporate and government sources. Assume, furthermore, that these contracts increase the wage earnings of ghetto workers and the profits of the contract recipients. In this situation, minority firms have successfully increased the flow of income into the ghetto, and a portion of this income flow will be spent at locally owned firms. Wage income resulting from this income flow will take the form of consumption expenditures at local retail and service establishments. The contract-holding firms will presumably use a portion of this income flow to purchase intermediate goods from local suppliers. Finally, part of the income flow will appear in local financial institutions in the form of checking and savings accounts. The spending and saving activities resulting from the initial income flow will generate a second round of spending and saving activities within the ghetto. The strength of ensuing rounds of spending (and saving) is directly dependent upon the degree to which the recipient firms (and their employees) shop within the inner city: more locally owned firms imply more rechanneling of these funds and more respending within the local economy. The greater the degree of local respending, the stronger the ghetto multiplier effect and hence the greater the resultant impact on ghetto incomes and employment.

Note that the streams of spending and respending percolating through the local economy were, in this example, entirely dependent on manufacturing and construction contracts that firms received from the outside economy: no inflow means no multiplier effect. The ghetto-oriented business community is fundamentally *reactive* to levels of income flows that are influenced by outside factors. The ghetto business that competes in the broader marketplace, in contrast, actually shapes the flow of income into the ghetto economy. Furthermore, its prospects are not held hostage by intraghetto income levels; its prospects are linked to its ability to compete in the broader economy.

ID. The Development Potential of Black Enterprise

I have characterized a ghetto economy whose poverty is partially maintained by:
1. Outflows of capital in several forms: savings, housing stock, and infrastructure.
2. Outflows of incomes exacerbated by weak internal income flows and a low resultant regional multiplier.

3. Outflows of many intelligent, capable, and imaginative young people by way of the educational system and the high-wage economy.

Stripped of capital and entrepreneurial talent, the ghetto economy really has no prospect of generating the internal economic development needed to produce jobs and incomes for its residents. The strategy of creating and expanding black-owned businesses and financial institutions can potentially alleviate all of these outflows, but this approach is fraught with risks due to lack of capital, weak ghetto markets, and related factors.

An economic development program that envisions utilizing black entrepreneurship as a tool for improving the ghetto economy must combine three elements. These three vital elements are (1) capital, (2) markets, and (3) talented and capable entrepreneurs. If any of these three elements are lacking, the development potential of black enterprise is seriously jeopardized. The natural functioning of the ghetto economy tends to produce weak internal markets as well as capital flight and a drain of highly educated people. Government programs to assist minority enterprise commonly focus upon only one of the three essential elements of business viability, typically either capital or markets. Some of these government programs perversely insist that evidence of entrepreneurial talent is grounds for denying assistance in the realms of capital and markets.[8]

Entrepreneurial ability is highly correlated with both education and income levels: successful business operators tend to be above average in both categories. The question that invariably arises when government assistance accrues to higher-income, well-educated black entrepreneurs is "Why help those who are already successful?" This objection can be addressed at two levels. First, programs that target assistance to lower-income, less educated entrepreneurs simply produce mass business failure.[9] Second, the capable entrepreneurs are the ones who are likely to produce the desired result, economic development, provided, of course, that the other ingredients of business success (capital and markets) are present. It is the viable firm, after all, that creates jobs. Its profits support investments that, in turn, permit further business expansion and job creation. The presence of business success stories lures younger, better-educated blacks into self-employment, and this further promotes the economic development thrust of black entrepreneurship. Similarly, existing firms in less profitable lines of business are induced by the success story phenomenon to reorient their operations to areas that offer greater profit potential; once again, economic development is promoted. The resource drains that exacerbate ghetto poverty all tend to be reversed if this business development process is successful:

1. Capital is invested in the ghetto economy; profitable operation creates additional capital and reinvestment.

2. As the network of locally owned businesses spreads, internal ghetto income flows are strengthened.

3. Capable business people, instead of being drawn into the dominant economy, are retained in the inner city, where they function to create incomes and jobs.

II. THE DATA BASE

Briefly, key ingredients of small-business viability are sufficient capital, available markets, and capable entrepreneurs. Yet the economic dynamics of the ghetto tend to preserve poverty, produce capital flight, and drain out highly educated people. Whether the growth of black entrepreneurship has eroded or reversed any of these tendencies is an empirical question. The size and scope of the black business community has broadened considerably in the last two decades, in part, due to an influx of self-employed individuals into lines of business in which minority representation has historically been minimal. In the most rapidly growing lines of black enterprise, such as finance and wholesaling, well over half of those individuals establishing firms have attended four or more years of college. Creation of the Characteristics of Business Owners (CBO) data base makes it possible to investigate black business behavior at levels as specific as individual zip codes. The CBO data base is specifically designed to address the sorts of issues raised above in my discussion of black business performance in a ghetto context.

The CBO survey was conducted in late 1986 and the data base was compiled by the U.S. Bureau of the Census in 1987. The CBO data base is the first data base of national scope that describes self-employed people as individuals as well as describing traits of businesses these people own, such as sales, earnings, employees, capital inputs, etc.[10] The CBO survey drew its sample from business owners included in the 1982 Survey of Minority-Owned Business Enterprises. This survey, in conjunction with the 1982 Survey of Women-Owned Businesses, identified firm owners as women, minority, or nonminority males. These two surveys were drawn from the universe of persons who filed in 1982 one of the following types of federal income tax forms: (1) Schedule C, Form 1040 (sole proprietorships); (2) Form 1065 (owners of partnerships); (3) Form 1120s (owners of subchapter S business corporations). In some instances, one owner of several firms is picked up in the sample; in other cases, multiple owners of one firm are encountered. In this study, each firm has a unique owner; multiple-owner firms are included through the designation of a representative owner (Bates [1990]). Among persons filing Schedule C forms, many are not small-business owners according to the commonly understood meaning of the term. Small-business owners are identified as the subset of the sample where owners had (1) a financial-capital investment in the business that was greater than zero and (2) annual sales of at least $5,000 in 1982. Observations not meeting these criteria were dropped from further consideration. For example, 21,127 responses (representing an 84.5 percent response rate) were received from owners of firms classified as "white male owned": 30.4 percent of these observations were dropped because the owners reported 1982 sales of less than $5,000. Of the remaining 14,707 observations, 28.2 percent were dropped because owners reported no financial-capital inputs at the point of business entry. This reduced the sample size to 10,556 owners, and 8.5 percent of this group was dropped because of nonresponse problems on certain key questionnaire items. The remaining 9,662 owners were connected with 7,960 firms, 3,513 of which were entered before 1976; the remaining 4,447 firms were entered by owners during the 1976-82 time period. Thus 21,127 responses to the CBO survey produced a sample of 7,960 businesses owned by white males. This sample is representative, regarding industry mix and geographic location, of all white male small-business proprietorships, partnerships, and small-business corporations that file tax returns, subject to the constraints that they (1) were operating in 1982 and (2) produced total annual sales of at least $5,000 in that calendar year. Selection of the sample of black-owned businesses was based upon the same procedures. Among black owners, a slightly lower 77.0 percent response rate produced a smaller sample of firms and over 40 percent of the respondents were dropped because the owners reported sales for 1982 of under $5,000.

This chapter analyzes black business in an urban context, focusing particularly upon firms operating in inner-city minority communities. The data are drawn from CBO information on firms that are located in 28 of the nation's largest metropolitan areas – in fact, Los Angeles, Chicago, New York, Philadelphia, Houston, Washington, D.C., Detroit, Dallas, and Atlanta account for over half of the businesses analyzed. Selection of the 28 areas is described in the Appendix.

Exact variable definitions of the variables from the CBO survey used in this study are summarized below:

Ed2: for owners completing four years of high school, the value of Ed2 = 1; otherwise, Ed2 = 0.

Ed3: for owners completing at least one but less than four years of college, the value of Ed3 = 1; otherwise, Ed3 = 0.

Ed4: for owners completing four or more years of college, the value of Ed4 = 1; otherwise, Ed4 = 0.

Those with less than 12 years of formal schooling are treated as the default group.

Age2: for owners between the ages of 35 and 44, Age2 = 1; otherwise, Age2 = 0.

Age3: for owners between the ages of 45 and 54, Age3 = 1; otherwise, Age3 = 0.

Age4: for owners 55 or older, Age4 = 1; otherwise, Age4 = 0.

Owners who are younger than 35 are the default group.

Sex: for male owners, Sex = 1; otherwise, Sex = 0.

Management: for owners who had worked in a managerial capacity prior to owning the business they owned in 1982, Management = number of years thusly worked.

Input: average number of hours per week that the owner devoted to operating the business under consideration.

Ongoing: method of acquiring the business, if the owner entered a business that was already in operation, Ongoing = 1; if the owner was the original founder of the business, Ongoing = 0.

Two variables describe how long ago the owner acquired or started the business, with businesses that started during 1976 to 1979 (and still continuing in 1982) serving as the default:

Time82: if the business was started or ownership was acquired during 1982, then Time82 = 1; otherwise, Time82 = 0;

Time80: if the business was started or ownership was acquired during 1980 or 1981, then Time80 = 1; otherwise, Time80 = 0.

Those businesses still operating in 1986 [11] are referred to as active firms; those that closed down between the start of 1983 and the end of 1986 are discontinued.

Debt: amount of borrowed money used to start or become an owner of the business, measured in thousands of dollars.

Equity: financial capital other than borrowed money used to start or become an owner of the business, measured in thousands of dollars. The dollar value of business assets contributed by the owner at the point of business entry is also included as equity.

Leverage: The ratio of debt to equity; the value of this ratio is constrained not to exceed 19 by the way questions about start-up investment and borrowing by the owners were formulated on the questionnaire.

Log capital: the logarithm of the sum of debt and equity capital.
The dollar amounts measured in Debt, Equity, and Log capital have not been adjusted for inflation.

Minority market: for firms having at least 75 percent minority customers in 1982, Minority market = 1; otherwise, Minority market = 0.

Minority area: for firms located in large SMSA communities in which over 40 percent of the residents are minorities, Minority area = 1; otherwise Minority area = 0. "Community" is measured by zip code: racial composition was calculated separately for each zip code within the large SMSAs.

Open market: for firms having over 25 percent nonminority customers in 1982, Open market = 1; otherwise, Open market = 0.

III. EMPIRICAL ANALYSIS: BLACKS OPERATING BUSINESSES IN LARGE METROPOLITAN AREAS

Black businesses as a group lag far behind the nonminority small-business community: their firms are, on average, smaller, less profitable, and more prone to failure than those operated by nonminorities. Smaller financial investments by black owners at the point of business start-up, less equity as well as less access to debt, are clearly linked to creation of smaller, less viable black-owned businesses. Beyond financial-capital input, a second trait that clearly delineates black from white firms concerns access to markets. Black businesses typically sell to other minorities, and this is particularly true among black firms that are located in minority communities of the nation's largest metropolitan areas. Findings by Handy and Swinton [1984] indicate that the local black clientele is still an overwhelmingly important market for black–owned businesses. They found that growth in black business receipts between 1972 and 1977 was powerfully influenced by the strength of local black purchasing power.

The state of the ghetto business community reflects the fact that the internal ghetto market is weak due to the low incomes of most of its residents. Table 10.1 indicates that both black and white firms differ systematically in terms of sales, employment, and discontinuance rates when they are divided into two groups: (1) those serving a clientele that is largely or entirely minority, and (2) those serving a clientele that is either diverse racially or largely nonminority. The firms described in table 10.1 are classified as minority-market oriented if 75 percent or more of their

customers are minorities; others are classified as competing in the nonminority marketplace. White-owned firms that are minority-market oriented actually have a higher discontinuance rate than blacks among the
business groups that service this market segment.

Among black firms doing business in large metropolitan areas (table
10.1), personal service lines of business are most reliant upon the minority
market; construction firms are least reliant on a minority clientele. The
majority of black firms in three industry groups, construction, manufacturing, and business services, sell to a clientele that is either racially diverse
or largely nonminority. Fewer than 15 percent of the personal service
firms, in contrast, compete in the nonminority marketplace. Traditional
lines of black enterprise, typified by personal services, are largely small-
scale, ghetto-based firms that serve minority customers. Finance, insurance, and real estate (FIRE) is an emerging line of business that has
attracted highly educated black entrepreneurs; nonetheless, table 10.1
shows that its customer base is predominantly minority. While the
tendency of emerging lines of enterprise is to compete actively in the
nonminority marketplace, it is nonetheless common for black college
graduates to enter skill-intensive service industries, FIRE in particular,
professional services to a lesser extent, that cater to a clientele that is
largely minority. For professionals as well as high-school dropouts, black
self-employment in the minority-market sector is associated with very
small firms. A comparison of mean 1982 sales for all blacks and whites in
the CBO samples who run businesses in the FIRE industry is revealing:

mean sales

black firms	$ 36,759
white male firms	$156,533

The only major sector of the service industry that has lower sales than FIRE
is personal services; black-owned firms in that sector produced mean 1982
sales of $26,634.[12]

Tiny firms serving a minority clientele are certainly numerous, but they
are not the only type of black-owned business operating in large metropolitan areas. Table 10.2 presents summary statistics describing the entire
samples of black- and white-owned firms that are operating in the 28 large
metropolitan areas under consideration. For the 23 percent of the black
businesses (table 10.2) that utilize paid employees, mean sales in 1982 were
$153,116 (versus $27,445 for the zero-employee firms) and 82.4 percent of
these firms were still operating in late 1986; 71.4 percent of the nonem-
ployers were still operating in 1986. Yet the contrasts (table 10.2) between
black and white-owned firms, whether employers or otherwise, are stark.

Table 10.1
Racial Ethnic Composition of the Customers of the Sample Firms Operating in 28 Large
Metropolitan Areas

	Black Firms	White Male Firms
A. Firms Oriented Toward the Minority Marketplace* (mean values):		
1982 sales	$49,362	$96,501
Number of employees	0.6	1.0
% still active, 1986	73.5%	69.8%
B. Firms Competing in the Nonminority Marketplace (mean values):		
1982 sales	$70,211	$174,593
Number of employees	1.0	2.1
% still active, 1986	74.7%	79.0%

C. Black-owned Firms: Degree of Reliance on the Minority Market

1. Lines of business relying most heavily on the minority market:[*]
   a. personal services
   b. retailing
   c. finance, insurance, and real estate (F.I.R.E.)

2. Lines of business relying most heavily on the nonminority market:[**]
   a. construction
   b. manufacturing
   c. business services

Notes: *Minority marketplace is defined to mean that 75% or more of the firm's customers in 1982 were minorities.
[*]Ranked in order from highest to lower percent of customers who are people of color
[**]Ranked in order from lowest to higher percent of customers who are people of color

259

Table 10.2
Business Characteristics of Firms Operating in Large Metropolitan Areas

	All Businesses		Employers Only	
	Black firms	White Male Firms	Black Firms	White Male Firms
1. Business traits (mean values) :				
a. total sales,1982	$56,342	$166,762	$153,116	$393,806
b. No. of employees, 1982	0.7	2.0	3.2	5.8
2. Owner traits:				
a. Total financial capital*	$16,059	$37,314	$28,204	$63,937
b. Equity capital*	$8,448	$20,867	$13,090	$34,532
c. Debt capital*	$7,611	$16,447	$15,114	$29,405
d. % with under 4 years of high school	21.9%	13.0%	18.6%	12.5%
e. % with 4 or more years of college	27.3%	41.0%	30.8%	42.5%
3. % of firms still in business, 1986	73.9%	78.1%	82.4%	85.4%
Observations (N)	2,318	1,815	533	630

Note: * Mean value at the date of entry into self-employment ($ figures are not inflation adjusted).

White firms utilizing paid employees are relatively more numerous than black employers: their mean sales are over twice as high and their financial capital inputs dwarf those reported by black enterprises.

The white-owned businesses are, of course, much less likely than blacks to cater to a minority clientele, and their spatial distribution within the metropolitan area differs sharply. Black firms are located largely in inner-city minority communities, while the white-owned enterprises are rarely observed in these environs. This locational distinction has great significance for comprehending both the laggard overall performance of black enterprise and the growth trajectory of the more successful small-business subset. Consider the following figures on black-owned firms that began operations between 1976 and 1982 in the 28 large metropolitan areas:

	Black Firms Located in Minority Communities	Black Firms Located in Nonminority Areas
Total financial capital (mean)	$15,096	$27,865
% of owners with four or more years of college	27.4%	41.3%

The largest disparity for these two groups of firms concerns debt capital: mean debt for the nonminority-area black businesses was $16,859, versus $5,994 for those located in minority communities. This difference accounts for most of the difference in total capital reported above.

Table 10.2 reveals substantial financial-capital disparities between black and white businesses. One important source of that disparity is rooted in the fact that debt capital is much more readily available to black-owned firms that are not located in urban minority communities. The practice whereby firms get smaller loans due to their location in minority residential areas is often called redlining.

Table 10.2's data are broken down into borrower and nonborrower groups below to highlight the role debt capital plays in determining total firm capitalization; these data are for firms formed between 1976 and 1982 only:

Table 10.3
Linear Regression Models Explaining Debt-Capital Inputs for Bank-Loan Recipients Entering Business in the 1976-1982 Time Period and Operating in Large Metropolitan Areas

	Black Firms	White Male Firms:
Constant	47.286	-25.964
	(38.528)	(28.177)
Sex	9.175	—
	(23.022)	—
Ed2	-5.403	30.827
	(28.085)	(29.727)
Ed3	-26.044	0.222
	(29.741)	(30.615)
Ed4	38.628*	34.110
	(26.806)	(28.118)
Age2	-29.285	-4.830
	(23.153)	(18.612)
Age3	-32.657	-5.280
	(26.390)	(23.042)
Age4	-24.641	-24.205
	(36.914)	(28.443)
Equity capital	.893*	1.791**
	(.165)	(.224)

Management	.784 (1.565)	2.134* (1.207)
Ongoing	24.770 (20.177)	49.996** (17.515)
Minority area††	−39.564** (18.117)	−4.180 (26.236)
Observations (N)	271	248
R-squared (adj)	.164	.301
F-value	5.31	10.21

Notes: Standard errors are in parentheses below the corresponding regression coefficients.
Debt and equity are measured in thousands of dollars.
*Statistically significant at the 10% level.
**Statistically significant at the 5% level.
††For the black-owned firms, minority area means that over 40% of the residents of the firm's zip code are minority, whereas for white-owned firms, it means that at least 20% of the residents are minority.

Mean Values	Borrowers Only		Nonborrowers Only	
	Black Firms	White Firms	Black Firms	White Firms
total financial capital	$33,937	$64,815	$8,545	$22,692
equity	$11,330	$23,210	$8,545	$22,692
debt	$22,607	$41,605	—	—
% receiving bank loans	47.2%	55.6%	—	—
N	574	446	797	572

The white-owned businesses are more likely to borrow than blacks and when they do borrow, average loan size ($41,605) is nearly double the corresponding $22,607 figure for black-owned firms. Most loan dollars come from commercial banks, particularly among black business borrowers: mean debt for those receiving bank loans was $33,860, versus $12,543 for black owners borrowing from nonbank sources.

Table 10.3 investigates sizes of bank loans received by white and black business owners operating in the 28 relevant large metropolitan areas. Among these bank-loan recipients, 63.1 percent of the black borrowers were located in minority areas of their respective metropolitan areas; 8.8 percent of the white business borrowers, in contrast, were located in minority communities. Multiple linear regression models (table 10.3) are utilized to explain relationships between debt capital received by bank borrowers and four types of explanatory variables: (1) owner equity-capital inputs, (2) owner human-capital traits, (3) owner demographic traits, and (4) geographic location of the firm. Direct relationships are hypothesized to exist between the size of debt capital at the point of business start-up and (1) equity capital as well as (2) human-capital and demographic traits that are associated with business viability. Considerations of both supply by the lender and demand by the borrower are relevant to loan-amount decisions; this econometric approach reflects judgments about which factor will dominate. The stronger borrower is expected to get the larger loan; debt and equity are complements rather than substitutes. While weaker borrowers may have a greater demand for credit – particularly to overcome equity-capital deficiencies – supply-side limitations are expected to limit loan access for the less attractive borrowers.[13]

The choice of owner human-capital and demographic traits for inclusion in this study's econometric exercises is shaped by previous findings on factors associated with business viability.[14] Overall, loan-amount determination is assumed to be a supply-side-dominated decision in the case of small-business start-ups. Lenders such as commercial banks are hypothesized to approve larger loans to borrowers who possess relatively large inputs of equity capital as well as human-capital and demographic traits that are associated positively with business viability. Attractive human-capital and demographic traits include (1) high education levels, (2) owners who lie in the middle, as opposed to the tails, of the age distribution, and (3) managerial experience. In addition, purchase of ongoing firms is seen as a likely shortcut to establishing business viability. Businesses located in minority communities are hypothesized to receive smaller loans, whether the firm in question is owned by whites or blacks, for the reasons described above: urban minority neighborhoods provide an unfavorable environment for most types of business.

Table 10.3 broadly indicates that highly educated owners possessing large equity-capital inputs are typically receiving the greater debt-capital inputs – unless their firms are located in large SMSA minority communities. Linear regression models explaining debt input levels are run separately for blacks and whites and they apply solely to bank-loan recipients whose firms are located in 28 very large metropolitan areas. In both of table 10.3's regression equations, coefficients were consistently large and statistically significant for the equity-capital explanatory variable. The fact that black owners in the large metropolitan areas who received bank loans possessed, on average, less equity capital than their white counterparts suggests that they can expect to receive less debt capital. Similarly, these same black owners were less likely to be college graduates: 33.6 percent of them had completed four or more years of college, versus 45.6 percent of their white counterparts. However, it is the racial difference in the coefficients attached to equity and minority-area variables (table 10.3) that provides the clearest explanation of the racial differential in loan size. While the coefficients favor white borrowers with respect to all criteria except for Ed4 (at least four years of college), the most striking difference, by a factor of two, is for the coefficient of equity capital: the white business bank-loan recipient in a large metropolitan area gets $1.79 in debt capital per dollar of equity-capital input he supplies, other things equal, while the black business borrower generates only $0.89 in debt capital for each dollar of equity-capital input he supplies.

Differential commercial bank treatment of black and white business borrowers accounts for much of the difference in mean debt inputs –

$49,679 for whites, $33,860 for blacks receiving bank loans – and this is particularly applicable for firms located in minority neighborhoods. Controlling for owner equity investment and demographic and human-capital traits, the black business located in the minority community receives substantially less in loan funds relative to the black borrower whose firm is located in a nonminority area! This is the essence of redlining. It is the location of one's firm that is the largest single determinant of loan size for the black business that receives a bank loan, according to table 10.3's black borrower regression analysis.

This relation between loan size and firm location for black-owned businesses is statistically highly significant and is invariant with respect to definitional changes regarding what constitutes a minority neighborhood. In the regression for black-owned businesses in table 10.3, the zip code area in which the business was located was classified as "minority" if over 40 percent of the total residents were minority, as measured by the 1980 census of population. In fact, black-owned businesses are rather frequent in zip codes that have more than 40 percent but less than 50 percent minority inhabitants. Reestimating this equation by defining a zip code as minority if over 50 percent of its inhabitants are minorities yields the same finding that banks are discriminating against black firms located in minority areas.

While most of the black firms were, in fact, located in zip codes that were over 50 percent minority in terms of racial or ethnic composition, white male firms were nearly nonexistent in these areas. Only five of the white firm bank-loan recipients analyzed in table 10.3 were located in zip code areas where the population racial composition was over 50 percent minority. The very small number of white borrowers in minority areas makes it hard to determine (statistically) if these firms are also being redlined by banks. In the regressions in table 10.3, white male firms were classified as being in minority areas if the zip code in which the borrowing firm was located had at least 20 percent minority population. Utilizing minority cutoff points of 40 percent and 50 percent to define "minority area," the table 10.3 regression equation was reestimated for white borrowers and the resultant minority-area variable coefficients suggest the following levels of loan reduction for white firms in various areas:

Change in Loan Size:

20-40% minority population	–$4,180
40-50% minority population	–$9,594
50% or more minority population	–$16,782

As minority population rises, it appears that white-owned firms in the area receive smaller and smaller loans, even when human-capital characteristics are held constant. Thus white borrowers appear to be redlined by banks, although to a lesser degree than black-owned firms, but the small sample size makes it difficult to confirm this relationship in terms of statistical significance.

Table 10.3's regression equation was reestimated for a pooled sample of all 519 black and white bank-loan recipients: this pooled model contained binary variables for minority area (meaning at least 20 percent minority) as well as race of owner. Two conclusions emerged from this exercise:

1. Firms located in minority areas, whether black- or white-owned, received an estimated $35,489 less than borrowers located in nonminority sections of metropolitan areas. These loan size differentials, other factors constant, were statistically significant at the 5% level.

2. After controlling for minority area and other factors, race of owner was not a statistically significant determinant of loan size.[15]

It therefore appears that bank redlining is applicable to geographic areas where minorities reside;[16] it handicaps black-owned businesses disproportionately because most of them are located in minority communities. Black owners that do business outside of minority areas do not appear to be discriminated against by banks to a significant degree with respect to average loan size. They may indeed be discriminated against at an earlier stage in the lending process – the point at which bankers decide whether to accept or reject loan applications – but that is a separate issue.[17] Among all firms doing business in nonminority sections of large metropolitan areas, the CBO data do indicate that black firms are less likely than whites to receive bank loans (irrespective of amount), but it is not possible to distinguish firms that were denied loans from those that never applied for bank loans.

IV. DISCRIMINANT ANALYSIS OF BUSINESS VIABILITY

The earlier discussion of ghetto dynamics argued that lack of capital and weak internal markets are the major problems facing black-owned firms that operate in ghetto areas. The evidence indicates that these two barriers to black business viability handicap all firms that operate in minority communities of large metropolitan areas. Black firms that rely most heavily upon a minority clientele are very small in size and are heavily overrepresented in two traditional lines of business: retailing and personal

Table 10.4
Discriminant Analysis: Blacks Entering Business During 1976-1982

Variable	1st Model: Black Firms in Large SMSA Minority Communities Only			2nd Model: Black Firms in Large SMSA Nonminority Communities Only		
	Discriminant Function	Group Mean Vectors		Discriminant Function	Group Mean Vectors	
	Standardized Coefficients	Active Firms	Discontinued Firms	Standardized Coefficients	Active Firms	Discontinued Firms
Sex	.004	.741	.724	-.129	.760	.768
Ed2	-.322	.280	.317	.399	.277	.260
Ed3	-.274	.246	.276	.521	.203	.204
Ed4	-.101	.283	.256	.654	.420	.401
Age2	-.228	.335	.369	.074	.415	.408
Age3	.055	.309	.240	.163	.233	.225
Age4	-.354	.114	.154	.217	.111	.056
Log capital	.324	8.759	8.539	.341	8.893	8.643
Leverage	.213	2.499	1.695	.156	3.105	2.418
Management	-.077	3.527	3.644	-.099	4.022	3.923
Input	.062	42.023	39.389	.195	41.792	37.250
Ongoing	-.436	.206	.292	-.142	.199	.232
Minority market	.224	.657	.596			
Open market				.095	.559	.515

Time80	-.661	.329	.423	-.620	.416	.472
Time82	-.600	.216	.282	-.858	.199	.330
Observations (N)	621		312		296	142

Notes: Multivariate test for differences between the two groups:

1st Model:
Wilks lambda statistic = .937
F = 4.07: so the group differences are statistically significant at the .01 level.

2nd Model:
Wilks lambda statistic = .927
F = 2.91: so the group differences are statistically significant at the .01 level.

Table 10.5
Discriminant Analysis: Whites Entering Business During 1976-1982

Variable	Discriminant Function Standardized Coefficients	Group Mean Vectors	
		Active Firms	Discontinued Firms
Ed2	-.142	.239	.325
Ed3	.211	.219	.214
Ed4	.383	.456	.269
Age2	.025	.338	.329
Age3	.095	.196	.182
Age4	.185	.134	.111
Log capital	.405	9.375	9.018
Leverage	-.210	2.842	3.211
Management	-.135	5.995	5.650
Input	.249	44.881	42.537
Ongoing	.251	.230	.159
Time80	-.539	.397	.472
Time82	-.651	.154	.238

Minority market	−.211	.087	.119
Minority area	−.075	.120	.123
Observations (N)		766	252

Notes: Multivariate test for differences between the two groups:
Wilks lambda statistic = .948
$F = 4.63$: so the group differences are statistically significant at the .01 level.

services. Black firms located in minority communities are very small, in part, because they have restricted access to credit: they are less likely to borrow and when they do borrow, they receive loans that are substantially less than those received by their counterparts located in nonminority areas.

Discriminant analysis exercises (tables 10.4 and 10.5) attempt to sort out and clarify the relative importance of the diverse factors impacting the viability of black firms that do business in large metropolitan areas.[18] The measure of firm viability is, by definition, whether or not the business was still operating in late 1986. Businesses that were still operating are "active" firms; those that had closed down are "discontinued." Explanatory variables utilized in tables 10.4 and 10.5 include human-capital, demographic, and business-location variables used previously, as well as variables measuring racial composition of the firm's clientele, age of the firm (Time80 and Time82), labor input of the owner (Input), financial-capital inputs, and leverage, as defined in section II. Log capital and Input are hypothesized to be directly related to firm viability, while the other new variables – Leverage, Minority market, Time80, and Time82 – are expected to be inversely related to viability.

The choice of explanatory variables for inclusion in the discriminant analysis requires elaboration. Entrepreneurial ability is clearly important in the determination of which firms remain in business. A pioneering model by Lucas [1978] concluded that persons having relatively more entrepreneurial ability became entrepreneurs, while those possessing relatively less became workers. In the Lucas model, business formation and discontinuances involved "marginal" managers characterized solely by a known managerial ability parameter. A more realistic model developed by Jovanovic [1982] assumes not only that individuals differ in their entrepreneurial abilities; they are also unsure of their abilities. Those who enter self-employment gradually learn about their managerial abilities by engaging in the actual running of a business and observing how well they do. As they learn more about their abilities, their entrepreneurial behavior changes through time: those who revise their ability estimate upward tend to expand output, while those embracing downward estimates tend to contract or to dissolve their businesses. Over time, surviving entrepreneurs acquire through experience precise estimates of their abilities, whereas younger firms exhibit relatively more variable behavior because they have less precise estimates of their true abilities.

Entry into an ongoing business is expected to be associated with increased viability, other things equal. Purchasing an existing (ongoing) business may permit a new owner to benefit from established managerial procedures; some degree of client goodwill may be present. Consistent with Jovanovic's model, the new owner who is unsure of his managerial abilities may reduce his uncertainty by buying into a firm where managerial practices of the previous owners are embodied in the business.

The black sample of business start-ups was divided into two groups: (1) those located in minority areas of large metropolitan areas[19] and (2) all others. Discriminant functions were estimated for each of these subsamples. Due to the very small number of white firms located in minority areas, this sample was not similarly divided. Instead, "minority area" was used as an explanatory variable in the table 10.5 discriminant analysis for white firms. Discriminant function standardized coefficients are reported in tables 10.4 and 10.5; these permit comparisons of the relative explanatory power of the independent variables. The objective of discriminant analysis is to weigh and combine the explanatory variables in a fashion that forces the groups to be as statistically distinct as possible. The exercises are successful in the sense that the explanatory variables are statistically able to distinguish active and discontinued firms at the 1 percent level.

The size of financial-capital inputs (log capital) exhibited a strong, direct relationship to firm viability in all sample groups. However, the leverage variable produced striking racial differences in the standardized coefficients. The applicable coefficient for white firms was –.210 (table 10.5), suggesting that high levels of indebtedness indeed do raise the probability of business failure. The exact opposite pattern was observed among both samples (table 10.4) of black firms: for blacks doing business in minority areas, the leverage coefficient was +.213; for other black businesses, the leverage coefficient was +.156. The remarkable fact is that highly leveraged black firms consistently appear to be more viable relative to other firms. Note that the mean value for leverage was lowest among black firms in minority communities (1.695 for discontinued firms) and highest for active black-owned businesses in nonminority areas (3.105 for active firms), with white firms falling well inside these bounds and with those white firms still active in 1986 being less leveraged at their start-ups than those white firms that were discontinued.

Thus the more viable (in the sense of still being active in late 1986) black firms at the point of start-up have greater access to debt: (1) they borrow more heavily than their weaker counterparts; (2) they create larger-scale operations. Among black owners, the discontinued firms as a group were much less highly leveraged than the active firms. The fact that the leverage coefficient was negative for whites and positive for blacks is completely consistent with the finding that supply-side capital-access constraints are tighter for black owners than for whites.

In general, the variables most successful (in terms of absolute size of standardized coefficients) at distinguishing active from discontinued firms, whether black or white, were Time80 and Time82. This is consistent with the Jovanovic [1982] model, which indicated that small-business owners know least about their entrepreneurial abilities at the point where they first enter self-employment. The Time82 variable identifies the newest of the businesses in the business samples: among white males, for example, firms formed in 1982 – 17.3 percent of the total sample – accounted for 23.8 percent of the 1986 discontinuances. The same pattern characterized the black groups. The newest firms, other things equal, were most likely to fail (between 1982 and 1986) and the Time82 coefficients indicate that this factor was the strongest single determinant of business viability. Similarly, firms entered during the 1980-81 period (Time80) were more likely to discontinue operations by 1986 than those who entered between 1976 and 1979; they were less likely to discontinue relative to those entered in 1982. The longer the period since the owner had entered his business, the more likely it was that the business would remain active in 1986.

Reliance on a minority clientele is positively associated with firm viability among black firms operating in minority communities; the exact opposite pattern prevails among white-owned businesses as well as black firms not located in minority areas. This striking result is related to differing findings on the impact of owner education on firm survival in the various samples. In nonminority areas, highly educated owners are the most likely to be involved in business start-ups that remain active. Among the white owners, for example, possessing four or more years of college is more directly related to firm viability than any other human-capital or demographic trait (table 10.5). The standardized coefficients for Ed3 and Ed4 (table 10.4) indicate that a similar, somewhat stronger relationship between education and viability characterizes the black sample of firms that are not located in large SMSA minority communities. Within minority areas, in contrast, the least educated owners are the ones that are most likely to remain in business. The high-school dropouts (this group corresponds to the default variable Ed1 excluded from tables 10.4 and 10.5) are least associated with viable businesses, except in the case of the black minority-community sample, where they are the education group that is most directly associated with continuing business operations.[20] Again there are striking racial differences in viability, in this case compounded with education and minority area.[21]

All of these results suggest that the economic development prospects of black businesses located in large metropolitan-area minority communities are really quite dismal. This particular group of firms clearly has the least access to financial capital, relative to other black as well as white male businesses. Their firms are, on average, the smallest, utilizing the fewest employees, and they are more likely to remain in business by catering to a predominantly minority clientele. In complete contrast to small-firm start-ups in general, the least educated are the most likely to remain in business! What sorts of firms thrive on minimal financial- and human-capital inputs as well as a clientele that excludes most higher-income customers? In fact, personal service firms are the line of business that is most heavily overrepresented: relative to all other black business industry groups, they are (1) most concentrated in minority areas, (2) least reliant upon nonminority clients, and (3) smallest in terms of financial-capital inputs at start-up. Although their mean 1982 sales per firm were the lowest reported by any industry group, the black-owned personal service firms reported lower discontinuance rates over the time period 1982 to late 1986 than other black firms as well as the sample of all white male businesses.

Other discriminant analysis variables produced standardized coefficient values that often diverged across the black and white and minority/nonminority business samples. Age variables were generally more important explanatory variables for black owners than for whites and in minority areas, blacks in the 45 to 54 age bracket (Age3) were generally more likely to remain in business than their younger or older counterparts. Even more striking, purchasing an Ongoing business was found to be a shortcut to business viability for whites but not for black owners. Business buyouts are frequently financed by loans from former owners, but this practice is much less common for blacks than whites; relative to blacks, white owners purchasing ongoing firms are nearly three times more likely to be financed by the former owner. Greater assistance from former owners may explain why whites are more successful than blacks in creating viable firms from buyout situations. Further, buyouts in minority areas are concentrated in the high risk retail sector.

The perverse behavior of the management experience variable is the one discriminant analysis result that is difficult to interpret. Having managerial experience is, for every sample of firms, directly associated with business discontinuance. Alternative forms of this variable, measured as number of years of management experience, were investigated, as were various functional forms. The fact that the management measure is highly correlated with age and education suggests that multicollinearity problems are compromising its usefulness.

V. ACHIEVING BUSINESS VIABILITY BY REDUCING CONTACT WITH THE MINORITY COMMUNITY?

If a major goal of minority business development is, indeed, to aid the economic development process in minority communities, then something of a dilemma is posed by the fact that the group of black firms possessing the greater development prospects is the one that is not located in the minority areas of large metropolitan areas. Talented and capable minority entrepreneurs, access to capital, and access to markets are the ingredients identified with minority economic development. Among the black-owned firms not located in the large urban minority communities, this development formula has direct applicability: (1) over half of the owners starting firms have attended college; (2) businesses most likely to remain active are the ones started by owners with four or more years of college; (3) firms with the larger financial capital inputs and a racially diverse clientele are the ones that are most likely to remain in business.

Within the minority communities, in contrast, capital access is constrained and the black business start-ups that survive consist disproportionately of tiny firms serving a minority clientele. Remaining in business in this milieu is directly associated with minimal owner education: the high-school dropouts often hang on by running small firms such as beauty parlors – firms that typically have no paid employees and minimal prospects for alleviating ghetto economic underdevelopment. It appears likely that many of these firms may be incapable of competing in the broader marketplace. Unless greater financial capital is forthcoming and better-educated owners are induced to remain in business, the black business community that is located in the minority neighborhoods of large urban areas is going to continue to stagnate. For the black (or white) college graduate seeking to start a viable business, the rational choice of locations is likely to be outside of the minority community.

The evidence indicates that inner-city minority communities are not favorable environments for the development of most lines of business. Yet these communities desperately need the capital and entrepreneurial talent that are prerequisites for reversing ghetto resource drains and generating growth. The financial capital and the entrepreneurial talent that have been drawn into the black business community, however, have increasingly chosen to locate either in the central business district or in outlying, largely nonminority suburban areas. The most sought-after business locations do not necessarily differ substantially with respect to owner race or ethnicity: businesses prosper in environs where financial capital and markets are readily accessible.

Two decades of progress in the black business development realm have not substantially altered the economic processes that maintain ghetto poverty. Financial capital continues to flow out; internal income flows are still weak; intelligent and capable young people continue to depart by way of the educational system and the high-wage economy. Weak internal markets, lack of capital, and related economic problems have not been overcome. Yet the nature of the black business community is profoundly different today than it was twenty five years ago. The size and scope of the black business community has expanded; industry diversity has flourished; highly educated entrepreneurs are the norm in many lines of business; bank credit is much more widely available. Yet these positive developments have been most pronounced in locations removed from minority communities. Job creation is an important effect of black enterprise development, and minority-community residents certainly benefit from the expansion of firms that employ a labor force that is largely minority.[22] But job creation alone does not reverse the resource drains that help to maintain ghetto poverty.

An important barrier to inner-city development may be political rather than economic. Markets can be found for larger-scale ghetto enterprises, especially through minority business set-aside and procurement programs. Such programs have been most beneficial to minority firms that are located in nonminority sections of urban America. Government regularly serves as a source of financial capital for various industries and interest groups, both domestically and abroad. Yet government efforts such as Small Business Administration loan programs have focused largely on very small-scale firms that have little economic development potential. Decisions about the use of public resources are made largely by people who do not reside in urban minority communities. In normal times, they prefer to ignore ghetto problems.

APPENDIX: SELECTION OF THE LARGE SMSAS USED IN THIS STUDY

The 28 Standard Metropolitan Statistical Areas (SMSAs) analyzed in this study all had the following traits: (1) substantial black population, (2) identifiable ghetto areas, and (3) numerous black-owned businesses. Ghetto areas were identified as existing in a SMSA if there were five or more census tracts that had a poverty rate of 40 percent or more in 1980. Several large SMSAs such as San Antonio and San Jose had relatively few blacks in census tracts where the poverty rate was 40 percent or higher, these SMSAs were excluded. Several very large SMSAs, such as San Diego and Seattle, were dropped because they lacked a sufficient number of census tracts with high poverty rates. Other SMSAs lacked sufficient black-owned businesses. The applicable SMSAs included in this study therefore are not merely the nation's largest SMSAs, although most of the SMSAs having one million or more residents in 1980 are listed in the group of 28 appearing below. Rather, the three criteria led to the inclusion of several southern SMSAs with fewer than one million residents (such as Richmond, Jackson, and Nashville) as well as one northern SMSA, Gary, Hammond, and East Chicago, Indiana.

The list of 28 was dominated by 14 large SMSAs in the sense that most of the sample of minority-area large SMSA black businesses were, in fact, located in these SMSAs:

1. Chicago	8. Dallas-Fort Worth
2. Los Angeles	9. New Orleans
3. New York	10. St. Louis
4. Detroit	11. San-Francisco-Oakland
5. Houston	12. Atlanta
6. Washington, D.C.	13. Baltimore
7. Philadelphia	14. Cleveland

The other 14 SMSAs were:

1. Indianapolis	8. Birmingham
2. Jacksonville	9. Newark
3. Milwaukee	10. Gary
4. Jackson	11. Nashville
5. Shreveport	12. Kansas City
6. Omaha	13. Richmond
7. Columbus	14. Memphis

and (5) white males. Samples 1, 2, and 3 overlap substantially with sample 4 (women). This study is based upon data drawn from samples 2 (blacks) and 5 (white males) only. All black and white male observations located in these 28 metropolitan areas that meet the restrictions described in section II (sales, data completeness) are included in the empirical analyses of sections III and IV.

11
Discrimination, Returns to Education, and Teenage Childbearing

Elaine McCrate

T he U.S. black teenage birth rate is approximately twice as high as the white teenage birth rate. In 1985, there were 97.4 births per thousand black women aged 15-19, and 42.8 births per thousand white women of the same age cohort in the United States (National Center for Health Statistics, 1987). Most contemporary policy discussions have emphasized that early childbirth reduces educational attainment and hence lifetime incomes (Hofferth and Moore [1979]). This logic emphasizes the effect of young women's individual fertility decisions on their human-capital formation and hence on their later economic status. Insofar as the higher black teenage birth rate explains part of racial income differentials among women, this reasoning accordingly reduces the possible role of discrimination in explaining such income disparities.

But why would a young woman have a baby when the economic consequences are apparently so negative? Why are black women so much more likely to become teenage mothers? Addressing a wide range of inner-city problems, from crime to adolescent parenthood, some human-capital theorists have extended the definition of human capital to include a positive cultural disposition toward work and school (Chiswick [1983b]; Loury [1984]; Sowell [1983]). They would contend that women who become teenage mothers do not have as great an endowment of cultural human capital as other women: they do not value school and work as highly. Moreover, these cultural differences are apparently exogenous – they exist independently of the operation of the labor market.

The purpose of this chapter is to provide a contrasting explanation of teenage childbearing, one that emphasizes the effect of differences in economic opportunities on childbearing decisions. Rather than attributing greater teenage childbearing to exogenous cultural human-capital differences, this chapter takes a more unabashedly economistic view.[1] Teenage mothers, on average, do not value education and work any less than other women. Rather, it is hypothesized that they correctly anticipate smaller average economic rewards for postponing birth and focusing more exclusively on their schooling. In other words, because they receive, on average, lower-quality education and/or because they expect job discrimination,[2] they also anticipate lower returns to education. The lower are these expected returns to education, the lower is the incentive to avoid a teenage birth.

This perspective reverses the usual direction of emphasis in most policy discussions. Rather than focusing on the effect of early births in reducing later incomes, the focus is on the effect of anticipated income differentials, which exist independently of early childbearing, on the probability of adolescent motherhood. I thus argue for a greater emphasis on discrimination in explaining racial income differentials among women: premarket or market discrimination[3] causes unequal returns to education, which contributes to early motherhood.[4]

The balance of this chapter contains a brief review of "culture of poverty" theories, then discusses the relevance of segmented labor market theory (Gordon, Edwards, and Reich [1982]) and of radical educational theory (Bowles and Gintis [1976]). I investigate the plausibility of the claim that adolescent women have, on average, accurate expectations of their future economic opportunities. Finally, I present the results of wage regressions from the 1986 National Longitudinal Survey of Youth (NLSY), one of a few large data sets to combine information on fertility, schooling, and work over a number of years for the same individuals (the women respondents were all aged 21-28 in 1986).

A test for possible effects of early births on returns to education is conducted. The results demonstrate that returns to education do differ dramatically by race and age at first birth: the coefficient on education is lowest for black teenage mothers, intermediate for white teenage mothers and black older mothers/nonmothers, and highest for white older mothers/nonmothers. However, these differences do not appear to be the *result* of teenage motherhood. The wage regressions also provide some insight into wage inequality among women *within* race groups.

I. THE CULTURE OF POVERTY VS. THE ECONOMICS OF POVERTY

In 1965, the most eminent proponent of the culture of poverty thesis, Daniel Patrick Moynihan, emphasized that the main problem behind contemporary black poverty was cultural, not economic. Widespread teenage childbearing and other urban problems were cause and consequence of a "culture of poverty" in which the poor replicate the conditions of their own deprivation. Moynihan asserted that while racism had explained most black social problems in the past, "the present tangle of [black cultural] pathology is capable of perpetuating itself without assistance from the white world" (Moynihan [1965]). More recently, Moynihan and numerous popular writers have reasserted these points (Moynihan [1985]; Kaus [1986]; Lemann [1986]).

It is undeniable that poor people live in a very different culture than people whose basic needs are being met. Culture also has economic ramifications. However, the Moynihan thesis involves several dubious assertions.

First, it explains teenage births by invoking the culture of poverty, to the complete neglect of the contemporary economics of poverty. Poverty is viewed as primarily cultural/psychological rather than economic. Moreover, such a theory is tautological: crime, substance abuse, teenage motherhood, and so on appear in the theory both as their own cause and consequence.

A related problem with extreme cultural determinism is its portrayal of teenage mothers as "unmotivated" or economically irrational. These women apparently fail to use available educational and work opportunities to improve their economic status. This assumption involves the untested belief that such opportunities are in fact available.

Finally, Darity and Williams present another objection to culture of poverty theory [1985]. Why does job competition not generalize the economically superior culture? What barriers exist to the transmission of more economically functional attitudes? Until the culture of poverty theorists identify such impediments, the argument remains incomplete.

II. SECONDARY JOBS, INFERIOR EDUCATION, AND TEEN-AGE CHILDBEARING

It is simply unnecessary to invoke a cultural determinist argument to explain adolescent motherhood. A young woman's expectation – conscious or unconscious – that her efforts to augment her education will not pay off reduces the incentive to avoid an early birth.

The possibility of unequal returns to education has long been recognized by the theory of segmented labor markets (Gordon, Edwards, and Reich [1982]). It contends that secondary labor markets, where black women are disproportionately concentrated, offer very small economic payoffs both to quantity and quality of schooling. Returns to schooling would of course be further reduced by lower-quality education. According to Bowles and Gintis' "correspondence principle," it is precisely those students who are being prepared for lower-status jobs who get lower-quality education.

Segmented labor market theory posits two fundamentally different types of jobs: primary and secondary.[5] The theory explains labor-market outcomes – pay, promotion, etc. – more in terms of the industrial, occupational, and firm-specific characteristics of the *jobs* than the productivity-related characteristics of the *workers*.[6] The "secondary" labor market is the arena of bad jobs. Secondary jobs typically are located in firms with lower profit rates and more arbitrary systems of worker supervision and in occupations with less worker control over the labor process. These jobs offer low pay, few chances for advancement, and low job security. Also, education does not pay off for workers in these jobs: in economic terms, the "returns to investment in education" – as well as to experience and tenure – are significantly lower for workers in secondary labor markets (Doeringer and Piore [1971]; Edwards [1979]). Examples of these jobs are many food service and cleaning occupations and some clerical occupations. Primary-sector jobs (for example, engineering, managerial work, and unionized craft jobs) have opposite characteristics.

A fundamental assertion of segmented labor market theory is that primary jobs are rationed by a nonprice mechanism: that is, not everyone who wants and is qualified for primary-sector jobs can get them. In particular, blacks and other people of color are disproportionately restricted to the secondary sector. This has been shown empirically several times on data sets covering male workers. More recently, some evidence has appeared that confirms the pattern among women as well: women of color are more likely than white women to be in the secondary sector and even to have lower wages than white women within the secondary sector (Kitchel [1988]).

Bad jobs ordinarily go together with lower-quality schooling and not just because the latter causes the former. Bowles and Gintis' "correspondence principle" [1976] posits a similarity between the types of social relations and skills in the jobs people will eventually get and the type of schooling they receive. Schools teach children of different gender, race, and social class to cultivate the social skills that will ultimately be most important in surviving or succeeding at their position in the labor hierarchy. Schools of privileged children teach them to be self-directed and creative. Schools teach working-class (especially black) students to obey rules and to respond to external authority. Teaching methods more often involve rote learning. School facilities are, on average, poorer, due to long standing inequities in school finance. Thus there is mutual causation between quality of education and quality of jobs.

III. YOUNG WOMEN'S EXPECTATIONS OF THEIR ECONOMIC FUTURES

Young women are not necessarily conscious of the process by which they relate childbearing decisions to economic expectations. "Social reproduction," the process by which economic class is maintained throughout and across generations, greatly reduces the ability of young people to conceptualize an alternative to their own class background.

For example, residential segregation by race and class probably contributes to accurate, if not conscious, expectations of the future. If black teenagers see older blacks in their neighborhoods who have completed high school but are still marginally employed or unemployed, they are likely to be pessimistic about the ability of education to improve their economic status. As argued above, schooling itself is another way that social reproduction affects economic expectations. Thus poor young women do not deliberately decide to have a baby because they know the exact trade off between mothering and schooling. Similarly, more fortunate young women do not necessarily decide to contracept or abort because they can precisely calculate the economic effect of early motherhood on their careers. Rather, the class and race differentiation of young people's hopes and expectations is so thorough and so pervasive by the time they reach adolescence that they are probably most often not aware of how it affects their childbearing decisions.

Table 11.1

Educational Attainment of Women Aged 21-28 by Race and Age at First Birth: May 1, 1986*

| | Age at First Birth | | |
	Less Than 18	18 and Over, or No Birth	% Difference
Blacks**			
Mean education completed (years)	11.5	13.0	–11.5%
Percent completing at least 12 years	63.3%	89.1%	–29.0%
Whites**			
Mean education completed (years)	10.6	13.0	–18.5%
Percent completing at least 12 years	52.3%	92.7%	–43.6%

Notes: *Receiving a general equivalency diploma and completing no further education counts as completing grade twelve.
**All Latinas excluded.

Source: National Longitudinal Survey of Youth, 1986

IV. TEENAGE CHILDBEARING, SCHOOLING, AND SECONDARY JOBS: THE EVIDENCE

Teenage childbearing indisputably reduces educational attainment, although less so for black women than for whites. Table 11.1 gives the percentage change in the proportion of women completing at least high school (or getting a general equivalency diploma) in the NLSY sample. This measurement is based on the 1986 survey, when all respondents were 21-28 years old. A "teenage mother" is defined as a woman who had her first child at age 17 or under, the years in which school is supposed to be one's major preoccupation. Only about half of white teenage mothers finished high school, compared to nine-tenths of their counterparts who postponed birth. The percentage reduction in the proportion of white women completing twelve years of schooling associated with teenage motherhood was 43.6 percent. In contrast, the percentage reduction in the proportion of black women completing twelve years of schooling was only 29.0 percent. This racial difference is due both to higher educational levels among black teenage mothers and to lower educational levels among black older mothers/nonmothers.

The greater success of black teenage mothers in completing high school, compared to their white counterparts, is one possible reason for higher black teenage birth rates: the educational penalty associated with early childbearing is smaller for blacks than whites. (This may be due to the greater support of the black extended family for its young mothers. See Ladner [1971]; Stack [1975].)

However, there still is a significant educational penalty associated with early births. Why would a young woman have a child when she is most likely aware of its consequences for schooling? If schooling itself is not effective in improving her economic status, the opportunity cost of an early birth is substantially reduced. The regression results presented here suggest that because of the rationing of primary jobs and/or because of lower-quality schooling, the positive economic effect of postponing motherhood and increasing education is smaller for black women than for white women.

The natural logarithm of the hourly wage was regressed on its usual determinants – education, experience, experience squared, region, government employment, self-employment, union status, and health – for four different groups: black teenage mothers, white teenage mothers, black older mothers and nonmothers, and white older mothers and nonmothers. (Women who did not reside in the United States when they were fourteen years old were excluded, because they probably had no way to form expectations of U.S. labor markets.) The variables listed all refer to characteristics of the worker and of the job with the most hours worked during the interview week of 1986.

A teenage birth could easily reduce returns to education for women who attend school after the birth: caring for a young child certainly reduces the time and attention available for other activities, including studying. In order to investigate whether the teenage birth itself significantly reduced returns to education, an interactive term, Compschl, which is the product of the education variable and a dummy variable, is also included. This dummy variable equals one if the month of first birth preceded the month last enrolled in school, and zero otherwise.

Other potential estimation problems arise from the possibility of differences between teenage mothers and other women that are correlated with the wage. Estimates of the wage functions would then be biased. To some extent, this is an omitted-variable problem. One remedy is to include any variables that would vary by age at first birth *and* by the wage.

Few of the other variables ordinarily included in studies of teenage fertility (for example, religion, abortion cost, etc.) have important direct effects on the wage. Others have potentially significant indirect effects that are captured by other variables already in the wage regression. For example, teenage welfare recipiency or teenage marriage may reduce labor supply, which would already be measured in the experience variable.

Moreover, each of these regressions included the inverse Mills ratio to measure possible selectivity effects and to give consistent estimates of all the coefficients in the wage regression. (This is the standard treatment of censored samples developed by Heckman (1979), which treats sample selection bias as a specification error.) Respondents had to be employed, with no military experience, not full-time students, and not unpaid family workers in order to be included in the wage sample. The probit equation that predicted inclusion in the wage sample and that generated the inverse Mills ratio was very similar to a labor-supply equation. It had the following explanatory variables: education, experience, experience squared, region, health, property income, level of public transfer payments to the respondent (and also to her spouse, if married), a dummy variable indicating whether anyone other than her husband paid for half or more of her support, spouse's (or cohabiting partner's) earnings (if married or cohabiting; otherwise, zero), and the interactive term described above. I do not list the coefficients here, but simply report that they generally had the predicted signs with acceptable levels of significance. (A table of coefficients and t-statistics is available upon request.)

The probit inclusion equations generated an inverse Mills ratio for each individual in the wage sample. The full wage regression was then

$$\ln(\text{wage})_{ij} = a + \mathbf{X}_{ij}\mathbf{b}_j + c_j l_{ij} + e_{ij},$$

where j designated one of the four race-by-age-at-first-birth groups and $\mathbf{X}_{ij}$ was the vector of observed explanatory variables:

Educ86: Years of education.

Compschl: Interactive term equalling education times a dummy that is 1 if the month of first birth preceded the month last enrolled in school, 0 otherwise.

Exphrs and Exphrs2: Experience/100 and experience/100 squared, where experience was measured in hours since the year in which the respondent turned 18 years old.

Region: Location of residence, where south = 1, non-south = 0.

Gvmt: For government employee, Gvmt = 1; otherwise, Gvmt = 0.

Selfemp: For self-employed, Selfemp = 1; otherwise, Selfemp = 0.

Union: If covered by a collective bargaining agreement, Union = 1; otherwise, Union = 0.

Health: If respondent has health problem that limits kind or amount of work she can do, Health = 1; otherwise Health = 0.

In addition to these X variables, there is the variable l_{ij}:

Mills: the inverse Mills ratio.

The coefficient of Mills, c_j, is the covariance between the errors in the probit and the wage equation, so that $\mathbf{X}_{ij}\mathbf{b}_j$ gives a consistent estimate of each person's wage offer, whether the wage is observed or not.

These results are provisional due to the simultaneity between expected wages and level of schooling completed. While coefficients in wage regressions are always biased due to this problem, it is a special issue here because the endogeneity of educational attainment is a special feature of the logic underlying the model. The coefficients on education are therefore expected to be upwardly biased. Also, selection into teenage motherhood is endogenous.

Table 11.2 gives the results of ordinary least squares regressions on this equation for the full sample of 21-28 year-olds. Regressions were also run for 24-28 year-olds only, but small sample sizes reduced t-statistics too much for reliable interpretation.

The most important result is that the coefficients on education for each of the four groups rank in the predicted order: the lowest returns to

Table 11.2
Wage Regressions for White and Black Older Mothers/Nonmothers
and for White and Black Teenage Mothers Aged 21-28 in 1986

	Black Older Mothers/ Nonmothers	White Older Mothers/ Nonmothers	Black Teen-age Mothers	White Teen-age Mothers
Intercept	.689 (2.34)	.591 (3.97)	1.631 (4.40)	1.51 (3.09)
Educ86	.069 (6.98)	.083 (15.75)	.022 (.89)	.049 (1.89)
Compschl	.0004 (.11)	.004 (1.03)	.005 (.65)	.005 (.62)
Exphrs	.00008 (.27)	.002 (1.34)	-.003 (.90)	-.004 (.79)
Exphrs^2	.00001 (.97)	5.6 E-7 (.11)	.00002 (2.05)	.00002 (.89)
Region	-.122 (3.49)	-.069 (3.14)	-.160 (2.05)	.158 (1.82)
Gvmt	.139 (3.25)	-.027 (.78)	.127 (1.64)	.071 (.44)

Selfemp	-.149 (1.05)	-.144 (2.78)	.150 (.82)	.362 (2.14)
Union	.084 (2.17)	.137 (4.08)	.180 (2.22)	.187 (1.47)
Health	.011 (.10)	-.167 (2.60)	-.238 (1.20)	.004 (.02)
Mills	-.082 (.56)	-.144 (1.75)	-.349 (2.23)	-.133 (.70)
Observations (N for wage equation)	504	1,549	105	99
Observations (N for probit equation)	967	2,475	256	229
R-squared (adj)	.334	.263	.324	.082

Note: T-statistics are in parentheses.

education are for black teenage mothers; white teenage mothers and black older mothers/nonmothers have intermediate returns to education; and white older mothers/nonmothers have the highest returns to education. At the extreme ends, the coefficient on schooling for white older mothers/ nonmothers is over three times as large as that for black teenage mothers. Differences in returns to education between the teenage mothers and older mothers/nonmothers of each race group were significant at the 1 percent level. Moreover, the coefficient on education for black teenage mothers is statistically insignificant (although this could be a consequence of sample size).

The coefficients of Compschl are never negative, quite small, and never statistically significant, indicating that the teenage birth itself did not itself reduce returns to education via some of the obvious possibilities such as reduced attention to school, etc. The experience variable was affected by a collinearity problem with the inverse Mills ratio. (The collinearity problem was diagnosed using a procedure described by Belsley, Kuh, and Welsch [1980].) The inverse Mills ratio, coverage by a collective bargaining contract, and region are the only significant variables for black teenage mothers (both of the latter with the expected signs). The consistently negative and sometimes significant coefficient on the inverse Mills ratio implies that the higher the probability of being included in the wage sample, the lower the wage; in other words, the highest potential earners within each race-by-age-at-first-birth group are outside the wage sample. There is far more noise in the data for white teenage mothers: this equation has exceptionally low adjusted coefficients of determination. Nonetheless, education, self-employment, and region were significant determinants of wages. Region, union coverage, and government employment have significant coefficients with the expected signs for black older mothers/nonmothers. Region, union coverage, and health have significant coefficients with the expected signs for white older mothers/nonmothers. Interestingly, self-employment (or typical characteristics of self-employed persons) seems to have opposite effects for teenage mothers and other women.

V. CONCLUSION

The results reported here constitute preliminary evidence for the argument that postponing first birth in order to concentrate on school is not equally effective for all women as a means of getting higher wages. It is especially ineffective for the black women who become teenage mothers. It seriously calls into question the assumption of cultural determinist theories that teenage mothers must be irrational or that they must value education and work less than other women. Rather, expected premarket and market discrimination appears to explain a great deal about these young women's decisions to become mothers. Further, the results reported here are consistent with the notion that the labor market is segmented in significant ways.[7]

The results in this chapter suggest that an important strategy for reducing teenage childbearing is the upgrading of education and jobs for poor women. Education must provide real skills, not just credentials. Young women must be guaranteed meaningful jobs with opportunities for advancement if they complete high school. (Community groups in Los Angeles, Boston, and other cities are already implementing this tactic.) Unions must bargain for significant job ladders that reward workers for education. The problem behind teenage childbearing is not cultural deficiencies, but the structure of economic opportunity.

12
Earnings of Black Immigrants: Implications for Racial Discrimination

Stephen A. Woodbury

Although several studies have documented significant improvement in the labor-market status of American blacks, especially since 1964 (Freeman [1981]; O'Neill, Cunningham, Sparks, and Sider [1986]; Smith and Welch [1989]), there remains a significant black/white earnings differential that is unexplained by observed variables such as education and work experience. By many accounts, this unexplained differential is attributable largely to discrimination, although recently this attribution has been challenged by the view that "culture," or differences in unobserved human capital, may be at the root of the unexplained differential (Sowell [1981b], [1983]; Chiswick [1983a], [1983b]). In view of the controversy over discrimination versus culture, Glen Cain [1986: 781] seems justified in his appraisal that

the econometric work [on discrimination] has ... been useful, but to my eyes more so for its descriptive content than for testing hypotheses or for providing estimates of causal relations.

The goal of this chapter is to throw additional light on the nature of earnings differentials – and in turn on the importance of discrimination and culture in the determination of earnings – by exploring the earnings of black immigrants to the United States. In particular, I address three sets of questions that have received scant attention.

First, how do the earnings of black men who immigrate to the United States compare with the earnings of native-born black men? Chiswick, in a pathbreaking 1978 paper, found that the earnings of white immigrants who have been in the United States for many years equal or exceed the earnings of native-born whites who have the same education, labor-market experience, and so on. Chiswick gave this finding a dynamic interpretation, viewing it as evidence that immigrants assimilate rapidly; that is, their earnings grow so rapidly that they catch up with the earnings of white native-born workers within ten to fifteen years of immigrating to the United States.[1] One set of questions to be addressed here is similar: How do the earnings of black immigrants compare with the earnings of native-born blacks? Is the relationship between the earnings of black immigrants and native-born blacks similar to that observed for whites? A related but subsidiary question will also be addressed: How do the earnings of the most recent black immigrants compare with the earnings of blacks who immigrated earlier?

Second, how do the earnings of black immigrants compare with the earnings of other groups of workers who have immigrated to the United States? There exists extensive work on the earnings of white and Hispanic immigrants (see, for example, Chiswick [1978], [1986]; Borjas [1982], [1985], [1988]). A comparison of the experience of black immigrants with that of other immigrants should offer clues about the degree to which race poses a barrier to success in the labor market, apart from the problems posed by an individual's culture or origin outside of the United States.

Third, it will become clear in the course of exploring these first two issues that the English-language proficiency of black immigrants is an important determinant of their success in the U.S. labor market. This should hardly be surprising, either intuitively or in view of recent work on Hispanic immigrants by McManus [1985], Tainer [1988], and Kossoudji [1989]. Accordingly, it will be appropriate to ask how the earnings of black immigrants whose native tongue is English differ from the earnings of black immigrants who speak English as a second language. More generally, how does the English-language proficiency of an immigrant influence his earnings in the U.S. labor market?

I. DISCRIMINATION AND "CULTURE"

Why examine these questions as a way of improving our understanding of black/white wage differentials? Basically, an examination of black immigrants' earnings may offer a way of choosing between two interpretations of the black/white wage differential. The first is the familiar interpretation of any portion of the black/white wage differential that cannot be explained by differences in education, work experience, and other observed variables as a measure of discrimination (Blinder [1973];

Oaxaca [1973]).

The second is the more recent interpretation of an unexplained wage differential as the result of "culture" or unobserved human capital. The cultural/human-capital interpretation of wage differentials can be traced to Thomas Sowell [1981b, 1983] and Barry Chiswick [1983a, 1983b], who have argued that unexplained wage differentials should not be taken as evidence of racial discrimination. Rather, as Sowell has stated, "Whether in an ethnic context or among peoples and nations generally, much depends on a whole constellation of values, attitudes, skills, and contacts that many call a culture and that economists call 'human capital'" [Sowell 1981b: 282].[2]

Sowell and Chiswick point to the prosperity of ethnic groups such as Chinese, Japanese, and Jews in the United States as evidence that groups who have been subjected to discrimination can nevertheless perform well in the U.S. labor market. For example, Chiswick [1983a: 212] concludes from his examination of American-born Chinese and Japanese men that "it is incorrect to assume that racial minority status in the United States and racial discrimination per se result in lower observed levels of earnings, schooling, employment, and rates of return to schooling. More care may be needed in attributing to racial discrimination the disadvantageous outcomes for other, less successful racial and ethnic minorities."

Is it possible to educe empirical evidence that would allow us to choose between the discriminatory and the cultural/human-capital interpretations of unexplained black/white wage differentials? Empirical evidence is more often circumstantial than demonstrative and it would be unrealistic to hope for settlement of a question as contentious and subtle as the discrimination/culture issue. Nevertheless, it should be possible to form some hypotheses (or empirical expectations) about the earnings of immigrants that would be consistent with the cultural interpretation. We can then sift through the data and appraise the degree to which the actual earnings of immigrants conform to these hypotheses. Deviations from this set of hypotheses we would attribute to other mechanisms, such as discrimination.

Suppose for the moment that there were no discrimination. Then any earnings differential that could not readily be explained by observed variables could be attributed to differences in culture or unobserved human capital. I would propose two sets of hypotheses about the earnings of immigrants in such a world.

First, we would expect immigrants whose only language is English to start at an earnings advantage compared with those who speak English as a second language. Also, we would expect those who speak English as a second language to show a higher rate of earnings growth. The reason is that English proficiency is a form of human capital that should translate into higher earnings. Immigrants who speak English well upon arrival should reap immediate benefits, although immigrants who must learn English should show more rapid earnings growth as they acquire English. Also, based on early empirical findings by Chiswick [1978], Carliner [1980], Long [1980], and others, we would expect the earnings of immigrants whose only language is English to approach the earnings of native-born workers of the same race or ethnicity.[3]

Second, in comparing the earnings of different groups of immigrants, some variation would be expected and interpretable as the result of differences in culture or unobserved human capital. That is, some groups of immigrants might well bring more human capital with them than others, and this human capital might not be in forms that are readily measurable (for example, quality of education, which is difficult to measure, as opposed to years of education, which are easy). We would generally expect immigrants whose only language is English to have higher earnings than immigrants whose English is less good (other things equal), regardless of race or ethnicity. Also, we would expect immigrants whose only language is English to receive higher rates of return to education than would immigrants whose English is less good, since English-proficiency should be related to ability to take advantage of the economic benefits of education, regardless of their race or ethnicity (Chiswick [1983a], [1983b]).

Deviations from these expectations could be interpreted as evidence that culture (or unobserved human capital) cannot alone explain the otherwise unexplained earnings differential. Rather, we might well attribute deviations from these expectations to discrimination.[4]

II. CHARACTERISTICS OF BLACK IMMIGRANTS

The only available data base offering a sample of black immigrants that is large enough to support the proposed analysis is the 1980 Census of Population 5 percent sample (the so-called A sample). I follow Chiswick [1978], who used the 1970 Census of Population to analyze the earnings of white foreign-born men, in restricting the sample analyzed in three ways. First, only men aged 25 to 64 who worked at least one week during 1979 and reported wage, salary, or self-employment earnings are included in the sample. Second, workers living outside the fifty states and the District of

Columbia are excluded. Third, workers born in an outlying area of the United States (such as Puerto Rico) or born abroad of American parents are excluded from the sample. These exclusions, although perhaps arbitrary in some cases, reduce random variation in the sample, make for simpler interpretation of the results, and allow comparisons with earlier results obtained by Chiswick [1978] and others. The black workers analyzed using this sample will be referred to interchangeably as black immigrants and foreign-born blacks.

The country of origin and year of immigration of this sample of black immigrants are shown in table 12.1. These tabulations suggest two main points. First, nearly 60 percent of the black immigrants living in the United States in 1980 had immigrated from the Caribbean, with Jamaica, Haiti, and Trinidad being by far the largest suppliers of black immigrants to the United States (Barbados is also a major Caribbean supplier of black immigrants to the United States). Countries outside of the Caribbean that contributed the most black immigrants to the United States are, in order of importance, Nigeria, Guyana, Panama, and Ghana.

Given the importance of the Caribbean in contributing black immigrants to the United States, it is puzzling that so few are from Spanish-speaking Caribbean countries, such as the Dominican Republic. The only Spanish-speaking country that, as of 1980, had contributed a sizable number of black immigrants was Panama. There are three possible explanations for this. First, it may be that Spanish-speaking Caribbeans report themselves as Puerto Rican in order to avoid legal problems with the Immigration and Naturalization Service (INS). (The 1965 amendments to the Immigration and Nationality Act first placed limits on the number of immigrants from Western Hemisphere countries.) Second, race is self-reported in the census and it is possible that Spanish-speaking Caribbeans who might be considered black by American cultural norms report their race as white. Accordingly, some Spanish-speaking Caribbean immigrants who might be considered black are classified as Hispanic. Third, Spanish-speaking Caribbeans may have ample opportunity to emigrate to other Spanish-speaking countries and may find those countries more attractive destinations than the United States.

The second main point suggested by the figures in table 12.1 is that nearly three-quarters of the foreign-born black men in the United States in 1980 had arrived in the United States between 1965 and 1980. The apparent post-1965 increase in immigration of black men seems to hold for nearly all countries of origin; only arrivals of black men from countries in South America (including Panama), North America, Europe, and the

Table 12.1
Black Male Immigrants by Region, Country of Origin, and Year of Immigration to the United States

Region/Country of Origin	Total	Year of Immigration					
		Pre-1950	1950-59	1960-64	1965-69	1970-74	1975-80
Caribbean:	5,671 [60.00%]	250 (4.41%)	450 (7.94%)	521 (9.19%)	1,501 (26.47%)	1,763 (31.09%)	1,186 (20.91%)
Jamaica	2,089 [22.10%]	107 (5.12%)	176 (8.43%)	166 (7.95%)	541 (25.90%)	641 (30.68%)	458 (21.92%)
Haiti	1,193 [12.62%]	8 (0.67%)	36 (3.02%)	105 (8.80%)	315 (26.40%)	404 (33.86%)	325 (27.24%)
Trinidad	717 [7.59%]	29 (4.04%)	27 (3.77%)	34 (4.74%)	247 (34.45%)	246 (34.31%)	134 (18.69%)
Barbados	351 [3.71]	17 (4.84%)	37 (10.54%)	39 (11.11%)	71 (20.23%)	118 (33.62%)	69 (19.66%)
Other English-Speaking-Caribbean	945 [10.00%]	71 (7.51%)	125 (13.23%)	103 (10.90%)	237 (25.08%)	257 (27.20%)	152 (16.08%)
Other Non-English-Speaking Caribbean	376 [3.98%]	18 (4.79%)	49 (13.03%)	74 (19.68%)	90 (23.94%)	97 (25.80%)	48 (12.77%)
Central America:	646 [6.83%]	41 (6.35%)	110 (17.03%)	120 (18.58%)	151 (23.37%)	136 (21.05%)	88 (13.62%)

	Total					
Panama	347 [3.67%]	28 (8.07%)	75 (21.61%)	65 (18.73%)	70 (20.17%)	60 (17.29%)	49 (14.12%)
Other Eng.-Speaking Cen. America	117 [1.24%]	4 (3.42%)	7 (5.98%)	20 (17.09%)	37 (31.62%)	36 (30.77%)	13 (11.11%)
Other Non-Eng. Speaking Cen. Amer.	182 [1.93%]	9 (4.95%)	28 (15.38%)	35 (19.23%)	44 (24.18%)	40 (21.98%)	26 (14.29%)
South America:	478 [5.06%]	14 (2.93%)	18 (3.77%)	35 (7.32%)	145 (30.33%)	151 (31.59%)	115 (24.06%)
Guyana	348 [3.68%]	7 (2.01%)	11 (3.16%)	19 (5.46%)	117 (33.62%)	107 (30.75%)	87 (25.00%)
Other So. America	130 [1.38%]	7 (5.38%)	7 (5.38%)	16 (12.31%)	28 (21.54%)	44 (33.85%)	28 (21.54%)
North America	116 [1.23%]	22 (18.97%)	18 (15.52%)	13 (11.21%)	14 (12.07%)	31 (26.72%)	18 (15.52%)
Pacific Ocean	3 [0.03%]	0 (0.00%)	0 (0.00%)	0 (0.00%)	0 (0.00%)	0 (0.00%)	3 (100.00%)
Europe	108 [1.14%]	14 (12.96%)	34 (31.48%)	16 (14.81%)	14 (12.96%)	17 (15.74%)	13 (12.04%)
Africa:	1,120 [11.85%]	23 (2.05%)	24 (2.14%)	73 (6.52%)	122 (10.89%)	437 (39.02%)	441 (39.38%)
Nigeria	402 [4.25%]	2 (0.50%)	5 (1.24%)	21 (5.22%)	29 (7.21%)	143 (35.57%)	202 (50.25%)

Table 12.1 (continued)
Black Male Immigrants by Region, Country of Origin, and Year of Immigration to the United States

Region/Country of Origin	Total	Year of Immigration					
		Pre-1950	1950-59	1960-64	1965-69	1970-74	1975-80
Ghana	196 [2.07%]	1 (0.51%)	6 (3.06%)	7 (3.57%)	29 (14.80%)	88 (44.90%)	65 (33.16%)
Other Africa	522 [5.52%]	20 (3.83%)	13 (2.49%)	45 (8.62%)	64 (12.26%)	206 (39.46%)	174 (33.33%)
Middle East	8 [0.08%]	0 (0.00%)	0 (0.00%)	0 (0.00%)	0 (0.00%)	4 (50.00%)	4 (50.00%)
Asia	50 [0.53%]	6 (12.00%)	12 (24.00%)	3 (6.00%)	4 (8.00%)	11 (22.00%)	14 (28.00%)
Soviet Union	56 [0.59%]	13 (23.21%)	13 (23.21%)	8 (14.29%)	6 (10.71%)	8 (14.29%)	8 (14.29%)
Country Not Specified	1,196 [12.65%]	386 (32.27%)	179 (14.97%)	79 (6.61%)	169 (14.13%)	198 (16.56%)	185 (15.47%)
Observations (N)	9,452 [100.00%]	769 (8.14%)	858 (9.08%)	868 (9.18%)	2,126 (22.49%)	2,756 (29.16%)	2,075 (21.95%)

Notes: Column percentages are shown in square brackets [ ].
          Row percentages are shown in parentheses ( ).

Source: Author's tabulations from the *1980 Census of Population 5 percent A sample*. The sample includes only those black male immigrants
          who were aged 25 to 64, worked at least one week and had earnings in 1979, and were living in one of the fifty states or the District of
          Columbia. Note that workers born in outlying areas of the United States (such as Puerto Rico) are not considered immigrants and
          hence are excluded from the sample.

Table 12.2
Descriptive Statistics for Native- and Foreign-Born Black Men Aged 25-64 in 1980

	Native-Born		Foreign-Born, English Only Language		Foreign-Born, English Second Language	
	Mean	Standard Deviation	Mean	Standard Deviation	Mean	Standard Deviation
Earnings ($)	12,790	8,759	12,729	9,222	11,314	8,664
Natural log of earnings	9.15	0.96	9.16	0.93	9.01	0.98
Education (years)	11.31	3.44	11.81	3.64	12.68	4.16
Age	39.90	11.06	39.74	10.58	37.66	9.66
Experience (age − education − 5)	23.59	12.68	22.92	11.96	19.97	11.18
Weeks worked	45.70	11.67	45.28	12.10	44.52	12.66
Natural log of weeks worked	3.75	0.48	3.74	0.50	3.71	0.52
Non-SMSA (%)	14.05	—	3.16	—	1.90	—
South (%)	53.25	—	23.89	—	23.44	—

Not married (%)	35.15	—	30.22	—	30.56	—
Foreign-born (%)	0.00	—	100.00	—	100.00	—
Year of Immigration (%):						
1975-1980	—	—	19.37	—	26.62	—
1970-1974	—	—	27.51	—	32.14	—
1965-1969	—	—	22.94	—	21.69	—
1960-1964	—	—	8.62	—	10.21	—
1950-1959	—	—	10.72	—	6.11	—
Pre-1950	—	—	10.85	—	3.23	—
Observations (N)	190,173	—	6,082	—	3,370	—

Source: Author's tabulations from the *1980 Census of Population* 5 percent A sample.

(—) : Denotes not applicable.

305

Soviet Union, all of which contributed a rather small number of black immigrants, failed to show a clear increase after 1965.

It is unlikely that the preponderance of post-1965 arrivals among foreign-born black workers can be attributed entirely to the aging of pre-1965 immigrants (which implies higher mortality and lower labor-force participation) or to reverse migration. Accordingly, the preponderance of post-1965 arrivals is puzzling because before 1965, an individual living elsewhere in the Western Hemisphere needed only to satisfy ordinary health, criminal, political, and self-sufficiency background requirements in order to enter the United States. But the 1965 amendments to the Immigration and Nationality Act for the first time placed limits on the number of immigrants from Western Hemisphere countries. Nevertheless, it appears that migration of black men from Western Hemisphere countries to the United States has increased since 1965. There appears to exist no research explaining this trend.

The reason for increases in migration from Eastern Hemisphere countries to the United States is clearer. Before 1965, the preference system for potential immigrants from countries in the Eastern Hemisphere favored two kinds of applicants: (1) those with skills or training that were considered "urgently needed" in the United States; and (2) those who were related to United States residents. Both of these aspects of the preference system tended to work against potential black immigrants from the Eastern Hemisphere in the years before 1965.

The differences between native- and foreign-born blacks can be seen in table 12.2, which displays descriptive statistics of three samples of workers: native-born black men, foreign-born black men whose only language is English (to be referred to as "English-only" immigrants), and foreign-born black men who speak English as a second language ("English-second-language" immigrants).[5]

A majority of foreign-born black men speak only English (6,082 out of 9,398, or 64 percent). This is not surprising because most black immigrants came from the West Indies (table 12.1). Table 12.2 shows at least three differences between the English-only and English-second-language black immigrants. First, the simple mean earnings of English-only immigrants were higher than those of English-second-language immigrants by over 12 percent. Second, English-only immigrants had *fewer* years of education than English-second-language immigrants, but were somewhat older. Third, a higher proportion of the English-only immigrants arrived in the United States before 1960, and a correspondingly smaller proportion of them arrived during the 1970s.

Table 12.2 also allows comparison of the characteristics of native-born blacks with the two groups of foreign-born blacks. Note first that the simple mean earnings of native-born blacks exceeded those of English-only black immigrants by less than 0.5 percent, but the mean earnings of native-born blacks exceeded those of English-second-language black immigrants by over 13 percent. Second, the average level of education of native-born blacks was lower than that of foreign-born blacks. Third, native-born blacks were much more likely to reside in the South or outside a Standard Metropolitan Statistical Area (SMSA). Fourth, a higher proportion of the native-born blacks were not married.[6] Other differences between the native- and foreign-born black men are less striking: the native-born blacks were somewhat older and worked somewhat more during 1979 than the foreign-born.

III. EARNINGS FUNCTIONS FOR BLACK IMMIGRANTS

The questions posed at the outset concern differences between the earnings of black immigrants and the earnings of three other broad classes of workers: native-born blacks, long-term black immigrants, and other groups of immigrants (white, Hispanic, and Asian). An additional question was posed about the differences between the earnings of black immigrants who speak only English and black immigrants who speak English as a second language.

The empirical framework needed to address these questions was developed by Chiswick [1978], based on Mincer's [1974] analysis of earnings. Many others have since used the same or a similar framework to analyze immigrants' earnings (Carliner [1980]; Long [1980]; Borjas [1982]; Stewart and Hyclak [1984]; Duleep and Sider [1986]; Abbott and Beach [1988]; Bloom and Gunderson [1989], among others), and I follow the same approach here.

The model specifies the natural logarithm of earnings in 1979 to be a linear function of the following explanatory variables:

- Years of education
- Years of experience (age minus years of education minus 5)
- Experience squared
- The natural logarithm of the number of weeks worked during 1979
- Whether the worker lived outside an SMSA (dummy variable equal to 1 if the worker lived outside an SMSA)
- Whether the worker lived in the South (dummy variable equal to 1 if

worker lived in the South)
- Whether the worker was not in the category "married, spouse present" (dummy variable equal to 1 if worker was not "married, spouse present")

For an immigrant, the year in which the worker arrived in the United States (modeled as a set of six dummy variables indicating whether the worker arrived in 1975-80, 1970-74, 1965-69, 1960-64, 1950-59, or before 1950).

In notation to be used later, the model may be written as follows:

$$(1) \quad Y_i = a_0 + a_1 X_{1i} + a_2 X_{2i} + \ldots + a_K X_{Ki} + b_1 M_{1i} + b_2 M_{2i} + \ldots \\ \ldots + b_6 M_{6i} + u_i,$$

where Y_i denotes the natural logarithm of the i'th worker's earnings, X_{1i} through X_{Ki} are the K explanatory variables listed above (other than year of immigration) that enter the earnings function, M_{1i} through M_{6i} are the dummy variables modeling the i'th worker's year of immigration, the a_ks and b_ts are parameters to be estimated, and ui is an error term that satisfies standard assumptions of normality and independence.

Since Y_i is in logarithmic terms, the a_ks and b_ts may be interpreted (to a first approximation) as percentage changes in expected earnings associated with a unit change in the corresponding explanatory variable (that is, partial elasticities), holding the other variables constant. [The exact percentage change in $E(Y_i)$ associated with a unit change in X_k (the k'th explanatory variable) would be $\exp(a_k) - 1$.]

Equation (1) has usually been estimated over a pooled sample of native- and foreign-born workers. In this context, two interpretations of the b_ts should be understood. The first is that they represent a profile of earnings differentials between immigrants and native-born workers. For example, if equation (1) were estimated over a sample of native- and foreign-born blacks, then b_t would show the earnings differential (usually negative) between native-born blacks and black immigrants who arrived in time period t. This interpretation is literal and uncontroversial. The second interpretation is Chiswick's dynamic interpretation – that the b_ts represent the path that the earnings differentials of a given cohort of black immigrants would follow over time. If $b_1 < b_2 < \ldots < b_6$, and higher-order b_ts approach zero, we would interpret this as evidence that black immigrants' earnings catch up to the earnings of native-born blacks. If higher-order b_ts approach zero rapidly, then we would take this as evidence of rapid assimilation. The dynamic interpretation requires the assumption that the estimated earnings function (equation 1) includes all determinants of earnings, omitting no relevant variable. The strength of this assumption makes the dynamic interpretation somewhat tenuous. Accordingly, it will be avoided for the most part in this chapter.[7]

The remainder of this section presents variants of the above model, estimated by ordinary least squares, using subsamples of workers from the *1980 Census of Population* 5 percent sample (or A sample). It will be simplest to start with the question of language proficiency, then to move on to the other issues.

IIIA. The Influence of Language Proficiency

Black immigrants are unique among immigrants in that a majority come to the United States with English as their only language. Moreover, table 12.2 shows that there are significant measurable differences between English-only and English-second-language black immigrants, even apart from language differences. It follows that the labor-market success of English-only black immigrants could differ markedly from that of English-second-language black immigrants.[8]

Column 1 of table 12.3 offers a preliminary estimate of the effects of English-language proficiency on the earnings of black immigrants. These are the results of estimating the earnings function over the full sample of native- and foreign-born blacks and including an "English Only Language" dummy variable equal to 1 for black immigrants whose only language is English, zero otherwise. (Specifically, the sample used in column 1 is the pooled sample of native- and foreign-born blacks – the aggregate of the three subsamples shown in table 12.2. Hence, the sample size is 199,625.) The coefficient of the English Only Language variable, 0.14, suggests that English-only black immigrants had 1979 earnings that were roughly 15 percent higher than English-second-language black immigrants, all else equal.[9]

This result tends to confirm that language proficiency is an important factor in the labor-market performance of black immigrants. But the estimates in column 1 of table 12.3 impose the assumption that English-only black immigrants receive a fixed earnings premium (in this case 15 percent) regardless of the year in which they immigrated. (The same point can be put differently: the profile of earnings differentials between English-only immigrants and native-born blacks is assumed to be the same as that between English-second-language blacks and native-born blacks, except for a fixed earnings premium received by English-only immigrants.) But

Table 12.3
Earnings Functions for Native- and Foreign-Born Adult Black Men

	(1) Native-Born and All Foreign-Born	(2) Native-Born and Foreign-Born, English Only Language	(3) Native-Born and Foreign-Born, English Second Language
Constant	4.6600 (0.0177)	4.6588 (0.0179)	4.6571 (0.0180)
Education	0.0586 (0.0006)	0.0592 (0.0006)	0.0592 (0.0006)
Experience	0.0215 (0.0006)	0.0215 (0.0006)	0.0212 (0.0006)
Experience^2/100	-0.0266 (0.0011)	-0.0263 (0.0011)	-0.0259 (0.0011)
Natural log of weeks worked	0.9891 (0.0037)	0.9882 (0.0037)	0.9894 (0.0037)
Non-SMSA	-0.1843 (0.0054)	-0.1833 (0.0054)	-0.1831 (0.0054)

South	-0.1780 (0.0037)	-0.1795 (0.0038)	-0.1801 (0.0038)
Not married	-0.2208 (0.0037)	-0.2230 (0.0038)	-0.2234 (0.0038)
Year of Immigration (Foreign-Born Only):			
1975-1980	-0.3911 (0.0197)	-0.2234 (0.0227)	-0.4293 (0.0260)
1970-1974	-0.2418 (0.0181)	-0.1054 (0.0191)	-0.2394 (0.0237)
1965-1969	-0.1653 (0.0203)	-0.0300 (0.0209)	-0.1606 (0.0288)
1960-1964	-0.1015 (0.0284)	0.0123 (0.0340)	-0.0658 (0.0420)
1950-1959	-0.1800 (0.0295)	-0.0526 (0.0305)	-0.1461 (0.0542)
Pre-1950	-0.1994 (0.1395)	-0.0679 (0.0303)	-0.1545 (0.0744)

Table 12.3 (continued)
Earnings Functions for Native- and Foreign-Born Adult Black Men

	(1) Native-Born and All Foreign-Born	(2) Native-Born and Foreign-Born, English Only Language	(3) Native-Born and Foreign-Born, English Second Language
English Only Language (Foreign-Born Only)	0.1395 (0.0169)	—	—
Observations (N)	199,625	196,255	193,543
R-squared (adj)	0.3524	0.3515	0.3524

Notes: The dependent variable is the natural logarithm of earnings in 1979. Estimates were obtained by ordinary least squares. Standard errors are in parentheses.

— denotes variable not entered in equation.

this assumption may be false; the premium earned by English-only black immigrants could vary with time spent in the United States. Because such variation would be important to an understanding of the assimilation of black immigrants, it is important to drop the assumption of a fixed wage premium. Accordingly, the estimates presented in the remainder of this chapter partition the sample of immigrants by their English-language proficiency, in effect relaxing the assumption of a fixed earnings premium received by those with greater English-language proficiency.[10]

IIIB. Differences Between Black Immigrants and Native-Born Blacks

The results of partitioning the sample of black immigrants into groups based on English-language proficiency can be seen in columns 2 and 3 of table 12.3. Column 2 shows the results of estimating the earnings function using a pooled sample of all native-born black men and the English-only black immigrants. Column 3 shows results from pooling all native-born black men and the English-second-language black immigrants.

The year-of-immigration dummy variables in columns 2 and 3 suggest large differences in earnings among different cohorts of black immigrants. In general, black immigrants who have been in the United States longer have higher earnings, all else equal. For example, English-only black immigrants who arrived during 1975-80 had earnings that were about 20 percent below the earnings of similar native-born blacks. But the earnings of English-only blacks who arrived during the 1950s, 1960-64, and 1965-69 differed insignificantly from the earnings of similar native-born blacks. Such a pattern is in accord with previous findings on white immigrants: both Chiswick [1978], using 1970 census data, and Borjas [1985], using 1980 census data, reported that the earnings of white immigrants who have been in the United States ten to fifteen years roughly equal the earnings of measurably similar native-born whites.[11]

But the year-of-immigration variables in column 3 present a different picture for English-second-language blacks. The English-second-language blacks who arrived during 1975-80 had earnings that were 35 percent below the earnings of similar native-born blacks. Moreover, the differential between English-second-language black immigrants and native-born blacks never quite disappears: the smallest such differential is about -6 percent (significant at the 12 percent level) for English-second-language immigrants who arrived during 1960-64.[12]

Figure 12.1
Earnings Differentials Between Native-Born Blacks and Black Immigrants

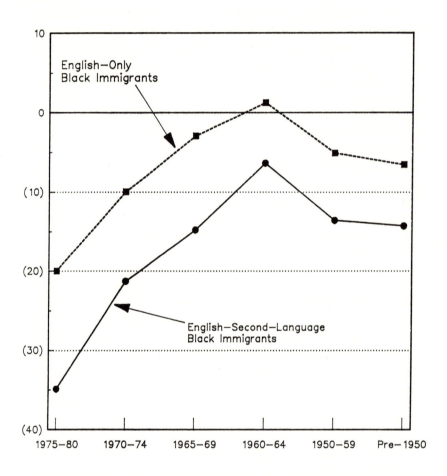

The earnings differentials between native-born blacks and the two groups of black immigrants are graphed in figure 12.1. These differentials are taken from the year-of-immigration dummy variables in columns 2 and 3 of table 12.3 (that is, by exponentiating each coefficient and subtracting 1). Figure 1 shows clearly that English-second-language black immigrants are at an earnings disadvantage compared with English-only black immigrants regardless of the year in which they immigrated. The figure also shows that the assumption that English-only black immigrants earn a fixed wage premium relative to English-second-language blacks is incorrect (this assumption was imposed in column 1 of table 12.3 and discussed in section IIIA). Rather, that wage premium, which is 15 percent for the 1975-80 group of immigrants, shrinks to 8 percent for the groups of immigrants who arrived in the early 1960s and before.

Overall, the results displayed in table 12.3 offer a mixed picture of the earnings of black immigrants relative to the earnings of native-born blacks. It is clear that black immigrants have markedly different success in the U.S. labor market depending on their English-language proficiency, as the human-capital approach would lead one to expect. English-only black immigrants have an earnings profile similar to that of white immigrants, in that the earnings of recent English-only black immigrants are well below the earnings of native-born blacks, but the earnings of English-only black immigrants who have been in the United States for ten to twenty years (that is, those who arrived during the 1960s) are about the same as the earnings of native-born blacks, other things equal. On the other hand, all groups of English-second-language blacks earn less than otherwise similar native-born blacks.

IIIC. Differences Between Recent and Long-Term Immigrants

The remainder of this section relies on the results of estimating eight earnings functions, one for each of eight subsamples of immigrants. Indexing the eight subsamples by g, these eight earnings functions can be written:

$$(2) \qquad Y_{gi} = a_{0g} + a_{1g}X_{1gi} + a_{2g}X_{2gi} + \ldots + a_{Kg}X_{Kgi} + b_{1g}M_{1gi} + b_{2g}M_{2gi} + \ldots + b_{6g}M_{6gi} + u_{gi}.$$

Equation (2) is similar to equation (1) above, with the addition of the g subscripts (for example, Y_{gi} denotes the log of earnings of the i'th worker in group g). Note that the specification allows a unique set of estimated coefficients for each subsample (for example, set g to BE for black English-only immigrants, WE for white English-only immigrants, and so on).[13]

Equation (2) is estimated for a total of eight mutually exclusive groups: four racial or ethnic groups – blacks, white non-Hispanics (hereafter "whites"), Asians, and Hispanic whites (hereafter "Hispanics") – each of which is subdivided into two language-proficiency groups. Black and

Table 12.4A
Earnings Functions for Foreign-Born Black and White Adult Men by Language Proficiency

	Black		White	
	English Only Language (1)	English Second Language (2)	English Only Language (3)	English Second Language (4)
Constant	4.6645 (0.1031)	4.5908 (0.1529)	4.2091 (0.0499)	4.7137 (0.0440)
Education	0.0449 (0.0031)	0.0394 (0.0038)	0.0643 (0.0013)	0.0452 (0.0010)
Experience	0.0298 (0.0036)	0.0198 (0.0049)	0.0473 (0.0015)	0.0328 (0.0013)
Experience^2/100	-0.0442 (0.0066)	-0.0298 (0.0094)	-0.0732 (0.0028)	-0.0526 (0.0023)
Natural log of weeks worked	0.9744 (0.0193)	1.0230 (0.0258)	1.0766 (0.0110)	1.0557 (0.0093)
Non-SMSA	-0.2086 (0.0569)	-0.0930 (0.0966)	-0.1686 (0.0147)	-0.0693 (0.0184)
South	-0.0772 (0.0235)	-0.0497 (0.0317)	-0.1013 (0.0104)	-0.0266 (0.0115)
Not married	-0.1281 (0.0213)	-0.0898 (0.0289)	-0.2615 (0.0099)	-0.2019 (0.0097)

316

Year of Immigration:

1975-1980	-0.1469 (0.0392)	-0.3035 (0.0810)	0.0394 (0.0158)	-0.2803 (0.0150)
1970-1974	-0.0107 (0.0373)	-0.0715 (0.0795)	-0.0005 (0.0186)	-0.1533 (0.0150)
1965-1969	0.0692 (0.0377)	0.0350 (0.0801)	0.0724 (0.0157)	-0.0709 (0.0143)
1960-1964	0.1140 (0.0454)	0.1461 (0.0852)	0.0084 (0.0142)	-0.0216 (0.0146)
1950-1959	0.0430 (0.0419)	0.0443 (0.0904)	0.0136 (0.0108)	0.0030 (0.0121)
Pre-1950	*	*	*	*
Observations (N)	6,082	3,370	31,168	41,237
R-squared (adj)	0.3622	0.4032	0.3522	0.3369

Notes: The dependent variable is the natural logarithm of earnings in 1979. Estimates were obtained by ordinary least squares. Standard errors are in parentheses.

* Immigration before 1950 is the reference category.

Table 12.4B
Earnings Functions for Foreign-Born Asian and Hispanic Adult Men by Language Proficiency

	Asian		Hispanic White	
	English Very Good	English Less Good	English Very Good	English Less Good
	(5)	(6)	(7)	(8)
Constant	4.3978 (0.0756)	5.0032 (0.0720)	4.3611 (0.0696)	5.2854 (0.0467)
Education	0.0793 (0.0019)	0.0477 (0.0018)	0.0637 (0.0015)	0.0357 (0.0010)
Experience	0.0352 (0.0022)	0.0231 (0.0022)	0.0319 (0.0021)	0.0202 (0.0016)
Experience^2/100	-0.0633 (0.0051)	-0.0442 (0.0041)	-0.0443 (0.0041)	-0.0315 (0.0027)
Natural log of weeks worked	0.9991 (0.0150)	0.9784 (0.0126)	1.0430 (0.0155)	0.8971 (0.0089)
Non-SMSA	0.0589 (0.0289)	-0.0233 (0.0335)	-0.1192 (0.0270)	-0.0469 (0.0175)
South	-0.0581 (0.0150)	-0.0056 (0.0185)	-0.0401 (0.0218)	-0.0873 (0.0087)
Not married	-0.2072 (0.0157)	-0.1734 (0.0173)	-0.2161 (0.0142)	-0.1409 (0.0103)

Year of Immigration:				
1975-1980	-0.3788 (0.0326)	-0.3855 (0.0368)	-0.1876 (0.0282)	-0.3157 (0.0228)
1970-1974	-0.1519 (0.0325)	-0.2128 (0.0377)	-0.0961 (0.0256)	-0.1242 (0.0223)
1965-1969	-0.0592 (0.0329)	-0.1490 (0.0392)	-0.0134 (0.0245)	-0.0493 (0.024)
1960-1964	-0.0216 (0.0357)	-0.0915 (0.0454)	0.0606 (0.0232)	0.0177 (0.0229)
1950-1959	-0.0145 (0.0347)	-0.1151 (0.0457)	0.0228 (0.0229)	0.0416 (0.0233)
Pre-1950	*	*	*	*
Observations (N)	13,928	12,835	13,843	36,535
R-squared (adj)	0.4159	0.4196	0.3756	0.2950

Notes: The dependent variable is the natural logarithm of earnings in 1979. Estimates were obtained by ordinary least squares. Standard errors are in parentheses.

* Immigration before 1950 is the reference category.

white immigrants are subdivided into the English-only and English-second-language groupings that have already been used for blacks. Because few if any Asians or Hispanics speak only English, these latter groups are subdivided into different language-proficiency groups: those who speak English only or English very well (referred to as the "English Very Good" group), and those who speak English well, not very well, or not at all (the "English Less Good" group).

Estimates of equation (2) for each of the eight subsamples are displayed in tables 12.4A and 12.4B. The first reason for estimating these equations is to see how the earnings of recent immigrants of each group compare with the earnings of longer-term immigrants of that same group. (Additional uses of these equations are pursued in section IIID.) The year-of-immigration variables in each equation yield the desired differentials. For example, the coefficient of the 1975-80 year-of-immigration variable in column 1 (−0.147) suggests that, other things equal, black English-only immigrants who arrived during 1975-80 had earnings that were lower by about 14 percent than the earnings of English-only blacks who arrived before 1950. But the coefficient of the 1960-64 variable (0.114) suggests that black English-only immigrants who arrived during 1960-64 had earnings that were 12 percent above the earnings of English-only blacks who arrived before 1950.

Inspection of the eight sets of year-of-immigration variables reveals three patterns of differentials between recent and long-term immigrants. First, white English-second-language immigrants, both Asian groups, and both Hispanic groups of immigrants show similar patterns in the following sense: the differentials are largest for the most recent immigrants and tend to diminish for longer-term immigrants within each group. Second, white English-only immigrants show a rather flat pattern of differentials with no clear trend. Third, for both groups of black immigrants, the differential is largest for the most recent groups of immigrants and then diminishes, but only through the 1960-64 cohort of immigrants; that is, the profile has a sharp kink at 1960-64. Also, black immigrants who arrived in the United States before 1950 appear to earn less than those who arrived during the 1950s or 1960s. Both of these features of black immigrants' earnings profiles make black immigrants unusual.

The profiles for white, Asian, and Hispanic immigrants are consistent with the cultural/human-capital interpretation of wage differentials. But the unusual profiles for black immigrants seem to require a different explanation. A possible explanation is that recent black immigrants have experienced less labor-market discrimination than have the longest-term black immigrants. Existing evidence suggests that a variety of factors — such as anti-discrimination legislation and improved education — combined, starting in the mid-1960s, to allow blacks to achieve greater success in the labor market (Leonard [1984]; Smith and Welch [1989]; Bound and Freeman [1989]; and chapter 13 by James Heckman in this volume). It would follow that for black immigrants, we should observe (as we do) higher earnings for those who arrived in the 1960s and later relative to the longest-term immigrants.

IIID. Differences Between Black Immigrants and Other Immigrants

The estimates presented in tables 12.4A and 12.4B also provide the basis for an examination of differences between black immigrants and other groups of immigrants. Two issues are addressed here: first, whether rates of return to education differ across the various groups of immigrants; second, whether adjusted earnings profiles differ across the various groups.

1. *Differences in returns to education.* The rate of return to education offers a good measure of the rewards received from investing in an activity that many believe enhances productivity. The estimated rate of return to education for black English-only immigrants is about 4.5 percent per annum (see the coefficient of the education variable in column 1 of table 12.4A). This rate of return is below that for white English-only immigrants (6.6 percent), Asian English-very-good immigrants (8.3 percent), and Hispanic English-very-good immigrants (6.6 percent). Indeed, it is similar to the rates of return experienced by black English-second-language immigrants (4.0 percent) and other immigrants who speak English as a second language or less well: white English-second-language immigrants (4.6 percent), Asian English-less-good immigrants (4.9 percent), and Hispanic English-less-good immigrants (3.6 percent).

There are at least three possible interpretations of the finding that black English-only immigrants receive a lower return to education than other immigrants whose English is very good. One, suggested by Chiswick's work [1983a, 1983b], would be the cultural/human-capital interpretation - that black English-only immigrants are less well equipped to take advantage of the benefits of education than are other immigrants who speak English very well. A second is that the quality of education received by blacks is lower than that received by other immigrants; this lower quality would in turn be the result of discrimination. A third is that the labor market simply fails to reward black English-only immigrants who receive education as gener-

Table 12.5
Unexplained Earnings Differentials Between White English-Only Immigrants and Other
Immigrant Groups

Immigrant Group	Year of Immigration					
	1975-80	1970-74	1965-69	1960-64	1950-59	Pre-1950
White, English only	0.000 [15,334]	0.000 [15,963]	0.000 [19,040]	0.000 [17,466]	0.000 [17,048]	0.000 [17,707]
White, English second language	0.328 [9,658]	0.116 [12,489]	0.123 [14,158]	0.023 [15,840]	0.013 [16,544]	0.015 [16,321]
Black, English only	0.599 [6,905]	0.382 [9,335]	0.413 [11,184]	0.278 [11,929]	0.368 [10,109]	0.378 [9,058]
Black, English second language	0.938 [5,337]	0.570 [8,415]	0.602 [10,176]	0.393 [12,189]	0.506 [10,036]	0.457 [9,003]
Hispanic, English very good	0.377 [8,514]	0.230 [10,574]	0.220 [12,493]	0.054 [14,529]	0.109 [13,708]	0.112 [13,342]
Hispanic, English less good	0.573 [6,052]	0.319 [8,492]	0.373 [9,623]	0.235 [10,444]	0.164 [10,085]	0.120 [8,798]
Asian, English very good	0.484 [9,985]	0.142 [16,002]	0.146 [19,276]	0.053 [20,746]	0.081 [18,725]	0.175 [16,939]
Asian, English less good	0.536 [7,713]	0.469 [11,286]	0.336 [12,758]	0.292 [13,354]	0.362 [12,236]	0.190 [10,599]

Notes: Figures in brackets show mean dollar earnings of each immigrant group.

Unbracketed figures show the proportional increase in mean earnings that each immigrant group would experience if its members' earnings were determined in the same way as the earnings of white English-only immigrants who arrived in the same period. For example, the figure 0.599 for black English-only immigrants who arrived during 1975-80 indicates that if these immigrants had been treated like white English-only immigrants who arrived in 1975-80, their earnings would have been about 60 percent higher than was actually observed. Mean earnings of black English-only immigrants arriving during 1975-80 were $6,905, so their earnings if treated like white English-only immigrants arriving during 1975-80 would have been ($6,905)(1.599) = $11,041. Using the notation developed in the text, the unexplained earnings differential for black English-only immigrants in period t is $(\hat{Y}_{BE,t} - Y_{BE,t})/Y_{BE,t}$.

ously as it rewards other immigrants who speak English well, which again would be evidence of discrimination based on race.[14]

The findings seem to belie the cultural interpretation that black English-only immigrants are less able to benefit from education. The cultural interpretation implies that immigrants with higher English proficiency can be expected to receive higher returns to education. After all, individuals whose English is better should be able to gain more from education conducted in English and to turn their education to better use in the labor market. Indeed, for whites, Asians, and Hispanics, this expectation is fulfilled. But black English-only immigrants receive roughly the same rate of return to education as black English-second-language immigrants and as other groups of immigrants whose English is less good. In other words, black English-only immigrants pose an anomaly for the cultural interpretation. The evidence seems to point to the alternative interpretation – labor-market discrimination against black English-only immigrants.[15]

2. *Differences in adjusted earnings profiles.* A final question is perhaps the most important of all: How do the earnings of black immigrants compare with the earnings of other groups of immigrants? The question can be rephrased more analytically: How much would black immigrants earn if their earnings were generated by the same function that generates the earnings of some reference group of immigrants – white English-only immigrants, say?

This question can be addressed by a well-known method developed by Blinder [1973] and Oaxaca [1973], which is discussed elsewhere in this volume by Harriet Duleep and Nadja Zalokar (chapter 8) and Solomon Polachek and Charng Kao (chapter 9). Let $Y_{BE,t}$ denote the actual mean earnings of black English-only immigrants who arrived in period t, and let $\tilde{Y}_{BE,t}$ denote the (econometrically simulated) mean earnings that black English-only immigrants who arrived in period t would receive if their earnings were generated in the same way (that is, by the same earnings function) as white English-only immigrants who arrived in period t. Then the differential $(\tilde{Y}_{BE,t} - Y_{BE,t})/Y_{BE,t}$ is the proportional increase in earnings that black English-only immigrants would experience if they were treated in the labor market as white English-only immigrants. Such differentials have often been considered as discriminatory in that they are unexplained by measured differences between black and white English-only immigrants. These differentials will be referred to as unexplained earnings differentials in what follows.

Table 12.5 displays the unexplained earnings differentials between

Figure 12.2

Unexplained Earnings Differentials Between White English-Only Immigrants and Other Immigrant Groups

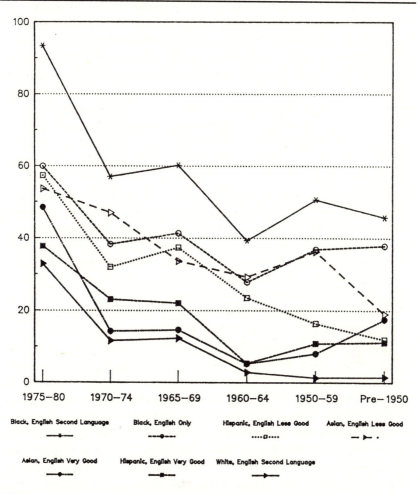

Black, English Second Language

Black, English Only

Hispanic, English Less Good

Asian, English Less Good

Asian, English Very Good

Hispanic, English Very Good

White, English Second Language

NOTES: Differentials shown come from Table 12.5. See the discussion in section III.D.2.

various groups of immigrants and white English-only immigrants. For example, the figure 0.599 for black English-only immigrants who arrived during 1975-80 indicates that these immigrants' earnings would have been 60 percent higher had they been treated like white English-only immigrants in the labor market. The unexplained earnings differentials displayed in table 12.5 are plotted for each group of immigrants in figure 12.2. It will be useful to discuss two aspects of the profiles shown: first, the sizes of the unexplained differentials, and second, the slopes of the profiles.

Regarding first the sizes of the unexplained differentials, the white English-second-language profile can be used as a reference. For these immigrants, the unexplained differential is high for recent immigrants, but nearly zero for immigrants who have been in the United States since 1964 or earlier. But for none of the other groups of immigrants does the unexplained earnings differential come so close to vanishing. For Hispanic and Asian immigrants whose English is very good, the unexplained differential is as low as 5 percent for immigrants who arrived during 1960-64, but higher for earlier groups of immigrants.

Black English-second-language immigrants have larger unexplained earnings differentials than any other group of immigrants. Black English-only immigrants have unexplained earnings differentials that are clearly larger than those of other immigrants whose English is very good (that is, white English-only, Hispanic English-very-good, and Asian English-very-good immigrants) and are generally about as large as the unexplained differentials of Asian and Hispanic immigrants whose English is less good.

There are at least two possible explanations of the relatively high unexplained earnings differentials observed for black immigrants. First, there could be important unmeasured characteristics of black immigrants – culture or human capital – that result in lower productivity and earnings, regardless of how long they are in the U.S. labor market. That is, the large unexplained differential for black immigrants would be explained if we had more and better data on workers. Second, there could be significant discriminatory barriers faced by black immigrants who participate in the U.S. labor market.

Even if we admit that unmeasured characteristics could account for part of the unexplained earnings differentials of blacks, it is difficult to rationalize all of such a large differential as the result of omitted variables. Indeed, the finding that black English-only immigrants have unexplained differentials as large as Hispanic and Asian immigrants whose English is less good suggests that labor-market discrimination poses a significant barrier for black immigrants.

It is also useful to examine the average slopes of the profiles shown in figure 12.2.[16] The average slopes are as follows, from steepest to flattest:

Hispanic, English Less Good	-1.25
Black, English Second Language	-1.14
Asian, English Less Good	-0.92
White, English Second Language	-0.82
Hispanic, English Very Good	-0.76
Asian, English Very Good	-0.68
Black, English Only	-0.49

Note that groups whose English is less good tend to have steeper profiles than those whose English is better. This is in accord with the cultural/ human-capital interpretation of earnings differentials. Acquisition of English by immigrants whose English is initially poor results in relatively rapid improvements in earnings. Black English-second-language immigrants are included in this relatively rapid improvement, although (as already noted) the disadvantage from which they start is the largest of any group.

Note also that Hispanics tend to have steeper profiles than Asians or blacks. This could be interpreted as evidence that Hispanics, many of whom are white, face fewer discriminatory barriers than do blacks or Asians. In particular, the profile for black English-only immigrants is the flattest of all. It follows that black English-only immigrants face the worst of both worlds – a relatively high unexplained differential to start out and relatively slow erosion of that differential. The flatness of the profile is at least partly consistent with the cultural/human-capital interpretation - if black English-only immigrants are proficient in English when they arrive in the United States, then English-language acquisition could not lead to accelerated earnings growth. But the magnitude of the unexplained differential is more difficult to rationalize without appealing to the existence of significant racial discrimination in the labor market.

IV. SUMMARY AND DISCUSSION

Four main points emerge from the results presented here. First, the earnings of black immigrants differ markedly depending on whether English is their only language or their second language. Specifically, the earnings of recent black English-only immigrants are well below the earnings of native-born blacks, but the earnings of black English-only immigrants who have been in the United States for ten to twenty years are

about the same as the earnings of native-born blacks with similar education, labor-market experience, and so on. In contrast, the earnings of black
English-second-language immigrants are below the earnings of otherwise
similar native-born blacks regardless of how long the black English-
second-language immigrants have been in the United States. (On these
results, see figure 12.1 and the discussion in section IIIB.)

Second, earnings profiles of black immigrants are distinctly different
from the earnings profiles of other groups of immigrants. Whereas the
profiles for other groups of immigrants suggest that immigrants who have
been in the United States longer have higher earnings, those for black
immigrants suggest that some early groups of black immigrants earn less
than more recent groups. This finding could be interpreted as evidence of
less severe discrimination against more recent groups of black immigrants.
(On these results, see the year-of-immigration dummy variables in tables
12.4A and 12.4B and the discussion in section IIIC.)

Third, the rate of return to education for black English-only immigrants
is unusually low compared with that for other immigrants whose only
language is English or whose English is very good. Indeed, the rate of return
for black English-only immigrants is similar to that for black English-
second-language immigrants, which in turn is similar to the return received by other immigrants whose speak English as a second language or
less well. (See the coefficients of the education variable in tables 12.4A
and 12.4B, and the discussion in section IIID1.)

Fourth, unexplained earnings differentials for English-second-language
blacks greatly exceed those for any other group of immigrants. That is,
English-second-language blacks are rewarded less well for measurable
characteristics that are correlated with earnings than are other groups of
immigrants. For black English-only immigrants, the unexplained earnings
differentials are also very large – as large as those of Asian and Hispanic
immigrants whose English is less good. (See figure 12.2 and the discussion
in section IIID2.)

Two questions remain. First, can the differences in labor-market
outcomes between black and other immigrants be explained wholly by
differences in culture (or human capital), or do we need to resort to
discrimination for at least part of the explanation? Second, what do the
findings imply about earnings differentials between native-born blacks and
whites?

The issue of culture versus discrimination is difficult precisely because
we cannot directly observe or measure either culture or discrimination.
Nevertheless, some of the findings do pose anomalies for the cultural/

human-capital interpretation of earnings differentials and point in turn to the existence of significant labor-market discrimination against black immigrants: (1) The profiles of earnings differentials between recent and long-term black immigrants are unusual and suggest the existence of past discrimination against black immigrants (which may have lessened since the mid-1960s). (2) Black English-only immigrants have a rate of return to education that is low (compared with other immigrants whose English is very good) and similar to that of immigrants whose English is less good (including black English-second-language immigrants). (3) Unexplained earnings differentials for black immigrants meet or exceed the unexplained differentials of other groups of immigrants regardless of language proficiency.

The cultural interpretation would need to be stretched considerably to fully accommodate these findings. To argue that culture can explain completely the findings just listed, one would need to maintain that any difference that cannot be explained by observed variables is at root a matter of culture or human capital. This approach is probably undesirable because it would tend to reduce the cultural interpretation to a tautology – to a dictum without empirical content.

There can be little doubt that unobserved human-capital differences between various groups of immigrants account in some degree for differences in labor-market success. But a cultural interpretation that avoids tautology needs to place limits on the differences that are attributed strictly to culture. In particular, the three findings noted above seem to be anomalous within the framework of culture and human capital. Why would we expect the profiles of earnings differentials between recent and long-term black immigrants to be unique? Why are black English-only immigrants rewarded less well for education than are other groups of immigrants whose English is very good? Why do black English-only immigrants experience labor-market success similar to that of Asians and Hispanics whose English is less good? Why do black English-second-language immigrants have by far the largest unexplained earnings differentials of any group of immigrants? If we weigh these findings, it is difficult not to conclude that black immigrants have faced greater and more daunting discriminatory barriers than have other groups of immigrants.

What, if anything, do the findings imply about whether earnings differentials between native-born blacks and whites are the result of culture or discrimination? If the earnings and earnings profiles of black immigrants were similar to those of other groups of immigrants - especially Asians and Hispanics – then it would be tempting to conclude that discrimination against native-born blacks did not extend to black immigrants. In turn, discrimination against native-born blacks could be interpreted as discrimination against a black American culture (however perceived), rather than against a race. But the empirical findings suggest that black immigrants are at a disadvantage compared with other immigrants and this suggests in turn that discrimination against blacks extends to all blacks regardless of nativity. That is, discrimination against blacks is to be interpreted as discrimination against a race (as defined by skin color), not against a culture. The implication is that if black Americans were to adopt a different set of cultural values – to assimilate, in the sense that immigrants are believed to assimilate – they would not eradicate the black/white earnings differential. Clearly, some form of antidiscrimination policy is suggested by this line of reasoning.

This chapter has attempted a systematic examination of black immigrants' earnings using data from the 1980 *Census of Population*. Although I believe that the evidence supports the existence of significant labor-market discrimination – and suggests certain limits to the applicability of the cultural/human-capital explanation of earnings differences – ambiguities remain. In particular, anyone willing to stretch the cultural explanation might still argue that unobserved variables wholly account for earnings differentials that are otherwise unexplained and might otherwise be attributed to discrimination.

It seems unlikely that the ambiguities will be resolved simply or soon, but I would suggest at least two lines of research that might prove fruitful. First, estimation of cohort effects (Borjas [1985]) would give a picture of how the "quality" of immigrants (that is, their capacity to perform well in the labor market) has changed over time for each group of immigrants. It follows that an understanding of cohort effects could limit the applicability of either the cultural or the discriminatory interpretations of earnings differentials. The problem, of course, is that estimating cohort effects must await data from the 1990 census. Second, data on the earnings of immigrants before they migrated to the United States, or better use of existing data (for example, careful disaggregation of immigrant groups by country of origin or by age at time of immigration), could add significantly to the list of observable characteristics of immigrants.[17] More data or better use of existing data could either reduce the unexplained differential or provide ways of understanding the degree to which unexplained differentials are the result of culture or discrimination. Of course, whether research along the suggested lines would actually narrow the scope for disagreement is an open question.

13
Accounting for the Economic Progress of Black Americans

James J. Heckman

This chapter explores one topical and controversial aspect of black economic progress: the role of government policy and social activism in elevating the status of blacks. The economics profession is currently divided in its assessment of the contribution of federal civil-rights and affirmative-action policy to the elevation of black economic status. The new National Research Council (NRC) volume *A Common Destiny: Blacks and American Society* (Jaynes and Williams [1989]) puts together a variety of pieces of evidence from several disciplines that shed valuable new light on this important issue.

One prevailing school of thought within our profession emphasizes the importance of long-term secular trends in migration and educational advancement in explaining black economic progress. Another school of thought focuses on the discontinuous improvement of black status that appears in the aggregate time series of relative black earnings and wages and in other indicators of black status after the passage of Title VII of the Civil Rights Act and initiation of affirmative-action plans. Two very different views of the labor-market experience of black Americans are offered. Does continuous or discontinuous change characterize the recent economic history of black Americans?

The importance of the continuous-improvement view to the argument that government played a negligible role is illustrated by the following quotation from James Smith and Finis Welch:

The racial gap narrowed as rapidly in the 20 years prior to 1960 (and before affirmative action) as during the 20 years afterward. This suggests that the slowly evolving historical forces we have emphasized ... education and migration - were the primary determinants of long-term black economic improvement. At best affirmative action has marginally altered black wage gains around this long-term trend. (Smith and Welch [1989: 519])

In fact, there is ample evidence of discontinuous change in the improvement of black status during the crucial period 1965-75, even in the studies that claim continuity. The sources of black improvement differ across decades. Migration of blacks out of the South played a major role until 1960 but accounted for little of the 1960-80 change. The decline in the labor market for the unskilled accounts for the post-1975 stagnation in black relative progress. At issue is what accounts for black progress between 1960 and 1975. Proponents of the continuity hypothesis rely on improvements in the quantity and quality of black schooling during this period. For the trend in black progress to be the same in 1960-80 as it was in 1940-60, the contribution of education and educational quality must have accelerated in this period, because the contribution of migration diminished.

The temporal coincidence of a discontinuous increase in the relative earnings data in the period 1960-75 and the creation of federal policy has led many scholars to assign a central role to government policy in elevating black status. A major difficulty with this argument is that the evidence supporting it is indirect – in large part due to the absence of convincing policy measures. Time-series studies that show an upward jump in the relative status of black earnings after 1964 have convinced few that the measured shift is anything but a temporal coincidence (Ashenfelter [1976]). An apparent enigma that must be explained by those who claim that federal policy was important is that policy-agency budgets were small and federal enforcement powers were weak during the period of the greatest black relative wage gains. If enforcement efforts were weak, how could the effect of federal activity have been so strong?

The key to resolving these issues is to disaggregate the data on black economic progress by region and by time period and to take a broader view of the full range of federal policies developed to eliminate discrimination. Disaggregation of the data reveals the central role of developments in the South for explaining black economic progress. This is hardly surprising since the majority of blacks - the vast majority in 1940 - live in that region. Once it is understood that black economic progress in the period 1960-75 is predominantly southern black economic progress and that federal policy was directed toward the South in that period, the evidence for a positive policy impact becomes more convincing.

I. BASIC FACTS OF BLACK ECONOMIC PROGRESS: DISCONTINUITY AND THE CENTRAL ROLE OF THE SOUTH

The aggregate data reveal an upward jump in the time series of black male earnings and relative wages beginning in the mid-1960s (Freeman [1973], [1981]). Much of the jump can be attributed to a jump in the North Central region imposed on a southern upward trend that started before 1965 (Butler and Heckman [1977]; Donohue and Heckman [1991]). Relative improvements in the North Central region died off by 1975. Those in the South did not. The South was the region of the greatest black economic advance in the 1960s. Two-thirds of the growth in black status between 1960 and 1970 occurred there. Blacks made their greatest advance in operative occupations in southern manufacturing (Butler, Heckman, and Payner [1990]). There is evidence of substantial desegregation of firms in the South in the period 1966-70 (Ashenfelter and Heckman [1976]). Bound and Freeman [1989] used Current Population Survey (CPS) annual March Demographic Files to estimate relative earnings and wage equations for males aged 20-64 over the period 1963-84. Controlling for age, region, urban status, race, and education, they documented an upward jump in black status after 1965. The period 1966-74 witnessed the greatest black economic gains. After 1975, black status stagnated, a finding later reproduced by other scholars. Especially noteworthy was the dramatic decline in the percentage wage gap between blacks and whites in the South after 1965, controlling for productivity characteristics. It dropped from 38.5 percent in 1965 to 12.6 percent in 1975, accounting for much of the aggregate improvement of black male status. Smith and Welch [1986: tables A.1 and A.2] corroborated this finding. They found that new entrants to the labor market in the South experienced a dramatic decline in the wage gap between blacks and whites. There was dramatic improvement across all cohorts of workers in the South in the period 1970-80 that they speculated might be a consequence of the fact that "racial discrimination is waning in the South" (Smith and Welch [1986: 49]).

The recent growth in black status in the South contrasts with the historical record of relative stagnation. A large body of scholarly literature beginning with Myrdal [1944] and continuing with Dewey [1952], Becker [1957], Wright [1986], [1988], and Margo [1990] documented the stability of black/white occupational status in the South over the period 1910-50 in the face of rising relative quantities and qualities of black schooling. Blacks were excluded from new industries and new occupations during this period. Black relative advance of the sort documented by Smith [1984] occurred because of migration to the North. Secular trends of improving black education and advancing industrialization do not explain the stagnant relative status of blacks in the South over this period (Margo [1990]). Heckman and Payner [1989] documented the stability of patterns of racial exclusion in South Carolina textiles over the period 1910-65. Through two world wars, the Great Depression, and the Korean War, the share of blacks remained low and stable. A dramatic breakthrough in black employment and wages occurred in the industry only after 1964. The story of blacks in the South is one of stability in relative status up to 1950 in the face of rising relative educational levels and rising industrialization, followed by rapid improvement that was concentrated in the period 1965-75, but began before 1964.

II. UNDERSTANDING THE CHANGE

The central role of black relative improvement in the South in accounting for aggregate black relative improvement in the period 1965-75 helps to resolve some of the controversy concerning the efficacy of government civil-rights and affirmative-action policy. One leading explanation of black relative progress advanced by proponents of the continuity hypothesis refers to rising relative levels of black schooling and schooling quality. Smith and Welch have been forceful advocates of this point of view. However, it is important to note that more than 80 percent of their estimated contribution of education to black relative progress is in the improvement in the "return to" (price of) black schooling relative to white schooling during the period 1960-80. The direct contribution of measured improvement in years of schooling is generally much smaller for workers in most work-experience classes. Smith and Welch relied on improvement in schooling coefficients as the main source of the contribution of black schooling to black status. Yet improvements in black schooling coefficients may be due to changing discrimination against blacks or changing "quality" of schooling.

There is as yet no microeconomic evidence supporting the claim that increasing black schooling quality raised the "return to" (price of) black schooling relative to that of white schooling. Aggregate data on relative schooling expenditures and length of school term in southern segregated facilities show marked improvement in the mid-1940s. Cohorts of black children fully educated in these schools appeared in the labor market in the mid-1960s. Thus there is a real possibility that increasing school quality may account for a substantial fraction of black economic advance in the South in the 1960s.

Before this conclusion is embraced too warmly, however, it is important to note the following qualifications. First, the rapid growth in teacher salaries in southern schools in the 1940s was due to a successful salary equalization program waged by the National Association for the Advancement of Colored People (NAACP) (Bullock [1967]). The same teachers were paid more. One form of blatant discrimination was removed by federal court order. Evidence that teacher quality actually improved is weak. The Coleman report [1966] revealed that by 1965 younger teachers in black schools were relatively more inferior compared to their white counterparts than were older black teachers. Second, the growth in schooling quality for blacks found in the aggregate data may be a consequence of the large outmigration from the rural South, where black/white disparities were particularly large. The current micro evidence that growth in relative schooling quality raised black status is weak. Yet if stronger evidence is found, there will be irony in this for the quality-of-schooling argument. It was government action in response to NAACP court cases that raised the quality of black schooling.

Direct measures of federal employment policy indicate low enforcement effort during the crucial 1960-70 period. Butler and Heckman [1977] and Smith and Welch [1984] noted that the greatest black gains occurred in a period (1966-72) when the two main civil-rights employment and affirmative-action enforcement agencies — the Office of Federal Contract Compliance (OFCC) and the Equal Employment Opportunity Commission (EEOC) — had limited budgets and weak enforcement powers. Many knowledgeable first-hand observers have commented that both agencies were ineffective in their early years. Estimates of OFCC impact summarized in Donohue and Heckman [forthcoming] provide no support — pro or con — for the proposition that the agency had a substantial impact on aggregate black relative wages.

If we take a broader view of the law and the measurement of the impacts of the law and recognize the full range of federal antidiscrimination programs, the case for a positive effect of the law is strengthened. Federal policy was directed toward the South in the crucial period 1965-75. (see Gold [1985]). By noting that civil-rights policy was directed toward an unwilling South, it is easy to counter the argument that civil-rights laws were merely manifestations of preexisting social trends that would have led to black progress under any event. By further noting that black improvement was most rapid in the South, the credibility of a policy effect is substantially strengthened.

The NRC report (Jaynes and Williams [1989]) is particularly helpful in documenting the full range of federal efforts directed toward the South during the period 1965-75. Direct measures of affirmative-action and civil-rights enforcement activity that have preoccupied previous discussions understate the full thrust of federal activity in the region. The NRC report documents how black voter registration in the South rose from 28 percent in 1962 to 67 percent in 1970. Fifty percent of all charges filed by the EEOC were filed against firms and establishments in the South during the period 1966-72. Southern schools were the most segregated in 1968 and the least segregated by 1972. These statistics document the full range of federal civil-rights activity directed toward the South. In the case of voter registration and school desegregation, they also reveal the success of the policy.

There is evidence that southern employers were eager to employ blacks if they were given the proper excuse. This produced a strong leverage effect for the new laws. Enforcement budgets could have been small and the law could still have been quite effective. The "enigma" of small budgets and rapid black advance is an artifact of a narrow view of the operation of antidiscrimination laws. Butler, Heckman, and Payner [1990] documented that employment of blacks in South Carolina textiles slowed down the growth of labor costs and kept the industry competitive in the period 1965-75 in the face of foreign competition. Integration of geographically isolated textile mills required integration of housing, schooling, and employment. The multithrusted federal effort in all areas of racial exclusion in southern life facilitated employment desegregation. It opened new supplies of labor to southern entrepreneurs.

An entire pattern of racial exclusion was challenged. This helps to explain how an apparent straw (the Equal Employment Opportunity Commission and the Office of Federal Contract Compliance) could have broken the back of southern employment discrimination. They were only the tip of a federal iceberg launched against the South.

Evidence of stability in racial status in the South during the period 1910-50 coupled with dramatic improvement in that region in the period 1965-75 is consistent with the multiple-equilibrium "community-norms" model of George Akerlof [1980]. Wright [1988] documented numerous failed attempts at marginal experimentation with the employment of black workers by southern textile firms. Social sanctions apparently played a major role in preserving the southern way of life against marginal experimentation by entrepreneurs. Massive government intervention on a number of interrelated fronts helped move the South from one equilibrium to another and broke down the racial code. Entrepreneurs were apparently willing to embrace the new laws and make them effective.

However, it is incorrect to attribute all of the black improvement in the South to civil-rights laws. The upward trend in black status in the South began before Title VII became law. Social activism in the South and improvements in schooling quality and industrial development were also important contributors.

The "quality-of-schooling" hypothesis does not explain the large cross-cohort improvement in the relative status of blacks in the South in the 1970-80 era (Donohue and Heckman [forthcoming]). "Quality of schooling" is nothing more than the price paid per unit of schooling. The record from the South indicates that the labor market shifted favorably toward blacks in a fashion that can most economically be accounted for by assigning a major role to federal civil-rights policy.

Notes

PREFACE AND DEDICATION

1. This overview of Dr. Alexander's life is drawn from Jablow [1980]. *Who's Who Among Black Americans* [1988], Boyd [1989], St. George [1989], and Fraser [1989].

CHAPTER 1

This chapter is a revised version of a paper presented at the Middlebury College Conference on Discrimination, April 1989. Richard Cornwall made helpful comments on the earlier draft.

1. Rhonda Williams (in section IIA of chapter 4) uses the concept of "marginalization rates" in order to combine unemployment statistics with those on involuntary part-timing and discouraged workers. Daniel Lichter [1988:776] comments that "Official government statistics routinely underestimate joblessness and related employment problems. Indeed, there is much speculation that the unemployment rate camouflages racial inequality...[and] appears to mask the extent of black-white differences in joblessness."

2. I leave it to Rhonda Williams (chapter 4, section IV) to describe the ways in which the supply and demand sides of the labor market are dependent on each other. I draw the supply-demand distinction overly sharply in part for the purpose of simplicity and in part because the lack of data on individual workplaces has allowed econometricians to focus on the characteristics of workers to the exclusion of explicit demand-side considerations (see section III of this chapter). Culp and Dunson [1986:233], for example, comment that "for reasons of theory and data availability, most social scientists, particularly economists, have focused on supply questions" in the analysis of black employment problems. In terms of causality, the premarket/in-market distinction is hard to justify theoretically, let alone empiri-

cally. Nonetheless, it is entirely on this basis that the human-capital explanation of racial inequality is constructed.

3. Hashemzadeh and Long [1985:15] detrend black and white unemployment to conclude that "with the onset of a recession, blacks . . . tend to be laid off or switched to part-time employment several weeks earlier than their white counterparts. As the economy picks up, blacks as a group are not among the first round beneficiaries of expanding employment opportunities." This last hired-first fired pattern would be exacerbated if the secular trend of increasing unemployment were included in their analysis.

4. For more detail on the connection between human-capital theory and unemployment, see section II of chapter 2 by William Darity, Jr. It is also worth noting that the alternative explanation of the convergence of black and white human capital – that low-wage blacks have dropped out of the labor force in increasing numbers, thereby raising the average human capital of those remaining – also cannot account for the persistence of the unemployment gap since persons in low-wage jobs have the highest turnover rates. Sample selection bias would thus be expected to reduce the unemployment gap in the same manner that it is alleged to reduce the wage gap. James J. Heckman has recently reiterated the dropout thesis in the *Wall Street Journal* [1989]; see Smith and Welch [1989:551-552] for a refutation.

5. This is done by a simple weighting procedure; $BUR^* = (FB_i \times UR_i)$, where FB_i is the fraction of black workers in occupational/industrial category i, UR_i is the unemployment rate for category i as a whole, and BUR^* is the black unemployment rate that would exist if blacks within each occupational/industrial category experienced the same unemployment rate as the category as a whole. Calculations were made with data from the *1989 Statistical Abstract of the United States*.

6. If a more detailed set of occupational categories were employed, more impact on black unemployment would be found, but even a greater degree of disaggregation and more complicated estimation techniques have failed to explain more than about a fifth of the unemployment gap on the basis of relative occupational distributions. See Shulman [1984a:164].

7. Smith and Welch are inconsistent about where black employment problems are concentrated. They focus on younger blacks in their 1986 monograph (see p.109) and on older blacks in their 1989 paper (see p.551). The contrast is striking since their later paper is largely a reiteration of their earlier monograph, and it underscores the confusion that black employment declines create for their optimistic assessment of black progress. To preserve this assessment, they blame black employment problems on the increasing elasticity of the black male labor supply curve "as opportunities in the nonmarket sector improved (i.e., welfare, crime)" [Smith and Welch 1989:551]. No evidence is introduced to support this remarkable conclusion; indeed, the drop in per recipient real aid to families with dependent children benefits as well as the increasingly punitive response to crime and drugs would lead one to expect that the opposite would be the case. Nor do they apply the same argument to whites despite the fact that relatively more rapid increases in black market opportunities would lead one to expect relatively more rapid increases in white nonmarket activities. Since Smith and Welch believe that market opportunities for blacks have steadily increased, they are forced to argue

that the drop in black employment must be due to nonmarket opportunities increasing even more. Though this conclusion cannot be verified and appears to be unreasonable, they refuse to qualify their aggressively optimistic assertions about black progress.

8. In contrast to the method shown in note 5, here the effort is to establish what the black unemployment rate would be if blacks had the same distribution as whites between categories but experienced their actual unemployment rates within categories: $BUR^{**} = (FW_i \times BUR_i)$, where BUR^{**} is the black unemployment rate which would exist if blacks had the same distribution as whites between categories.

9. Reynolds Farley [1986:14], for example, notes that "high unemployment rates and low rates of labor force participation are not restricted to young black men, to those in central cities, or to those who dropped out of school . . . For almost all age groups - including those in the suburbs and those with five years of college - the unemployment rate for blacks was double that of comparable white men, and the proportion who were out of the labor force in 1985 or who did not work in 1984 was much higher."

10. The Braddock and McPartland study [1987] and the studies cited by Baron in chapter 6 are important exceptions to this generalization; they are discussed in section IV.

11. Culp and Dunson [1986:251] also conclude that "many observers believe that demand issues can be safely ignored . . . [Yet] employer behavior is an important topic that begs further inquiry by research on black youth unemployment." However, it is worth noting that the data pertinent to the analysis of employment discrimination are no less "innocent" than the data on worker characteristics. As Baron comments in chapter six of this volume, "Organizations [not only] shape the reality of discrimination, but also . . . manipulate the very statistics and perceptions that frame public policies and discussions concerning discrimination. . . . [T]he social scientist's datum or trend is often the manager's strategically created fiction."

12. A possible exception to this conclusion is if the law forbids occupational segregation and wage discrimination. In that case, prejudiced employers may compensate by discriminating in their hiring decisions [Beller 1978]. Compositional shifts in discrimination are discussed below, but in and of itself this argument cannot account for unemployment differentials prior to the advent of civil-rights and affirmative-action laws. It is also worth noting (as Richard Cornwall has pointed out to me) that Becker's model is itself implicitly biased: why is it presumed that segregation results from white distaste at associating with blacks rather than black distaste at associating with whites?

13. This is not the only radical model of discrimination, although that is the way it is sometimes described [Shulman 1989]. Marxist economists are more prone to subscribe to it than Marxist sociologists and historians, who tend to be more sophisticated about these matters. The economistic reduction of race to class (originated by Oliver C. Cox [1948] and propounded today in a more simplistic version by authors such as Robert Cherry [1988:128-130] and Michael Reich [1981]) is "by no means seen by contemporary Marxists as an adequate analysis of the complex historical determinants of racism or of the relationship between

racism and capitalist social relations," as Solomos [1986:87] comments. The model of employment discrimination ultimately developed here falls under the radical classification since it shares the presumption of class conflict; however, it refuses to reduce race relations to a mere manifestation of class relations, describing them instead as mutually determinant and constitutive.

14. The limits of divide-and-conquer models are again a theme at the start of section IV in chapter 4 in Williams' contribution to this volume. Also see Shulman 1989.

15. This point renders moot Reich's argument [1981:ch. 4] that the differing models of discrimination can be usefully distinguished in terms of their distributional consequences. Since discrimination may benefit both white workers (with job security) and capitalists (with productivity and stability), or harm one at the expense of the other (wages versus profits), its distributional consequences are historically contingent rather than logically preordained. See Shulman 1989.

16. I mention only wages, occupations, and employment due to my focus on labor markets. Housing discrimination is at least as important, especially in terms of the (mal)distribution of public resources. Any complete account must also include social segregation, racial ideologies (e.g., the myth of the black criminal), and discrimination in governmental policies. The last presents an interesting contrast since overt policies have largely been antidiscriminatory while covert policies (e.g., the financing of public education) have worked distinctly and more powerfully to the disadvantage of blacks. I am currently at work on a book that will attempt to show that these different aspects of discrimination constitute a self-reinforcing system of class/race domination.

17. This is in essence the argument made by Beller [1978]. She shows that firms may respond to legal pressures to reduce wage discrimination by reducing their demand for black labor (i.e., increasing their hiring preferences for whites). However, she fails to explain why the overall intensity of discrimination would not fall in the face of governmental efforts to eradicate it.

18. Baron notes in chapter 6 that "we often find more evidence of egalitarian *reforms* by organizations than we do of egalitarian *outcomes*." His argument has some intriguing implications for the contrast in governmental policies mentioned in footnote 16.

19. "Hegemonic control" refers to a system of labor-power extraction exercised through the shared interests and beliefs between management and labor. It may supplement or supplant the straightforward repression of labor by capital. It corresponds to the transition from simple control to technical and bureaucratic control as methods of eliciting desired work behavior from workers [Edwards 1979]. However, my terminology emphasizes that managerial control is social as well as technological or organizational; consequently, the mechanisms that control white male labor may well differ from those that control black and female labor. Hegemonic control indicates that the ability of capital to dominate labor depends in part upon labor's identification (both ideological and material) with capital. This identification can be in terms of race and gender and as such can offset class differentiation. Other ideologies, such as individualism, serve the same function.

CHAPTER 2

The author is grateful to James Heckman for his valuable remarks on an earlier draft of this paper.

1. The notion of "imperfections" as deviations from the neoclassical ideal of perfect competition is explored at the start of chapter 4 by Rhonda Williams.

2. That is, what matters is the responsiveness of the productivity of a firm's workers to the wage it pays where this responsiveness depends on the amount of monitoring of workers' effort, the amount of unemployment, etc.

3. That is, what matters is the dependence of the effort or productivity of a firm's workers on the wage it pays compared to the wages paid by other firms, the amount of unemployment, etc.

4. For example, Wachter [1986] takes trade-union power for granted and uses transaction costs based on a description of institutional "law and economics" to argue that the range of options in firm-union bargaining is very limited, resulting in considerable inertia in union wage patterns.

5. Keynes (1973: 106) wrote in his 1937 contribution to the Irving Fisher festschrift, "Indeed, the condition in which the elasticity for output as a whole is zero is, I now think, the most convenient criterion for defining full employment."

6. In the case of Stiglitz and Weiss's argument [1981: 395] for the plausibility of credit rationing based on adverse selection by potential borrowers, this is presented in passing as a detail to be taken for granted: "Obviously, we are not discussing a 'price-taking' equilibrium."

7. Thus Stiglitz [1987: 26] only considers piece-rate systems as an alternative to hourly wages in describing the costs of monitoring.

8. It should be noted that Bowles [1985: footnote 14] acknowledges this possibility.

9. Shapiro and Stiglitz [1984: 441]: "In general, it is not possible to ascertain whether the equilibrium entails too much or too little employment."

10. Bielby and Bielby [1988: 1050]. However, chapter 3 by Michael Robinson and Phanindra Wunnava presents evidence in table 3.3 that there are gender differences in the trade-offs between wage premia and supervision costs that are consistent with EWT.

11. The end of Section I of the following chapter takes the opposite view of the propensity to separate. In chapter 9, Solomon Polachek and Charng Kao call this intermittency and trace the idea that intermittency affects investments in human capital.

12. The discussion of the realism of the NeoKeynesian theories of discrimination in the rest of this section is drawn from Rhonda Williams' evaluation of these theories in the paper she presented at the Middlebury Conference in April 1989. It was moved to this chapter to consolidate this discussion in one place in this volume.

13. Bulow and Summers [1986] also suggest that "disadvantaged" workers may be crowded into the secondary sector because they are liquidity constrained – there are constraints on borrowing. That is, the disadvantaged cannot accept deferred payment schemes (or post bonds) in the primary sector. Bulow and Summers seem to be saying that black youth are too poor to accept low starting

wages in the primary sector (although the wage will rise over time?) but can accept permanently lower wages in the secondary sector: This makes little sense. Also, this argument does not explain why many white youth start in the secondary sector and leave, but black youth tend to stay (see Williams [1984]).

Bulow and Summers also suggest (401) the possibility that black youth, being statistically discriminated against, might accept a lower wage than white youth in primary-sector jobs to "prove themselves" and would be willing to trust the employer to increase these wages after the trial period or to have the employer post a bond. They then dismiss this possibility on the grounds that it is incompatible with their model, but one might dismiss it for more realistic reasons relating to incentive effects of invidious comparisons of human worth and incentive compatibility problems for the employer as both payer of the bond and judge of the release of the bond.

14. See the chapters by Stephen Woodbury and Elaine McCrate in this volume as well as Darity [1989] for clear limits to the appropriateness of taking "cultural prescriptions" as exogenous and as enlightening.

15. See the chapter by Rhonda Williams for a more detailed examination of how labor intensity affects wages.

CHAPTER 3

We would like to thank Steven Shulman, Richard Cornwall, Alan Dillingham, and other participants of the Middlebury Conference for their valuable comments on an earlier draft of this chapter. The usual caveat applies.

1. Goldin [1986] presents evidence from manufacturing around 1890 on the relationship between monitoring costs and occupational segregation.

2. See the preceding chapter by William Darity for arguments confronting efficiency wage explanations of the existence of involuntary unemployment and discrimination.

3. Here we assume that the probability of a false positive detection of shirking is zero.

4. Note that the preceding chapter of this volume cites evidence by Bielby and Bielby [1988] that questions this distinction by sex in the relation between work effort and wage premia.

5. Meitzen [1986] and Viscusi [1980] examine sex differences in quit rates.

6. Of course, in equilibrium the cost of worker effort to the firm is the same for both males and females if one assumes diminishing marginal effects of supervision and wage premiums on effort. It is only the mix of wage premia and supervision that will vary between males and females, not the final cost to the firm.

7. This is not dissimilar to the explanation for sexual segregation given by William Bielby in chapter 5.

8. The difference between the coefficients of large and small plant sizes is statistically significant at the 1 percent level.

9. In order to compute this, we assume that the male coefficients are the nondiscriminatory coefficients. Thus the difference between the male and female coefficients times the mean supervision cost for females gives the unexplained

differential due to supervision cost coefficient differentials: $(.0826 - .00373)$ x $.702 = .0554$. The total log differential between male and female wages in this sample is 0.376. Therefore, the unexplained differential due to supervision variable would be approximately $.147 (= .0554/.376)$.

10. Note that equation 9 indicates that for profit maximization, firms will set the ratio of the marginal benefits of wage premia (in terms of effort) equal to the marginal benefits of supervision to the costs of supervision. Hence in general, we would expect that increasing supervision costs would lead to higher wage premia. If there is a difference between males and females in either their responsiveness to wage premia or to supervision, this trade-off will occur at different rates. Suppose in the extreme case that females are totally unresponsive to wage premia; then one would expect that increasing supervision costs would not lead to higher wages for females. Thus the coefficient of the supervisory variable in the wage regressions for males should be greater than that for females. The decomposition is just to give an idea of how important this difference is for the overall male/female wage differential.

CHAPTER 4

1. Krueger and Summers [1987]. Japan, Korea, and Sweden rank among the countries whose industrial wage structures correlate closely with that of the United States. Although Japan once colonized Korea, Koreans are a small minority of the Japanese citizenry; to the best of my knowledge, "race" has not been deeply constitutive of cultural identity in Korea and Sweden.

2. These models of rent sharing are described further at the end of section II of chapter 2 by William Darity.

3. This chapter explores the material base for intra-working-class conflict within white supremacist, or, more generally, ethnically divided capitalist societies. I take as a given that actually existing Western civil society is patriarchal and that gender relations mediate race and class relations within these societies. See section IV for further discussion.

4. Here I am following Marx's method by beginning with an analysis of capital as a whole and successively adding ever more degrees of specificity en route to creating the "thought concrete."

5. Shaikh [1982b]: 159.

6. Friedman [1953]. My statement paraphrases the instrumentalist argument.

7. It is also worth noting that "false" antecedents can generate "true" consequences. As Caldwell notes [1982: 181-182], if we desire explanatory theories, predictive accuracy is insufficient to assure that result. His chapters 8 and 9 provide a very useful discussion of modern positivism and economic methodology.

8. As Resnick and Wolff [1987] rightly observe, the Marxian tradition abounds in epistemological standpoints. Rationalists and essentialists have left their marks; indeed, they have defined, for both leftist "sympathizers" and those openly hostile to and/or ignorant of the tradition, "the" Marxist perspective. Resnick and Wolff offer the following typology: Empiricists reside within and outside the Marxian tradition. Their signature is the belief in the autonomous

existence of a "factual" reality; for the empiricist, there is a singular reality that all theories confront. Observation is unmediated by meaning, and our senses directly appropriate the world. The best theories are those that correspond to the essential reality. For Marxist empiricists, Marxist theory is preferred because it better corresponds to the historical "truth." Rationalists also believe in an essential reality, but argue that we can only access its phenomenal form. For the rationalist, theory's goal is to express the essence that underlies form. Marxist rationalists believe that Marx captured the truth of social reality.

Resnick and Wolff struggle to define an overdeterminist perspective amidst philosophical hostility to Althusser's overdeterminist construction of "process without subject." For the record, this author does not equate the use of an overdeterminist epistemology with *either* structural determinism *or* the denial of embodied human subjects who shape, and are shaped by, their social formations.

9. Darity identifies the Stiglitzian roots of this literature, that is, the assumption of the existence of persistent "imperfections" in the economic world that condition maximizing behavior. As he so pointedly notes, the immutability of these "barriers" to entrepreneurial agency is never addressed.

10. It is interesting to note the similarities between the neoclassical "idea" that firms must elicit effort and the long standing Marxian distinction between "labor power" and "labor." For neoclassical theorists, this "idea" implies the existence of imperfect labor markets and, as Darity points out in chapter 2, this often means slipping an assumption of monopsony "under the door." For Marx, capitalist accumulation requires the successful imposition of surplus labor time upon the working class, that is, capitalists must *impose* surplus labor time upon the workers from whom they have purchased labor power. For Marxists, analysis of the social relations of production has been and continues to be crucial to our understanding of capital. However, we do not view the underdetermined and political nature of the wage-labor contract as an "imperfection" or deviation from some perfect capitalist world.

11. Shaikh [1981a] and Roberts [1988] provide good introductions to the labor theory of value; each piece also offers a response to Neo-Ricardian critiques of value theory.

12. This chapter obviously does not rigorously examine the ideological conditions that underlie capitalistic social relations. Marxists have, of course, frequently asked why workers consent to capital's domination and have come to varied conclusions. Some posit "false consciousness," others point to capital's cultural hegemony. Still others suggest that capitalist democracy flourishes because it can, for many people much of the time, satisfy the short-term material interests encouraged and rewarded therein (see Cohen and Rogers [1983]).

13. See Lang, Leonard, and Lilien [1987] for a discussion of imperfect competition, wage differentials, and unemployment.

14. As is evident from this terminological straddling, this discussion attempts to bridge two theoretical worlds, neoclassical and Marxist. The author hopes that this difficult process will enable neoclassically trained readers to explore Marxist theory. A more detailed exposition would distinguish between the technical composition of capital (TCC) and the organic composition of capital (OCC). For many readers, the TCC is a more familiar concept: TCC equals the capital/labor

ratio in physical units. The ratio of a firm's expenditures on the means of production (constant capital) to its total labor costs (purchases of labor power or variable capital) is the OCC: the ratio of the value of the means of production to the value of labor purchased. See Marx [1894], ch. 8, and Weeks [1981], 197-198.

15. Marx [1867], ch. 25, p. 620.

16. Ibid., 628.

17. See Braverman [1974] for a discussion of the U.S. reserve army in the late twentieth century. Cherry [1988, 1989] and Christensen [1988] discuss and document the increasing proportion of black youth who survive in the reserve army. Because it focuses on the United States, this chapter does not examine the particularities of the global reserve army.

18. See chapter 1 (Shulman), where Figure 1.1 shows that since the mid 1950s the difference between these two rates has increased and the ratio has remained roughly constant, *even ignoring the decline in the EPR for black men compared to white men.* (For an overview of changes in the EPRs, see David Swinton in Dewart [1989], 27-30).

19. In volume 1 of *Capital*, Marx examines in detail the reserve armies of his era (see ch. 25). *The Imperiled Economy* (Book II) (Cherry et. al. [1988]), part 2 also provides insight into the current composition of the reserve army.

20. See Rubery [1978]; Darity [1982b, 1989]; Darity and Williams [1985]; Williams [1987b].

21. Botwinick [1988], p. 123.

22. Ibid., 126.

23. Hill [1984, 1985, 1989].

24. See Darity [1982b,1989]; Rubery [1978]; Williams [1987b].

25. Hartmann [1981] discusses the role of the state in constructing husbands and fathers as family heads recognized by that same state, that is, husband patriarchy; Pateman [1988] explores the patriarchal foundations of civil society and contract theory.

26. See Shulman's discussion in chapter 1 of how these costs of changing the social relations of production by changing the amount of discrimination plausibly depend on the amount of unemployment, the size of the reserve army. In section IV, I discuss the costs of labor substitutes in the context of a racially self-defined working class.

27. See Semmler [1984], part 1 for a discussion of the monopoly-capital tradition. Leiman [1987] discusses race and class in the monopoly-capital tradition. Reich [1981] presents a bargaining-power model of the firm wherein price-taking "competitive" behavior is rendered consistent with black/white wage inequality. Baran and Sweezy [1966] argue for the abandonment of theory rooted in competition.

28. Clifton [1977]; Shaikh [1980, 1982a, 1982b]; Semmler [1984]; Weeks [1981].

29. Semmler's [1984] discussion of theories of competition is quite helpful. His empirical studies strongly suggest that monopoly power theories cannot explain consistently the distribution of profits and prices; that distribution can, however, be explained with Classical and Classical Marxian tools. Semmler proposes that market structure is not the source of corporate power; rather, modern corporate

power is rooted in firm size, vertical integration, and diversification.

30. Botwinick [1988]: chapter 5, develops this point at length.

31. Recall the distinction between these two ideas made in note 14.

32. See Botwinick [1988], 193-194 for a summary of this argument and see his chapter 5, part 2, for a more detailed discussion of profit cycles and profit rates.

33. This is an appropriate point at which to contrast this chapter with previous works (e.g., Darity and Williams [1985]; Williams [1987b]). Earlier works did not develop the analysis of regulating capitals or the subtleties of Marxian competition among capitals; rather, we developed the foundations of Classical and Marxian competition and applied the latter to worker competition. This chapter further develops the dynamics of capitalist competition; in so doing, we have a richer analysis of the competitive conditions between capitals that condition (and are conditioned by) competition among workers.

34. Botwinick presents a three-tiered analysis of competition and differential wage rates, beginning with a review of Marx's incomplete theory of wage differentials and concluding with analyses of wage differentials among regulating and nonregulating capitals, respectively ([1988]: chs. 4, 6, 7). I will restrict my attention to his first two tiers.

35. See Botwinick [1988], ch. 6, for a more detailed presentation of the analysis of regulating capitals and ch. 7 for the discussion of nonregulating capitals.

36. (1) $p^* = c + r^*(K/Q)$,
where p^* is the regulating price of production, c is regulating unit costs, r^* is the rate of profit for regulating capitals, and K/Q = regulating capital/output ratio. Then the profit margin, PM, can be written as follows:

(2) $PM = p^* - c = r^*(K/Q)$, and

(3) $r^* = (p - c)/(K/Q)$.

Thus from (2) and (3), if K/Q is constant, then $\partial PM/\partial c < 0$ and $\partial r^*/\partial c < 0$. We are here abstracting from both multiperiod capital and secondary feedback effects. The former implies that all capital is used in one period; the latter means that we are not considering the impact of a local wage increase on the cost of other inputs. From (3), it is clear that the equalization of profit rates across industries requires that profit margins be proportional to capital/output ratios. See five notes below and Botwinick [1988], 247.

37. Botwinick [1988], 232-233.

38. Ibid., 237.

39. Ibid., ch. 6 for simple algebraic derivations and examples of each limit.

40. Ibid., 245.

41. From five notes above, $PM = r^*(K/Q)$. But, $K/Q = (K/L)(L/Q)$, and therefore $PM = r^* (K/L)(L/Q)$, or $PM/(L/Q) = r^*(K/L)$. Thus Limit one = $PM/(L/Q)$. The intuition is this: each unit of output requires L/Q labor units and each unit of labor receives the hourly wage increase. The total wage increase (increase per worker multiplied by workers per unit output) cannot be so large that it eliminates the profit margin.

42. For two industries, A and B, also note that equal r^*'s implies

$$[PM/(L/Q)]_A / [PM/(L/Q)]_B = [K/L]_A / [K/L]_B$$

43. Equation 1 seven notes above can be used to derive a precise condition involving the unit costs of the two capitals and their capital/output ratios to ensure that the regulating capital maintains its position.

44. Botwinick [1988]: 250-260.

45. Ibid., 260.

46. Botwinick also discusses capital intensity of production and market structure as structural conditions that mediate the bargaining relationship.

47. Botwinick [1988], 281. I have not examined inter- and intraindustry wage differentials that arise because of the differential conditions of productivity within industries. Botwinick develops this analysis, but space limitations preclude my reviewing his argument in detail here. However, my concerns in the next section warrant at least a summary of his findings. As would be expected, Botwinick finds that within an industry, the less efficient capitals face far more stringent limits to wage increases. Their higher unit costs and higher unit labor requirements make them less fertile ground for workers seeking wage increases. Thus capital's intraindustry diversity is clearly significant to job competition among workers.

48. The neo-Marxian models also fail to address the particularities of capital vis-à-vis worker-supported discrimination. In other words, the specific conditions of capitalist competition – the availability of labor power, the intensity and specifics of the struggle for profits and market shares, etc. – will condition capitalists' willingness to challenge or accept worker-based discrimination. Although Leiman [1987] works within the monopoly-capital tradition, I am very sympathetic to his call for the need to analyze capital's racial strategies in an intertemporal and dynamic context.

49. The prevalent misuse of such "dummies" is not restricted to econometrics. Spelman [1981] describes "additive analyses" in literature that describe race and gender as separate oppressions, the effects of which can simply be added. Spelman links this to the "white solipsism" described by Adrienne Rich and to denial of the "particularity of experience," which, in statistical work, can only be captured by sorting workers into race-gender groups.

50. The idea that racial and ethnic inequality may be due to more than atomistic and asocial capitalistic market pressures has been a key focus of earlier works by Darity and Williams. This view stands in stark opposition to the perspective underlying chapter 9 by Solomon Polachek and Charng Kao. Polachek and Kao endeavor to tie all differentials in earnings and employment to differences in productivity or human capital. Darity's remarks [1989: 357] challenge human-capital theorists' efforts to distinguish premarket from in-market discrimination: "The putative line of demarcation between market and extra-market discrimination becomes meaningless." Clearly the wage hierarchy and the social hierarchy are closely linked.

51. In her discussion of occupational sex segregation, Reskin [1988] also presents a compelling case for the restoration of oppositional agency within the working class. More concretely, she argues that the gender wage gap is a political problem and must be understood as constitutive of male privilege, privilege many men are not willing to cede without a fight. Hence strategies like comparable worth

and occupational integration are being and will be resisted; also, because men set the rules, they have the authority to change them to preserve their advantages in the labor market. I like Reskin's agency-oriented discussion; I find it lacking in that she does not explicitly address racial divisions among men and women.

CHAPTER 5

1. However, studies that control for wages, job opportunities, and other work traits show that there are no net differences in the quit behavior of men and women (Viscusi [1980]; Blau and Kahn [1981]). Weiss' [1984] study of job turnover in a manufacturing firm showed that women were *less* likely to quit than otherwise identical, equally paid men in the same jobs.

2. In chapter 7 of this volume, David Fairris and Lori Kletzer present evidence that the barriers described here are also visible at a much more aggregated level in the distribution of men and women across working conditions.

3. In the following chapter, James Baron expands on the evidence of organizational inertia and on the importance of organizational form.

4. In the following chapter, Baron cites evidence showing that social cognition shapes how jobs are defined and compensated as well as how individuals are assigned to jobs.

5. One possible exception is the concept of "hegemonic control," noted in Steven Shulman's chapter in this volume. Neo-Marxist scholars have attempted to use this concept to explain how control can be exercised through beliefs shared by dominant and subordinate groups.

CHAPTER 6

This chapter was partially completed while the author was a fellow at the Center for Advanced Study in the Behavioral Sciences; support from the Alfred P. Sloan Foundation and from the center staff is gratefully acknowledged. The National Research Council's Panel on Pay Equity Research, the Stanford Graduate School of Business, and faculty fellowships from the Business School Trust and from Robert M. and Anne T. Bass helped support the research described in this chapter, for which the author is appreciative. I thank Pamela Pommerenke for research assistance and thank David Baron, William Bielby, James Heckman, Rod Kramer, Ed Lazear, Jeffrey Pfeffer, John Roberts, and the Middlebury Conference participants for very helpful comments on the ideas in this chapter.

1. I use the terms *discrimination* and *ascription* in this chapter to refer to job assignments or reward allocations influenced directly (intentionally or not) by employees' ascriptive characteristics – in other words, where group membership has an effect on opportunities and outcomes that is not simply due to straightforward differences in human capital and labor supply across social groups.

2. Because most of my own work has focused on these issues as they relate to gender inequality, I concentrate on this aspect of discrimination more than on

ethnicity, age, or other ascriptive characteristics.

3. For instance, Bielby and Baron [1986] analyzed job titles occurring in "mixed occupations" (i.e., detailed *Dictionary of Occupational Titles* categories having between 20 and 80 percent female incumbents in their sample of establishments). Even in this sample of work roles where both sexes were employed, men commanded roughly 59 percent of the one-person titles, while representing less than 48 percent of the employees.

4. For instance, "experimental psychologist" and "industrial psychologist" are enumerated as distinct master job titles. Within the former, the synonymous titles of "comparative" and "physiological" psychologist are listed, whereas the synonyms of "market-research analyst," "military personnel psychologist," and "personnel psychologist" are enumerated within "industrial psychologist."

5. While the conventional economic argument is that such misperceptions would be eroded by competitive forces, I suggest below some reasons for these biases to persist. Moreover, note that the idiosyncratic nature of specialized job titles may vitiate external comparisons and market pressures.

6. Social psychologists have also shown that individuals tend to make reward comparisons against those in the same job categories and sociodemographic groups. Therefore, by contributing to ascriptive segregation, specialized job titles also conveniently reduce the tendency for women and nonwhites to compare their reward outcomes to those of white males (see Lansberg [1989]).

7. As an example of historical conditions affecting the subsequent operation of private firms, William Bielby's chapter in this volume cites the enduring legacy of "protective legislation" restricting women's access to certain types of work.

8. Many state agencies have a mandate based on a specific piece of enabling state legislation. However, others have a mandate at the federal level or in the state constitution. We predicted that the latter agencies would be more insulated from scrutiny and sanctions with respect to job-integration outcomes than agencies that essentially serve purely at the behest of the legislature.

9. We distinguished agencies that provide objective performance measures in their annual reports and budgetary requests from those that do not. We predicted that agencies (such as the Coastal Commission) that cannot document their operating efficiency on purely technical or objective criteria may face more external scrutiny and pressure for egalitarian reform than agencies possessing a "bottom line" (such as the Franchise Tax Board, which collects state income taxes).

10. In our statistical analyses, we examined annual data for agencies between 1979 and 1985. Each agency's target level in a given year was specified to be an exponential function of the average extent of job-title proliferation and gender imbalance throughout the previous year. The rate of adjustment in a given year was specified to be a linear function of the organizational characteristics, with a one-year lag for variables that were not temporally invariant.

11. The effects of age were actually curvilinear: the oldest state agencies also exhibited somewhat faster desegregation. We attribute this finding to the fact that ours was a sample of survivor agencies and there is probably a selection process at work. The very survival of the oldest agencies is due in part to the success with which they have learned to adapt to changes in their environments. Their ability

to integrate the workplace by sex more rapidly no doubt illustrates this adaptive capacity. Moreover, consistent with other research on governmental organizations (Meyer and Brown [1977]), one by-product of longevity among California state agencies appears to be more meritocratic systems of personnel administration.

12. Specifically, we calculated how segregated each agency would appear to be if the gender composition in each of its jobs was identical to the gender composition in the relevant occupation within the entire state civil service. We then took the ratio between each agency's observed segregation index and this corresponding "expected" value of segregation (see Bridges [1982]). Values greater than one for this ratio denote agencies in which jobs tend to be more segregated than their corresponding occupations or labor markets are within the statewide civil-service system, whereas values less than one denote agencies in which there is a more balanced distribution in jobs than one observes across the relevant occupations statewide.

13. Specifically, the effects almost vanish once period (year) effects are included in statistical models.

14. Borjas [1980] used related reasoning in econometric analyses of wage determination in federal agencies. He found that greater social heterogeneity within an agency (measured by the standard deviations of tenure, education, and age) resulted in lower average salaries, which he attributed to the problems of mobilizing a diverse constituency.

15. Stinchcombe [1965: 149] argued that this is also true early in the life cycle of organizations, when the lack of an adequate experiential record upon which to base decisions encourages members to rely on more general social and cultural norms.

16. Note that the absence of clear performance standards makes for greater uncertainty about what a given position and individual is worth, not only among those who dispense rewards, but also among those occupying the position, thereby rendering collective action more difficult.

17. As Parsons [1954] noted long ago, social and cultural forces influence what is rational and efficient in the first place, and not merely which of the equally efficient forms a given organization adopts. Hayek [1988, especially ch. 1] makes a similar argument, emphasizing the role of cultural customs, traditions, and rules in shaping the means and ends of economic action.

CHAPTER 7

We have benefited from the useful comments of Elaine McCrate and participants in presentations at Vassar College, Williams College, and the Eleventh Annual Middlebury Conference on Economic Issues. We are grateful for support from a Williams College research grant and for the able research assistance of Anne MacEachern.

1. More specifically, it is argued that, given the need in many occupations for significant on-the-job training, people make occupational decisions early on in their work lives and thereby reap the rewards from this initial specific human capital acquisition over their remaining years in the labor force. Because women

generally plan to take time out of the labor force to raise children, thereby decreasing the amount of time they have to recoup specific human-capital investments, and because human capital is assumed to depreciate when not in use, women may rationally choose occupations requiring little on-the-job training, but also resulting in lower rates of wage growth with years of experience. For statements of the theory and empirical tests, see Mincer and Polachek [1974] and Polachek [1981] as well as chapter 9 of this volume. England [1982] presents contradictory empirical evidence.

2. A firm utilizing internal labor markets to allocate labor generally contains a few jobs with ports of entry open to the external labor market, but the majority of jobs are filled from inside the firm through well-defined job ladders and lines of progression based on a combination of merit and seniority. Wages are attached to jobs, not to people, and the "value" of a job is often arrived at through formal job-evaluation procedures.

3. For ease of exposition, we have assumed the compensating payments to be equal in the two segments.

4. For a discussion of these issues, see the preceding chapter by James Baron in this volume.

5. See Osterman [1975] for the details of actual categorization of occupations used in this chapter.

6. This literature suggests that it is possible to further reduce the male coefficient by using more detailed occupation variables (Treiman and Hartmann [1981]). We were unable to use more disaggregated measures of occupation due to small sample sizes.

7. A similar pattern emerges in the secondary labor market (table 7.4). In the subordinate primary labor market (table 7.3) however, an interesting pattern emerges: women appear to be segregated in such a way that they are no more prominent in the worse-paying occupations than in the better-paying ones. The results suggest that women are nonetheless relegated to the worst-paying jobs within broadly defined occupations.

8. Using the specification in column 1, there are structural differences between the two sectors ($F^* = 1.5373$, F_c (25,707) = 1.52). Note that the returns to education follow the results of the segmented labor markets literature: earnings rise steadily with educational attainment in the subordinate primary sector, while in the secondary sector, generally only graduate training earns a statistically significant return. The returns to tenure are also marginally greater in the subordinate primary sector. The results on labor market experience, however, are rather puzzling, as we find no statistically significant evidence of returns to experience in the subordinate primary sector, while in the secondary sector, earnings rise with experience.

9. We can reject the null hypothesis that the working-conditions coefficients are jointly zero: $F^* = 2.087$, F_c (11,556) = 1.79.

10. We can reject the null hypothesis that the working-conditions coefficients are jointly zero: $F^* = 2.969$, F_c (11,129) = 1.86.

11. We are hesitant, however, to attribute the existence of positive compensating payments in the secondary sector solely to competitive labor-market mechanisms. Our secondary labor-market sample contains a number of union members

and when the nonunion subsegment was analyzed separately, no positive and significant compensating payments were found. For a discussion of the role unions may play in altering the pattern of wages across working conditions, see Fairris [1989].

12. We estimated separate male/female wage equations for the specifications of columns 1 and 3 for each sample: the subordinate primary, the secondary, and both segments combined. Using the Blinder [1973]/Oaxaca [1973] technique, we decomposed the average wage gap into explained (due to differences in observables) and unexplained (due to differences in estimated coefficients and intercepts) portions. In each case, the unexplained portion of the average wage gap followed the direction of our reported change in the gender coefficient in moving from the column 1 specification to the column 3 specification. These results are available from the authors upon request.

13. The empirical results of the present chapter were reproduced using an alternative categorization procedure developed by Gordon [1986]. A major difference between Gordon's and Osterman's procedures for allocating jobs to labor-market segments is that Gordon distinguished between core and periphery industries and assigned semiskilled and unskilled workers in the periphery to secondary labor-market status independent of their detailed occupation. Gordon also created a separate segment as part of the independent primary sector for craft workers. The results associated with this alternative categorization procedure are very similar to those presented in this chapter, including results on the pattern of compensating payments across segments. Interestingly, however, the estimated male/female wage gap falls in the secondary labor market when working-conditions controls are added to the equation, which is directly counter to the results presented here. A number of attempts to further segment the subordinate primary sample produced no increased tendency toward the equalization of differences (see the segmentations discussed in the two endnotes following the next note as well as the last endnote below).

14. See the preceding chapters by James Baron and William Bielby in this volume.

15. Treiman [1979] argued that there is some evidence to suggest that job-evaluation schemes in the subordinate primary sector contain different weights for assessed job characteristics between office jobs, held disproportionately by women, and production jobs, held disproportionately by men. We estimated separate wage equations for the blue-collar and white-collar subsegments of the subordinate primary sector, but found no evidence of significant differences in the weights attached to either working-conditions or human-capital variables.

16. We estimated separate wage equations for men and women in the subordinate primary labor market, but could not reject the null hypothesis of no differences in working-conditions coefficients.

17. Note that this may be viewed as largely a statistical artifact owing to insufficient data. That is, with accurate measures of workers' specific human-capital endowments, as opposed to simply using tenure with the firm, for example, these wage differences would disappear. Put somewhat differently, tenure with the firm is an imperfect proxy for "position in the job ladder" if otherwise similar people experience different rates of progression through the rungs. The issue is then one

of employment discrimination as opposed to pure wage discrimination.

18. The literature on gender discrimination has more recently taken a critical stance on the usefulness of the segmented labor markets paradigm for understanding the dynamics of gender discrimination. It has been argued, for example, that the dead-end jobs associated with pink-collar occupations have characteristics resembling secondary labor-market jobs more than they do jobs in the subordinate primary sector. We analyzed a sample containing pink-collar occupations (defined here as sales, clerical, and service occupations in the subordinate primary sector with percent female exceeding 70 percent) and could reject the hypothesis of no structural difference with the secondary sector of the labor market. However, the pink-collar sample proved to be structurally different from the rest of the subordinate primary sector as well.

CHAPTER 8

The principal author of this chapter is Harriet Orcutt Duleep, with additional contributions made by Nadja Zalokar. The chapter also benefited from extensive discussions with James S. Cunningham and draws from *Incomes of Americans* studies prepared by economists at the U.S. Commission on Civil Rights. We gratefully acknowledge comments by Barbara Bergmann, Glen Cain, Richard Cornwall, David Neumark, Mark Regets, and Phanindra Wunnava. The opinions expressed in this chapter do not necessarily reflect the views of the U.S. Commission on Civil Rights.

1. See Duleep and Sider [1986], O'Neill, et al. [1986], Duleep [1988], and Zalokar [1990].

2. Of course, the choice of weights in this measure of discrimination is somewhat arbitrary; one can replace $\hat{\beta}^{maj}$ by $\hat{\beta}^{min}$ in (1), and X_j^{min} by X_j^{maj} in (2). For ease of exposition, we refer, as is commonly done, to the Oaxaca decomposition as yielding an estimate of the amount of discrimination experienced by the average minority person. Note, however, that if any of the X_j's enter the wage equation in nonlinear form (e.g., quadratic or spline), the Oaxaca decomposition, which provides an estimate of the average amount of discrimination experienced by the minority group, is clearly not equivalent to an estimate of the amount of discrimination experienced by the average member of the minority group. As an example, consider the earnings equation $\ln y_i = \beta X_i^2 + u_i$. An estimate of discrimination experienced by the average minority person would be what he earns minus what he would earn in the absence of discrimination, or $(\hat{\beta}^{min} - \hat{\beta}^{maj})\overline{X}^2$. The Oaxaca decomposition yields as the estimate of the amount of discrimination experienced on average by the minority group, $(\hat{\beta}^{min} - \hat{\beta}^{maj})\overline{X^2}$. Of course, when all the X_j's are linear, the two are exactly the same.

3. The questions we raise are, of course, supplemented by the question of the extent to which adjusted earnings differentials can be assessed accurately. For example, as chapter 7 by David Fairris and Lori Kletzer illustrates, conventionally computed adjusted earnings differentials may understate or overstate wage differentials by gender, depending on the sector of the labor market, if working

conditions are not allowed for.

4. For instance, in Becker's model of employee discrimination by employees who are perfect substitutes for members of the minority group, no market discrimination results. Instead, workers become segregated into majority and minority firms. Minority workers would not have access to jobs in majority firms, and vice versa. Similarly, in the case of employer discrimination where there is a sufficient number of nondiscriminating firms to absorb all minority workers at nondiscriminatory pay rates, some firms (those with discriminatory employers) will refuse to hire minority workers. This illustrates an important outcome of Becker's analysis: namely, that market mobility can equalize wages even when some employers discriminate.

5. Note that if the lower response rate to a minority worker's job search results in unemployment, then we would expect this unemployment experience to result in lower earnings. This provides a good argument for using earnings instead of wages for measuring discrimination, and to the extent that longer job search affects labor-force participation, this would argue for including labor-force dropouts in discrimination analyses.

6. One exception is Polachek [1981], who focused on occupational outcomes rather than earnings outcomes for women. Polachek estimated a model in which occupations and characteristics are determined simultaneously and found that in this case, there is no feedback effect whereby women's occupational opportunities affect their human-capital investments.

7. Elaine McCrate (chapter 11) argues that greater teenage childbearing may not be due to exogenous cultural/human-capital differences, but instead lower-quality schooling and/or expected market discrimination may reduce the incentive to avoid a teenage birth. In other words, according to McCrate, teenage mothers correctly anticipate *smaller* economic incentives (due to premarket and anticipated market discrimination) for postponing childbearing.

8. The effect of intermittent labor-force participation on human-capital investment has been thoroughly explored by Solomon Polachek and Charng Kao (chapter 9). Their analysis indicates that adjusting for the flow of human-capital investments in light of intermittent labor-force participation would narrow the unexplained wage gap between men and women. Of course, as pointed out by Barbara Bergmann, intermittent labor-force participation may itself be affected by sex discrimination: "There is kind of a vicious-circle phenomenon here. The kinds of jobs to which women are relegated are those which offer little career development and, therefore, little incentive to avoid dropping out [of the labor force] for considerable periods. The propensity of these bored women in unchallenging jobs to drop out of the labor force in order to devote themselves to housewifery for long periods is then used as a reason for excluding them from jobs where continuity pays off to employer and employee" (Bergmann [1973: 154]).

9. Note that the time frame in which decisions and responses to a discriminatory situation are made may span generations. For instance, the discrimination encountered by Asian immigrants of the early twentieth century likely provided the impetus for their high self-employment rates. Higher education may have been seen as an alternative, less taxing route for avoiding discrimination faced by Asians in labor markets utilizing unskilled labor. This may explain the large intergenera-

tional growth in education among Asians (and also Jews) and their concomitant decline in self-employment.

10. The survey analysis of Waldinger [1989] suggested that group cohesiveness lowers the cost of pursuing self-employment not only through financial cooperation, but perhaps more importantly from the sharing of information. Bates [1989a] supported and updated Light using data on business start-ups from 1976 to 1982 by finding that nearly three times as much start-up capital came from "friends" for Asian Americans as for nonminorities. However, by far the largest source of start-up capital was commercial bank loans, and Bates found strong evidence of discrimination in this credit market pushing Asian Americans into small-scale retailing, consistent with the hypothesis here.

11. On the other hand, note that chapter 10 by Timothy Bates presents strong evidence that in the period 1976-82, economic incentives led black entrepreneurs (as well as white entrepreneurs) to invest primarily in areas where the clientele was *not* predominantly black.

12. Becker, [1971: 133-134].

13. In 1940, 4.7 percent of black women and 19.1 percent of white women in the South were professionals. Among professional southern women, 87 percent of blacks and 51 percent of whites were teachers. (Among nonsouthern professional women, roughly half of both whites and blacks were teachers.) If southern white women had had the same education, age, and urban/rural distribution as southern black women, however, 6 percent of southern white women would have been professionals. On the other hand, 4.1 percent of southern black women and 9.7 percent of southern white women were teachers; and 2.6 percent of southern white women would have been teachers if they had had the characteristics of southern black women.

14. Glen Cain in his written comments on this chapter (February 1990) pointed out that both supply responses and earnings differentials provide important information: "On the one hand, it is useful to know about sources of discrimination for legal purposes, even if the victims respond in ways that permit them to end up with equal incomes. On the other hand, it is useful to know whether the market as a whole is sufficiently open and flexible to permit equality to be attained. Supply elasticities reflect the quality of alternatives, and the alternatives are part of what the market offers. ... For example: minority X faces worse discrimination than minority Y in applying for jobs in industry A, but minority X has better alternatives than minority Y and ends up with higher incomes than Y. Stronger legal sanctions may be appropriately directed at industry A because of their discrimination against X. Nevertheless, the market [as a whole] is less discriminatory against X than Y in terms of the earnings outcomes."

15. Butler [1982] has also demonstrated labor-supply elasticity's effect on measures of market discrimination. He considered a case where the majority and the minority's labor-supply elasticities differ.

16. Closely related to search costs are group-specific limitations to access to information channels, internal labor markets, and unions, which Steven Shulman argues in chapter 1 have historically been important in maintaining racial inequality. Similarly, William Bielby (chapter 5) and James Baron (chapter 6) add substantial detail to the basis for the term "discrimination" by examining empiri-

cally social cognition, organizational inertia, sex-specific norms of entitlement, and competing interests.

17. Minority members who face greater discrimination in one market may also face greater discrimination in other markets and hence have poorer alternatives elsewhere as well.

18. Note, however, that this problem could be overcome with traditional approaches to measuring discrimination as long as measures of all productive characteristics, including ability, were available.

19. Note that if we are only interested in measuring the average extent of discrimination experienced by a minority group, then differential responses to discrimination in particular labor markets according to unmeasured productive attributes of individual minority members do not pose a problem; even in the absence of a fully comprehensive model, the overall adjusted earnings differential will give us an approximately correct answer as long as the unmeasured factors are equal across the minority/majority groups as a whole.

20. The analogy is very loose because market discrimination only measures a difference in prices, not the corresponding area under a Hicksian compensated demand curve, and because figure 8.6 shows an ordinary demand curve, not a compensated demand curve.

21. The inequality between market discrimination and potential discrimination shown in figure 8.6 is, in this realm of analogies, similar to the usual relation that compensating variation (CV) is less than or equal to equivalent variation (EV) and that these two concepts bound the usual Marshallian measure of economic surplus. This suggests developing an analogue to Willig's procedure for estimating bounds when using Marshallian surplus to approximate CV or EV. However, since we are dealing with an analogue to equivalent surplus rather than equivalent variation, it would be necessary to invent a Randall-Stoll procedure (see Cornwall [1984: 634]) to adapt to quantities being held fixed. However, the omission of consideration of and measurement of the utility costs stemming from "psychic" damages caused by discrimination makes such a theoretical venture not very promising.

22. Examples of an experimental approach to measuring labor-market discrimination include Jowell and Prescott-Clarke [1970], McIntosh and Smith [1974], Henry and Ginzberg [1985], Riach and Rich [1987], and Cross et al. [1990].

CHAPTER 9

Thanks are due to W. Stanley Siebert for correcting an error in an earlier version, and to Phanindra Wunnava and Richard Cornwall for their editorial assistance.

1. See Chiswick [1986]. His explanation is that recent immigrants have low levels of education, training, and English fluency.

2. One should note that work expectations are important for other demographic groups as well, such as singles and marrieds, blacks and whites, and Hispanics and Anglos.

3. See chapter 8 by Harriet Duleep and Nadja Zalokar for a very critical appraisal of measuring discrimination based on the conventional residual analysis.

4. For another view of this specialization, see chapter 5 by William Bielby.

5. See Polachek [1975b] for a discussion of this. Butler [1982] also provides a similar discussion.

6. Human capital should be taken more broadly than usual. In this chapter it denotes any worker outlay, including forgone wages, resulting in future earnings augmentation, regardless of effects on actual on-the-job productivity. The term "human-capital investment" is used for lack of a better term.

7. Uncertainty as in the Levhari and Weiss [1974] model also could be considered but would not change the implications. Neither would making labor-force participation endogenous, as considered by Heckman [1976] and Killingsworth and Heckman [1986].

8. It would be equally possible to illustrate this using a life-cycle model having a "family" orientation, as in Polachek [1975b], or even in the context of a Nash-bargaining-type family model of the type presented by Brown and Mancer [1980] or McElroy and Horney [1981].

9. Specific training models that in equilibrium imply that the workers' shares of training costs equal their benefits should yield similar results. See Kuratani [1973] or Hashimoto [1981] for a similar version.

10. See Becker and Stigler [1974], Lazear [1979], and Lazear and Moore [1984].

11. Many variations of equation (12) appear in the human-capital literature. Examples include Ben-Porath [1967], Heckman [1975], Haley [1976], Johnson [1978], Weiss and Gronau [1981], Hanushek and Quigley [1985].

12. The Hamiltonian is here defined on the assumption that no corner solutions are binding.

13. Exceptions are Polachek [1975a]; Goldin and Polachek [1987]; and Kao [1989]. In addition Sandell and Shapiro [1980] illustrate the empirical importance of intermittency expectations on initial age-earnings profile slopes.

14. If measured correctly, X should incorporate what Becker [1985] calls "effort."

15. This is most succinctly described in Ben-Porath [1967].

16. The classic example is Mincer [1974a]. Capacity earnings are observed earnings augmented by period t's gross investment. Thus $\ln E(t) = \ln y(t) - \ln [1-K'(t)]$. As indicated, these computations are performed for each schooling level.

17. See Polachek [1975a] for an elaboration of this derivation.

18. See Willis and Rosen's [1979] adaptation of Heckman [1979].

19. Comparable results for the U.S. 1960 census are given in Polachek [1975a]. However, note that these percentages are only approximate. To be technically correct, one would need to evaluate at $(e^b - 1)$.

CHAPTER 10

Research reported in this chapter was carried out as an American Statistical Association/National Science Foundation//Census Research Fellow and as a visiting scholar at the Joint Center for Political Studies. It was supported by the National Science Foundation under grants SES84-01460 and SES87-13643, "On-Site Research to Improve the Government-generated Social Science Data Base." The research was conducted at the U.S. Bureau of the Census while I was a participant in the American Statistical Association/Census Bureau Research Program, which is supported by the Census Bureau and NSF. The extensive research assistance of Richard Greene is gratefully acknowledged. Any findings or conclusions expressed herein are mine and do not necessarily reflect the views of the Census Bureau or NSF.

1. For an elaboration of this discussion of ghetto defining mechanisms, see chapter 10 in Bates and Fusfeld [1984].

2. Chapter 12 by Stephen Woodbury explores the situation for immigrants and finds a "recent-arrival" effect.

3. The notion that cultural differences combined with differences in power lead to cultural racism is explored by Jones [1986].

4. See Browne [1971].

5. Bates and Fusfeld [1984: 138-140].

6. See Bates and Bradford [1979], chapters 1, 2, and 5 for more detailed discussions of ghetto financial flows.

7. See Bates and Bradford [1979: 66-71].

8. See Bates [1981].

9. See Bates [1975].

10. The survey is described in detail in Bates [1990].

11. Note that the total sample contains only firms started between 1976 and 1982 and still operating in 1982.

12. These sales figures for FIRE and personal services combine firms serving minority markets with those serving nonminority markets.

13. This argument and the results in table 10.3 are clearly consistent with Stiglitz and Weiss' [1981] rationale for credit rationing and supply-side determination of who receives loans. The perspective offered by William Darity in chapter 2 on Stiglitz and Weiss's NeoKeynesian approach is relevant here.

14. For a more detailed discussion of this, see Bates [1989b].

15. However, this conclusion must be tempered by the fact that the pooled regression only contained a dummy variable for race. The possibility of purely racial inequality in the treatment by banks of loans to new businesses cannot be ruled out. See discussion of the education variables in the discriminant analysis in section IV.

16. A similar conclusion for the market in home mortgages was found by Bradbury, Case, and Dunham [1989].

17. A study by Faith Ando [1988] concluded that after risk is controlled for, black business owners of established firms are substantially less likely than nonminorities to have their loan applications accepted by commercial banks.

18. Alternative statistical techniques such as logit analysis could be used in these exercises to establish the statistical significance of the individual explanatory

variables. However, the particular use of logit in tables 10.4 and 10.5 would be inappropriate because multicollinearity problems would compromise the interpretation of individual variable coefficients. Age, education, and management variables are often highly correlated. Thus logit's power to establish variable coefficient significance is sacrificed, but the choice of the discriminant technique has produced clear-cut results without resorting to violating the underlying assumptions that discriminant analysis is built upon.

19. Minority area again means that over 40 percent of the residents are minorities.

20. If the shut-down point for owner-operated businesses is where net profits are equal to alternative wage opportunities, we would expect that those entrepreneurs with the least human capital would be the least likely to shut down, especially in ghettos where other opportunities are severely limited.

21. The finding that having at least some college education is more important for black entrepreneurs in nonminority areas compared to white entrepreneurs in the same areas suggests that lack of college education may sometimes serve as a proxy for racial discrimination. Thus Dovidio and Gaertner [1986: 78] found substantial psychological evidence to support "the hypothesis that when a racially biased response can be rationalised or attributed to factors other than race even well-intentioned people will discriminate."

22. See Bates [1988].

CHAPTER 11

This chapter is part of a larger project on teenage mothers that has been supported by a University of Vermont faculty summer research fellowship, a postdoctoral fellowship at the Center for Afro-American Studies of the University of California at Los Angeles, a research grant from the Institute of American Cultures at UCLA, and the Jesse Smith Noyes Fellowship at the Mary Ingraham Bunting Institute of Radcliffe College. I wish to thank all these institutions for their support. I am also grateful to Samuel Bowles, Nancy Folbre, Melva Minnis, Manuel Pastor, and Steven Shulman for helpful discussions. Thanks also are due to Mel Widawski for programming assistance, and to Laura Branden for providing information about the data base. None of these individuals or institutions is responsible for any errors or opinions expressed here.

1. Woodbury in chapter 12, while examining labor-market discrimination against black immigrants, also challenges the cultural human-capital explanations of earnings differences.

2. Steven Shulman in chapter 1 provides a demand-side rationale for the existence of such discrimination and Rhonda Williams in chapter 4 provides a model of racial inequality stemming from the interaction of labor and capital markets.

3. Harriet Duleep and Nadja Zalokar in chapter 8 show how the economic measurement of discrimination is affected by the fact that groups that are subject to discrimination may respond to such discrimination by altering their characteristics/behavior in the labor market, for example, adjusting their decisions about how much education to pursue as a response to facing discrimination.

4. Solomon Polachek and Charng Kao in chapter 9 explore the effects of expectations about future intermittent labor-force participation on investments in human capital.

5. David Fairris and Lori Kletzer in chapter 7 find rather striking rather differences by gender in how these two sectors compensate for working conditions. Using 1977 Quality of Employment Survey data, they find that estimates of the male/female wage gap that do not control for differences in working conditions may underestimate the extent of wage discrimination in the secondary sector (i.e., this may be because women tend to have worse working conditions than men for those conditions with positive compensating payments).

6. William Bielby in chapter 5 offers a list of non-human-capital factors, along with supporting evidence, that contribute to sexual discrimination: social psychological notions of entitlement norms that guide the relation between a worker's effort and wage, organizational history, and organizational inertia, as well as segregation by job titles. James Baron in chapter 6 extends Bielby's overview by offering a comprehensive survey of the institutional factors that segment the labor market, especially internal labor markets, by gender.

7. Thus this chapter and the chapters by Fairris and Kletzer, Bielby, and Baron serve to reinforce the conjecture that labor markets are segmented.

CHAPTER 12

An earlier version of this chapter was presented at the Eleventh Annual Middlebury Conference on Economic Issues in April 1989. I am grateful for discussions with David Bloom, Richard Cornwall, John V. Craven, William A. Darity, Cotton Mather Lindsay, Susan Pozo, David Shapiro, Hal Sider, James Stewart, and Phanindra Wunnava. Douglas R. Bettinger and Eric Chua provided excellent research assistance.

1. Borjas [1985] has pointed out that such a dynamic interpretation of cross-sectional data may give a biased picture of earnings growth. Although, in a practical sense, the existence and direction of bias can be appraised only by examining a single cohort over time, useful information can still be gained from examining a single cross-section.

2. Elaine McCrate (in chapter 11 of this volume) treats the application of the cultural/human-capital explanation to a different issue, differences between blacks and whites in teenage childbearing.

3. In fact, the existing research does not distinguish among immigrants of differing language proficiencies, so this hypothesis is more speculative. Whether the earnings of immigrants whose second language is English would ever equal the earnings of native-born workers is an open question.

4. Another possibility, raised by Darity [1989], is that socioeconomic status before immigration is an important determinant of earnings after immigration. Lack of pre-immigration data on individuals makes it difficult to explore this possibility, although data on country of origin and pre-immigration education might be used to shed light on the question. This is a topic for future research.

5. The foreign-born black sample is identical to that used in table 12.1. The

native-born black sample is made up of black men born in the fifty states or the District of Columbia who were aged 25 to 64 in 1979, worked at least one week during 1979, and reported earnings.

6. Both in the text and tables, workers who are *not* in the category "married, spouse present" are referred to simply as not married.

7. Nevertheless, it is worth noting that Bloom and Gunderson [1989] have obtained similar findings about the earnings growth of Canadian immigrants from a cross-section and from quasi-longitudinal data, suggesting that the dynamic interpretation may give a fairly accurate picture in some cases.

8. See McManus [1985], Tainer [1988], and Kossoudji [1989] on the importance of English-language proficiency to the labor-market performance of Hispanic immigrants. For black immigrants, the influence of English-language proficiency on earnings could also be treated as a country-of-origin effect, since most of the immigrants with English as their only language come from Jamaica, Trinidad, Barbados, and other countries where English is the main language.

9. The earnings premium is 15 percent because $\exp(0.14) - 1$ equals approximately 0.15.

10. The same results could be obtained by fully interacting English-language proficiency with the explanatory variables.

11. The results in table 12.3 differ from Borjas's findings [1985: table 2], which suggest few differences in earnings among cohorts of foreign-born blacks. The disparity between table 12.3 and Borjas's results may derive from Borjas's use of a subsample of 2,287 foreign-born black men from the 1980 census. The results in table 12.3 are based on a larger sample of 9,452. The results in table 12.3 are in accord with findings reported by Chiswick [1980], who analyzed a sample of 565 foreign-born black men from the 1970 census.

12. Note that the negative differential of the pre-1960 immigrants exceeds that of the 1960-64 immigrants. As discussed at the end of section IIIC, this could be a cohort effect explainable in part by reduced discrimination faced by black immigrants who arrived after 1959.

13. Note also that since equation (2) is to be estimated over a sample of immigrants, one of the year-of-immigration dummy variables must be omitted and treated as a reference category. In the estimates reported below (and in tables 12.4A and 12.4B), M_6 has been omitted.

14. A difficulty in interpreting immigrants' rates of return to schooling is that we do not know whether the schooling was received in the home country or the United States. So far, my attempts, using the available data, to distinguish schooling received in the home country from schooling received in the United States have been unsatisfactory.

15. Note that black English-second-language immigrants receive roughly the same return to education as other immigrants whose English is less good – that is, they are at no disadvantage, either culturally or through discrimination, with respect to returns to education. This tends to reinforce the interpretation of the relatively low return to education experienced by black English-only immigrants as discriminatory: if black English-second-language immigrants are at no cultural disadvantage, then we would not expect black English-only immigrants to be culturally disadvantaged. The low return to education for black English-only

immigrants would thus seem to be discriminatory.

16. For each profile, the average slope is computed by a regression in which the dependent variable is the unexplained differential in each time period (six observations for each profile). This variable is regressed on a constant and on the midpoint of the period to which each differential applies (for example, 1962 for the 1960-64 period). The coefficient of the midpoint is the average slope of each profile – that is, the average number of percentage points by which the unexplained differential falls annually.

17. On the importance of preimmigration socioeconomic status, see Darity [1989]. For a treatment of age at time of immigration, see Kossoudji [1989].

CHAPTER 13

This research was supported by NSF grant 87-11845.

References

Abbott, Michael G. and Charles M. Beach. 1988. "Immigrant Earnings Differentials and Cohort Effects in Canada." *Queen's Papers in Industrial Relations* Queen's University Industrial Relations Centre, Kingston, Ontario (December).

Aigner, Dennis J. and Glen C. Cain. 1977. "Statistical Theories of Discrimination in Labor Markets." *Industrial and Labor Relations Review* 30, 2 (January): 175-187.

Akerlof, George A. 1980. "A Theory of Social Custom, of Which Unemployment May Be One Consequence." *Quarterly Journal of Economics* 94, 4 (June): 749-775.

———. 1982. "Labor Contracts as Partial Gift Exchange." *Quarterly Journal of Economics* 97, 4 (November): 543-569.

———. 1984. "Gift Exchange and Efficiency Wages: Four Views." *American Economic Review* 74, 2 (May): 79-83.

Akerlof, George A. and Janet L. Yellen. 1988. "Fairness and Unemployment." *American Economic Review* 78, 2 (May): 44-49.

Ando, Faith. 1988. *An Analysis of Access to Bank Credit.* Los Angeles: UCLA Center for Afro-American Studies.

Ardener, Shirley. 1964. "The Comparative Study of Rotating Credit Associations." *Journal of the Royal Anthropological Institute* 94, 2.

Ashenfelter, Orley. 1976. "Comment." *Industrial and Labor Relations Review* 29 (July): 576-581.

Ashenfelter, Orley and James Heckman. 1976. "Measuring the Effect of an Antidiscrimination Program." in O. Ashenfelter and J. Blum (eds.) *Evaluating the Labor-Market Effects of Social Programs.* Princeton, N.J.: Industrial Relations Section.

Ashmore, Richard D. and Frances K. Del Boca. 1981. "Conceptual Approaches to Stereotypes and Stereotyping." pp. 1-35 in Hamilton [1981].

Austin, William. 1977. "Equity Theory and Social Comparison Processes." pp. 279-305 in J. Suls and R. Miller (eds.) *Social Comparison Theory: Theoretical and Empirical Perspectives*. Washington, D.C.: Hemisphere Publishing.

Averitt, Robert. 1968. *The Dual Economy*. New York: Horton.

Baker, George P., Michael C. Jensen, and Kevin J. Murphy. 1988. "Compensation and Incentives: Practice Versus Theory." *Journal of Finance* 43, 3 (July): 593-616.

Baran, Paul and Paul Sweezy. 1966. *Monopoly Capital*. New York: Monthly Review Press.

Baron, James N. 1988. "The Employment Relation as a Social Relation." *Journal of the Japanese and International Economies* 2 (December): 492-525.

Baron, James N. and William T. Bielby. 1984. "The Organization of Work in a Segmented Economy." *American Sociological Review* 49, 4 (August): 454-473.

————. 1985. "Organizational Barriers to Gender Equality: Sex Segregation of Jobs and Opportunities." pp. 233-251 in A. S. Rossi (ed.) *Gender and the Life Course*. New York: Aldine.

————. 1986. "The Proliferation of Job Titles in Organizations." *Administrative Science Quarterly* 31 (December): 561-586.

Baron, James N., Frank Dobbin, and P. Devereaux Jennings. 1986. "War and Peace: the Evolution of Modern Personnel Administration in U. S. Industry." *American Journal of Sociology* 92, 2 (September): 350-383.

Baron, James N., Brian S. Mittman, and Andrew E. Newman. 1991. "Targets of Opportunity: Organizational and Environmental Determinants of Gender Integration within the California Civil Service, 1979-1985." *American Journal of Sociology* 96, 3 (May): 1362-1401.

Baron, James N. and Andrew E. Newman. 1989. "Pay the Man: Effects of Demographic Composition on Prescribed Wage Rates in the California Civil Service." pp. 107-130 in Michael, Hartmann, and O'Farrell [1989].

————. 1990. "For What It's Worth: Differences Across Organizations, Occupations, and the Value of Work Done by Women and Nonwhites." *American Sociological Review* 55, 2 (April): 155-175.

Bates, Timothy. 1975. "Government as Financial Intermediary for Minority Entrepreneurs: An Evaluation." *Journal of Business* 48, 4 (October): 542-553.

————. 1981. "Black Entrepreneurship and Government Programs." *Journal of Contemporary Studies* (Fall): 59-69.

————. 1988. "Do Black-owned Businesses Employ Minority Workers? New Evidence." *Review of Black Political Economy* 16 (Spring): 52-56.

————. 1989a. "Asian-Owned Businesses." unpublished paper (August).

————. 1989b. "Business Viability in the Urban Ghetto Milieu." *Journal of Regional Science* (November): 625-643.

—————. 1990. "The Characteristics of Business Owners Data Base." *Journal of Human Resources* (Fall).

Bates, Timothy and William Bradford. 1979. *Financing Black Economic Development.* New York: Academic Press.

Bates, Timothy and Daniel Fusfeld. 1984. *Political Economy of the Urban Ghetto.* Carbondale: Southern Illinois University Press, 1984.

Becker, F. M. 1934. *Administration of the Personnel Program in the State of California.* Sacramento: State of California Archives (Administration: Personnel Board, Historical).

Becker, Gary S. 1957; 2d ed. 1971. *The Economics of Discrimination.* Chicago: University of Chicago Press.

—————. 1985. "Human Capital, Effort, and the Sexual Division of Labor." *Journal of Labor Economics* 3, 1, pt. 2 (January): 33-58.

Becker, G. and G. Stigler. 1974. "Law Enforcement, Malfeasance, and Compensation of Enforcers." *Journal of Legal Studies* 3, 1 (January): 1-18.

Beller, Andrea H. 1978. "The Economics of Enforcement of an Antidiscrimination Law: Title VII of the Civil Rights Act of 1964." *Journal of Law and Economics* 21, 2 (October): 359-380.

—————. 1984. "Trends in Occupational Segregation by Sex and Race, 1960-1981." pp. 11-26 in Reskin [1984].

Belsley, D.A., E. Kuh, and R.E. Welsch. 1980. *Regression Diagnostics.* New York: John Wiley and Sons.

Ben-Porath, Y. 1967. "The Production of Human Capital Over the Life Cycle." *Journal of Political Economy.* 75, 4 (August): 352-365.

Berger, Joseph, Susan J. Rosenholtz, and Morris Zelditch. 1980. "Status Organizing Processes." *Annual Review of Sociology* 6: 479-508.

Berger, Joseph, Morris Zelditch, Jr., Bo Anderson, and Bernard P. Cohen. 1972. "Structural Aspects of Distributive Justice: A Status Value Formulation." pp. 119-146 in J. Berger, M. Zelditch, and B. Anderson (eds.) *Sociological Theories in Progress,* vol. 2. Boston: Houghton Mifflin.

Bergmann, Barbara. 1973. "Comment on 'Sex Discrimination in Wages' by Ronald Oaxaca." pp. 152-154 in Orley Ashenfelter and Albert Rees (eds.) *Discrimination in Labor Markets.* Princeton, N.J.: Princeton University Press.

—————. 1986. *The Economic Emergence of Women.* New York: Basic Books.

—————. 1989. "Does the Market for Women's Labor Need Fixing?" *Journal of Economic Perspectives* 3, 1 (Winter): 43-60.

Bielby, William T. and James N. Baron. 1984. "A Woman's Place Is with Other Women: Sex Segregation within Organizations." pp. 27-55 in Reskin [1984].

—————. 1986. "Men and Women at Work: Sex Segregation and Statistical Discrimination." *American Journal of Sociology* 91, 4 (January): 759-799.

—————. 1987. "Undoing Discrimination: Comparable Worth and Job

Integration." in Christine Bose and Glenna Spitze (eds.) *Ingredients for Women's Employment Policy*. Albany: State University of New York Press.

Bielby, William T. and Denise D. Bielby. 1988. "She Works Hard for the Money: Household Responsibilities and the Allocation of Work Effort." *American Journal of Sociology* 93, 5 (March): 1031-1059.

——————. 1989. *The Hollywood Writers Report, 1989 Update*. West Hollywood, Calif.: Writers' Guild of America, West.

——————. 1991. "I will Follow Him: Family Ties, Gender-Role Beliefs, and Reluctance to Relocate for a Better Job." Forthcoming, *American Journal of Sociology* 94.

Binger, B. R. and E. Hoffman. 1988. *Microeconomics with Calculus*. Glenview, Ill.: Scott, Foresman.

Blau, Francine D. 1977. *Equal Pay in the Office*. Lexington, Mass.: Lexington Books.

Blau, Francine and Lawrence M. Kahn. 1981. "Race and Sex Differences in Quits by Young Workers." *Industrial and Labor Relations Review* 34, 4 (July): 563-577.

Blau, Peter and Otis Dudley Duncan. 1967. *The American Occupational Structure*. New York: Wiley.

Blauner, Robert. 1972. *Racial Oppression in America*. New York: Harper and Row.

Blinder, Alan S. 1973. "Wage Discrimination: Reduced Form and Structural Estimates." *Journal of Human Resources* 8, 4 (Fall): 436-455.

Bloom, David E. and Morley Gunderson. 1989. *An Analysis of the Earnings of Canadian Immigrants*. Working Paper no. 3035. Cambridge, Mass.: National Bureau of Economic Research (July).

Bonacich, Edna. 1976. "Advanced Capitalism and Black/White Race Relations in the United States: A Split Labor Market Interpretation." *American Sociological Review* 41, 1 (February): 34-51.

——————. 1979. "The Past, Present, and Future of Split Labor Market Theory." pp. 17-64 in Cora Marrett and Cheryl Leggon (eds.) *Race and Ethnic Relations* vol. 1.

Borjas, George J. 1980. "Wage Determination in the Federal Government: The Role of Constituents and Bureaucrats." *Journal of Political Economy* 88, 6 (December): 1110-1147.

——————. 1982. "The Earnings of Male Hispanic Immigrants in the United States." *Industrial and Labor Relations Review* 35 (April): 343-353.

——————. 1985. "Assimilation, Changes in Cohort Quality, and the Earnings of Immigrants." *Journal of Labor Economics* 3 (October): 463-489.

——————. 1986. "The Self-Employment Experience of Immigrants." *Journal of Human Resources* 21, 4 (Fall): 485-506.

——————. 1988. *International Differences in the Labor Market Performance of Immigrants*. Kalamazoo, Mich.: W. E. Upjohn Institute for Employment

Research.

Bose, Christine E. and Peter H. Rossi. 1983. "Gender and Jobs: Prestige Standings of Occupations as Affected by Gender." *American Sociological Review* 48, 3 (June): 316-330.

Boston, Thomas D. 1988. *Race, Class, and Conservatism.* Boston: Unwin Hyman.

Botwinick, Howard I. 1988. "Wage Differentials and the Competition of Capitals: A New Explanation for Inter- and Intra-Industry Wage Differentials Among Workers of Similar Skill." Ph.D. diss. New School for Social Research. This is forthcoming from Princeton, N.J.: Princeton University Press.

Bound, John and Richard Freeman. 1989. "Black Progress: Erosion of the Post-1965 Gains in the 1980s?" ch. 2 in Shulman and Darity [1989].

Bowles, Samuel. 1985. "The Production Process in a Competitive Economy: Walrasian, Neo-Hobbesian, and Marxian Models." *American Economic Review* 75, 1 (March): 16-36.

Bowles, Samuel and Herbert Gintis. 1976. *Schooling in Capitalist America: Educational Reform and the Contradictions of Economic Life.* New York: Basic Books.

Boyd, Herb. 1989. "Sadie Alexander, 2nd Black Woman Ph.D., Dies." *New York Amsterdam News* (November 11): 59.

Bradbury, Katherine L., Karl E. Case, and Constance R. Dunham. 1989. "Geographic Patterns of Mortgage Lending in Boston, 1982-1987." *New England Economic Review* (September/October): 3-30.

Braddock II, Jomills Henry, and James M. McPartland. 1987. "How Minorities Continue to Be Excluded from Equal Employment Opportunities: Research on Labor Market and Institutional Barriers." *Journal of Social Issues* 43, 1: 5-39.

Braverman, Harry. 1974. *Labor and Monopoly Capital.* New York: Monthly Review Press.

Brewer, Marilynn B. and Roderick M. Kramer. 1985. "The Psychology of Intergroup Attitudes and Behavior." *Annual Review of Psychology* 36: 219-243.

Bridges, William P. 1980. "Industry Marginality and Female Employment: A New Appraisal." *American Sociological Review* 45, 1 (February): 58-75.

————. 1982. "The Sexual Segregation of Occupations: Theories of Labor Stratification in Industry." *American Journal of Sociology* 88, 2 (September): 270-295.

Bridges, William P. and Robert L. Nelson. 1989. "Markets in Hierarchies: Organizational and Market Influences on Gender Inequality in a State Pay System." *American Journal of Sociology* 95, 3 (November): 616-658.

Brown, Charles. 1980. "Equalizing Differences in the Labor Market." *Quarterly Journal of Economics* 95 (February): 113-134.

Brown, Clair. and Joseph A. Pechman (eds.) 1987. *Gender in the Workplace.*

Washington, D.C.: Brookings Institution.

Brown, M. and M. Mancer. 1980. "Marriage and Household Decision Making: A Bargaining Analysis." *International Economic Review* 21, 1 (February): 31-44.

Browne, Robert. 1971. "Cash Flows in a Ghetto Economy." *Review of Black Political Economy* (Spring): 28-29.

Bullock, Henry. 1967. *A History of Negro Education in the South*. Cambridge, Mass.: Harvard University Press.

Bulow, Jeremy and Lawrence H. Summers. 1986. "A Theory of Dual Labor Markets with Application to Industrial Policy, Discrimination, and Keynesian Unemployment." *Journal of Labor Economics* 4, 3 (July): 376-414.

Burstein, Paul. 1985. *Discrimination, Jobs, and Politics*. Chicago: University of Chicago Press.

Butler, Richard J. 1982. "Estimating Wage Discrimination in the Labor Market." *Journal of Human Resources* 17, 4 (Fall): 606-621.

Butler, Richard and James Heckman. 1977. "The Government's Impact on the Labor Market Status of Black Americans: A Critical Review." ch. 9, pp. 235-281, in Leonard J. Hausman (eds.) *Equal Rights and Industrial Relations*. Madison, Wis.: Industrial Relations Research Association.

Butler, Richard, James Heckman, and Brook Payner. 1990. "The Impact of the Economy and State on the Economic Status of Blacks." ch. 6 in David W. Galenson (ed.) *Markets in History: Economic Studies of the Past*. Cambridge, England: Cambridge University Press.

Cain, Glen G. 1986. "The Economic Analysis of Labor Market Discrimination: A Survey." pp. 693-785 in Orley Ashenfelter and Richard Layard (eds.) *Handbook of Labor Economics*, vol. 1. Amsterdam: North-Holland.

Cain, Pamela S. and Donald J. Treiman. 1981. "The *Dictionary of Occupational Titles* as a Source of Occupational Data." *American Sociological Review* 46, 3 (June): 253-278.

Caldwell, Bruce. 1982. *Beyond Positivism: Economic Methodology in the Twentieth Century*. Boston: Allen and Unwin.

Callahan-Levy, Charlene M. and Lawrence A. Messe. 1979. "Sex Differences in the Allocation of Pay." *Journal of Personality and Social Psychology* 37, 3 (March): 433-446.

Calvo, Guillermo A. and Stanislaw Wellisz. 1978. "Supervision, Loss of Control, and the Optimum Size of the Firm." *Journal of Political Economy* 86, 5 (October): 943-952.

Carliner, Geoffrey. 1980. "Wages, Earnings, and Hours of First, Second, and Third Generation American Males." *Economic Inquiry* 18 (January): 87-102.

Cartter, Allan. 1975. *Theory of Wages and Unemployment*. Westport, Conn.: Greenwood Press.

Chase, Richard X. 1979. "Production Theory." in Alfred Eichner (ed.), *A Guide* to *Post-Keynesian Economics*. White Plains, N.Y.: M.E. Sharpe.

Cherry, Robert. 1988. "Black Youth Employment Problems." in Robert Cherry (eds.) *The Imperiled Economy*, Book II. New York: URPE.

—————. 1989. *Discrimination: Its Impact on Blacks, Jews, and Women*. Lexington, Mass.: D. C. Heath.

Chiswick, Barry R. 1978. "The Effects of Americanization on the Earnings of Foreign-Born Men." *Journal of Political Economy* 86, 5 (October): 897-921.

—————. 1980. *An Analysis of the Economic Progress and Impact of Immigrants*. Final Report to the Employment and Training Administration. U. S. Department of Labor. NTIS PB 80-200454. University of Illinois at Chicago (June): ch. 7.

—————. 1983a. "An Analysis of the Earnings and Employment of Asian-American Men." *Journal of Labor Economics* 1 (April): 197-214.

—————. 1983b. "The Earnings and Human Capital of American Jews." *Journal of Human Resources* 18 (Summer): 313-336.

—————. 1986. "Is the New Immigrant Less Skilled Than the Old?" *Journal of Labor Economics* 4, 2 (April): 168-192.

Christensen, Kimberly. 1988. "Political Determinants of Racial Income Differentials." paper presented at National Economic Association/Union for Radical Political Economics Session, Allied Social Sciences Association Meetings, New York, N.Y.

Cialdini, Robert B. 1988. *Influence*. 2d ed. Glenview, Ill: Scott, Foresman.

Clifton, James. 1977. "Competition and the Evolution of the Capitalist Mode of Production." *Cambridge Journal of Economics* 1, 2 (June): 137-151.

Cohen, Joshua and Joel Rogers. 1983. *On Democracy: Toward a Transformation of American Society*. New York: Penguin Books.

Cohen, M. S. 1971. "Sex Differences in Compensation." *Journal of Human Resources* 6, 4 (Fall): 434-447.

Cohen, Yinon and Jeffrey Pfeffer. 1986. "Organizational Hiring Standards." *Administrative Science Quarterly* 31, 1 (March): 1-24.

Cohn, Samuel R. 1985. "Clerical Labor Intensity and the Feminization of Clerical Labor in Great Britain, 1857-1937." *Social Forces* 63, 4 (June): 1060-1068.

Coleman, James S. 1966. *Equality of Educational Opportunity*. Washington, D.C.: U.S. Government Printing Office.

—————. 1990. *Foundations of Social Theory*. Cambridge, Mass.: Harvard University Press.

Collins, Randall. 1975. *The Credential Society*. New York: Academic Press.

Conk, Margo A. 1978. "Occupational Classification in the United States Census, 1870-1940." *Journal of Interdisciplinary History* 9, 1 (Summer): 111-130.

Corcoran, Mary and Gregory J. Duncan. 1979. "Work History, Labor Force Attachment, and Earnings Differences Between the Races and Sexes."

Journal of Human Resources 14, 1 (Winter): 3-20.

Corcoran, M., G. Duncan and M. Ponza. 1983. "Longitudinal Analysis of White Women's Wages." *Journal of Human Resources* 18, 4 (Fall): 497-520.

Cornwall, Richard R. 1984. *Introduction to the Use of General Equilibrium Analysis.* New York: North-Holland.

Cox, Oliver C. 1948. *Caste, Class, and Race: A Study in Social Dynamics.* Garden City, N.Y.: Doubleday.

——————. 1970. *Caste, Class, and Race.* New York: Monthly Review Press.

Crosby, F. 1982. *Relative Deprivation and Working Women.* New York: Oxford University Press.

Cross, Harry, Genevieve Kenney, Jane Mell, and Wendy Zimmermann. 1990. *Employer Hiring Practices: Differential Treatment of Hispanic and Anglo Job Seekers.* Washington, D.C.: Urban Institute.

Culp, Jerome and Bruce H. Dunson. 1986. "Brothers of a Different Color: A Preliminary Look at Employer Treatment of White and Black Youth." in Freeman and Holzer [1986].

Darity, William A., Jr. 1982a. "The Human Capital Approach to Black-White Earnings Inequality: Some Unsettled Questions." *Journal of Human Resouces* 17, 1 (Winter): 72-93.

——————. 1982b. "Economists, the Minimum Wage, and the Underclass." in Clement Cottingham (ed.), *Race, Poverty, and the Urban Underclass.* Lexington, Mass.: D. C. Heath.

——————. 1984a. "Reflections on the State of the Art in Labor Economics." in Darity [1984b].

——————. (ed.) 1984b. *Labor Economics: Modern Views.* Boston: Kluwer-Nijhoff.

——————. 1989. "What's Left of the Economic Theory of Discrimination?" in Shulman and Darity [1989].

Darity, William A., Jr. and Bobbie L. Horn. 1983. "Involuntary Unemployment Reconsidered." *Southern Economic Journal* 49, 1 (January): 717-733.

——————. 1987-88. "Involuntary Unemployment Independent of the Labor Market." *Journal of Post-Keynesian Economics* 10, 2 (Winter): 216-224.

Darity, William A., Jr. and Samuel L. Myers, Jr. 1980. "Changes in Black-White Income Inequality, 1968-1978: A Decade of Progress?" *Review of Black Political Economy* 10, 4 (Summer): 354, 356-379.

——————. 1984. "Does Welfare Dependency Cause Female Headship? The Case of the Black Family." *Journal of Marriage and the Family* 46 (November): 765-779.

——————. 1987. "Do Transfer Payments Keep the Poor in Poverty?" *American Economic Review* 77, 2 (May): 216-222.

Darity, William A. and Rhonda M. Williams. 1985. "Peddlers Forever? Culture, Competition, and Discrimination." *American Economic Review: Papers and Proceedings* 75, 2 (May): 256-261.

Darley, J. M. and R. H. Fazio. 1980. "Expectancy Confirmation Sequences." *American Psychologist* 35, 10 (October): 867-881.

Davis, Kingsley and Wilbert E. Moore. 1945. "Some Principles of Stratification." *American Sociological Review* 10, 2 (April): 242-249.

Dean, Jayne. 1988. "Sex Segregation, Relative Wages, and the Technical Conditions of Production: A Theoretical and Empirical Analysis." Ph.D. diss., New School for Social Research.

Deaux, Kay. 1985. "Sex and Gender." *Annual Review of Psychology* 36: 49-81.

Dewart, Janet (ed.). 1989. *The State of Black America, 1989.* National Urban League.

Dewey, Donald. 1952. "Negro Employment in Southern Industry." *Journal of Political Economy* 60, 4 (August): 279-293.

Dickens, William T. and Lawrence Katz. 1987. "Industry Characteristics and Interindustry Wage Differences." pp. 48-89 in Lang and Leonard [1987].

Dickens, William T. and Kevin Lang. 1985. "A Test of Dual Labor Market Theory." *American Economic Review* 75 (September): 792-805.

—————. 1988. "The Reemergence of Segmented Labor Market Theory." *American Economic Review* 78, 2 (May): 129-134.

DiMaggio, Paul J. and Walter W. Powell. 1983. "The Iron Cage Revisited: Institutional Isomorphism and Collective Rationality in Organizational Fields." *American Sociological Review* 48, 2 (April): 147-160.

Doeringer, Peter B. and Michael J. Piore. 1971. *Internal Labor Markets and Manpower Analysis.* Lexington, Mass.: Heath.

Donohue, John and James Heckman. 1991. "Continuous Versus Episodic Change: The Impact of Affirmative Action and Civil Rights Policy on the Economic Status of Blacks." Forthcoming. *Journal of Economic Literature* (December).

Dovidio, John F. and Samuel L. Gaertner. 1986. "The Aversive Form of Racism." ch. 3, pp. 61-89, in John Dovidio and Samuel Gaertner (eds.) *Prejudice, Discrimination, and Racism.* Orlando, Fla.: Academic Press.

Duleep, Harriet Orcutt. 1988. *The Economic Status of Americans of Asian Descent: An Exploratory Investigation.* Washington, D.C.: U.S. Commission on Civil Rights.

Duleep, Harriet Orcutt and Hal Sider. 1986. *The Economic Status of Americans of Southern and Eastern European Ancestry.* Clearinghouse Publication 89. Washington, D.C.: U. S. Commission on Civil Rights (October).

Duncan, Otis Dudley. 1968. "Inheritance of Poverty or Inheritance of Race?" pp. 85-110 in Daniel P. Moynihan (ed.) *On Understanding Poverty.* New York: Basic Books.

Duncan, Otis Dudley and Beverly Duncan. 1955. "A Methodological Analysis of Segregation Indices." *American Sociological Review* 20, 2 (April): 210-217.

Dunlop, John T. 1957. "The Task of Contemporary Wage Theory." pp. 3-27 in

John T. Dunlop (ed.), *The Theory of Wage Determination*. London: Macmillan.

Edelman, Marian Wright. 1987. *Families in Peril: An Agenda for Social Change*. Cambridge, Mass.: Harvard University Press.

Edwards, Richard. 1979. *Contested Terrain: The Transformation of the Workplace in the Twentieth Century*. New York: Basic Books.

Edwards, Richard and Michael Podgursky. 1986. "The Unraveling Accord: American Unions in Crisis." in R. Edwards, P. Garonna, and F. Todtling (eds.) *Unions in Crisis and Beyond: Perspectives from Six Countries*. Dover, Mass.: Auburn House.

Elbaum, Bernard S. 1984. "The Making and Shaping of Job and Pay Structures in the Iron and Steel Industry." pp. 71-108 in Paul Osterman (ed.) *Internal Labor Markets*. Cambridge, Mass.: MIT Press.

England, Paula. 1982. "The Failure of Human Capital Theory to Explain Occupational Sex Segregation." *Journal of Human Resources* 17 (Winter): 358-370.

————. 1984. "Wage Appreciation and Depreciation: A Test of Neoclassical Economic Explanations of Occupational Sex Segregation." *Social Forces* 62.

England, Paula, Marilyn Chassie, and Linda McCormack. 1982. "Skill Demands and Earnings in Female and Male Occupations." *Sociology and Social Research* 66, 2 (January): 147-168.

England, Paula and Dana Dunn. 1988. "Evaluating Work and Comparable Worth." *Annual Review of Sociology* 14: 227-248.

England, Paula, George Farkas, Barbara S. Kilbourne, and Thomas Dou. 1988. "Explaining Occupational Sex Segregation and Wages: Findings from a Model with Fixed Effects." *American Sociological Review* 53, 4 (August): 544-558.

Fairris, David. 1989. "Compensating Wage Differentials in the Union and Nonunion Sectors." *Industrial Relations* 28 (Fall): 356-372.

Fama, Eugene. 1980. "Agency Problems and the Theory of The Firm." *Journal of Political Economy* 88, 2 (April): 288-307.

Farley, Reynolds. 1984. *Blacks and Whites: Narrowing the Gap?* Cambridge, Mass.: Harvard University Press.

————. 1986. "Assessing Black Progress: Employment, Occupation, Earnings, Income, Poverty." *Economic Outlook USA* 13, 3 (Third Quarter).

Filer, Randall K. 1983. "Sexual Differences in Earnings: The Role of Individual Personalities and Tastes." *Journal of Human Resources* 18 (Winter): 82-99.

————. 1985. "Male-Female Wage Differences: The Importance of Compensating Differentials." *Industrial and Labor Relations Review* 8 (April): 426-437.

————. 1989. "Occupational Segregation, Compensating Differential, and

Comparable Worth," pp. 153-170 in Michael, Hartmann, and O'Farrell [1989].

Fine, Sidney A. 1968. *The 1965 Third Edition of the Dictionary of Occupational Titles – Content, Contrasts, and Critique*. Kalamazoo, Mich.: Upjohn Institute for Employment Research.

Fiske, Susan T. and Shelley E. Taylor. 1984. *Social Cognition*. New York: Addison-Wesley.

Fosu, Augustin K. 1987. "Explaining Post-1964 Earnings Gains by Black Women: Race or Sex?" *Review of Black Political Economy* 15, 3 (Winter): 41-55.

Frank, Robert M. 1984. "Are Workers Paid Their Marginal Products?" *American Economic Review* 74, 4: 549-571.

Fraser, C. Gerald. 1989. "Sadie T. M. Alexander, 91, Dies; Lawyer and Civil Rights Advocate." *New York Times* (November 3): D18.

Fredrickson, George M. 1981. *White Supremacy: A Comparative Study in American and South African History*. Oxford: Oxford University Press.

—————. 1988. "Colonialism and Racism: The United States and South Africa in Comparative Perspective." in George M. Fredrickson (ed.) *The Arrogance of Race* Middletown CT: Wesleyan University Press.

Freeman, Richard B. 1973. "Changes in the Labor Market for Black Americans, 1948-1972." *Brookings Papers on Economic Activity* 1: 246-295.

—————. 1981. "Black Economic Progress After 1964: Who Has Gained and Why?" pp. 247-294 in Sherwin Rosen (ed.) *Studies in Labor Markets*. Chicago: University of Chicago Press for the National Bureau of Economic Research.

Freeman, Richard B. and Harry J. Holzer (eds.) 1986. *The Black Youth Employment Crisis*. Chicago: University of Chicago Press.

Freeman, Richard and James Medoff. 1982. "Substitution Between Labor and Other Inputs in Unionized and Nonunionized Manufacturing." *Review of Economics and Statistics* 64, 2 (May): 220-233.

Friedman, Milton. 1953. "The Methodology of Positive Economics." in *Essays in Positive Economics*. Chicago: University of Chicago Press.

Friedman, Samuel. 1984. "Structure, Process, and the Labor Market." in Darity [1984b].

Fuchs, Victor. 1971. "Male-Female Differentials in Hourly Earnings." *Monthly Labor Review* 94, 5 (May): 9-15.

Galbraith, John K. 1967. *The New Industrial State*. Boston: Houghton Mifflin.

Gilman, Harry J. 1965. "Economic Discrimination and Unemployment." *American Economic Review* 55 (December): 1077-1095.

Gilroy, Curtis. 1974. "Black-White Unemployment: The Dynamics of the Differential." *Monthly Labor Review* (February).

Glenn, Evelyn Nakano. 1985. "Racial Ethnic Women's Labor: The Intersection of Race, Gender, and Class Oppression." *Review of Radical Political Economics* 17, 3: 86-108.

Gold, Michael. 1985. "Grigg's Folly: An Essay on the Theory Problems and Origin of the Adverse Impact Definition of Employment Discrimination and a Recommendation for Reform." *Industrial Relations Law Journal* 7 (December): 231-238.

Goldin, Claudia. 1986. "Monitoring Costs and Occupational Segregation by Sex: A Historical Analysis." *Journal of Labor Economics* 4, 1 (January): 3-27.

Goldin, Claudia and Solomon W. Polachek. 1987. "Residual Differences by Sex: Perspectives on the Gender Gap in Earnings." *American Economic Review: Papers and Proceedings* 77, 2 (May): 143-151.

Gordon, David M. 1986. "Procedure for Allocating Jobs into Labor Segments." Mimeo. New School for Social Research (May).

Gordon, David, Richard Edwards, and Michael Reich. 1982. *Segmented Work, Divided Workers: The Historical Transformation of Labor in the United States.* Cambridge, England: Cambridge University Press.

Gordon, Francine E. and Myra H. Strober. 1978. "Initial Observations on a Pioneer Cohort: 1974 Women MBA's." *Sloan Management Review* 19 (Winter) 15-23.

Granovetter, Mark. 1985. "Economic Action and Social Structure: The Problem of Embeddedness." *American Journal of Sociology* 91, 3 (November): 481-510.

—————. 1988. "The Sociological and Economic Approaches to Labor Market Analysis: A Social Structural View." pp. 187-216 in George Farkas and Paula England (eds.) *Industries, Firms, and Jobs: Sociological and Economic Approaches.* New York: Plenum Press.

Groshen, Erica L. 1989. "Do Wage Differences Among Employers Last?" Working Paper 8906, Federal Reserve Bank of Cleveland.

Hahn, Frank. 1987. "On Involuntary Unemployment." *Economic Journal* 97, 385 (Conference volume) (March): 1-16.

Haley, W. 1976. "Estimated Earnings Profiles from Optimal Human Capital Accumulation." *Econometrica* 44, 6 (November): 1223-1238.

Hamilton, David L. (ed.) 1981. *Cognitive Processes in Stereotyping and Intergroup Behavior.* Hillsdale, N.J.: Erlbaum.

Handy, John and David Swinton. 1984. "The Determinants of the Rate of Growth of Black-owned Businesses." *Review of Black Political Economy* 12, 4 (Spring): 99-102.

Hannan, Michael T. and John H. Freeman. 1984. "Structural Inertia and Organizational Change." *American Sociological Review* 49, 2: 149-164.

Hanushek, E. and J. Quigley. 1985. "Life Cycle Earnings Capacity and the On-the-Job Training Investment Model." *International Economic Review* 26, 2 (June): 365-385.

Harris, Abram. 1927. "Economic Foundations of American Race Division." *Social Forces* 5, 3.

Hartmann, Heidi I. 1981. "The Family as Locus of Gender, Class, and Political

Struggle." *Signs* 6, 3 (Spring): 366-394.

——. 1982. "Capitalism, Patriarchy, and Job Segregation by Sex." in A. Giddens and David Held (eds.) *Classes, Power, and Conflict: Classical and Contemporary Debates*. Berkeley: University of California Press.

——. (ed.) 1985. *Comparable Worth: New Directions for Research*. Washington, D.C.: National Academy Press.

——. 1987. "Internal Labor Markets and Gender: A Case Study of Promotion." pp. 59-105 in Brown and Pechman [1987].

Hashemzadeh, Nozar and Burl F. Long. 1985. "Cyclical Aspects of Black Unemployment: An Empirical Analysis." *Review of Regional Studies* 15, 1 (Winter): 7-19.

Hashimoto, Masanori. 1981. "Firm Specific Human Capital as a Shared Investment." *American Economic Review* 71, 3 (June): 475-482.

Hayek, F. A. 1988. *The Fatal Conceit*. Chicago: University of Chicago Press.

Hechter, Michael. 1983. *The Microfoundations of Macrosociology*. Philadelphia: Temple University Press.

Heckman, James J. 1975. "Estimates of a Human Capital Production Function Embedded in a Life Cycle Model of Labor Supply." pp. 227-264 in N. Terleckyi (ed.) *Household Production and Consumption*. New York: National Bureau of Economic Research.

——. 1976. "A Life-Cycle Model of Earnings, Learning, and Consumption." *Journal of Political Economy* 84, 4, pt. 2 (August): S11-S44.

——. 1979. "Sample Selection Bias as a Specification Error." *Econometrica* 47, 1 (January): 153-161.

——. 1989. "Murky Numbers on Black Economic Progress." *Wall Street Journal* (August 22).

Heckman, James J. and Thomas MaCurdy. Forothcoming. "Empirical Tests of Labor Market Equilibrium." Mimeo. Department of Economics, Yale University.

Heckman, James J. and Brook Payner. 1989. "Determining the Impact of Federal Anti-discrimination Policy on the Economic Status of Blacks: A Study of South Carolina." *American Economic Review* 79 (March): 138-177.

Henry, Frances and Effie Ginzberg. 1985. *Who Gets the Work? A Test of Racial Discrimination in Employment*. Toronto: Urban Alliance on Race Relations and the Social Planning Council of Metropolitan Toronto.

Higgs, Robert. 1989. "Black Progress and the Persistence of Racial Economic Inequalites." ch. 1 in Shulman and Darity [1989].

Hill, Herbert. 1976. "Affirmative Action and the Quest for Job Equality." *Review of Black Political Economy* 6, 3 (Winter).

——. 1984. "Race and Ethnicity in Organized Labor: The Historical Sources of Resistance to Affirmative Action." *Journal of Intergroup Relations* 13, 4.

——. 1985. *Black Labor and the American Legal System: Race, Work, and the Law*. Madison: University of Wisconsin Press (originally published in 1977).

——————. 1989. "Black Labor and Affirmative Action: An Historical Perspective." ch. 8 in Shulman and Darity [1989].

Hofferth, Sandra L. and Kristin A. Moore. 1979. "Early Childbearing and Later Economic Well-Being." *American Sociological Review* 44, 5 (October): 784-815.

Holmstrom, Bengt R. and Jean Tirole. 1989. "The Theory of the Firm." pp. 61-133 in Richard Schmalensee and Robert Willig (eds.) *Handbook of Industrial Organization*. vol. 1. Amsterdam: North-Holland.

Holzer, Harry. 1988. "Can We Solve Black Youth Unemployment?" *Challenge* 31, 6 (December): 43-49.

Jablow, Martha. 1980. "Madam Chairman." *50 Plus* (November): 32-33.

Jackson, Peter and Edward Montgomery. 1986. "Layoffs, Discharges, and Youth Unemployment." in Freeman and Holzer [1986].

Janiewski, Dolores E. 1986. *Sisterhood Denied: Race, Gender, and Class in a New South Community*. Philadelphia: Temple University Press.

Jaynes, Gerald D. 1990. "The Labor Market Status of Black Americans, 1939-1985." *Journal of Economic Perspectives* 4, 4 (Fall): 9-24.

Jaynes, Gerald D. and Robin Williams. 1989. *A Common Destiny: Blacks and American Society*. Washington, D.C.: National Academy Press.

Jensen, Michael and William Meckling. 1976. "Theory of the Firm: Managerial Behavior, Agency Costs, and Ownership Structure." *Journal of Financial Economics* 3, 4: 305-360.

Jiang, F. and S. Polachek. 1986. "Investment Dependent Labor Supply." Paper presented at the Eastern Economic Association Meetings, Philadelphia.

Jiobu, Robert M. 1988. *Ethnicity and Assimilation*. Albany: State University of New York Press.

Johnson, T. 1978. "Time in School: The Case of the Prudent Patron." *American Economic Review* 68, 5 (December): 862-872.

Jones, James M. 1986. "Racism: A Cultural Analysis of the Problem." ch. 10, pp. 279-314, in John F. Dovidio and Samuel L. Gaertner (eds.) *Prejudice, Discrimination, and Racism*. Orlando, Fla.: Academic Press.

Jones, Stephen R. G. 1987. "Minimum Wage Legislation in a Dual Labor Market." *European Economic Review* 31, 6: 1229-1246.

Jovanovic, Boyan. 1982. "Selection and Evolution of Industry." *Econometrica*. 650-653.

Jowell, Roger and Patricia Prescott-Clarke. 1970. "Racial Discrimination and White-Collar Workers in Britain." *Race* 11: 397-417.

Kamalich, R. and S. Polachek. 1982. "Discrimination: Fact or Fiction? An Examination Using an Alternative Approach." *Southern Economic Journal* 49, 2 (October): 450-461.

Kanter, Rosabeth Moss. 1977. *Men and Women of the Corporation*. New York:

Basic Books.

Kao, C. 1989. "A Human Capital Approach to Male-Female Wage Differentials in Taiwan." Ph.D. diss. SUNY-Binghamton.

Katz, Lawrence F. 1986. "Efficiency Wage Theories: A Partial Evaluation." in Stanley Fischer (ed.), *NBER Macroeconomics Annual*. Cambridge, Mass.: MIT Press.

Katznelson, Ira. 1986. "Working Class Formation: Constructing Cases and Comparisons." in Katznelson and Zolberg [1986].

Katznelson, Ira and Aristide Zolberg (eds.) 1986. *Working-Class Formation: Nineteenth-Century Patterns in Western Europe and the United States.* Princeton:, N.J. Princeton University Press.

Kaus, Mickey. 1986. "The Work Ethic State." *New Republic* 7 (July): 22-33.

Kerr, Clark. 1954. "The Balkanization of Labor Markets." pp. 92-110 in E. Wight Bakke, Philip Hauser, Gladys Palmer, C. Myers, Dale Yoder, and Clark Kerr (eds.) *Labor Mobility and Economic Opportunity*. Cambridge, Mass.: MIT Press.

Keynes, John Maynard. 1936. *The General Theory of Employment, Interest, and Money.* London: Macmillan.

————————. 1973. "The Theory of the Rate of Interest." originally in A. D. Gayer (ed.) 1937. *The Lessons of Monetary Experience: Essays in Honour of Irving Fisher.* Holt, Rinehart and Winston. Page citations here are taken from the reprinted version in Donald Moggridge (ed.) *The Collected Writings of John Maynard Keynes*, vol. 14. London: Macmillan.

Killingsworth, Mark R. 1985. "The Economics of Comparable Worth: Analytical, Empirical, and Policy Questions." pp. 86-115 in Hartmann [1985].

Killingsworth, M. and J. Heckman. 1986. "Female Labor Supply: A Survey." pp. 103-204 in O. Ashenfelter and R. Layard (eds.) *Handbook of Labor Economics*, vol. 1. Amsterdam: North-Holland.

Kim, Marlene. 1989. "Gender Bias in Compensation Structure: A Case Study of Its Historical Basis and Persistence." *Journal of Social Issues* 45, 4 (Winter): 39-50.

Kitchel, Marc. 1988. "The Secondary Labor Market and Local Labor Markets." Mimeo,.Amherst, Mass.: University of Massachusetts.

Kniesner, Thomas J. and Arthur H. Goldsmith. 1987. "A Survey of Alternative Models of the U.S. Labor Market." *Journal of Economic Literature* 25, 3 (September): 1241-1280.

Kossoudji, Sherrie A. 1989. "Immigrant Worker Assimilation: Is It a Labor Market Phenomenon?" *Journal of Human Resources* 24 (Summer): 494-527.

Krueger, Alan B. and Lawrence H. Summers. 1987. "Reflections on the Inter-Industry Wage Structure." ch. 2, pp. 17-47, in Lang and Leonard [1987].

Kuratani, M. 1973. "A Theory of Training, Warnings, and Employment: An Application to Japan." Ph.D. diss. Columbia University.

Ladner, Joyce A. 1971. *Tomorrow's Tomorrow: The Black Woman*. Garden City, N.Y.: Doubleday.

Lang, Kevin and Jonathan S. Leonard (eds.) 1987. *Unemployment and the Structure of Labor Markets*. New York: Basil Blackwell.

Lang, Kevin, J. S. Leonard, and D. M. Lilien. 1987. "Labor Market Structure, Wages, and Unemployment." ch. 1, pp. 1-16,. in Lang and Leonard [1987].

Lansberg, Ivan. 1989. "Social Categorization, Entitlement, and Justice in Organizations: Contextual Determinants and Cognitive Underpinnings." *Human Relations* 41: 871-899.

Lazear, Edward P. 1979. "Why Is There Mandatory Retirement?" *Journal of Political Economy* 87, 6 (December): 1261-1284.

————. 1989. "Pay Equality and Industrial Politics." *Journal of Political Economy* 97, 3 (June): 561-580.

Lazear, Edward P. and R. Moore. 1984. "Incentives, Productivity, and Labor Contracts." *Quarterly Journal of Economics* 99, 2 (May): 275-296.

Lee, Lung-Fei. 1978. "Unionism and Wage Rates: Simultaneous Equations Model with Qualitative and Limited Dependent Variables." *International Economic Review* 19 (June): 415-433.

Leiman, Melvin. 1987. "The Political Economy of Racism." *Insurgent Sociologist*.

Lemann, Nicholas. 1986. "The Origins of the Underclass." *The Atlantic Monthly* 257, 6 (June): 31-55; 258, 1 (July): 54-68.

Lenney, Ellen. 1977. "Women's Self-Confidence in Achievement Settings." *Psychological Bulletin* 84, 1 (January): 1-13.

Lenski, Gerhard. 1966. *Power and Privilege: A Theory of Social Stratification*. New York: McGraw-Hill.

Leonard, Jonathan S. 1984. "The Impact of Affirmative Action on Employment." *Journal of Labor Economics* 2 (October): 439-463.

————. 1987. "Carrots and Sticks: Pay, Supervision, and Turnover." *Journal of Labor Economics* 5, 4, pt. 2 (October): S136-S152.

————. 1989. "Women and Affirmative Action." *Journal of Economic Perspectives* 3, 1 (Winter): 61-75.

————. 1990. "The Impact of Affirmative Action Regulation and Equal Employment Law on Black Employment." *Journal of Economic Perspectives* 4, 4 (Fall): 47-63.

Levhari, D. and Y. Weiss. 1974. "The Effect of Risk on the Investment of Human Capital." *American Economic Review* 64, 6 (December): 950-963.

Lichter, Daniel T. 1988. "Racial Differences in Underemployment in American Cities." *American Journal of Sociology* 93, 4 (January): 771-792.

Light, Ivan H. 1972. *Ethnic Enterprise in America*. Berkeley: University of California Press.

Lindbeck, Assar and Dennis J. Snower. 1988. "Cooperation, Harassment, and Involuntary Unemployment." *American Economic Review* 78, 1 (March):

167-188.

Long, James E. 1980. "The Effects of Americanization on Earnings: Some Evidence for Women." *Journal of Political Economy* 88, 3 (June): 620-629.

Loury, Glen. 1984. "Internally Directed Action for Black Community Development: The Next Frontier for 'The Movement.'" *Review of Black Political Economy* 13, 1 (Summer): 31-46.

Lucas, Robert. 1978. "On the Size Distribution of Business Firms." *Bell Journal of Economics* 9, 2 (Autumn): 510-518.

Lyson, Thomas A. 1985. "Race and Sex Segregation in Occupational Structures of Southern Employers." *Social Science Quarterly* 66: 281-295.

McArthur, Leslie. 1985. "Social Judgment Biases in Comparable Worth Analysis." pp. 53-70 in Hartmann [1985].

McCrate, Elaine. 1990. "Labor Market Segmentation and Relative Black/White Teenage Birth Rates." *Review of Black Political Economy* (Winter/Spring).

McElroy, M. and M. J. Horney. 1981. "Nash-Bargained Household Decisions: Toward a Generalization of the Theory of Demand." *International Economic Review* 22, 2 (June): 333-349.

Machung, Anne. 1989. "Talking Career, Thinking Job: Gender Differences in Career and Family Expectations of Berkeley Seniors." *Feminist Studies* 15, 1 (Spring) 35-58.

McIntosh, Neil and David J. Smith. 1974. *The Extent of Racial Discrimination.* vol. 40 broadsheet no. 547. London: Political and Economic Planning, The Social Science Institute.

McManus, Walter S. 1985. "Labor Market Assimilation of Immigrants: The Importance of Language Skills." *Contemporary Policy Issues* 3 (Spring): 77-89.

McNulty, D. 1967. "Differences in Pay Between Men and Women Workers." *Monthly Labor Review* 90, 12 (December): 40-43.

Magura, Michael and Edward Shapiro. 1987. "The Black Dropout Rate and the Black Youth Unemployment Rate: A Granger-Causal Analysis." *Review of Black Political Economy* 15, 3 (Winter): 56-67.

Major, Brenda and Blythe Forcey. 1985. "Social Comparisons and Pay Evaluations: Preferences for Same-Sex and Same-Job Wage Comparisons." *Journal of Experimental Social Psychology* 21, 4 (July): 393-405.

Major, Brenda, Dean B. McFarlin, and Diana Gagnon. 1984. "Overworked and Underpaid: On the Nature of Gender Differences in Personal Entitlement." *Journal of Personality and Social Psychology* 47, 6 (December): 1399-1412.

Malkiel, B. and J. Malkiel. 1973. "Male-Female Pay Differentials in Professional Employment." *American Economic Review* 63, 4 (September): 693-705.

Margo, Robert. 1990. *Segregated Schools in the American South: A Quantitative History, 1880-1950.* Chicago: University of Chicago Press.

Marks, Stephen R. 1977. "Multiple Roles and Role Strain: Some Notes on Human Energy, Time, and Commitment." *American Sociological Review* 42, 6

(December): 921-936.

Marx, Karl. 1849. *Wage-Labour and Capital.* New York: International Publishers, 1983.

———. 1857. *Grundrisse.* New York: Vintage Books, 1973.

———. 1863. *Theories of Surplus Value.* Moscow: Progress Publishers, 1967.

———. 1867. *Capital.* vol. 1. New York: International Publishers, 1967.

———. 1885. *Capital.* vol. 2. New York: International Publishers, 1967.

———. 1894. *Capital.* vol. 3. New York: International Publishers, 1967.

———. 1970. "Wages, Price, and Profit." in *Karl Marx and Frederick Engels: Selected Works.* New York: International Publishers.

Meitzen, Mark E. 1986. "Differences in Male and Female Job-Quitting Behavior." *Journal of Labor Economics* 4, 2 (April): 151-167.

Messick, David M. and Diane M. Mackie. 1989. "Intergroup Relations." *Annual Review of Psychology* 40: 45-81.

Meyer, John W. and Brian Rowan. 1977. "Institutionalized Organizations: Formal Structure as Myth and Ceremony." *American Journal of Sociology* 83, 2 (September): 340-363.

Meyer, Marshall W. 1975. "Leadership and Organization Structure." *American Journal of Sociology* 81, 3 (November): 514-542.

Meyer, Marshall W. and M. Craig Brown. 1977. "The Process of Bureaucratization." *American Journal of Sociology* 83, 2 (September): 364-385.

Michael, Robert T., Heidi I. Hartmann, and Brigid O'Farrell (eds.) 1989. *Pay Equity: Empirical Inquiries.* Washington, D.C.: National Academy Press.

Mies, Maria. 1986. *Patriarchy and Accumulation on a World Scale.* London: Zed Press.

Milgrom, Paul and John Roberts. 1988. "An Economic Approach to Influence Activities in Organizations." *American Journal of Sociology* 94 (Supplement): S154-S179.

Milkman, Ruth. 1980. "Organizing the Sexual Division of Labor: Historical Perspectives on 'Women's Work' and the American Labor Movement." *Socialist Review* 10, 1 (January/February): 95-150.

———. 1987. *Gender at Work: The Dynamics of Job Segregation by Sex During World War II.* Urbana: University of Illinois Press.

Mill, John Stuart. 1900. *Principles of Political Economy.* vol. 1. New York: Colonial Press.

Mincer, Jacob. 1971. "On-the-Job Training: Costs, Returns, and Some Implications." in Burton et al. (eds.) *Readings in Labor Market Analysis.* New York: Holt, Rinehart and Winston.

———. 1974. *Schooling, Experience, and Earnings.* New York: Columbia University Press and National Bureau of Economic Research.

———. 1978. "Family Migration Decisions." *Journal of Political Economy* 86, no. 5 (October): 749-773.

Mincer, Jacob and Solomon W. Polachek. 1974. "Family Investments in Human

Capital: Earnings of Women." *Journal of Political Economy* 82, 2, pt. 2 (March/April): S76-S108.

Moe, Terry M. 1987. "An Assessment of the Positive Theory of 'Congressional Dominance.'" *Legislative Studies Quarterly* 12, 4: 475-520.

Moore, Kristin A., Sandra L. Hofferth, Steven B. Caldwell, and Linda J. Waite. 1979. *Teenage Motherhood - Social and Economic Consequences*. Washington, D.C.: Urban Institute.

Moynihan, D. P. 1965. "The Negro Family: The Case for National Action." in Lee Rainwater and William L. Yancey (eds.) *The Moynihan Report and the Politics of Controversy*. Cambridge, Mass.: MIT Press.

───────. 1985. "Family and Nation." Godkin Lectures. Harvard University.

Murray, Charles. 1984. *Losing Ground: American Social Policy, 1950-1980*. New York: Basic Books.

Myrdal, Gunnar. 1944. *An American Dilemma: The Negro Problem and Modern Democracy*. New York: Harper and Row.

National Center for Health Statistics, U.S. Department of Health and Human Services. 1987. "Advance Report of Final Natality Statistics, 1985." *Monthly Vital Statistics Report* 36, 4, Supplement. Washington, D.C.: U.S. Government Printing Office.

Oakland, William, Frederick Sparrow, and H. Lewis Stettler. 1971. "Ghetto Multipliers: A Case Study of Hough." *Journal of Regional Science* 11, 3 (July): 337-345.

Oaxaca, Ronald L. 1973. "Male-Female Wage Differentials in Urban Labor Markets." *International Economic Review* 14, 2 (October): 693-709.

O'Farrell, Brigid and Susan Harlan. 1984. "Job Integration Strategies: Today's Programs and Tomorrow's Needs." pp. 267-291 in Reskin [1984].

O'Neill, June. 1987. "Discrimination and Income Inequality." *Social Philosophy and Policy* 5, 1 (Autumn).

───────. 1990. "The Role of Human Capital in Earnings Differences Between Black and White Men." *Journal of Economic Perspectives* 4, 4 (Fall): 25-45.

O'Neill, June, James Cunningham, Andy Sparks, and Hal Sider. 1986. *The Economic Progress of Black Men*. Clearinghouse Publication 91. Washington, D.C.: United States Commission on Civil Rights (October).

Oster, Gerry. 1979. "A Factor Analytic Test of the Theory of the Dual Economy." *Review of Economics and Statistics* 61 (February): 33-39.

Osterman, Paul. 1975. "An Empirical Study of Labor Market Segmentation." *Industrial and Labor Relations Review* 28 (July): 508-521.

Parcel, Toby L. 1989. "Comparable Worth, Occupational Labor Markets, and Occupational Earnings: Results from the 1980 Census." pp. 134-152 in Michael, Hartmann, and O'Farrell [1989].

Parsons, Talcott. 1951. *The Social System*. Glencoe, Ill: Free Press.

───────. 1954. "The Motivation of Economic Activities." pp. 50-68 in *Essays in Sociological Theory*. Rev. ed. Glencoe, Ill: Free Press.

Pateman, Carole. 1988. "The Fraternal Social Contract." in John Keane (ed.) *Civil Society and the State*. New York: Verso Press.

Perrow, Charles. 1979. *Complex Organizations*. 2d ed.. Glenview, Ill: Scott, Foresman.

Pfeffer, Jeffrey. 1981. *Power in Organizations*. Marshfield, Mass.: Pitman.

Pfeffer, Jeffrey and Alison Davis-Blake. 1987. "The Effect of the Proportion of Women on Salaries: The Case of College Administrators." *Administrative Science Quarterly* 32, 1 (March): 1-24.

Phelps, E. S. 1972. "The Statistical Theory of Racism and Sexism." *American Economic Review* 62, 4 (September): 659-661.

Polachek, Solomon W. 1975a. "Differences in Expected Post-School Investment as a Determinant of Market Wage Differentials." *International Economic Review* 16, 1 (June): 451-470.

——————. 1975b. "Potential Biases in Measuring Male-Female Discrimination." *Journal of Human Resources* 10, 2 (Spring): 205-229.

——————. 1979. "Occupational Segregation Among Women: Theory, Evidence, and a Prognosis." pp. 137-157 in C. B. Lloyd, E. S. Andrews, and C. L. Gilroy (eds.) *Women in the Labor Market*. New York: Columbia University Press.

——————. 1981. "Occupational Self-Selection: A Human Capital Approach to Sex Differences in Occupational Structure." *Review of Economics and Statistics* 63 (February): 60-69.

Raff, Daniel M. G. and Lawrence H. Summers. 1987. "Did Henry Ford Pay Efficiency Wages?" *Journal of Labor Economics* 5, 4, pt. 2 (October): S57-S86.

Ragan, James F., Jr. and Sharon P. Smith. 1981. "The Impact of Differences in Turnover Rates on Male/Female Pay Differentials." *Journal of Human Resources* 16, 3 (Summer): 343-365.

Rebitzer, James B. 1988. "Unemployment, Labor Relations, and Unit Labor Costs." *American Economic Review* 78, 2 (May): 389-394.

Reich, Michael. 1981. *Racial Inequality: A Political-Economic Analysis*. Princeton, N.J.: Princeton University Press.

——————. 1984. "Segmented Labor: Time Series Hypotheses and Evidence." *Cambridge Journal of Economics* 8 (March): 63-82.

Remick, Helen. 1984. "Major Issues in a Priori Applications." pp. 99-117 in Helen Remick (ed.) *Comparable Worth and Wage Discrimination: Technical Possibilities and Political Realities*. Philadelphia: Temple University Press.

Reskin, Barbara F. (ed.) 1984. *Sex Segregation in the Workplace: Trends, Explanations, Remedies*. Washington, D.C.: National Academy Press.

——————. (ed.) 1988. "Bringing the Men Back In: Sex Differentiation and the Devaluation of Women's Work." *Gender and Society* 2, 1 (March): 58-81.

Reskin, Barbara F. and Heidi I. Hartmann (eds.) 1986. *Women's Work, Men's*

Work: Sex Segregation on the Job. Washington, D.C.: National Academy Press.

Resnick, Stephen and Richard D. Wolff. 1987. *Knowledge and Class: A Marxian Critique of Political Economy.* Chicago: University of Chicago Press.

Riach, Peter A. and Judith Rich. 1987. "Testing for Sexual Discrimination in the Labour Market." *Australian Economic Papers* (December): 165-178.

Roberts, Bruce. 1988. "What Is Profit?" *Rethinking Marxism* 1, 1.

Roos, Patricia A., and Barbara F. Reskin. 1984. "Institutional Factors Contributing to Sex Segregation in the Workplace." pp. 235-260 in Reskin [1984].

Rosen, Sherwin. 1974. "Hedonic Prices and Implicit Markets." *Journal of Political Economy* 82 (January/February): 34-55.

Rosenbaum, James E. 1985. "Jobs, Job Status, and Women's Gains from Affirmative Action: Implications for Comparable Worth." pp. 116-136 in Hartmann [1985].

Rosenthal, Robert and Donald B. Rubin. 1978. "Interpersonal Expectancy Effects: The First 345 Studies." *Behavioral and Brain Sciences* 1, 3 (September): 377-386.

Rubery, Jill. 1978. "Structural Labor Markets, Worker Organization, and Low Pay." *Cambridge Journal of Economics* 2, 1 (March).

Rumberger, Russell W. and Martin Carnoy. 1980. "Segmentation in the US Labour Market: Its Effects on the Mobility and Earnings of Whites and Blacks." *Cambridge Journal of Economics* 4 (June): 117-132.

Runciman, Walter G. 1966. *Relative Deprivation and Social Justice* London: Routledge and Kegan Paul.

Said, Edward. 1979. *Orientalism.* New York: Vintage.

St. George, Donna. 1989. "Lawyer Sadie Alexander, a Black Pioneer, Dies at 91." *Philadelphia Inquirer* (November 3): A1.

Salancik, Gerald R. 1979. "Interorganizational Dependence and Responsiveness to Affirmative Action: The Case of Women and Defense Contractors." *Academy of Management Journal* 22, 2: 375-394.

Sandell, S. and D. Shapiro. 1980. "Work Expectations, Human Capital Accumulation, and the Wages of Young Women." *Journal of Human Resources* 15, 3 (Summer): 335-353.

Scott, W. Richard. 1987. *Organizations: Rational, Natural, and Open Systems.* 2d ed. Englewood Cliffs, N.J.: Prentice-Hall.

Scoville, James G. 1969. *Concepts and Measurements for Manpower and Occupational Analysis.* Report to Office of Manpower Research, U. S. Department of Labor, Washington, D.C.

Semmler, Willi. 1984. *Competition, Monopoly, and Differential Profit Rates: On the Relevance of the Classical and Marxian Theories of Production Prices for Modern Industrial and Corporate Pricing.* New York: Columbia University Press.

Shaeffer, Ruth G. and Edith F. Lynton. 1979. *Corporate Experiences in Improving*

Women's Job Opportunities. Conference Board Report no. 755. New York: Conference Board.

Shaikh, Anwar. 1978. "Political Economy and Capitalism: Notes on Dobb's Theory of Crisis." *Cambridge Journal of Economics*. 2, 2 (June): 233-251.

——————. 1980. "Marxian Competition vs. Perfect Competition: Further Comments on the So-called Choice of Technique." *Cambridge Journal of Economics* 4, 1 (March): 75-83.

——————. 1981a. "The Poverty of Algebra." in Ian Steedman et al. (eds.) *The Value Controversy*. London: Verso Editions and New Left Books.

——————. 1981b. "Advanced Political Economy." Unpublished lecture notes, New School for Social Research.

——————. 1982a. "The Effect of Regulating Capitals on the General Rate of Profit." Unpublished manuscript, New School for Social Research.

——————. 1982b. "Neo-Ricardian Economics: A Wealth of Algebra, A Poverty of Theory." *Review of Radical Political Economics* 14, 2 (Summer): 67-83.

Shapiro, Carl and Joseph E. Stiglitz. 1984. "Equilibrium Unemployment as a Worker Discipline Device." *American Economic Review* 74, 3 (June): 433-444.

Shefter, Martin. 1986. "Trade Unions and Political Machines: The Organization and Disorganization of the American Working Class in the Late Nineteenth Century." in Katznelson and Zolberg [1986].

Shulman, Steven. 1984a. "Changing Patterns of Labor Market Discrimination: Differentials in the Probability of Employment by Race and City." Ph.D. diss. University of Massachusetts at Amherst.

——————. 1984b. "Competition and Racial Discrimination: The Employment Effects of Reagan's Labor Market Policies." *Review of Radical Political Economics* 16, 4: 111-128.

——————. 1987. "Discrimination, Human Capital, and Black/White Unemployment: Evidence from Cities." *Journal of Human Resources* 22, 3 (Summer): 361-376.

——————. 1989. "Racial Inequality and White Employment: An Interpretation and Test of the Bargaining Power Hypothesis." *Review of Black Political Economy*.

Shulman, Steven and William Darity, Jr. 1989. *The Question of Discrimination: Racial Inequality in the U.S. Labor Market*. Middletown, Conn.: Wesleyan University Press.

Simpson, Lorenzo. 1987. "Values, Respect, and Recognition: On Race and Culture in the Neoconservative Debate." *Praxis International* 7, 2.

Smith, Adam. 1937. *The Wealth of Nations*. New York: Modern Library.

Smith, James. 1984. "Race and Human Capital." *American Economic Review* 74 (September): 685-698.

Smith, James P. and Finis R. Welch. 1984. "Affirmative Action and Labor

Markets." *Journal of Labor Economics* 2, 2 (April): 269-301.

—————. 1986. *Closing the Gap: Forty Years of Economic Progress for Blacks.* Santa Monica, Calif.: Rand Corporation (February).

—————. 1989. "Black Economic Progress After Myrdal." *Journal of Economic Literature* 26 (June): 519-564.

Smith, Robert S. 1979. "Compensating Wage Differentials and Public Policy: A Review." *Industrial and Labor Relations Review* 32 (April): 339-352.

Solomos, John. 1986. "Varieties of Marxist Conceptions of 'Race,' Class, and the State: A Critical Analysis." in John Rex and David Mason (eds.) *Theories of Race and Ethnic Relations* New York: Cambridge University Press.

Solow, Robert M. 1980. "On Theories of Unemployment." *American Economic Review* 70, 1 (March): 1-11.

Sowell, Thomas. 1981a. *Ethnic America.* New York: Basic Books.

—————. 1981b. *Markets and Minorities.* New York: Basic Books.

—————. 1983. *The Economics and Politics of Race: An International Perspective.* New York: William Morrow.

Spelman, Elizabeth V. 1981. "The Erasure of Black Women." *Quest* 5, 4: 36-62.

Spero, Sterling and Abram Harris. 1931. *The Black Worker: The Negro and the Labor Movement.* New York: Columbia University Press.

Stack, Carol B. 1975. *All Our Kin: Strategies for Survival in a Black Community.* New York: Harper and Row.

Starr, Paul. 1987. "The Sociology of Official Statistics." pp. 7-57 in William Alonso and Paul Starr (eds.) *The Politics of Numbers.* New York: Russell Sage Foundation.

Stewart, James B. and Thomas Hyclak. 1984. "An Analysis of the Earnings Profiles of Immigrants." *Review of Economics and Statistics* 66 (May): 292-296.

Stiglitz, Joseph. 1973. "Approaches to the Economics of Discrimination." *American Economic Review* 63, 2 (May): 287-295.

—————. 1986. "Theories of Wage Rigidity." pp. 153-206 in James L. Butkiewicz et al. (eds.) *Keynes' Economic Legacy: Contemporary Economic Theories.* New York: Praeger Publishers.

—————. 1987. "The Causes and Consequences of the Dependence of Quality on Price." *Journal of Economic Literature* 25 (March): 1-48.

Stiglitz, Joseph and Andrew Weiss. 1981. "Credit Rationing in Markets with Imperfect Information." *American Economic Review* 71, 3 (June): 393-410.

Stinchcombe, Arthur L. 1965. "Social Structure and Organizations." pp. 142-193 in J. G. March (ed.) *Handbook of Organizations.* Chicago: Rand McNally.

—————. 1979. "Social Mobility in Industrial Labor Markets." *Acta Sociologica* 22, 3: 217-245.

Strang, David G. and James N. Baron. 1990. "Categorical Imperatives: The Structure of Job Titles in California State Agencies." *American Sociological Review* 55 (August): 479-495.

Strober, Myra H. 1982. "The MBA: Same Passport to Success for Women and Men?" ch. 2, pp. 25-44 in Phyllis A. Wallace (ed.) *Women in the Workplace*. Boston, Mass.: Auburn House.

——. 1984. "Toward a General Theory of Occupational Sex Segregation: The Case of Public School Teaching." pp. 144-156 in Reskin [1984].

Strober, Myra H. and Carolyn L. Arnold. 1987. "The Dynamics of Occupational Segregation Among Bank Tellers." pp. 107-148 in Brown and Pechman [1987].

Summers, Lawrence H. 1988. "Relative Wages, Efficiency Wages, and Keynesian Unemployment." *American Economic Review* 78, 2 (May): 383-388.

Swinton, David H. 1983. "Orthodox and Systemic Explanations for Unemployment and Racial Inequality: Implications for Policy." *Review of Black Political Economy* 12, 3 (Spring): 9-25.

Tabb, William K. 1970. *The Political Economy of the Black Ghetto*. New York: Norton.

Tainer, Evelina. 1988. "English Language Proficiency and the Determination of Earnings Among Foreign-Born Men." *Journal of Human Resources* 23 (Winter): 108-122.

Tetlock, Phil E. 1985. "Accountability: The Neglected Social Context of Judgment and Choice." pp. 297-332 in L. L. Cummings and B. M. Staw (eds.) *Research in Organizational Behavior*, vol. 7. Greenwich, Conn.: JAI Press.

Thaler, Richard and Sherwin Rosen. 1975. "The Value of Saving a Life: Evidence from the Labor Market." pp. 265-297 in Nestor E. Terleckyi (ed.) *Household Production and Consumption*. New York: National Bureau of Economic Research.

Theil, Henri and Anthony J. Finizza. 1971. "A Note on the Measurement of Racial Integration of Schools by Means of Informational Concepts." *Journal of Mathematical Sociology* 1, 2: 187-193.

Thurow, Lester. 1975. *Generating Inequality*. New York: Basic Books.

Tolbert, Pamela S., and Lynne Zucker. 1983. "Institutional Sources of Change in Organizational Structure: The Diffusion of Civil Service Reform, 1880-1930." *Administrative Science Quarterly* 28, 1 (March): 22-39.

Treiman, Donald J. 1977. *Occupational Prestige in Comparative Perspective*. New York: Academic Press.

——. 1979. *Job Evaluation: An Analytic Review*. Interim Report of the Committee on Occupational Classification and Analysis to the Equal Employment Opportunity Commission. National Research Council. Washington, D.C.: National Academy of Sciences.

Treiman, Donald and Heidi Hartmann (eds.). 1981. *Women, Work, and Wages: Equal Pay for Jobs of Equal Value*. Report of the Committee on Occupational Classification and Analysis. Washington, D.C.: National Academy Press.

Treiman, Donald J., Heidi I. Hartmann, and Patricia A. Roos. 1984. "Assessing Pay Discrimination Using National Data." pp. 137-154 in Helen Remick (ed.) *Comparable Worth and Wage Discrimination: Technical Possibilities and Political Realities*. Philadelphia: Temple University Press.

U.S. Commission on Civil Rights. 1982. *Unemployment and Underemployment Among Blacks, Hispanics, and Women*. Clearinghouse Publication 74. Washington, D.C.: (November).

U.S. Department of Commerce, Bureau of the Census. 1987. *1982 Characteristics of Business Owners*. Washington, D.C.: U.S. Government Printing Office.

—————. 1988. *Employment and Earnings*.

U. S. Department of Labor (USDoL). 1965. *Dictionary of Occupational Titles*, 3d ed. Washington, D.C.: U. S. Government Printing Office.

—————. 1984. *Educational Attainment of Workers, March 1982-83*. Bulletin 2191 (April).

—————. 1986a. *Geographic Profile of Employment and Unemployment, 1985*. Bulletin 2266 (September).

—————. 1986b. *Linking Employment Problems to Economic Status*. Bulletin 2270 (September).

Viscusi, W. Kip. 1980. "Sex Differences in Worker Quitting." *Review of Economics and Statistics* 62, 3 (August): 388-398.

Wachter, Michael L. 1986. "Union Wage Rigidity: The Default Settings of Labor Law." *American Economic Review* 76, 2 (May): 240-244.

Walby, Sylvia. 1986. *Patriarchy at Work*. Minneapolis: University of Minnesota Press.

Waldinger, Roger. 1989. "Structural Opportunity or Ethnic Advantage? Immigrant Business Development in New York." *International Migration Review* (Spring): 48-72.

Weeks, John. 1981. *Capital and Exploitation*. Princeton, N.J.: Princeton University Press.

Weick, Karl E. 1976. "Educational Organizations as Loosely Coupled Systems." *Administrative Science Quarterly* 21, 1 (March): 1-49.

Weiss, Andrew. 1984. "Determinants of Quit Behavior." *Journal of Labor Economics* 2, 3 (July): 371-387.

Weiss, Y. and R. Gronau. 1981. "Expected Interruptions in Labor Force Participation and Sex Related Differences in Earnings Growth." *Review of Economic Studies* 48, 4 (October): 607-619.

Welch, Finis R. 1984. "Affirmative Action and Labor Markets." *Journal of Labor Economics* 2 (April): 269-301.

—————. 1986. *Closing The Gap*. Santa Monica, Calif.: Rand Corporation.

—————. 1989. "Black Economic Progress After Myrdal." *Journal of Economic Literature* 27 (June): 519-564.

West, Cornel. 1982. *Prophesy Deliverance! An Afro-American Revolutionary*

Christianity. Philadelphia: Westminster Press.

Who's Who Among Black Americans. 1988. Northbrook, Ill.: Who's Who Among Black Americans Publishing.

Williams, Rhonda M. 1984. "The Methodology and Practice of Modern Labor Economics: A Critique." pp. 23-52 in Darity [1984b].

——————. 1987a. "Culture as Human Capital: Methodological and Policy Implications." *Praxis International* 7, 2 (July): 152-163.

——————. 1987b. "Capital, Competition, and Discrimination: A Reconsideration of Racial Earnings Inequality." *Review of Radical Political Economics* 19, 2: 1-15.

——————. 1988. "Beyond Human Capital: Black Women, Work, and Wages." Working Paper 183, Wellesley College Center For Research on Women.

——————. 1990. "Beyond 'Bad Luck': The Racial Dimensions of Deindustrialization." Technical Paper. Washington, D.C.: Joint Center for Political Studies.

Williamson, Oliver E. 1964. *The Economics of Discretionary Behavior*. Englewood Cliffs, N.J.: Prentice-Hall.

——————. 1975. *Markets and Hierarchies*. New York: Free Press.

——————. 1985. *The Economic Institutions of Capitalism*. New York: Free Press.

Willis, R. and S. Rosen. 1979. "Education and Self-Selection." *Journal of Political Economy* 87, 5, pt. 2 (October): S7-S36.

Wright, Gavin. 1986. *Old South, New South*. New York: Basic Books.

——————. 1988. "Segregation and Racial Wage Differentials in the South Before World War II." Working Paper, Department of Economics, Stanford University.

Yellen, Janet L. 1984. "Efficiency Wage Models of Unemployment." *American Economic Review* 74, 2 (May): 200-205.

Zalokar, Nadja. 1990. *The Economic Status of Black Women: An Exploratory Investigation*. Washington, D.C.: U.S. Commission on Civil Rights.

Index

About the Editors and Contributors

James N. Baron is a professor of organizational behavior and sociology at the Graduate School of Business and a professor of sociology at Stanford University in Stanford, California 94305-5015. He has degrees from Reed College, the University of Wisconsin at Madison, and the University of California at Santa Barbara. His current research interests include economic sociology, complex organizations, labor markets, and socioeconomic inequality.

Timothy Bates is Director of the Urban Policy Analysis Program at the New School for Social Research in New York, New York 10011. He was at the University of Vermont from 1974 to 1990. He also held appointments as a visiting scholar at the Joint Center for Political Studies and as a research fellow of the American Statistical Association. He received a B.S. from the University of Illinois, and a M.S. and Ph.D. from the University of Wisconsin. His current research is on the economics of urban poor and ethnic groups.

William T. Bielby was educated first in electrical engineering at the University of Illinois at Urbana and then received a Ph.D. in sociology from the University of Wisconsin. He is a professor in the Department of Sociology at the University of California at Santa Barbara, California 93106. His statistical work on social differences by gender have spread well outside the discipline of sociology and make econometricians take notice of sociological insights.

Richard R. Cornwall is chairperson of the Department of Economics at Middlebury College in Middlebury, Vermont 05753. He was educated at Princeton University and at the University of California at Berkeley and then taught at Princeton and the University of California at Davis. His interests include microeconomic and general equilibrium theory as well as the interaction between social inequality and economic markets.

William A. Darity, Jr., is the Cary C. Boshumer professor of economics at the University of North Carolina at Chapel Hill, North Carolina 27599-3305. From 1978 to 1983 he was at the University of Texas at Austin. Darity received a B.A. from Brown University and a Ph.D. from MIT. His major research interests include equality, distribution and growth, post-Keynesian economics, and the economics of the family.

Harriet Orcutt Duleep is a senior economist at the U.S. Commission on Civil Rights in Washington, D.C. 20425. She was with the Social Security Administration from 1979 to 1985. Duleep received a B.A. from the University of Michigan and a Ph.D. from MIT. Her current research focuses on discrimination, immigration, and the determinants of income differentials.

David Fairris teaches economics at the University of California at Riverside, California 92521. He received a B.A. from Washington University in St. Louis and a Ph.D. from Duke University. Most of his published research involves a political-economic analysis of work and the work place.

James J. Heckman is the Henry Schultz professor of economics at the University of Chicago. Earlier, he taught at Yale University and Columbia University. He received his graduate training at Princeton University. Heckman has received numerous awards including the prestigious the John Bates Clark Award in 1983. Heckman's research has changed the face of labor economics, econometrics, and demography. His work on panel data and selection problems has set the standard for analysis of microeconomic cross-section, time-series data. The technique he originally proposed in 1976 for handling sample selectivity bias has become so universal that students of econometrics are routinely taught how to "heckit" regression equations. He serves on the editorial boards of numerous scholarly journals, such as the *Journal of Labor Economics, Journal of Economic Perspectives,* and *Econometrica*. His areas of research include microdynamics, fertility, earnings, selectivity bias, and the evaluation of social programs.

Charng Kao is an associate research fellow and deputy director of the First Institute at the Chung-Hua Institution, Center for Economic Research in Taipei, Taiwan (ROC). He received B.A. and M.A. degrees from the National Chung-chi University in Taiwan and received a Ph.D. from the State University of New York at Binghamton. His topics for research include economics of education, mainland China's economy, and development of economic relations between Taiwan and mainland China.

Lori G. Kletzer is an assistant professor of economics at Williams College in Williamstown, Massachusetts 01267. She received a B.A. from Vassar College and a Ph.D. from the University of California at Berkeley. Her research interests include the effects in labor markets of job displacement, college choice and returns to college, and long-term unemployment.

Elaine McCrate is an assistant professor of economics at the University of Vermont in Burlington, Vermont 05405. She has recently been a postdoctoral fellow at the Center for Afro-American Studies at the University of California at Los Angeles and a fellow at the Mary Ingraham Bunting Institute of Radcliffe College. She was educated at the University of Massachusetts at Amherst. Her interests include teenage childbearing and feminist responses to rational choice models of family decision-making.

Solomon W. Polachek is a professor of economics at the State University of New York at Binghamton, New York 13902-6000. Polachek was at the University of North Carolina at Chapel Hill prior to his move to SUNY and before that was a postdoctoral fellow at the University of Chicago. During 1979-80 he served as a national fellow at the Hoover Institute at Stanford University. Polachek received a B.A. from George Washington University and a Ph.D. from Columbia University. He has done pioneering work developing earnings functions for women. In addition to his work on discrimination, Polachek has made significant contributions applying the life-cycle human-capital model to understand geographic and job mobility and union-earnings profiles as well as developing an innovative way to measure buyer and seller information in markets. He has also applied economic methodology to understand international political conflict. He serves on the editorial boards of *Conflict Management and Peace Science* and the *International Studies Quarterly*.

Michael D. Robinson is an assistant professor of economics at Mount Holyoke College in South Hadley, Massachusetts 01075-1461. He taught at Middlebury College during 1987-88. He received a B.A. from Washington University in St. Louis and a Ph.D. from the University of Texas at Austin. His areas of research include labor economics and econometrics.

Steven Shulman is an associate professor of economics at Colorado State University, Fort Collins, Colorado 80523. He received his Ph.D. from the University of Massachusetts at Amherst. He works in the fields of labor economics, poverty and discrimination. He is the co-editor (with William Darity, Jr.) of *The Question of Discrimination: Racial Inequality in the U.S. Labor Market* (Wesleyan University Press, 1989).

Rhonda M. Williams is at the Afro-American Studies Program and the Economics Department at the University of Maryland in College Park, Maryland 20742. She received a B.A. from Harvard and a Ph.D. from MIT and then taught at the University of Texas at Austin and at the New School for Social Research. Her interests include capitalist development and the evolution of gender and ethnic divisions of labor.

Stephen A. Woodbury is currently an associate professor of economics at Michigan State University in East Lansing, Michigan 48824-1038 and also holds a research appointment at the W. E. Upjohn Institute for Employment Research in

Kalamazoo, Michigan. He received a B.A. from Middlebury College in Vermont and a Ph.D. from the University of Wisconsin at Madison. His interests focus on labor markets - particularly on wage and nonwage compensation, social insurance, and unemployment.

Phanindra V. Wunnava is an associate professor of economics at Middlebury College in Middlebury, Vermont 05753 and is also a research associate in economics at the State University of New York at Binghamton. He received Bachelor of Commerce and Master of Commerce degrees from Andhra University in India, a Doctor of Arts degree from the University of Miami, and a Ph.D. from the State University of New York at Binghamton. His main areas of interest are life-cycle union wage/benefit effects, firm size effects, gender discrimination, efficiency wage models, charitable contributions towards higher education, frontier estimation, and pooled cross-section time-series analysis.

Nadja Zalokar is an economist at the U.S. Commission on Civil Rights in Washington, D. C. 20425. She was educated at Wesleyan University and then at Princeton and earlier taught at the University of Florida and at Haverford College. Her interests center on gender differences, the economic status of minority women, and education.

AGL1645   6/15/92   X hill

HD4903
N48
1991

KFS